Cases on Electronic Commerce Technologies and Applications

Mehdi Khosrow-Pour, D.B.A.
Editor-in-Chief, Journal of Cases on Information Technology

IDEA GROUP PUBLISHING
Hershey • London • Melbourne • Singapore

Acquisitions Editor: Michelle Potter
Development Editor: Kristin Roth
Senior Managing Editor: Amanda Appicello
Managing Editor: Jennifer Neidig
Typesetter: Diane Huskinson
Cover Design: Lisa Tosheff
Printed at: Integrated Book Technology

Published in the United States of America by
        Idea Group Publishing (an imprint of Idea Group Inc.)
        701 E. Chocolate Avenue, Suite 200
        Hershey PA 17033
        Tel: 717-533-8845
        Fax: 717-533-8661
        E-mail: cust@idea-group.com
        Web site: http://www.idea-group.com

and in the United Kingdom by
        Idea Group Publishing (an imprint of Idea Group Inc.)
        3 Henrietta Street
        Covent Garden
        London WC2E 8LU
        Tel: 44 20 7240 0856
        Fax: 44 20 7379 0609
        Web site: http://www.eurospanonline.com

Library of Congress Cataloging-in-Publication Data

Cases on electronic commerce technologies and applications / Mehdi Khosrow-Pour, editor.
        p. cm.
  Summary: "This book presents a wide range of real-life cases that describe the successful and unsuccessful adoption of e-commerce, e-business, e-government, mobile commerce, and Web services technologies"--Provided by publisher.
  Includes bibliographical references and index.
  ISBN 1-59904-402-1 (hardcover) -- ISBN 1-59904-403-X (softcover) -- ISBN 1-59904-404-8 (ebook)
  1. Electronic commerce--Case studies. I. Khosrowpour, Mehdi, 1951-
  HF5548.32.C3655 2006
  658.8'72--dc22
                        2006008079

British Cataloguing in Publication Data
A Cataloguing in Publication record for this book is available from the British Library.

The views expressed in this book are those of the authors, but not necessarily of the publisher.

Cases on Information Technology Series

ISSN: 1537-9337

Series Editor
Mehdi Khosrow-Pour, D.B.A.
Editor-in-Chief, *Journal of Cases on Information Technology*

- Cases on Database Technologies
  Mehdi Khosrow-Pour, Information Resources Management Association, USA
- Cases on Electronic Commerce
  Mehdi Khosrow-Pour, Information Resources Management Association, USA
- Cases on Global IT Applications and Management: Success and Pitfalls
  Felix B. Tan, University of Auckland, New Zealand
- Cases on Information Technology and Business Process Reengineering
  Mehdi Khosrow-Pour, Information Resources Management Association, USA
- Cases on Information Technology and Organizational Politics and Culture
  Mehdi Khosrow-Pour, Information Resources Management Association, USA
- Cases on Information Technology Management In Modern Organizations
  Mehdi Khosrow-Pour, Information Resources Management Association, USA & Jay Liebowitz, George Washington University, USA
- Cases on Information Technology Planning, Design and Implementation
  Mehdi Khosrow-Pour, Information Resources Management Association, USA
- Cases on Information Technology, Volume 7
  Mehdi Khosrow-Pour, Information Resources Management Association, USA
- Cases on Strategic Information Systems
  Mehdi Khosrow-Pour, Information Resources Management Association, USA
- Cases on Telecommunications and Networking
  Mehdi Khosrow-Pour, Information Resources Management Association, USA
- Cases on the Human Side of Information Technology
  Mehdi Khosrow-Pour, Information Resources Management Association, USA
- Cases on Worldwide E-Commerce: Theory in Action
  Mahesh S. Raisinghani, Texas Woman's University, USA
- Case Studies in Knowledge Management
  Murray E. Jennex, San Diego State University, USA
- Case Studies on Information Technology in Higher Education: Implications for Policy and Practice
  Lisa Ann Petrides, Columbia University, USA
- Success and Pitfalls of IT Management (Annals of Cases in Information Technology, Volume 1)
  Mehdi Khosrow-Pour, Information Resources Management Association, USA
- Organizational Achievement and Failure in Information Technology Management
  (Annals of Cases in Information Technology, Volume 2)
  Mehdi Khosrow-Pour, Information Resources Management Association, USA
- Pitfalls and Triumphs of Information Technology Management
  (Annals of Cases in Information Technology, Volume 3)
  Mehdi Khosrow-Pour, Information Resources Management Association, USA
- Annals of Cases in Information Technology, Volume 4 - 6
  Mehdi Khosrow-Pour, Information Resources Management Association, USA

IDEA GROUP INC.

Cases on Electronic Commerce Technologies and Applications

Detailed Table of Contents

The e-government initiative discussed in this case study (E-Tax) provided an additional service to individual Australian taxpayers by enabling them to file their tax returns online. The E-Tax case demonstrates how complex e-government projects can be and the need to take contextual factors into account in planning and evaluating e-government implementation.

ENI Company is an electronic commerce firm in South Korea. ENI Company provides English news items and English lessons to the subscribers through daily e-mail service that includes free English news-related question and answer sessions via e-mail. This case study deals with the struggle of this firm to establish and sustain its business in a less-developed national information infrastructure. This case is a good example of how to conduct an e-commerce in a county where national IT infrastructure is not ready for it.

Hardwarezone.com is rated the top IT media Web site in Singapore by Hitwise. It provides 100% proprietary and localized content on IT news, product releases, and numerous member-centric services, such as hardware pricelists and forums. This teaching case will chart the evolution of Hardwarezone's business model and strategies through its humble beginnings and the challenges to the company as a result of the dot-com crisis and thereafter.

E*Trade revolutionized the securities brokerage industry by "creating" Internet trading. E*Trade's original strategy was to deliver cost savings to customers while amortizing fixed costs over a greater number of accounts. E*Trade established a popular Web site offering the convenience and control of automated stock, options, and mutual fund order placement at low commission rates. This case presents E*Trade's successes and also fierce competition and emerging ethical and operational problems.

This case analyzes a new digital music label, mVine.com. It discusses the turbulent context within which the company was launched and the particular individual strengths of the founding directors. A full description of how mVine operated initially as a virtual organization provides a full understanding of the benefits and challenges that such a company faces and the opportunity to discuss the strategies that mVine employed to overcome this.

The case describes a small locally run Washington, DC company facing several strategic decisions at the end of 1999; marketing its new high-tech products, securing sufficient venture capital financing, and creating a profit sharing plan for current and future employees.

This case uses ASDA.com, ASDA's home-shopping arm, to demonstrate the challenges in building and developing an online grocery business in the UK. Particularly, it delineates the operational aspects of B2C e-commerce in the grocery business: fulfillment center and fulfillment process. The case will also describe ASDA's efforts in overcoming problems with their home-shopping fulfillment model and present important elements of ASDA.com's virtual store and its operation.

The case study describes the process involved in EDI implementation in the Australian automotive industry. Buyer-supplier interactions during EDI implementation and its impact on technical, political, behavioral and trading partner trust aspects are discussed in this case study between Ford Australia (manufacturer) and Patents, Brakes and Replacements Limited (their first tier supplier).

Office Depot first introduced B2B e-commerce for larger corporate customers and realized that OfficeMax had already launched B2C e-commerce for the general public. This case describes how Office Depot quickly launched B2C e-commerce, and investigates critical factors managers should take into consideration in adopting new e-commerce strategies and technologies that will leverage corporate resources.

This case study presents an overview of the efforts of Texas Instrument's (TI's) internal and external ERP implementation, with a focus on linking its ERP system in a global e-commerce setting. This linkage is especially important since it had been stated in TI's strategic plan as an objective of this project to provide visibility of the ERP system to external constituents via Web linkages along with the objective of standardizing internal processes and important information technology systems to support market needs. Issues faced by TI are clearly outlined with future questions also posed in the final section.

Airgun Products, Inc. (API) is a small firm that sells airguns and related products directly to consumers. Since the introduction of the online channel, they have struggled with how to best utilize their complementary channels and produce a profit. Their current challenges are to identify which of their customers prefer which channel (market segmentation), identify and take advantage of the relative advantages of their two channels (paper vs. online catalogs), and identify opportunities for enhancing the value provided by their Web site.

Chapter XII

This case aims to analyze, in some detail, the major challenges in the widespread adoption of electronic commerce in the Spanish-speaking population. The case also provides a general overview of related issues in global e-commerce, specifically: language, localization, currency, cultural difference, export controls, payment methods, taxation issues, consumer protection, and legal issues. The chapter illustrates that while Latin America initially attracted many investors by offering one of the world's fastest growing online populations, the market was not large enough to accommodate all the new entrants.

This case discusses the challenges facing the music recording industry through the eyes of two of its most influential trade associations: the RIAA and the IFPI. First, readers of the case will learn about the history of the music recording industry and how new emerging technologies can impact individual organizations or entire industries and the music industry value chain and its various stakeholders. Second, they will learn about the strategic opportunities and business models being unleashed by the new emerging technologies, and the challenges facing music industry trade associations.

Margaret T. O'Hara, East Carolina University, USA
Hugh J. Watson, University of Georgia, USA

This case discusses how Student Advantage has successfully transformed itself from the brick and mortar company it began as in 1992 to become the leading online portal to the higher education community.

Anne Honkaranta, University of Jyväskylä, Finland
Airi Salminen, University of Jyväskylä, Finland
Tuomo Peltola, SysOpen Plc., Finland

The Finnish Centre for Pensions (FCP) is a government organization acting as the central body for private pension institutions in Finland. One of its central tasks is to produce and publish guideline documents for ensuring that the pension institutions carry out pension provisioning in a unified way. Due to problems in the maintenance of the documents and requests for faster information delivery by the Internet, FCP carried out a content management development initiative. The case follows the changes in components of the content management environment. The case highlights the challenges encountered and describes the tools utilized for redesign activities.

Theodore H. K. Clark, Hong Kong University of Science & Technology, Hong Kong
Karl Reiner Lang, Hong Kong University of Science & Technology, Hong Kong
Will W-K. Ma, Hong Kong University of Science & Technology, Hong Kong

This case concerns a recently launched retirement protection scheme, the Mandatory Provident Fund, in Hong Kong. The service has been implemented in two versions, a bricks model and a clicks model.

This case provides an overview of the roles of the Global Trade Point Network (GTPNet) in facilitating small- and medium-sized enterprises' (SMEs') adoption of the Internet and e-commerce technologies. The GTPNet puts potential and actual traders in the position of suppliers and users of strategic information. Using the services provided by a Trade Point, traders can identify markets for their products, complete export formalities and procedures, and meet other international trade related requirements on the spot.

This case covers the introduction and diffusion of retail banking in Egypt and the development in electronic delivery channels and payment systems in its marketplace. The case represents a model for the application of advanced information and communication technology in the context of a developing nation.

This case history takes place at the biggest flower auction of the world, the Aalsmeer Flower Auction. Directors of the Aalsmeer Flower Auction felt that the Internet might play an important role in the future of their business. The case study describes the different e-business initiatives taken and the responses from suppliers, customers, managers and other stakeholders on each of these initiatives. Readers will be challenged to analyze this material and offer advice to the management of the auction about future directions with respect to e-business.

This case study examines the impact of online reservation systems and e-commerce on the travel industry. Initial discussion concerns the impact of the American

Airlines SABRE system. The wider impact of remote-access, computerized reservation systems, or Global Distribution Systems, and e-commerce access to online reservations in the travel industry is analyzed. The case study concludes with a comparison of the impact of information technologies between the U.S. and European travel industries.

Savvas Papagiannidis, University of Newcastle upon Tyne Business
School, UK
Feng Li, University of Newcastle upon Tyne Business School, UK

In this article, we use the experience of Gaia Fulfilment to demonstrate the challenges of developing and deploying collateral fulfillment, i.e., short-run print on demand via the Web. By discussing the technological innovations that Gaia achieved we will outline their product development steps and the solutions the technology enabled. We also show the benefits of collateral fulfillment by presenting two examples of customers that use Gaia's technology.

Luvai Motiwalla, University of Massachusetts, Lowell, USA
Azim Hashimi, University of Massachusetts, Lowell, USA

This case's emphasis is on the reduction of the logistical aspects of adventure travel and increase in the customer base by using the Web-enabling information technology resources. A global travel company, Himalayan Adventures (HA), based in Pakistan wants to build a one-stop electronic commerce store for its customers.

Preface

During the past two decades, electronic commerce technologies and applications have revolutionized the basic fundamental use of information technologies in all aspects of our social and business infrastructures. Through the use of this technology, organizations of all types and sizes have managed to expand their market reach and the ways they serve their customers throughout the world. Many organizations have been very successful, and yet some have witnessed failure, in using this technology. There are many documented cases related to the utilization and management of electronic commerce that can provide significant insight in how successfully electronic commerce may be utilized in organizations. *Cases on Electronic Commerce Technologies and Applications*, part of Idea Group Inc.'s *Cases on Information Technology Series*, presents a wide range of real-life cases related to the adoption of e-commerce, e-business, e-government, mobile commerce and Web services technologies and applications in organizations worldwide.

The cases included in this volume cover a wide range of issues focusing on tax services online, an English e-mail service, a successful Singaporean dot-com venture, Internet trading, the creation of a digital music label, a company's implementation of a Web site, an online grocery business, business-to-business e-commerce in various industries, the adoption of e-commerce by office supplies industries, e-commerce enabled enterprise information systems, marketing products online, Spanish-speaking e-markets, MP3 players and the music recording industry, college markets online, e-government initiatives, a retirement protection scheme, e-commerce in developing nations, electronic banking, an online flower auction, e-commerce in the air travel industry, digital print business online, and the Web initiatives of a global travel company.

As electronic commerce technologies continue to prevail in organizations of all types and sizes, developers and managers of these technologies must keep up with emerging technologies as well as managerial issues related to the utilization and management of these technologies. *Cases on Electronic Commerce Technology and Applications* provides a much needed understanding of how to successfully implement e-technologies in organizations that can greatly benefit from the use of these technologies. Cases included in this volume will allow practitioners, educators and their students a better understanding of the issues, problems and challenges associated with the effective utilization of e-commerce, e-business, e-government, m-commerce and Web services in organizations. Lessons learned from the cases included in this publication will be very instrumental for those learning more about the issues and challenges in the field of e-technologies.

Note to Professors: Teaching notes for cases included in this publication are available to those professors who decide to adopt the book for their college course. Contact cases@idea-group.com for additional information regarding teaching notes and to learn about other volumes of case books in the IGI *Cases on Information Technology Series.*

ACKNOWLEDGMENTS

Putting together a publication of this magnitude requires the cooperation and assistance of many professionals with much expertise. I would like to take this opportunity to express my gratitude to all the authors of cases included in this volume. Many thanks also to all the editorial assistance provided by the Idea Group Inc. editors during the development of these books, particularly all the valuable and timely efforts of Mr. Andrew Bundy and Ms. Michelle Potter. Finally, I would like to dedicate this book to all my colleagues and former students who taught me a lot during my years in academia.

A special thank you to the Editorial Advisory Board: Annie Becker, Florida Institute of Technology, USA; Stephen Burgess, Victoria University, Australia; Juergen Seitz, University of Cooperative Education, Germany; Subhasish Dasgupta, George Washington University, USA; and Barbara Klein, University of Michigan, Dearborn, USA.

Mehdi Khosrow-Pour, D.B.A.
Editor-in-Chief
Cases on Information Technology Series
http://www.idea-group.com/bookseries/details.asp?id=18

Chapter I

Moving Personal Tax Online:
The Australian Taxation Office's E-Tax Initiative

Jeff Chamberlain, Deakin University, Australia

Tanya Castleman, Deakin University, Australia

EXECUTIVE SUMMARY

In exploiting the capabilities of online technologies, governments have developed policies and launched projects to conduct transactions and deliver their services through the Internet. The motivations for this include cost cutting, efficiency improvements, service enhancements, and leadership in business transformation. However, these diverse goals are not necessarily consistent, especially in the early stages of implementation. The e-government initiative discussed in this case study (E-Tax) provided an additional service to individual Australian taxpayers by enabling them to file their tax returns online. This case study provides an analysis of the E-Tax implementation in the first three years of its operation. Data on E-Tax use compared to other filing methods show that the package worked well technically, was favorably received by users, and was consistent with policy on e-government. However, adoption levels in the early stages did not meet government targets. The analysis suggests that impediments to a greater level of E-Tax use included entrenched patterns of filing, the nature of the taxation system, and political sensitivities. The E-Tax case demonstrates how complex e-government projects can be and the need to take contextual factors into account in planning and evaluating e-government implementation.

SETTING THE STAGE

Paying personal income tax is one of those melancholy, although necessary, duties that most adults have to perform. But think for a moment about those whose job it is to manage the system that facilitates this (usually annual) process. Surely technology can come to the rescue, making the process easier and more successful for the taxpayer and more efficient and less costly for the taxation office. Such a project would be a good example of e-government, especially consistent with governments' goals to transact with their citizens online, making their lives more convenient and, in the process, saving money for the taxpaying public. But what might be involved in such an implementation? What factors should be considered in mounting a project to file tax returns or other government documents online?

In this study, we report a case of a government using electronic service delivery for just such a purpose. We outline the experience of the Australian Taxation Office (ATO) in developing a simple, free system that allows taxpayers to submit their annual returns online. The system, known as E-Tax, was designed to reduce the ponderous inefficiencies and delays that are an unavoidable part of systems based on paper returns. It is a case that demonstrates the issues surrounding e-government initiatives as a form of electronic business or electronic government. It highlights the complexities in balancing gains in efficiencies for individual transactions, efficiency, and coherence across the whole system of service delivery with access for the diverse population of end users whose needs must be met. It also emphasizes the lengthy implementation period that such initiatives may require in order to achieve success.

We begin by describing the Australian government's policy framework for online services and e-business development. Like many other governments the world over (La Porte et al., 2001; McCartney & Wilson, 2001), Australia has sought to utilize information and communication technologies to improve government business processes (ANAO, 2000; Thibodeau, 2000) for the convenience of its clients (Power, 2001; Symonds, 2000; Tillet, 2000) and to provide an example of effective use of these technologies (Government On-line, 2000) for business and community. We then outline the E-Tax project and describe the early implementation period of this initiative. The discussion that follows points out the lessons this case holds, both for electronic government initiatives and for other service organizations embarking on similar ventures.

CONTEXT OF GOVERNMENT PROVISION OF SERVICE ONLINE

Governments as Managers and Providers

There are two main goals underlying initiatives for government online service delivery: increased government openness, including better provision of citizen services; and business process improvement (Chamberlain & Castleman, 2001). The prevailing motivation for electronic government initiatives appears to be their potential to improve business processes. They are seen to maximize business efficiency and effectiveness.

Such improvements relate primarily to the delivery of services to the public and information dissemination, typical transactions performed by governments every day (Public Management, 2000). Business efficiency and effectiveness can be measured principally against the reduced costs of administering citizen transactions. Reduced transaction costs are presented as major arguments by governments in justifying business cases for implementation of online innovations. In this way, governments also exercise their accountabilities to the public by demonstrating the effective allocation of public funds (Al-Kibsi et al., 2001; Colecchia, 1999; Girishankar, 1997).

Contemporary governments must legitimise themselves both as good managers of public resources and as providers of appropriate services to the population. It is in the best interest of governments to demonstrate that, by their online activities, they use public resources more rationally and more economically and can deliver better services. However, should those goals not be achieved through the implementation of this technology, a government will confront other political problems, especially those associated with rising expectations. Governments are working to understand how their initiatives to use the Internet for communication and transacting with citizens can achieve the desired outcomes and where the pitfalls in strategy and implementation lie. The apparently seamless rhetoric of benefit does not acknowledge that there may be conflicts between business efficiency and citizen service (Chamberlain & Castleman, 2002). The multiple agendas of governments must still be balanced.

Online Strategy of the Australian Government

Australia has a federated system of government. There are six state governments and two territory governments as well as the federal (national) commonwealth government. The Australian Commonwealth government's online strategy is expressed comprehensively in a document published by the Department of Communications, Information Technology and the Arts, titled Government On-line Strategy (Government On-line, 2000). It is in this strategy that the federal government recognizes that its own transition to the online environment is critical to instilling public confidence in that environment. The strategy includes provision for security, authentication, privacy, accessibility, navigability, and standards. Through this strategy, the government delegates to its agencies the decisions about which programs, such as citizen tax return administration, should be placed online first, how it will be done, and which applications are best not to go online.

The four stated objectives of the government online strategy are as follows:

1. An environment where almost all government services are available around the clock to anyone;
2. A complete range of high-quality, low-cost online services;
3. Tailored services that are easy to use and that allow people to interact with government in a way that is natural to them; and
4. Bringing government closer to people to encourage people to interact with government (Government On-line, 2000).

The Australian government believes that its online strategy is a natural and important step in the development of government and community interaction. It believes that it will enable a stronger service quality emphasis and that it will enhance the delivery of client needs by breaking down the traditional barriers typically faced by clients. It also believes that it will positively impact older and disabled Australians as well as those living in regional communities. It believes that greater public convenience will be facilitated via around-the-clock access to Web site information and services and that both business and government will experience reduced costs and faster operational processes (Government On-line, 2000).

ORGANIZATION BACKGROUND

E-Government and the Australian Taxation Office

As an agency of the government, the Australian Taxation Office (ATO) administers the majority of federal taxes in the country, including the administration and collection of income taxes from Australian citizens. The ATO is the government's prime revenue collector responsible for the collection of about 96% of revenue, which accounts for more than $140 billion in income taxes per year (e.g., more than $142 billion in 2004) (Australian Taxation Office, 2004). Income tax constitutes the majority of the federal revenue collections. In 2000, approximately 11.9 million taxpayers filed returns, and of these, individuals accounted for 85% of total taxpayers (more than 10,000,000 individuals representing 53% of the total Australian population as of June 2000), while companies accounted for about 5%, partnerships and trusts about 4%, and funds about 2% (Australian Taxation Office, 2003). The ATO Strategic Statement 2000-2003 acknowledges that one of the five key issues that will shape the future of Australia's revenue administration is the impact of internationalization and the growth of the Internet and electronic commerce (Australian Taxation Office, 2001).

In 2001, the ATO noted that internationalization along with the growth of e-commerce and the Internet would shape the future of Australia's revenue administration (Australian Taxation Office, 2001). To align itself with these trends, the ATO developed an online e-business strategy to steer the reengineering of its business processes and its relationships and interactions with the community. The ATO argued that, for the majority of its clients, interactions would be performed increasingly online. The ATO has long been recognized as a government leader in the provision of services online. This is exemplified through a number of its programs, including the following:

- Online registration by companies to receive their Australian Business Number (ABN);
- Online filing by companies of their quarterly sales tax statements;
- An online tax filing system used by tax agents and accountants; and
- E-Tax, an individual's tax return preparation and online filing program (Australian Taxation Office, 2000, 2001).

The ATO's e-commerce strategy was described as "revolutionis[ing] the way we do business and our relationship/interaction with the community" (Australian Taxation Office, 1999b, 1999c, 2000).

For several years, the ATO has been committed to service delivery, which is secure, low-cost, easy-to-access, and easy-to-use (Australian Taxation Office, 1999c). In pursuit of this objective, electronic techniques have been actively pursued both to replace and to enhance conventional forms of interaction with the community. The ATO aimed to be a leader in the effective use of electronic services. This approach to service delivery has been expressed explicitly in whole-of-government and whole-of-ATO terms.

A key driver of the ATO's pursuit of electronic service delivery has been the search for transactional efficiencies in its systems. These include the following:

- The technological transformation of businesses and associated processes and the opportunities offered by technology for gains in strategic and operational efficiency and effectiveness;
- The high levels of service consistently demanded by clients and their inherent expectations, as influenced by change in their general environment (e.g., an increasing exposure to the Internet and its capabilities); and
- Budgetary constraints that consistently require that more be done with less, thus influencing the selection of technologies and communications channels with a view to obtaining those with the potential to deliver the highest-quality service at the least cost to the ATO and to its clients (Australian Taxation Office, 1999d).

International experience has indicated that significant efficiency gains can be made by filing tax forms and managing data electronically (Al-Kibsi et al., 2001; EzGov, 2002; Faipo, 1999; Inland Revenue Service, 2002, 2003).

While seeking to improve the operational and cost effectiveness of its administration, the ATO also has been committed to supporting the government's larger agenda of developing online government and e-commerce capabilities more generally. As a result, it was outward-looking and policy-oriented, fully aware of the broader issues involved in the development of its online tax filing application.

The ATO has carefully observed the progressive adoption of the Internet by Australian industry and its clients and has seen this as a credible means through which to communicate and conduct business. The ATO has embraced leading-edge technological business applications delivered online (Australian Taxation Office, 2001).

CASE DESCRIPTION

The E-Tax Initiative

In 1997, the ATO introduced an electronic version of its traditional paper-based personal income tax form. The electronic version is called E-Tax and is the ATO's Internet-based income tax return preparation and filing software. Individuals can download the E-Tax package from the ATO's Web site to their personal computers. It assists clients (i.e., individual taxpayers) with the preparation of tax returns and then lodges those returns securely over the Internet. This is quite distinct from the electronic facility used by tax agents to lodge individual and business tax returns on behalf of their clients, which has been in use since 1992.

E-Tax assists users in determining whether they should file a tax return and, if so, proceeds by asking the user a series of questions, guiding them to complete the actual return. The E-Tax software user is "interviewed" and is required to respond to a series of relatively straightforward questions with yes and no answers, not unlike responding to an expert system. The E-Tax system analyzes responses as it receives them and proceeds by asking the user only those questions relevant to his or her personal tax affairs. This aids in the speed and accuracy of the completion of the return; in contrast, taxpayers using the paper return must work through more than 100 pages of publications. Anecdotal evidence suggests that E-Tax preparation can be completed in as little as half the time required for paper returns.

The E-Tax program collates all of the typically required tax return data, including information on the taxpayer's income, deductions, losses, tax offsets (rebates), the national health levy, and adjustments. It also provides an estimate of the taxpayer's assessment (i.e., the dollar amount of tax owing or refundable). Validation and consistency tests check answers, figures, and incomplete items. Public Key encryption technology is used to ensure security, privacy, authenticity, and integrity. Partially completed returns can be saved, and several members of a household can use this software on the same computer after downloading their individual secure electronic keys and digital certificates (Australian Taxation Office, 1999a; Thomas, 2000).

In the original proof of concept documentation, business arguments were presented in favor of the trial of the E-Tax product including the following:

- Improvements in the level of assistance to taxpayers in filling out their returns;
- Easier tax return preparation;
- Faster tax return preparation;
- Reduction in compliance costs (e.g., filing over the Internet); and
- Better data quality by virtue of client-keyed data and some software error checking (Australian Taxation Office, 1997; McCarthy, 1997).

These business arguments exemplify the efficiency and effectiveness objectives of governments when implementing such innovations. Expected gains included reductions in processing and compliance costs and increased effectiveness in terms of client service and data quality. All arguments reflected the ATO's wider strategic plans in place at that time.

E-Tax commenced in 1997 as a proof-of-concept project and continued as a pilot-only scheme in 1998. Technically, the program was a success, meeting both the functional and business objectives, and in 1999, the project was implemented fully. The ATO projected a rapidly rising use of E-Tax after the pilot phase. However, although the number of filings increased from 1999 to 2003, usage fell behind the ATO's imputed targets. These trends are shown in Figure 1.

It was encouraging to see the actual figures approaching the target figures more closely, but a different understanding of the E-Tax issue emerges when we look at E-Tax

Figure 1. Actual and expected E-Tax filings

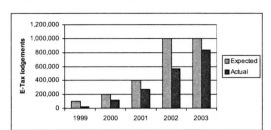

Table 1. Methods of filing for personal income tax returns in Australia in 2000

Filing Type	Number of Filings	Percentage of Filings
E-Tax	113,164	1.1%
Tax agent	7,708,302	76.8%
Paper forms	1,983,778	19.8%
Paper forms keyed and filed electronically through post offices	234,507	2.3%
Total	**10,039,751**	**100%**

Source: ATO mainframe data extracted November 2001, Australian Taxation Office

figures in contrast to other types of tax filing. Table 1 shows the number of taxpayers using various filing methods.

These figures show that during 2000, more than three-quarters of Australian personal income taxpayers sought professional accounting assistance to prepare their annual income tax returns. These filings were completed online. The next largest group used paper forms and accounted for nearly 20% of filings.

The problem for the ATO at that time was that, although E-Tax functioned well, not enough people used it, which undermined its ability to deliver the anticipated efficiencies. These efficiencies could be achieved only if people shifted from paper returns to E-Tax. The ATO would not gain any efficiencies if the majority of taxpayers who used tax accountants used E-Tax instead, since tax accountants already submit electronically. Individual taxpayers might benefit, if using E-Tax saves the cost of professional services and is a quick transaction, but that would not create any benefit for the ATO. This raises the question of whether E-Tax was a positive contribution to e-government in Australia or whether it was irrelevant in terms of improving government efficiency and taxpayer convenience.

Factors in E-Tax Adoption and Satisfaction

To understand the success and limitations of the E-Tax initiative, we analyzed the characteristics of taxpayers using E-Tax and the users' evaluations of it. This information comes from an analysis of anonymous filing data and responses to a survey of E-Tax users conducted online in 2001.

E-Tax Use and Evaluation Data

Official, complete, and accurate personal income tax return filing data for the years 1997 and 2001 were obtained from the ATO's mainframe computer. A total of 415,436 e-tax records were analyzed. Data examined included summaries of statistics pertaining to income, deductions, and tax rebates for major income tax lodgement methods (e.g., E-Tax, tax accountants, and paper filings). Other data also were obtained, including E-Tax user gender, residency status, age, residential postal code, filing date, occupation, income level, refund history, and counts of filings made from overseas.

The E-Tax software provides users with an opportunity to voluntarily participate in a 26-question electronic survey, which, when completed, is automatically sent to the ATO upon filing of the individual's income tax return. The survey was introduced in the 2001 filing year. The survey asked a series of questions requiring responses relating to user satisfaction with the E-Tax product and also requested a rating of the importance of various issues. It also canvassed users' views of the importance of a range of motivators that are considered to encourage use of the product. Summarized results of the survey, including responses from 26,662 people comprising 9.73% of all E-Tax users, were obtained and included in this study (the authors acknowledge that conclusions drawn from survey responses are limited to the extent of the sample population).

E-Tax users were unable to be interviewed due to privacy constraints, which inhibited the identification of individual taxpayers using the E-Tax product. The study provides minimal insight into users' motivations and meanings, and any inferences drawn are based on quantitative analysis only. It is important to note that interviewee responses to the E-Tax electronic survey may not represent the motivations and adoption characteristics of all E-Tax users. E-Tax user profiles were deduced from the available data only; however, it is significant to note that complete and official personal income tax return filing population data, rather than sample data, were used in the analysis.

User Satisfaction With the E-Tax Application

A high level of satisfaction was reported by users in the survey about various technical aspects of the system's operation (e.g., ease of download, installation, navigation) and the way they interacted with it. Ninety percent of respondents were either very satisfied or satisfied with the E-Tax interview method. Eighty-nine percent of respondents considered this to be a very important or important feature of E-Tax. Table 2 shows E-Tax users' evaluations of the time-saving and efficiency aspects of E-Tax and its overall popularity with its users. Over 90% of users responded that they were satisfied overall with E-Tax.

Survey questions about specific E-Tax features drew positive responses about the product. The vast majority (80%) of respondents indicated that they were either very satisfied or satisfied with the ability to locate E-Tax on the ATO Web site, and 90% believed that this was either a very important or important feature. Eighty-seven percent of respondents were either very satisfied or satisfied with downloading the E-Tax software from the Internet, while 81% indicated that they were very satisfied or satisfied with downloading the E-Tax security software. This is also pertinent, because the E-Tax software is about four megabytes and takes considerable time to download, especially over a typical telephone line connection and modem.

Table 2. User evaluation of E-Tax

Questions	Very Satisfied	Satisfied	Neither	Dissatisfied	Very Dissatisfied
How satisfied or dissatisfied were you with E-Tax?	45%	47%	4%	3%	1%
Downloading the E-Tax software from the Internet	36%	51%	5%	4%	4%
Downloading the E-Tax security software	37%	43%	5%	9%	5%
Installing the E-Tax software on your computer	42%	50%	3%	2%	3%
The interview approach (where it asks you yes/no questions)	39%	51%	5%	3%	1%
Navigating around E-Tax	33%	51%	7%	7%	1%
Automatic checking of return to identify incorrect or missed items	47%	43%	5%	3%	1%
Ability to check your return details before filing	48%	42%	4%	4%	1%
Automatic calculation of assessment	63%	32%	2%	2%	1%

Source: E-Tax user survey 2001 (number of respondents: 26,662)

These results show that, at least for those E-Tax users who responded to the survey as they filed their 2001 income tax returns, E-Tax was received favorably. Ninety-four percent indicated that they would use E-Tax again. As the questionnaire was anonymous, we do not know to what extent the views of the survey respondents reflect those of E-Tax users as a whole. But the positive responses strongly suggest that the package was well received by users and that, thus, it was a viable initiative.

Accessibility

If E-Tax was complicated and required skill and education levels beyond those of the majority of the population, its use might be limited. Was it possible that E-Tax was suitable only for a small group of highly sophisticated, technologically adept users?

Using data extracted from the ATO's mainframe database, we analyzed the occupations of E-Tax filers on the premise that occupations are related to education and that this gives some indication of a person's ability to use a system that requires technical competence. Occupations are broadly identified by the ATO with codes representing about 300 occupational descriptions that are based on the Australian Bureau of Statistics standard occupational classifications (ABS, 2005). To make the comparisons clearer, each code was considered and allocated a professional or non-professional status. Seventeen codes representing about 90 occupations were allocated professional status. The remainder were represented as non-professional. Examples of occupations considered to hold a professional status include parliamentarians, judges, managers, scientists, engineers, medical practitioners, teachers, lawyers, and business professionals. Examples of those occupations allocated a non-professional status include carpenters, bricklayers, painters, automobile mechanics, cabinetmakers, sales representatives, taxi drivers, and construction workers.

As with other innovations, the early adopters are very likely to be those with a high level of knowledge and skill. Our analysis of the complete E-Tax dataset for the three filing years 1999 through 2001 reveals a gradual decline in the proportion of users in profes-

Figure 2. Professional and non-professional E-Tax users 1999-2001

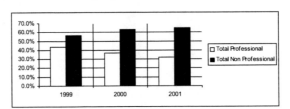

sional employment and an increase in the proportion whose non-professional occupations require less education (see Figure 2). In 1999, 43% of E-Tax users were identified as professionals, but in 2001, they represented only 31% of the E-Tax user base. Conversely, non-professional E-Tax users increased from 57% in 1999 to 65% in 2001. The fact that non-professionals are a majority and a growing proportion of E-Tax users indicates that the product is accessible not just for an elite group. In fact, the majority of E-Tax users are ordinary taxpayers with moderate levels of education.

E-Tax can be regarded as generally accessible, not just because of these positive assessments on the survey, but because the majority of Australian taxpayers are able to use computers and the Internet. Many Australian households have computers and Internet access, and other forms of provision are available.

The Australian Bureau of Statistics reported that in 2002, 66% of households had access to a computer, 53% had access to the Internet, and 58% of adults accessed the Internet (ABS, 2004). Thus, it is reasonable to conclude that, for the majority of taxpayers, E-Tax is an accessible and satisfactory product well within their competence to use.

E-Tax Ability to Deal With More Complex Tax Issues

Despite a thorough and targeted questioning of the user, there is some question about how well E-Tax deals with more complex tax issues. A deficiency in dealing with more complex tax issues would constitute a disincentive for some people to use E-Tax as opposed to tax agents. We examined this factor by identifying people whose tax affairs are likely to be more complicated. We had no direct measure of complexity, but, for this exercise, we assumed that people in the higher income brackets have more complex tax issues, because they are more likely to run larger operations and to have more items to claim as deductions.

Analysis of the income levels of E-Tax users during the three years 1999 through 2001 revealed that the predominant income range of E-Tax users was between $20,701 and $38,000, (middle-level incomes); 36% of users during the period were in that range. The second highest range fell between $5,401 and $20,700, representing an average of about 27% during the period. Together, these groups represent almost 63% of E-Tax users during the three filing years (see Figure 3). In 2001, the median individual income for people aged 15 years and over was approximately $18,000 per year (ABS, 2001).

Interestingly, E-Tax users receiving income in excess of $50,001 were a substantial group of around 17% of users during the period; however, the proportion of E-Tax users in this category declined substantially from 22% in 1999 to just over 10% in 2001,

Figure 3. Average income of E-Tax users 1999-2001

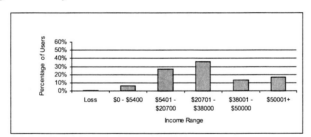

Table 3. Average income, deductions, and rebates by major filing methods in 2000

	E-Tax	Paper form	Tax agent
Total Average Income	$35,241	$24,360	$34,563
Total Average Deductions	$1,351	$856	$1,787
Total Average Tax Rebates	$730	$818	$808

Source: ATO Environmental Monitoring System, Australian Taxation Office, November 2001

reflecting again the broadening of the user base. These figures indicate that, as more people began using E-Tax, the profile of users became increasingly similar to the taxpayer population as a whole.

However, some differences in the groups can be noted. Table 3 shows that in 2000, the average annual income for E-Tax users was marginally higher than for those who used tax agents and significantly higher than for paper form users. However, their average level of deductions was lower than the deductions received by those who used tax accountants, and they had the lowest level of tax rebates among the three groups.

These figures lend further weight to the conclusion that using a tax accountant can help the taxpayer to maximize his or her refund. This is likely to be even more of an issue with the increasing complexity of Australian tax law (Australian Financial Review, 2004). The tradeoff is between a speedy return using E-Tax and a higher return via a tax accountant (although a fee is charged). Interestingly, only 24% of survey respondents reported that the simplicity of their tax affairs was an important or very important motivator for adopting E-Tax. Fifty-one percent indicated that they felt this was neither important nor unimportant. This suggests that the majority of E-Tax users file relatively uncomplicated income tax returns. However, it must be noted that, although the E-Tax application is unable to deal with very high levels of complexity (e.g., intricate property investment schemes and public shareholder investments), it can cope with a wide range of tax issues, such as employee work deductions, basic depreciation schedules, and tax refund estimates.

Speed of Processing

It is not uncommon for Australian taxpayers to receive a refund at the end of the financial year. A significant advantage of E-Tax is the speed with which a tax return can be filed and a refund provided. This is likely to be attractive to the majority of E-Tax users, and may, to some degree, contribute to its popularity. As pointed out earlier, the processing time for E-Tax is considerably shorter than for paper returns. The ATO indicates that an E-Tax assessment generally will be issued within 14 days, while the assessment of a paper-based tax return can take up to six weeks (ATO, 2005). It also is likely to be shorter than for many accountant-filed returns.

It may be expected, therefore, that E-Tax would be sought out by taxpayers expecting to receive a refund and of much less interest to those who expect to pay additional tax. In fact, the vast majority of E-Tax filers received a tax refund and, thus, had an incentive to use a system that would provide a refund as early as possible. Table 4 reveals that just over 86% of all E-Tax users received tax refunds for the 1999 and 2000 filing years. During the 2001 filing year, this figure had risen to about 90%.

Outcomes for Tax Payers

By far, the most common form of filing personal returns in Australia is via a tax accountant, who provides advice in addition to filling out and filing the returns (almost all accountants electronically file the returns that they prepare for clients). Hiring an accountant gives the taxpayer confidence that all potential tax deductions have been considered and included in income tax returns, where possible. This appears to be a well-founded perception. Taken as a group, filings through tax agents received the highest average level of claims for deductions of the major filing methods during the full E-Tax implementation period of 1999 through 2001. It would appear that tax accountants indeed may help taxpayers to increase their deductions and reduce their tax liability. A declining average refund for E-Tax users probably reflects the broader base of users, which, over the years, has included fewer people in professional occupations who will be more likely to have higher incomes.

To the extent that tax agent filings are recognized as the best way to increase tax deductions, E-Tax will be a less attractive form of filing. Even though E-Tax may provide

Table 4. E-Tax user refunds and additional payments, 1999-2000

Amount of Refund $	% of E-Tax Users
> 1,500	19.9%
1,000-1,499	11.2%
500-999	20.4%
1-499	34.6%
Percent receiving refund	86.2%

Source: ATO mainframe data extracted November 2001

Table 5. Motivators for adoption and user rating of significance

Adoption Motivators 2001	Very Important	Important	Total
How important, if at all, were the following motivations or reasons to encourage or convince you to use E-Tax?			
	%	%	%
I could do it anytime at home [convenience]	68	29	97
In-built calculation tools and help	40	48	89
Comfort with Internet and electronic transactions	37	52	89
I felt comfortable with the security software	46	42	88
Saving time	52	34	87
Less paperwork	45	35	81
My tax affairs were simple and straightforward	34	45	79
To save money (no filing agent fees)	43	29	72
To obtain a faster refund	32	38	70
My tax affairs were complex	7	17	24

users with prompts to alert them to the deductions that they might claim, it may not be able to match (or may not be perceived to match) the ability of tax accountants to identify allowable deductions.

Motivators for E-Tax Use

Despite the fact that a large majority of E-Tax users received refunds, the survey results did not indicate that speed of refund was as significant of a motivator for adoption as were convenience factors (see Table 5). Only 76% of respondents said that receiving a faster refund was very important and important as motivators to their use of E-Tax, which is about 10 percentage points less than the percentage of those who received a refund. This might be due to modest refunds for many of the respondents.

Saving money and accessing faster refunds were rated lowest among adoption motivators (although they still represented a sizeable majority of users), while users rated the time-saving convenience of the Internet as well as the instant online help and tools offered in the E-Tax product as more important. To the extent that these responses represent E-Tax users' real motivations, we could expect that they would be willing to use E-Tax, even if they weren't expecting to receive a refund.

Communicating E-Government Initiatives and Their Benefits

One of the issues to emerge about the launching of the E-Tax initiative was that many taxpayers appear not to have been aware of it, or they had difficulty locating the Web site to access it. An ATO marketing strategy document prepared in April 2001 revealed that the growth in the use of E-Tax occurred with only moderate promotion mainly through business as usual ATO channels. Examples of such channels include counter and telephone inquiries and advertising within the booklet containing the paper forms and other brochures.

The online survey asked E-Tax users how they found out about it. Table 6 shows the sources from which users learned of E-Tax for the 2001 filing year. The most common

Table 6. How users of E-Tax in 2001 learned about it

Publicity Medium	% of Users
Newspaper	7%
Booklet with paper tax forms	36%
Friend	21%
TV	7%
Internet	17%
Radio	3%
Other	9%
Total	100%

Source: E-Tax 2001 user online questionnaire summary, Australian Taxation Office

source of information was an advertisement in the paper form booklet (36% of users). The mass media were negligible sources of information, since there was no publicity campaign.

The fact that so few E-Tax users learned about the product through mass media indicates that the publicity strategy for E-Tax was inadequate and that it was insufficiently promoted through public channels. The majority of users found out about it through other sources. Without a public information campaign, it is unlikely that the diffusion rate of E-Tax or a similar application would have risen more swiftly. It might have been adopted in preference to paper forms, a private accountant, or one of the commercial providers of tax software. But this raises the question of how actively a government provider should compete in a market of private providers, individual tax accountants, and those selling commercial applications.

CURRENT CHALLENGES AND PROBLEMS FACING THE ORGANIZATION

The Broader Picture for E-Tax

Our analysis of Australia's E-Tax system suggests that it functions well, saves time, and is appropriate for a wide range of taxpayers. However, in the first four years, its uptake rate was lower than anticipated, and it may not be as cost effective for the ATO as originally hoped. Consequently, there appears to be a tension between e-government policy and the goals of efficiency and cost savings on the one hand and service to citizens on the other. Is it appropriate to invest in such online services, if insufficient numbers of people use them, thus rendering them uneconomical?

The E-Tax case exemplifies the issues that governments may face in attempting to balance the two objectives of increased government to citizen service provision and business process improvement. Here, we observe government pursuit of business efficiencies and effectiveness from improved online business processes, which also may threaten traditional citizen services and, therefore, citizen interaction with government. The contradiction here is that citizen interaction with governments is crucial in order for governments to serve the needs of citizens. Under-used online services are hard for governments to justify (Al-Kibsi et al., 2001).

Despite disappointing uptake levels, E-Tax performed well and was popular with its users. This case highlights the problems that governments have in balancing client services and business efficiency. E-Tax was effective largely in terms of e-government principles and met at least three of the government's policy objectives for the online environment by being widely available, easy to use, and low-cost. In meeting service objectives, E-Tax was successful for the small minority of taxpayers who use it. But it remained simply an additional channel, and the government did not see it as feasible to provide strong inducements to use it.

The overall contribution of E-Tax to the government's online strategy was, therefore, unclear, despite its ability to meet specific targets and comply with government policy directions. This is because E-Tax is not able to replace paper filings totally, neither now nor in the foreseeable future, especially for those taxpayers without IT skills or access to computers. There is a contradiction between its success as an application consistent with government strategy and policy principles and its lack of widespread acceptance as a method of personal tax filing.

REFERENCES

Al-Kibsi, G., de Boer, K., Mourshed, M., & Rea, N. (2001). Putting citizens on-line, not in line. *The McKinsey Quarterly, 2*.

Australian Bureau of Statistics (ABS). (2001). *Census 07/08/2001*. Retrieved January 15, 2005, from http://www.abs.gov.au/Ausstats/abs@census.nsf/4079a1bbd 2a04b80ca256b9d00208f92/7dd97c937216e32fca256bbe008371f0 !OpenDocument#Income

Australian Bureau of Statistics (ABS). (2004). *Measures of a knowledge-based economy and society. Australia information and communications technology indicators*. Retrieved October 20, 2004, from http://www.abs.gov.au/ausstats/abs@.nsf/ 94713ad445ff1425ca25682000192af2/7599f94ffdbadccbca 256d97002c8636!OpenDocument

Australian Bureau of Statistics (ABS). (2005). *Australian standard classification of occupations (ASCO)*. Retrieved January 28, 2005, from http://www.abs.gov.au/ Ausstats/abs@.nsf/66f306f503e529a5ca25697e0017661f/5c244fd9 d252cfc8ca25697e00184d35!OpenDocument

Australian Financial Review. (2004). *Push for business tax shake-up*. Retrieved October 10, 2004, from http://www.afr.com.au

Australian National Audit Office. (2000). *Electronic service delivery, including Internet use, by commonwealth government agencies* (Performance Audit). Australian National Audit Office.

Australian Taxation Office (ATO). (1997). E-tax trial scheduled for October. *The ATO Updater On-line*.

Australian Taxation Office (ATO). (1999a). E-tax ready for 1999 tax season. *The ATO Updater On-line*.

Australian Taxation Office (ATO). (1999b). *A new tax office for a new tax system.* Australian Taxation Office.

Australian Taxation Office (ATO). (1999c). *Supporting the community—1999-2002 plan.* Australian Taxation Office.

Australian Taxation Office (ATO). (1999d). *ATO electronic service delivery strategy version 1.1.* Australian Taxation Office.

Australian Taxation Office (ATO). (2000). *On-line eBusiness strategy, version 2.2.* Australian Taxation Office.

Australian Taxation Office (ATO). (2001). *On-line action plan 2001.* Australian Taxation Office.

Australian Taxation Office (ATO). (2003). Taxation Statistics. Australian Taxation Office.

Australian Taxation Office (ATO). (2004). Annual Report (Appendix 6, 330).

Australian Taxation Office (ATO). (2005). Retrieved January 25, 2005, from http://www.ato.gov.au/individuals/content.asp?doc=/content/DSHOB.NHOBWPS01.003670036.htm

Chamberlain, J., & Castleman, T. (2001). *National governments doing business online: An Australian look at current practice and future hazards.* Coffs Harbour, Australia: CollECTeR.

Chamberlain, J., & Castleman, T. (2002). EGovernment business strategies and services to citizens: An analysis of the Australian e-tax system. *Proceedings of the IFIP WG 8.4 2nd Conference on E-business: Multidisciplinary Research and Practice,* Copenhagen, Denmark.

Colecchia, A. (1999). Defining and measuring electronic commerce. Towards the development of an OECD methodology. *Proceedings of the Conference on the Measurement of Electronic Commerce*, Singapore.

EzGov. (2002). Web based tax filing. *EzGov.*

Faipo, C. A. (1999). E-commerce: The UK's taxation agenda. *The Tax Journal*, 17-19.

Girishankar, S. (1997). Feds get down to business with latest e-commerce push. *Internet Week, 688*, 18-19.

Government On-line. (2000). *Government On-line—The commonwealth government's strategy.* Department of Communications Information Technology and the Arts.

Inland Revenue. (2002). *Electronic business: Internet service for self assessment— Frequently asked questions.* Inland Revenue.

Internal Revenue Service. (2003). *IRS e-file for tax payers federal/state e-file.* Department of the Treasury, Internal Revenue Service.

La Porte, T. M., Demchak, C. C., et al. (2001). Webbing governance: Global trends across national-level public agencies. *Communications of the ACM, 44*(1), 63-67.

McCartney, I., & Wilson, R. (2001). *UK government: Civil service embraces the Internet.* Coventry: M2 Presswire.

McCarthy, J. (1997). Electronic tax pack to be piloted during 1997. *The ATO Updater On-line.*

Power, K. (2001). With liberty e-gov for all. *CIO Government*, 13-16.

Public Management. (2000). A guide to e-government and e-commerce. *Public Management, 82*(7), 1.

Symonds, M. (2000). Government and the Internet—The next revolution. *The Economist, 355*(8176), 3.

Thibodeau, P. (2000). E-government spending to soar through 2005. *Computerworld, 34*(17), 12-13.

Thomas, T. (2000). High hopes for on-line tax returns. *Business Review Weekly, 22*(25), 82.

Tillet, L. S. (2000). E-governments on the rise—In more municipalities, citizens go on-line instead of standing in line. *Internetweek, 818*, 24.

Jeff Chamberlain worked in national government administration for 20 years. Highlights of this included managing interactive Internet based projects, including involvement with the OECD and the exploration and implementation of the use of knowledge systems, intelligent agents and expert systems for government to citizen electronic services. He is now lecturing post graduate and undergraduate students at Deakin University, Australia, in electronic commerce, IT/IS project management and IT strategy and management. He holds two business degrees—one is a master's degree in electronic commerce. He has written a thesis on the Australian Government On-line and has published internationally on e-government and IS project management. His PhD studies focus on managerial and strategic issues in government electronic service delivery.

Tanya Castleman is a professor of information systems and head of the Deakin Business School at Deakin University. Her expertise in organisational sociology relates to her main area of research which is the social context of technology, particularly the commercial and social implications of electronic business and electronic government. She has conducted numerous research projects to identify ways in which these technologies are used to enhance business performance, achieve better customer service, derive cost savings, promote community and stimulate economic development. Small business issues and regional development have been a significant part of this research program. She publishes internationally on electronic commerce and electronic service delivery by governments.

This case was previously published in the *International Journal of Cases on Electronic Commerce*, 1(3), pp. 54-70, © 2005.

Chapter II

ENI Company

Ook Lee, Hansung University, Seoul, Korea

EXECUTIVE SUMMARY

ENI Company is an electronic commerce firm in South Korea. ENI Company provides English news items and English lessons to the subscribers through daily e-mail service that includes free English news-related question and answer sessions via e-mail. This case study deals with the struggle of this firm to establish and sustain its business in a less-developed national information infrastructure. Information on national information infrastructure and the Internet in South Korea is provided in order to facilitate understanding of the difficulty that ENI Company faces while conducting e-commerce in South Korea. The chronology of ENI Company evolution is described and the organizational structure of ENI Company is also presented. The marketing of ENI Company's products that is the biggest challenge for the firm is also discussed. This case is a good example of how to conduct an e-commerce in a county where national IT infrastructure is not ready for it.

BACKGROUND

Literature Survey

We can easily suggest that doing an e-commerce business in a developed country should be different from doing it in a less-developed country; here "development" refers mainly to the level of national IT infrastructure development. National IT infrastructure can be defined as the vision of broadband communications that are interoperable as though a single network, easily accessible and widely distributed to all groups within society bringing business, education, and government services directly to households and facilitating peer to peer communication throughout society (Kraemer et al., 1996). But this idealistic vision is hard to achieve for countries with less economic resources. By conducting a literature survey on e-commerce in developing countries, the following factors in addition to having a well-developed national IT infrastructure, were found to be necessary for a country in order to provide a fertile ground for e-commerce.

1. **Active use of credit cards in the Internet:** countries such as Philippines, India, and China, where credit cards are not widely used, can not find a workable payment method for e-commerce (Asuncion, 1997; Bhatnagar, 1997; Liu, 1997; Rao, 1998). In a way, South Korea is similar to these countries even though credit cards are widely used since many consumers on the Internet are very much reluctant to give out their credit card number. In the cultural point of view, another reason can be the fact that Koreans love to use cash in most business transactions even for a large sum just like people in Hong Kong (Westland et al., 1997). As for the payment method in e-commerce in Korea, many companies use money transfer through a bank account, that is, the buyer sends money to the bank account of the seller and the seller will send the goods to the buyer. This kind of pay-first-get-the goods-later payment method is obviously an obstacle for e-commerce to grow since many consumers feel insecure. Thus it is clear that without the full trust between consumers and e-commerce companies, even a country with widespread credit card use can not facilitate the growth of e-commerce.

2. **Fixed fee option of the unlimited use of local telephone lines:** Unlike the U.S., the South Korean telephone company is a government-owned monopoly. Even though it is trying to upgrade the communication lines with fiber-optic cables, its business policy has not changed, that is, there is no concept of separate billing for the unlimited local call option. In other words, if a person makes a local call to the Internet service provider and surfs the net for a long time, the person will get a very expensive phone bill. With this kind of environment, it is not easy to do e-commerce.

South Korean Internet Statistics

It is estimated that the number of Internet users in Korea is about 350,000 in 1996 as shown in Table 1(NCA, 1997).

In Figure 1 (NCA, 1997), we can see the rapid growth in the number of users of dedicated lines for their Internet use in Korea. The users are, in general, institutions which then provide Internet access to employees or students in the institution.

In Figure 2 (NCA, 1997), we can also see the rapid growth in the number of owners of PPP/Shell accounts for their Internet use in Korea. The owners are normally individual subscribers of commercial Internet service providers.

Table 1. Number of Internet users in Korea

	Commercial ISP users	Non-Commercial ISP users
Institution	51,850	69,000
Individual	231,226	221
Total	283,076	69,221

Figure 1. Number of dedicated line users (institutions) in Korea

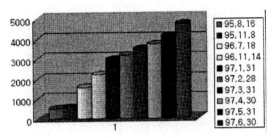

Figure 2. Number of owners of PPP/Shell account in Korea

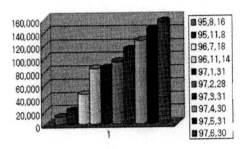

Using a Web-based survey (NCA, 1997), National Computerization Agency (NCA) of Korea was able to collect important statistics on the demographics of the Internet users in Korea. The total number of respondents who visited the survey Web site and completed the questionnaire was 1725 and following is the result of the survey.

- SEX: male (1463), female (262).
- AGE: under 15 (26), 15-20 (459), 21-25 (453), 26-30 (457), 31-35 (173), 36-40 (75), 41-45 (55), 46-50 (18), over 50 (9).
- OCCUPATION: college student (952), worker-non computer or Internet industry (305), worker-computer industry (125), primary and secondary school student (73), researcher (67), worker-Internet industry (52), teacher and professor (40), government (28), business executive (8), miscellaneous (75).
- EDUCATION: primary school (39), middle school (34), high school (754), two-year college (261), four-year college (471), master's (145), doctoral (21).
- PURPOSE OF USING INTERNET: information collection (1301), research (135), entertainment (151), business (82), miscellaneous (56).
- YEARS USING INTERNET: less than six months (147), six months to one year (854), one-two years (410), two-three years (161), over three years (153).

The result shows that the Internet in Korea is a new medium used mainly by young college students and professionals for non-business-related activity; this also means that user population is not very active in utilizing e-commerce as of 1997.

NCA also reports that the total number of e-commerce Web sites in Korea is 140 where only 50 have all the mechanisms for automated shopping, that is, the payment method using credit cards is workable for these sites as of March, 1998 (NCA, 1998). In the same report, NCA estimates the volume of e-commerce in 1998 to be around 9.4 billion won (US$7 million). Thus it is clear that e-commerce is in its infancy in Korea.

ENI Company Introduction

ENI Company (pseudonym is being used to protect the anonymity of the firm) is a South Korean firm that specializes delivering overseas news in English and its translation with lessons on English language to the subscribers via e-mail. The primary goal of this business is to educate the public in English reading comprehension as well as inform through up-to-date foreign current affair items. The business was formed in 1997 by a university professor who had extensive knowledge in world affairs. The business charges the subscribers a monthly fixed fee that was approximately US$10. The English news and its translation with lessons on English expressions are delivered everyday via e-mail to the subscribers. The subscribers can also ask questions regarding the content of the news item and its explanation and the firm answers them as soon as possible.

SETTING THE STAGE

Before we embark on presenting our case, we need to address following issues. Since our subject firm is an e-commerce firm in South Korea, it is bounded by the level of development of South Korean national IT infrastructure. Thus information on South Korean national IT infrastructure is given. Our subject firm also needs to conduct marketing in cyberspace and in order to facilitate understanding of the concept of cyberspace marketing, we introduce some background theories of cyberspace marketing.

South Korean National IT Infrastructure

South Korea embarked on building its national IT infrastructure in 1994 which was officially called "Korea Information Infrastructure (KII)" project (Jeong & King, 1996). The Korean government committed itself to promoting industries such as computer makers, telecommunication network builders and value-added service providers, multimedia firms, cable TV industries, and Internet-related companies. Major aspects of Korean national IT infrastructure are described in Tables 2 to 5 (Jeong & King, 1996).

E-commerce firms in South Korea have to struggle in a national IT infrastructure which is not adequate for effective commercial activity yet. This case shows that despite this kind of hardship, it is possible to create and run an e-commerce firm even though it will be difficult to generate a big financial bonanza.

Cyberspace Marketing

As many firms throughout the world try to conduct business on the Internet, the importance of marketing in the Internet has become an important issue to IS scholars and practitioners alike (Copfer, 1998). Some businesses are interested in setting up a WWW site to expand their reach to customers in addition to the physical entity in real world,

Table 2. Size of domestic PC market

Year	1991	1992	1993	1994
Quantity	614	665	773	1200

*In terms of PC's sold (thousand sets).

Table 3. Telephone lines per 100 population (1993)

Korea	U.S.	Japan	Germany	UK	France
38	53	47	46	47	53

*Units: thousand sets.

Table 4. Subscribers of mobile communications

	1993	1994
Mobile Telephones	472	960

*Units: thousand sets.

Table 5. Multimedia industry (1994)

Type	Sales (Billion Won)
Multimedia PC	94.5
CD-ROM drive	37.5
CD-ROM Title	38.0
Sound card	51.4
Image card	25.0
Tools	5.4
Total	251.8

whereas others try to establish a presence in the Internet without having any physical entity in the real world. In both cases, firms need to conduct marketing in order to solve vexing questions such as who the customers are, how to advertise effectively, etc. (Mosley, 1998).

In this case study we define those consumers who are using the Internet and/or an online information provider such as America Online as consumers of cyberspace. Now that cyberspace is born and all these users of cyberspace are reachable by the Internet and they, therefore, have become attractive consumers to the companies that always try to get any individual consumer's attention. For example, a consumer spend their awake time in watching TV or listening to the radio; this is the reason that advertisements exist in those mediums. Thus, similarly, more and more people are spending their time surfing the Internet, which means that companies should advertise in this medium too, since the consumers' precious attention span is being used here just as with TV and radio.

Thus how to advertise effectively in cyberspace has become a very important issue. To advertise effectively, a business should choose the right kind of tool in order to reach enough customers with a reasonable amount of time and money. Many businesses now have Web pages which were made for variety of purposes. For example, big corporations created Web pages to promote corporate image, thus these Web sites are not for trading goods and services. On the other hand, some firms created Web sites for the purpose of selling goods and services such as books, computers, flowers, etc. Among them, some exist only in Web sites, that is, no physical entity exists, while others have physical entities with Web sites used for additional business from cyberspace consumers. Except for corporations which created Web sites for public relations purposes, all other Web sites are engaged in profit-making ventures, which consequently need sophisticated marketing strategies and tools (Hansen, 1998). Thus, Internet marketing can be defined as marketing strategies and tools that are designed to enhance product purchases on the Internet. In other words, Internet marketing is geared toward consumers of cyberspace.

These consumers of cyberspace have some distinctive characteristics compared to real-world consumers. The main differences are as follows. The consumers of cyberspace choose only the Web sites which are of interest to them, which means that unlike TV, radio or print advertisement, it is difficult to promote a product to unsuspecting mass customers. In other words, people who are interested in adult-related products will go to those Web sites without wandering into some other Web sites, such as those selling flowers. Thus, making people aware of the existence of particular Web sites even though they are not of interest to the consumer at the moment is not easy. There are some technological breakthroughs such as PUSH technology which does provide Web site information to the consumer who seems to have potential interest in the particular area (Burke, 1997).

But even in PUSH technology, one can only push things after the information regarding the customers' behavior is gathered. Thus, with millions newly signing-up to the Internet everyday, the PUSH technology has its limits. Nowadays, Internet advertising is often done in banner ads which take up small space on a Web page, are supposedly noticeable and, hopefully, actually being read. But banner ads can appear only in Web pages which a particular consumer reads, that is, if the Web site is not visited by consumers, the ad becomes simply obsolete. There has to be a better way to market a product in the Internet in order to reach more people possibly in mass numbers.

Direct e-mail advertisement can be a good answer to solve the above stated problem in Internet marketing. One can not reach mass customers if only banner ads are used. Direct and bulk e-mailing literally means sending bulk or mass number of e-mails directly to unsuspecting users of cyberspace (Gustavson, 1997). The product that is advertised in a direct e-mail advertisement can be anything, which means that unlike PUSH technology which advertises only products considered to be of interest to consumers whose online browsing behavior is known, the direct e-mail advertisement can send promotional messages of any product to almost anybody who has an e-mail address. Thus, direct and bulk e-mailing is more or less similar to the direct marketing in real-world shopping. In direct marketing, shoppers are either called or sent a so-called junk-mail by the direct marketer.

Culnan (1993) investigated the consumer attitudes toward direct mail advertisement. In her paper, she claims that strategic uses of information technology based on personal information may raise privacy concerns among consumers if these applications do not reflect a common set of values. Her study addresses what differentiates consumers who object to certain uses of personal information from those who do not object. Data collected by questionnaire from young consumers are used to identify a research approach for investigating attitudes toward the secondary use of personal information for direct marketing. Secondary information use occurs when personal information collected for one purpose is subsequently used for a different purpose. While secondary information use is both widespread and legal, it may be viewed as an invasion of privacy when it occurs without the knowledge or consent of the consumer.

But in the case of direct e-mail advertisement, there is no prior knowledge or consent of the consumer, therefore there can be serious problems using direct e-mailing as a marketing tool. The setting for her study is the use of point-of-sale data from a supermarket frequent shopper program to generate direct mail solicitations. Control emerges as a clear theme in differentiating individuals with positive overall attitudes toward secondary information use from those with negative attitudes. Study participants with positive attitudes are less concerned about privacy (measured as control over personal information, that is, some people don't like to try hard to keep every aspect of his or her life under tight control while some people like to be secretive about almost everything; like to be in total control over one's life), perceive shopping by mail as beneficial, and have coping strategies for dealing with unwanted mail.

Notice that this result happens when the use of secondary information was already consented. Thus, in direct e-mailing advertisement, even people who have a tendency to favor less control over his/her life and are more tolerant of junk surface mail, can react negatively to those direct e-mail ads since there was no consent of their address for information use, whatsoever. But people who have tendency to tolerate junk surface mail, might still react positively since those e-mails contain information about products that can be useful or cheaper for the consumer.

Some merits of direct e-mail advertisement are as follows:

a.   Unlike direct marketing which can cost heavily, the cost of bulk e-mailing is very low since sending e-mail letters to any number of people in the world does not cost a dime, at least for the use of the communication line, that is, Internet communication is free. All the firm has to pay is a local phone bill and, if the firm does not own a server, to pay the Internet service provider which does not charge by the number of e-mail letters, but by the time spent online (sometimes, just a flat fee per a certain period time, say, a month).

b.   E-mail can cause a very direct response from the consumer since unlike junk letters in real world marketing, people tend to read e-mails even though those are advertisement (Martin, 1998). Junk-mails can be thrown out without even considering what the content could be. But junk or spam e-mails are harder to delete away because people tend to read any e-mail before they delete it. Once they read it, the information which is contained in the ad e-mail can be very effective in terms of getting attention from the customer.

CASE DESCRIPTION

Chronology of ENI Company

- **January 1997:** ENI Company was founded by a marketing professor who spent 10 years studying and working in the U.S. and Australia.
- **February 1997:** With 108 subscribers, ENI started to send English news via e-mail.
- **May 1997:** The number of subscribers: 220. ENI Company started an advertising campaign in the conventional media as well as cyberspace.
- **May 1998:** The number of subscribers: 1,002. The amount of projected annual sales revenue: 120,000 dollars. The amount of projected annual net profit: 30,000 dollars.

Organization of ENI Company

The founder, who is also the CEO, wanted to minimize bureaucracy which he regarded as a major cost center. Thus the organization of ENI Company is very flat, with primary workers being teachers whose main tasks include translating English news items and answering questions from subscribers. Currently ENI Company has 10 teachers who work in an autonomous environment where each teacher has the authority to work, that is, teachers have no management interference on how they write English news items and how they answer questions from subscribers. They are given a PC and an e-mail account for their work. Thus translating English news from sources such as AP or Reuters which provide up-to-date news in the Internet, and sending the translated English news plus explanations on English expressions in the news via e-mail, and answering e-mail questions from subscribers, all fall into each teacher's responsibility. With the current 1,000 subscribers, each teacher deals with 100 subscribers personally. Other staff include a computer technician and a secretary who also works as a bookkeeper. Figure 3 shows the organizational structure of ENI Company.

Figure 3. Organizational structure of ENI Company

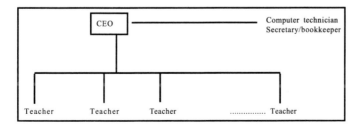

Marketing Strategy of ENI Company

The marketing strategy of ENI Company can be analyzed through marketing mix components as follows:

1. **Product:** ENI Company tried to differentiate its products from its competitors by giving a personal touch. In other words, by answering questions from subscribers promptly and paying attention to each subscriber's needs in English learning, ENI Company was successful in attracting loyal followers.
2. **Price:** ENI Company tried to differentiate its price from its competitors by offering a fixed monthly fee regardless of the number of questions answered. Other services charged customers by the length of time they spent on their service, since other services were available on the online information providers unlike ENI Company which supplies via e-mail.
3. **Place:** ENI Company did not see a presence in the Web as a viable option due to the small number of Internet surfers. Instead, ENI Company noticed that even though there were relatively small number of people surfing the Internet, many more people have e-mail accounts either from commercial Internet service providers or from non-commercial Internet service providers such as one's own schools and companies. Thus ENI Company decided to exist only in the e-mail form until there will be more Web surfers in Korea.
4. **Promotion:** ENI Company tried cyberspace advertising medium such as banner ads which failed due to the small number of Web surfers, and bulk e-mailing ads which failed due to the high telephone bill for modem-based mailing and the law against such bulk e-mailing ads for non-modem-based mailings. ENI Company relied more on conventional advertising medium such as magazine and newspaper ads.

In summary, Table 6 outlines the marketing strategy of ENI Company.

In the CEO's Own Words

The CEO of ENI Company provided detailed information on the firm. The following conversations are taken from the interview with the CEO.

Q: When and how was ENI created?

A: In the beginning of 1997 I created the firm since I thought that I could use my extensive knowledge on world affairs in helping Koreans understand foreign news and at the same time, teach them on English lessons using expressions used in the news items. The Koreans are very interested in improving their English skill, especially young students in high school or college since it is vital to acquire a good English skill in order

Table 6. Marketing strategy of ENI Company

Product	Personal Touch
Price	Fixed Fee
Place	E-mail Form
Promotion	Conventional Medium

to get into a good college and to land in a better job. My idea was that if ENI Company could provide attentive answers to questions regarding English promptly, many people would sign on to our service. It turned out to be true. But there was a serious difficulty in getting our company known to the general public."

Q: What are its short and long term objectives?
A: In short term, our objective is to create a critical mass of loyal subscribers whose size should be at least 1,000 people, which we achieved in a year. In long term, our objective is to move to the Web eventually and be able to serve multimedia English news and lessons when the IT infrastructure of Korea improves and the number of Internet users increases significantly.

Q: Who are ENI Company's competitors?
A: There are several similar services in the online information providers such as "Chollian" which is similar to AOL in U.S. But they don't send out individual e-mails; they put English news and lessons in the directory of online information providers. Thus they can not give the personal touch as ENI Company does. ENI Company is the only one that provides daily e-mail English news service to the individual subscribers in Korea.

Q: What were the challenges ahead? And how has ENI addressed the challenges?
A: The challenge was marketing, especially advertising. In order to get more subscribers, it was critical to do effective advertising campaign. We tried conventional advertising medium such as magazines, radio, and newspapers as well as cyberspace advertising medium such as banner ads in the Web page and direct e-mail ads. Besides conventional advertising medium whose effect was obvious, we thought that cyberspace ads could be effective too. At first, the banner ad in the Web page looked attractive but soon we realized that the number of people who browsed the Web pages in South Korea was still not big enough due to the low development of national IT infrastructure. We finally looked at mass mailing technique and it looked workable. We sent out direct e-mail ads and found out that modem-based bulk mailing used up so much telephone time that it was not financially feasible since there was no fixed fee option for local phone call in Korea. Non-modem-based bulk mailing through the Internet could not be used either since the Internet bulk mailing was already against the law in Korea. Thus we relied more on conventional medium such as magazine and newspaper ads.

Q: What were the critical events and outcomes in the evolution of ENI Company?
A: The critical event happened after we installed the mass mailer and used it for sending advertisement mails for ENI Company. We didn't realize how big the telephone bill could be when the dial-up connection was used for a long time. In other words, during the peak hours the performance of the mass mailer got downgraded, which resulted in taking much longer time to finish sending out all mails. This meant a disaster for ENI Company since the increased revenue from the bigger number of subscribers thanks to the mass mail advertisement was wiped out because of astronomical amount of the local phone bill. This event forced us to give up advertising through the mass mailer.

CURRENT CHALLENGES/PROBLEMS FACING THE ORGANIZATION

The following matters can be considered to be current challenges/problems for ENI Company.

First, how to sustain an e-commerce venture in a less-developed national IT infrastructure is a big concern for ENI Company. Effective e-commerce activity requires well-developed national information technology infrastructure such as well-connected fiber optic computer networks that cover the entire country, and easy availability of computers and affordable cost of network use among ordinary citizens of the country.

Second, how to conduct marketing for the venture is another big concern for ENI Company. Not only is it very difficult to establish a functioning e-commerce firm but it is even more difficult to do marketing on the Internet. The product of an e-commerce firm is usually advertised in banner-style ads in the Web page, which is a common practice and is considered to be a working solution in developed countries. However, in countries such as South Korea, not many people are surfing the Internet, that is, the number of people who can afford to surf the Internet for quite a long time are very limited due to the outdated billing practice of the government-owned monopolistic phone company. Thus, in this environment an e-commerce company which wants to sell a tangible product such as computer hardware components or software items has no choice but to create a Web page that sells those products and faces the problem of how to make its Web page noticeable to the small-number of Web surfers in Korea. Furthermore, those e-commerce companies who sell intangible goods face even more difficult challenge in advertising their products. The company which is the subject of this case sells English news and English lessons as products; they deliver these products to the individual's e-mail account. In short, any e-commerce company in Korea faces the same problem in marketing, which is how to advertise effectively in an environment where there are only small number of people who are surfing World Wide Web pages.

Third, how to establish a workable payment method is the biggest concern for ENI Company. This matter is a serious obstacle in the development of e-commerce even in developed countries such as the U.S. since consumers are worried that their credit card numbers might be stolen and might not get the ordered goods after paying with credit cards. In less developed countries such as South Korea, the consumers are, of course, very much worried when they order a product online or through the Internet, not because of the possibility that their credit card numbers might be stolen, but mostly because of the fact that the cash they have already paid might be robbed, that is, the goods never arrive. The reason is rather simple. In a less-developed country like South Korea, not many people have credit cards and even for those with credit cards, tend to prefer cash when the price of the good is not very high. For this reason, most online payment is made as follows: First, the customer goes to the bank and does a wire-transfer of cash to the designated bank account of the seller which is an e-commerce firm. Second, the e-commerce firm's employee goes to the bank and checks if a certain customer's cash was transferred. Last, if the money-transfer is confirmed then the firm sends out the good that was ordered by the customer. With this kind of payment method, the consumers are naturally worried, since in actual incidents some firms took the money and ran away, that is, no goods arrived.

Last, how to handle customer relations is also a concern for ENI Company. The subject of our case is a firm that claims to be attentive to the needs of the customers, that is, it promises to answer all questions regarding English news items and lessons using those news items that are delivered to the subscribers. But in reality, it is very difficult to give satisfying answers to every question from the customer. Thus, quality control of customer service is a challenging puzzle to solve.

REFERENCES

Asuncion, R. M. (1997). Potentials of electronic markets in the Philippines. *Electronic Markets, 7*(2), 34-37.

Bhatnagar, S. (1997). Electronic commerce in India: The untapped potential. *Electronic Markets, 7*(2), 22-24.

Burke, R. (1997). Do you see what I see? The future of virtual shopping. *Journal of the Academy of Marketing Science, 25*(4), 352-360.

Copfer, R. (1998). Marketing in an online world. *American Salesman, 43*(3), 19-21.

Culnan, M. (1993). 'How did they get my name?': An exploratory investigation of consumer attitudes toward secondary information use. *MIS Quarterly, 17*(3), 341-361.

Gustavson, J. (1997). Netiquette and DM. *Marketing, 102*(42), 46.

Hansen, G. (1998). Smaller may be better for Web marketing. *Marketing News, 32*(2), 10-11.

Jeong, K. H., & King, J. (1996). National information infrastructure initiatives in Korea: Vision and Policy Issues. *Information Infrastructure And Policy, 5*(2), 119-133.

Kraemer, K., Dedrick, J., Jeong, K. H., King, J., Thierry, V., West, J., & Wong, P. K. (1996). National information infrastructure: A cross-country comparison. *Information Infrastructure And Policy, 5*(2), 81-93.

Liu, Z. (1997). China's information super highway: Its goal, architecture and problems. *Electronic Markets, 7*(4), 45-50.

Martin, J. (1998). You've got junk mail. *PC World, 16*(4), 45-46.

Mosley, J. (January 19, 1998). Deck us all in on-line shopping. *Marketing News, 32*(2), 6.

NCA (National Computerization Agency of Korea). (1997). *A Study on the technical trend of the NIC (Network Information Center) and Internet technologies.* Retrieved from http://ncalib.nca.or.kr/HTML/1997/97066/f97066.htm

NCA (National Computerization Agency of Korea). (1998). The White Paper on Informatization of 1998. Retrieved from http://calsec.nca.or.kr/knowledgebase.htm

Rao, M. (1998). Ad convention: Indian advertising agencies urged to harness Internet technologies. *Electronic Markets, 8*(1), 48-49.

Westland, J. C., Kwok, M., Shu, J., Kwok, T., & Ho, H. (1997). Electronic cash in Hong Kong. *Electronic Markets, 7*(2), 3-6.

FURTHER READING

Kalakota, R., & Whinston, A. B. (1996). *Electronic commerce: A manager's guide.* Addison-Wesley.

Kalakota, R., & Whinston, A. B. (1996). *Frontiers of electronic commerce.* Addison-Wesley.

Keen, P. G. W., & Ballance, C. (1997). *On-line profits: A manager's guide to electronic commerce.* Harvard Business School Press.

Meeker, M., & Stanley, M. (1997). *The Internet advertising report.* HarperCollins.

O'Keefe, S. (1996). *Publicity on the Internet: Creating successful publicity campaigns on the Internet and the commercial online services.* John Wiley & Sons.

Sterne, J. (1997). *What makes people click: Advertising on the Web.* Que Education & Training.

Whinston, A. B., Stahl, D. O., & Choi, S. Y. (1997). *The economics of electronic commerce.* Macmillan Technical Publishing.

Wong, P. K. (1996). Implementing the NII vision: Singapore's experience and future challenges. *Information Infrastructure and Policy, 5*(2), 95-117.

Zeff, R. L., Aronson, B., & Zeff, R. (1997). *Advertising on the Internet.* John Wiley & Sons.

Ook Lee is a professor of information systems in the Department of Business Administration at Hansung University in Seoul, Korea. Previously, he worked as a project director at Information Resources, Inc., in Chicago, Illinois, and as a senior information research scientist at Korea Research Information Center in Seoul, Korea. His main research interests include electronic commerce, digital libraries, expert systems, neural networks, and critical social theory. He holds a BS in computer science and statistics from Seoul National University in Seoul, Korea, and an MS in computer science from Northwestern University in Evanston, Illinois. He also earned an MS and PhD in management information systems from Claremont Graduate University in Claremont, California.

This case was previously published in M. Raisinghani (Ed.), *Cases on Worldwide E-Commerce: Theory in Action*, pp. 186-200, © 2002.

Chapter III

Hardwarezone:
A Singaporean Success Story

Chee Chang Tan, Institute of Technical Education, Singapore

Gek Woo Tan, National University of Singapore, Singapore

EXECUTIVE SUMMARY

Hardwarezone.com is rated the top IT media Web site in Singapore by Hitwise, with more than 32 million page visits per month (Chellam, 2004). It provides 100% proprietary and localized content on IT news, product releases, and numerous member-centric services, such as hardware pricelists and forums. What started as a hobby for six undergraduates on an SGD $1,000 capital became a new-age media company with over SGD $200,000/month in advertising revenue and SGD $2 million in net assets within a short span of six years. Their success and continued growth today is exceptional, considering how most of its competitors and other dot-com ventures in Singapore have fallen by the wayside or stagnated after the dot-com crisis during mid-1999. This teaching case will chart the evolution of Hardwarezone's business model and strategies through its humble beginnings and the challenges to the company as a result of the dot-com crisis and thereafter.

ORGANIZATION BACKGROUND

Singapore Overclocker's Group

August 9, 2002—Eugene Low, General Manager and founding member of Hardwarezone, had just attended a company function celebrating the fourth anniversary of its founding and was in his office poring over some old photographs. One picture, in particular, made him smile. Dated four years ago, the slightly stained picture showed six friends, smiles and exuberance etched in their young faces, posing in what looked like an empty room totally devoid of any office equipment.

The room in the picture was, in fact, where Hardwarezone first began operations. It was a small factory space, measuring a mere six meters by four meters, rented from an IT company at JTC Block 71, Ayer Rajah Crescent in Singapore. As part of Eugene's personal ritual on this particular day of significance, he began to recall the story of Hardwarezone, its metamorphosis from its humble beginnings, through turbulent and exciting times, to the dynamic and fast-moving organization that it was that day.

Hardwarezone began as a hobby involving do-it-yourself (DIY) computers for six undergraduates from the computing and engineering faculties at the National University of Singapore. The initial manifestation of Hardwarezone was the Singapore Overclocker's Group, a special interest group founded in June 1998, hosted under the umbrella of SingaporeOne, a Singaporean government initiative.

The Singapore Overclocker's Group (SOG) served a niche community of CPU overclockers by allowing them to post their hardware configurations and overclocking results. Despite its niche roots and the relatively small size of the overclockers community in Singapore, SOG became so popular that the management of SingaporeOne had to tell the group to move out, as it was effectively taking up 90% of SingaporeOne's total bandwidth.

Based on the overwhelming popularity of SOG and the experience gained from managing it, the founders identified an unmet demand for a Web site that provides hardware reviews, prices, and comparisons among the community of DIY computer enthusiasts in Singapore. Assisted and endorsed by the management of SingaporeOne, the founders of Hardwarezone applied for and obtained an SGD $20,000 grant from the Infocomm Development Authority of Singapore, a statutory board developed by the Singaporean government to foster a world-class infocomm industry in Singapore.

With this grant and a mere SGD $1,000 initial investment, on August 9, 1998, Hardwarezone was founded in a rented factory space with an office running solely on home equipment. The name *Hardwarezone* came about because the founders believed that it was catchy, easy to remember, and, most importantly, the domain name was available. At the time, Hardwarezone was running on empty; it only had enough capital for one server and a mere six months of bandwidth charges.

The Dot-Com Bubble

From Hardwarezone's inception in August 1998 to mid-1999, the global economy was in a boom, and the IT sector was developing at an unprecedented rate, a phenomenon often referred to today as the *dot-com bubble*. The concepts of e-commerce and dot-coms quickly were being embraced by both major organizations and budding entrepreneurs worldwide.

The rapid development of the Internet; the business opportunities and promises it offered, as well as the declining prices of computer hardware as a result of technological advancement resulted in an increase in demand for PCs in general. Because of this increasing demand and the relative higher costs of off-the-shelf computers, DIY computers presented a more flexible and cost-effective alternative.

With the increasing demand for DIY computers, the information needs of DIY computer enthusiasts increased. However, particularly in Singapore, there was a lack of information on local IT products (e.g., product reviews and prices). With the maturing Internet technology and the rapid growth of Internet traffic, the founders of Hardwarezone identified the opportunity in using the many advantages offered by the Internet, such as its global nature, the low entry cost, the opportunity to reach millions, the existence of standard protocols, the interactivity it offered, the wide range of possibilities and resources, and the rapid growth of support infrastructures, such as the World Wide Web (O'Connell, 2000; Patel & McCarthy, 2000; Plant, 2000; Slywotzky & Morrison, 2000; Tapscott, 2000), to meet the increasing information needs of local DIY computer enthusiasts.

One of the main obstacles at this point was the intense competition already existing within the IT publications industry. Direct competitors in the online IT publications industry during this period included CNET, ZDNet, and PCWorld (see Appendix A). They were major players catering to the information needs of DIY computer enthusiasts globally over the Internet. These organizations were well funded and internationally recognized and had large global audiences. They also provided numerous quality IT product reviews and prices targeted mainly for the international audience.

In Singapore, there also were several Web sites dedicated to local IT product reviews. Hardware-One.com (see Appendix A) was one of the pioneers in the local IT publications industry providing localized product reviews and prices, catering to the needs of the Singaporean DIY computer enthusiast. The content generated was highly localized and catered to local needs.

Traditionally, DIY computer enthusiasts obtain product information from IT magazines. Therefore, indirect competitors during this period included local publications, such as *Chip*, *Tech*, *Gravity*, and *Singapore Computing Magazine*, as well as foreign magazines like *PCWorld* (backed and funded by the highly influential International Data Group), *Wired*, *ComputerWorld*, and *PC Magazine*. These off-line IT publications offered the same extensive coverage of IT products as their online counterparts and offered a certain degree of tangibility in having a physical product.

Market Strategies

Based on the experience gained from running the SOG and the feedback they received from its close-knit community, Hardwarezone identified two under-served needs of local DIY computer enthusiasts that none of their competitors fulfilled.

First, there was a need for comprehensive, up-to-date prices of local IT products. The prices of local IT products (e.g., from Sim Lim Square and Funan IT mall, major retail malls for computer parts and peripherals in Singapore) fluctuated frequently. They were highly subjected to the economic forces of demand and supply, and listed prices on a particular day could differ drastically from the previous day or from the prices listed in foreign IT publications. Product prices listed in local IT publications also tended to be incomprehensive (i.e., desired product not listed) or outdated (i.e., product prices not up-to-date).

Second, there was a need for comprehensive reviews of local IT products. The needs of local DIY computer enthusiasts were not met sufficiently by foreign IT publications, as their content is generated and targeted at the global audience (e.g., product reviewed may not be available locally) and may be irrelevant in the local context. Local IT publications also were inadequate, as the quality and quantity of product reviews often were lacking.

Based on this analysis, Hardwarezone quickly positioned itself as a provider of up-to-date prices of local IT products as well as a provider of comprehensive local product reviews, benchmarks, and compatibility reports, based on product tests conducted in its own test labs to cater to the needs of local DIY computer enthusiasts. This significantly reduced the amount of time and effort they spent physically visiting each store in order to obtain the required information.

During this period of boom and opportunities, Hardwarezone used several key market strategies with a strong emphasis on establishing market presence and credibility for its Web site.

One of its key strategies was to broaden its target market. The SOG, predecessor of Hardwarezone, targeted the PC overclockers (computer enthusiasts who were interested in overclocking their CPUs) market segment. By broadening its focus to IT products reviews, news, and prices, Hardwarezone broadened its market focus to encompass first-time computer builders, independent computer assemblers, and hardware enthusiasts.

Second, in order to distinguish itself from other existing online IT publications, Hardwarezone established hardware testing labs to generate its own product reviews. Thus, content generated by Hardwarezone was 100% proprietary. Its content also was generally perceived as more creditable, because all product reviews were created by genuine content authors, and more relevant in the local context, since testing was done only on products available in the local mainstream market.

Next, in order to establish its market presence firmly, members at Hardwarezone were not charged fees for the information they accessed. Its main source of revenue was from online advertising.

Another key strategy they used to establish market presence and credibility was the formation of strategic partnerships with local IT vendors. In order to obtain the latest IT product prices and information regarding their availability, Hardwarezone formed partnerships with many local vendors in Sim Lim Square, the biggest IT retail mall in Singapore, and offered publicity in exchange for information that Hardwarezone required. As a result, Hardwarezone was able to enhance the timeliness of their product information by updating their Web site on a daily basis.

Last and most important, Hardwarezone undertook extensive measures to nurture a strong sense of community among their users. First, management sought to enhance the interactivity of its discussion forum by replying directly to any user query. Second, social gatherings such as outings and barbecues were organized to add a physical dimension to the communities. Last, management identified key forum contributors and opinion leaders and invited them to the office for tea. Freebies such as t-shirts and forum moderator privileges also were handed out to ensure their loyalty to Hardwarezone. This last strategy, as the management of Hardwarezone found out later, proved to be an important foundation upon which future strategies and success were built.

Competitive Advantage

Hardwarezone held several important competitive advantages relative to its competitors, which contributed greatly to their early success.

First, Hardwarezone's content was geared specifically to suit the tastes of local IT enthusiasts. The content of foreign IT publications, mainly based in the United States, is both generated in the U.S. and geared toward the needs of the U.S. audience. For example, some of the products reviewed are not available locally, and listed product prices are not in Singapore dollars. Thus, the content may not be relevant or simply not up-to-date in the local context.

Second, capitalizing on the strategic partnerships with local IT vendors and immense dedication on the part of management, Hardwarezone provided a comprehensive and up-to-date coverage of local IT products. Despite the existence of a few local Web sites dedicated to local IT product reviews, due to a shortage of manpower and an even greater lack of funding, product reviews were not nearly as comprehensive or extensive as their foreign counterparts. By establishing a partnership with local IT vendors, Hardwarezone was able to get access to the latest IT news, products, and prices, and feature content that was more comprehensive and up-to-date than any of its local competitors.

A third advantage was credibility. Compared to local competitors, Hardwarezone also was able to create a greater sense of credibility due to the establishment of its own hardware testing labs. The credibility of Hardwarezone also was enhanced by its publicized partnerships with local IT vendors as well as its rapidly growing number of forum participants.

Last, compared to its indirect competitors (i.e., IT magazines), a key advantage of Hardwarezone is cost. While a typical IT magazine can cost anything from SGD $9.00 to SGD $15.00, the content on Hardwarezone's Web site is absolutely free. Moreover, past content is archived and organized to facilitate easy access, compared to tediously trying to purchase a back issue of a magazine.

Before the Dot-Com Crisis

The results achieved by Hardwarezone up until mid-1999 speak for themselves (see Table 1). Incorporated within two months of its launch, Hardwarezone quickly estab-

Table 1. Hardwarezone statistics for year 1998

		1998

1.	Revenue
	    a. Online Advertising
	    b. Off-line Advertising
		Total = SGD$300,000
		Online = SGD$300,000
		Off-line = SGD$0

2.	Net Profits	(SGD$300,000)
3.	Amount of capital investments in Hardwarezone	SGD$21,000 (inclusive of SGD$20,000 grant from IDA Singapore)
4.	Number of Employees	6
5.	Technical Infrastructure	One server residing at 1-Net

6.	Web Site Statistics
	    a. Number of page views per month
	    b. Official membership figures
		Page Views: 16,000,000
		
		Membership: 40,000

lished itself in Singapore as a massively popular online portal for price guides and tech reviews. Within a mere one-and-a-half years, online advertising revenue reached levels in excess of SGD $25,000/month. Membership for the Web site and discussion forum was well over 40,000 with an outstanding monthly page impression count of more than 16 million. Without a doubt, Hardwarezone, up until this point, was a resounding success, but new challenges were just about to arise.

SETTING THE SCENE

The Dot-Com Crisis

Stacking the albums of old photographs and storing them away in a meticulously organized cabinet in a corner of his office, Eugene settled into his usual work routine. Work that day consisted of analyzing the monthly financial data generated by the accounts department, and, to Eugene's relief, the data showed that Hardwarezone was in good financial shape for the past month, as it had been nearly every month since operations began.

There was, however, no room for complacency just yet. Eugene knew full well that in an industry as dynamic as IT, one can take nothing for granted. The phenomenal success of Hardwarezone in Singapore, where dot-com failures were the norm rather than the exception, was not without turbulence. Fresh in Eugene's mind was the biggest storm that Hardwarezone had to weather thus far, a storm that sunk many dot-com ventures worldwide—the bursting of the dot-com bubble.

The dot-com crisis reduced numerous multi-million-dollar ventures into high profiled failures. Many other sectors also were caught in its wake, and assets were destroyed on an immense scale. According to research conducted by the Deutsche Bank, market capitalization of listed companies plunged by 40% between 2000 and 2002, while the confidence of many private investors had been severely and perhaps even lastingly shattered (Heng et al., 2003).

The dot-com crisis was a very trying period for Hardwarezone, a pure-play dot-com company (see Table 2). The problems that arose threatened the company's survival.

Table 2. Hardwarezone statistics for year 2000

		2000

1.	Revenue
	   a. Online Advertising
	   b. Off-line Advertising
		Total = SGD$1,000,000
		Online = SGD$1,000,000
		Off-line = SGD$0

2.	Net Profits	(SGD$150,000)
3.	Amount of capital investments in Hardwarezone	SGD$1,501,000
4.	Number of Employees	10
5.	Technical Infrastructure	One rack of servers with about 10 servers

6.	Web Site Statistics
	   a. Number of page views per month
	   b. Official membership figures
		Page Views: 19,000,000
		
		Membership: 50,000

Advertisers were losing confidence in the effectiveness of online advertising, while the ensuing economic downturn also caused most companies to cut back on advertising spending. As a result, most advertisers were reducing or even stopping their online advertising. Dot-com companies that placed a heavy emphasis on online advertising for revenue had to compete fiercely with each other for advertisers with the pools of online advertisers shrinking fast.

As a result of the closure of many dot-com ventures, many venture capitalists that had invested their funds in these ventures were badly affected. Some sunk, together with their investments, while others had to reduce drastically the level of funding for existing dot-coms. Hardwarezone was one of those badly affected by the dot-com crisis. Three venture capitalists that had pledged funds to Hardwarezone's development had to withdraw, even though Hardwarezone faced no operational problems. The scarcity of funding subsequently led to intense competition for venture capital funds, as well.

In regard to Hardwarezone, there was also a drop in participation in the forums, with fewer repeat visits by members. Its Web site was losing "stickiness." The conversations in the forums were beginning to be dominated by a few members. It seemed that the novelty of the Web site had worn off for some of Hardwarezone's members.

Faced with seemingly insurmountable odds, the management of Hardwarezone decided that they must change in order to suit the current business environment and to remain competitive. They decided that the essence of Hardwarezone is in its content and not just its Web site or forums. Thus, it decided to refocus its efforts on delivering better content, in terms of quality of quantity, to its users.

At the height of the crisis, it had two choices: to scale down its operations in order to cut costs or to stake everything it had established thus far by scaling up its operations and finding alternate streams of revenue. Eugene recalled the tense meeting with Hardwarezone's investors and their astounded faces when told of management's decision. Eventually, after no small amount of persuasion, they bought management's idea that scaling up operations would provide a better chance of survival and progress and possibly benefit the existing business, as well.

CASE DESCRIPTION

Moving into Print

With their experience in managing Hardwarezone thus far, members of management decided that online advertising revenue would not provide a stable revenue stream. Based on a comprehensive analysis of existing and potential advertisers, they identified an untapped market of advertisers who were reluctant to advertise online. These advertisers had traditional and conservative mindsets, and, as Eugene noted, they wanted something that they could see, touch, and hold. Online advertising simply did not do it for them.

Instead of competing with other online companies for the shrinking market of current online advertisers, Hardwarezone wanted the more conservative-minded advertisers on board, as well. To cater to such conservative advertisers, the decision to deliver their content via off-line printed media was made.

This decision was not made without apprehension. The printing business involved a much larger working capital compared to the online business, which would affect Hardwarezone's immediate cash flow. The issues of getting enough advertisers, competing with other existing off-line IT publications (see Appendix B) for readership as well as advertising dollars, market acceptance, and, most importantly, sustainability were some of the concerns the management of Hardwarezone had. Also, the decision meant that Hardwarezone needed to expand its team, hire more people, increase office space, and acquire the knowledge and expertise of off-line publishing.

However, management foresaw that print advertising revenue, coupled with magazine sales revenue, would give them the steady revenue flow to survive the existing adverse economic climate. This steady revenue also would give them greater maneuverability, flexibility, and confidence to expand to other areas of interest, such as computer gaming. This decision eventually led to the launch of *HWM* magazine.

Starting with its current advertisers, Hardwarezone introduced its new magazine as a new advertising avenue. For existing advertisers, such as Canon, Sony, and Microsoft, increasing their advertising share through print media was a natural progression, but what really surprised the management of Hardwarezone was the ease at which the more conservative-minded advertisers were persuaded and the enthusiasm they displayed with regard to Hardwarezone's venture into print.

Strengthening the Hardwarezone Brand

With an existing base of community members in the Hardwarezone forums, selling the magazine was much easier. This ready eyeball base attracted advertisers even more. Eugene recalled with some satisfaction the win-win situation that contributed to *HWM*'s success. On one hand, the Hardwarezone community was ready to support Hardwarezone by buying its magazine. On the other hand, with *HWM* in newsstands, Hardwarezone's brand reach increased, and thus, it also could get more people to come to the Hardwarezone Web site.

In this aspect, Eugene firmly believes that Hardwarezone's strategy is unique. As he noted retrospectively, not many dot-coms today can reproduce their business off-line and not only maintain profitability and sustain their current momentum but grow bigger and more profitable than ever before.

The term *clicks and mortar* was coined by David Pottruck, President and Co-Chief Executive Officer of Charles Schwab & Co., to describe the integration of conventional physically located businesses mainly in the retail field and online businesses (Whitaker et al., 2001). Instead of the usual route of an off-line company going online, which many advocate as the conventional bricks-and-clicks or clicks-and-mortar strategy (Freeland & Stirton, 2000; Gulati & Garrino, 2000), Hardwarezone defied convention by going from a purely online presence to bricks-and-clicks as a complete online and off-line IT content aggregator.

The main advantage of the reverse clicks-and-mortar strategy over conventional clicks-and-mortar strategy is avoiding the problem of organizational inertia that commonly plagues established off-line companies when they try to move online. For established companies that have been operating for years and have invested heavily in improving productivity to reach their current level of operational efficiency, a strong business case and compelling reasons are often required for these companies to change the way they work (Doorley, 2000), which contributes to organizational inertia.

To make *HWM* work, management decided on a few strategic plans with the emphasis and focus on creating a stronger market presence and image for Hardwarezone.

First, management sought to further distinguish *HWM* from foreign publications by injecting a stronger local flavor in its IT publication. By introducing more local information to the magazine through means such as having local reviewers and writers, they wanted the readers to identify with *HWM* and its distinct Asian context. Other PC or IT magazines had foreign writers and editors, even though they label their magazines as Asian or Singapore editions. The management wanted the readers of *HWM* to see and feel the differences among its competitors and Hardwarezone. They wanted the support of Singaporean customers on the basis that it was a Singaporean brand.

Second, management recognized that the need for a large number of members of the Hardwarezone community to form the seed readership for *HWM*. It tried to create a sense of ownership of *HWM* among the Hardwarezone community by adding snippets of conversations from the online forums and quoting members in *HWM*. The aim of this strategy was to make community members feel recognized for their contributions, especially when these members saw their forum messages and names used in the magazine. Management hoped that this sense of ownership would increase the stickiness of their Web site as well as create a significant number of loyal readers.

Third, management practiced a philosophy that it termed *cyclic reinforcement*. The content in *HWM* and the Web site was complementary, and the Hardwarezone management ensured that the content featured in the Web site was not included in the magazine and vice versa. The strategy stemmed from the belief that there will not be a reason for readers to buy the magazine if content was duplicated and available for free on the Web site. By cross-highlighting or cross-advertising the articles so that people who go to the Web site can read more about it in the magazine and vice versa, the Hardwarezone Web site and *HWM* magazine became partners in delivering localized and personalized content to Singapore readers, complementing each other and inducing people to use both avenues.

Next, Hardwarezone sought to expand its product offering by diversifying its online content with the launch of GameAxis.com. GameAxis formerly existed as a special interest group within the Hardwarezone community, and, as Hardwarezone's gaming community expanded, many members of the community felt that the coverage of computer games on Hardwarezone was not extensive enough to sustain members' interests. This resulted in the formation of GameAxis with a sole focus on computer games. With GameAxis, Hardwarezone effectively tackled the growing community of gamers on a multitude of gaming platforms: PC, Console (e.g., PS2, Xbox), mobile gaming, and so forth. Its content was created by transposing and expanding the content generated in the previous forum features of the latest gaming news and reviews.

Last, Hardwarezone also tried to create a stronger physical presence by establishing Bubblezone, a bubble tea outlet in Sim Lim Square, to give Hardwarezone members a place to socialize and meet, adding an even greater physical dimension to their community. Wireless Internet access also was established at this bubble tea outlet to allow patrons to access Hardwarezone while patronizing the outlet. This value-added service allowed people the convenience of dropping by for refreshments while checking out information on the products available in Sim Lim Square before heading off to do their IT shopping.

CURRENT CHALLENGES FACING THE ORGANIZATION

Results Achieved

Looking at the cumulative operational statistics for the year 2002 (see Table 3), Eugene heaved a deep sigh of satisfaction. Official membership figures for Hardwarezone were now in excess of 100,000, while its Web site was generating close to 22,000,000 page views per month. Revenue from advertising, both online and off-line, was reaching levels of approximately SGD $200,000 since 1998, derived mainly from advertisers in the United States and Singapore. More encouragingly, the level of online advertising had begun to pick up again; it was close to the pre-dot-com crisis level and was expected to exceed off-line advertising revenue within a few years.

At present, Hardwarezone has a representative office in the United States as well as offices in Singapore, Malaysia, and Thailand, and employs more than 40 people worldwide (see Appendix C). After spending more than $200,000 since 1998 to improve its back-end infrastructure, it currently runs three full racks of about 20 servers, including five dedicated servers for the forum and two dedicated servers for advertisements alone. With the growing Internet traffic due to publicity from its *HWM* magazine, Hardwarezone constantly outgrows its servers.

HWM also experienced spectacular success since its launch in July 2001. With a healthy circulation of more than 20,000 copies a month, it quickly became the best-selling IT magazine in Singapore, edging out or even forcing the closure of several well established, well funded competitors such as *PCWorld* (Singapore), *Chip*, and *Singapore Computing Magazine*.

While satisfied with Hardwarezone's achievements thus far, Eugene gazed out the window of his swanky, well furnished ninth floor office at the Technopreneur Center in Singapore; his mind was focused intently on the challenges ahead.

Table 3. Hardwarezone statistics for year 2002

	2002
1. Revenue 　　a.　Online Advertising 　　b.　Off-line Advertising	Total = SGD$2,000,000 Online = SGD$600,000 Off-line = SGD$1,400,000
2. Net Profits	SGD$20,000
3. Amount of capital investments in Hardwarezone	SGD$1,501,000
4. Number of Employees	40
5. Technical Infrastructure	Three rack of servers with about 20 servers, load balanced
6. Web Site Statistics 　　a.　Number of page views per month 　　b.　Official membership figures	Page Views: 21,800,000 Membership: 110,000

Intensified Competition

As in the case of nearly every success story, imitation is inevitable. With sustained profitability and continued growth through its four years of operation, Hardwarezone saw that new entrants were emerging to challenge the market leadership it had established. Particularly troubling to Eugene was the news that several local IT vendors, some of whom were Hardwarezone's partners in the past, were now eying Hardwarezone's lucrative business.

Already on the horizon was the planned launch of Hardwarezoom.com in early 2003. Positioned to be Hardwarezone's direct competitor, even on the basis of its name, it was set to emulate Hardwarezone's online/off-line approach. Similar to Hardwarezone's Web site, Hardwarezoom's Web site provided proprietary content and forum facilities for members. Off-line, it also had established a strategic partnership with *PC Magazine* to be Hardwarezoom's official magazine.

With Hardwarezone's change in business strategy and new entrants imitating its value proposition as a provider of comprehensive local IT reviews, many of its competitive advantages were being eroded. Especially with Hardwarezone's entry into magazine publications (off-line IT publications), indirect competitors of the past were now competing directly with Hardwarezone. The cost advantage that it once possessed over these competitors was gone, and a key challenge to Hardwarezone at this point in time was to continue outperforming its competitors while charging a similar fee for the content that it provided.

Reevaluating Its Strengths

With a board meeting scheduled later in the afternoon to discuss Hardwarezone's new strategic direction for the next year, Eugene was bracing himself for the biggest challenge to Hardwarezone's continued profitability and growth since the dot-com crisis. Preparing notes for his presentation during the meeting, Eugene knew that Hardwarezone had to rely on its strengths, the foundations of its success that had been laid carefully since operations began in 1998.

Examining the advantages that Hardwarezone had over new entrants, such as Hardwarezoom and existing IT publications, Eugene realized that one of the main advantages on its side was its community. Fiercely loyal to Hardwarezone's cause and the source of numerous contributions and ideas, the community was the reason why *HWM* magazine succeeded in overcoming the challenge posed by foreign publications to become Singapore's best-selling IT magazine. The community also was responsible for the concept of GameAxis, initially providing much of its content.

Studying the makeup of the community, Eugene discovered a surprising statistic. As much as 60% of the members of Hardwarezone's community were not, in fact, from Singapore but from countries around the Southeast Asia region, such as Malaysia, Indonesia, Vietnam, and Thailand. But how could Hardwarezone leverage the multinational makeup of its community?

Another cornerstone of Hardwarezone's success and continued survival through the dot-com crisis was the conviction of its management to make painful changes that they deemed necessary. In defying convention and implementing an unprecedented reverse clicks-and-mortar strategy, the management of Hardwarezone had demonstrated an uncanny business mind, dogged determination, and a willingness to take risks. But what strategies could they pursue now that new entrants with similar product offerings were beginning to saturate the Singaporean IT publications industry?

Another important advantage that Hardwarezone had over its competitors was the strategic alliances it had formed with local IT vendors at the major IT retail malls in Singapore. This alliance was the key source of up-to-date product information and prices for which Hardwarezone was now renowned in Singapore. Now that some of these IT vendors were turning against Hardwarezone and threatening to disintermediate Hardwarezone from the process of disseminating product information to end consumers, what could Hardwarezone do to stop this from happening?

Recalling an earlier discussion with Jackie Lee, Chairperson, founding member, and CEO of Hardwarezone, the two options available to Hardwarezone in terms of strategic direction at this time were similar to the options that they had at the height of the dot-com crisis: to scale up or to scale down.

Scaling up their operations meant bringing Hardwarezone into regional countries in Southeast Asia, such as Malaysia, Thailand, Indonesia, and Vietnam, essentially replicating the reverse clicks-and-mortar strategy that had proved so successful in Singapore. This approach would leverage the multi-national makeup of Hardwarezone's community and, perhaps, even boost the credibility of its existing publications by acquiring the reputation of a local product that was good enough to go regional.

However, such an approach once again meant staking everything Hardwarezone had achieved up to this point and testing its business model in even greater uncertainty, given that regional markets, while similar to that of Singapore, undoubtedly would have its own nuances and cultural differences.

Scaling down its operations would mean consolidating its current resources, looking for ways to improve cost efficiencies within its current operations, and, perhaps, cementing its strategic alliances with local IT vendors with legally binding contracts. The advantages of such an approach, compared to scaling up, obviously would be to minimize risk. No additional inflow of capital would be needed, and Hardwarezone would continue to operate in a market that its management knew well and understood. The disadvantages of this approach, however, was that any competitive advantage derived from this approach was likely to be short-term, unless Hardwarezone could sustain its improved cost advantage in the long run.

Eugene's thoughts were interrupted by a familiar beep emitted from his desktop, an alarm he had set on his electronic organizer reminding him of the day's meeting. His brows were furrowed as he left his office, heading down the hallway toward the meeting room, knowing full well that the decision Jackie and he settled upon would require plenty of grit and determination from everyone onboard.

REFERENCES

Chellam, R. (2004). Singapore's very own Google guys? *The Business Times.*

Doorley, T. (2000). New model enterprises: How organizations must adapt for the new economy. *eAI Journal*, 78-81.

Freeland, G. D., & Stirton, S. (2000). Organizing for e-commerce. Retrieved January 27, 2004, from http://www.bcg.com/publications/files/organizing%20Ecommerce%20Apr%2000.pdf

Gulati, R., & Garino, J. (2000). Get the right mix of bricks and clicks. *Harvard Business Review*, 107-114.

Heng, S., Heymann, E., Lahusen, R., & Stobbe, A. (2003). Economics—Digital economy and structural change. *Deutsche Bank Research, 39*, 1-15.

O'Connell, B. (2000). *B2B.com: Cashing in on the business to business e-commerce bonanza.* Holbrook, MA: Adams Media Corporation.

Patel, K., & McCarthy, M. (2000). *The essentials of e-business leadership—Digital transformation.* New York: McGraw-Hill.

Plant, R. (2000). *E-commerce: Formulation of strategy.* NJ: Prentice Hall.

Slywotsky, A. J., & Morrison, D. J. (2000). *How digital is your business?* New York: Crown Publishing Group.

Tapscott, D., Ticoll, D., & Lowy, A. (2000). *Digital capital: Harnessing the power of business Webs.* Boston: Harvard Business School Press.

Whitaker, J., Murphy, J., Caldwell, A., & Palmieri, P. (2001). Impact of clicks on bricks: Principles of VET facilities planning in an information age—Literature search and review. Retrieved January 27, 2005, from http://www.flexiblelearning.net.au/clicks/res_libr/litesear/media/pdf/litrev_full.pdf

APPENDIXES

Appendix A: Selected Online Competitor Profiles

CNET Networks

CNet.com, ZDNet, and Gamespot.com are owned by the same parent company, CNET Networks, Inc. CNET Networks, Inc. was one of the pioneers of the online IT publications industry and has recently utilized complementary off-line media, such as print, research, in-person events, and wireless devices, to strengthen their market position. It has the largest global audience with more than 55,000,000 unique users with leading market positions in the U.S., Europe, and Asia. Audience profiles include technology professionals, business people, technology enthusiasts, and gamers. It generated US$237 million of revenue through advertising, marketing services, sales leads, content licensing, subscriptions, and other fee-based services.

PCWorld.com

PCWorld.com is published by PC World Communications, Inc. and is a subsidiary of IDG, the world's leading IT media, research, and exposition company. Its target audience includes management-level buyers and users of computer products; it averaged 1.7 million unique visitors per month. The site offers quick access to authoritative reviews of computer products, the most current product pricing information, continuously updated news, an extensive library of carefully evaluated freeware and shareware, interactive tools, and free newsletters. However, content is U.S.-based and caters more to the American audience.

Hardware-one.com

Hardware-one.com began around the same time as Hardwarezone and mirrored Hardwarezone in the early stages of development. It was started by several computing engineering undergraduates from the Nanyang Technological University and offered reports on breakthrough products, evaluation, and benchmarks of important systems. Its development and site content subsequently slowed down with only four product reviews in 2002. Unlike Hardwarezone, which had a very active discussion forum, Hardware-one.com had only a small community with low forum participation. According to Eugene Low, the founders of Hardware-one.com lacked the business sense required to turn their hobby into a business venture.

Hardwarezoom.com

Hardwarezoom.com was launched in 2003, and, according to industry sources, specifically targeted Hardwarezone as a direct competitor. The management of Hardwarezone believes the organization behind Hardwarezoom.com is an IT vendor in Sim Lim Square. Strategies employed by Hardwarezoom.com include giving free PC magazines to forum participants for every 10 forum postings and omitting Hardwarezone from its links section. Targeted audience and site content is very similar to Hardwarezone's, and, although forum participation is low compared to Hardwarezone, it is steadily increasing.

Appendix B: The IT Magazine Industry in Singapore

IT magazines generally can be classified as trade titles that target readers from the IT industry and consumer titles that target general end consumers and IT enthusiasts. In addition, IT magazines also can be classified based on their focus on hardware or software and communications technology.

Selected IT titles can be plotted on a two-by-two matrix based on the two different classifications (see Appendix Figure 1).

HWM (Singapore) is operating currently in quadrant 1 of the matrix. Its content is targeted for the general consumer with a strong focus on computer hardware reviews and with a few articles on the latest software, games, and communication devices and gadgets. Competitors targeting the general consumer market include *CHIP*, *PC Magazine*, the now defunct *PC World* (Singapore) and *Digital Life*.

PC Magazine

PC Magazine (Singapore) was launched in August 2003 by CR Media Ltd under a license agreement with Ziff Davis Media, which controls the licenses of other popular IT publications such as *Computer Gamine World*, *Eweek*, and *CIO Insight* worldwide. *PC Magazine* (Malaysia) was launched in the same month by CR Media Sdn. Bhd. This was followed in quick succession by the launch of *PC Magazine* (Indonesia) and *PC Magazine* (Thailand). The content within its pages is similar to *HWM* (Singapore) with a strong emphasis on hardware reviews and with occasional articles on software and

Appendix Figure 1.

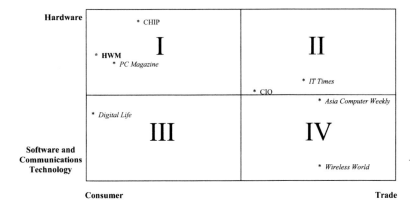

communications technology. While official circulation figures are unavailable, media industry sources cite *PC Magazine* (Singapore) as *HWM*'s (Singapore) closest competitor with more than 15,000 copies sold per month.

CHIP

Launched in 1978 by the Vogel Media Group with more than 2,500,000 readers worldwide, *CHIP* magazine has a strong European presence with separate editions in Germany, Poland, Italy, Ukraine, Hungary, Rumania, Greece, Turkey, and the Czech Republic. It established its presence in Asia with editions published in India, China, Saudi Arabia, and Singapore around 1998. Current estimates cite *CHIP* Singapore's circulation figures at more than 5,000 copies per month. While *CHIP* Singapore does not have a Web site, it maintains its online presence with a discussion forum with more than 100 members.

Digital Life

Digital Life is a weekly tabloid covering the latest news in information technology, including hardware, software, and communications technology targeted at the general consumer. It is included with *The Straits Times*, Singapore's most established English newspaper, and is available free of charge. While its coverage of local IT products is not as extensive as *HWM* (Singapore), it has a massive reach with a circulation of more than 380,000.

Appendix C: Hardwarezone Organization Chart

Hardwarezone Pte Ltd (HQ Division)

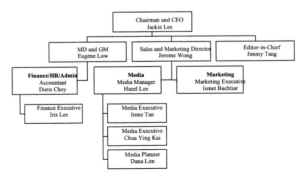

Hardwarezone Pte Ltd (Strategic Business Units)

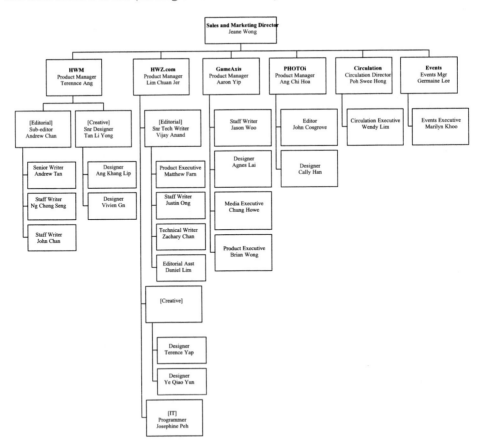

Tan Chee Chang is a lecturer in the Business Information Technology Department at the Institute of Technical Education (Singapore). He graduated from the National University of Singapore where he received his BComp in information systems. His research interests include knowledge management, e-commerce strategies and business models, and customer relationship management.

Tan Gek Woo is an assistant professor in the School of Computing at the National University of Singapore (NUS). She received her MSc in computer science from Indiana University (IU) and a PhD in business administration from the University of Illinois at Urbana-Champaign (UIUC). Her primary research focuses on information sharing in supply chain network. In recent years, she has moved into Web site design and knowledge management. Her research work has been published in IEEE Transactions on Engineering Management, Journal of Organizational Computing and Electronic Commerce, *and* International Conference on Information Systems *(ICIS).*

This case was previously published in the *International Journal of Cases on Electronic Commerce*, 1(3), pp. 37-53, © 2005.

Chapter IV

E*Trade Securities, Inc., Poineer Online Trader, Struggles to Stay on Top

Adam T. Elegant, University of Colorado, Boulder, USA

Ramiro Montealegre, University of Colorado, Boulder, USA

EXECUTIVE SUMMARY

E*Trade revolutionized the securities brokerage industry by "creating" Internet trading. E*Trade's original strategy was to deliver cost savings to customers while amortizing fixed costs over a greater number of accounts. In 1997, several competitors established Internet sites and E*Trade was dethroned as the price leader. Its management team introduced a strategic initiative to transform the company into a financial, one-stop shop for investors. The initiative included expanding its information technology, improving its marketing and advertising program, and developing new strategic alliances. By early 1999, E*Trade had established a popular Web site offering the convenience and control of automated stock, options, and mutual fund order placement at low commission rates. E*Trade's success pleased management but was challenged by fierce competition and emerging ethical and operational problems.

BACKGROUND

The Securities Brokerage Industry

Before the securities industry deregulation on May 1, 1975, full-service brokerages charging fixed commissions were the only firms in the industry (Glasgall, 1999). A full-service broker is a stockbroker who gives personal attention and advice to clients and charges a flat fee or percentage of the transaction. Such a broker acts as an agent, providing advice and buying or selling securities for the client. The client interacts with the broker face to face or over the telephone. Full-service brokers provide a wide array of services, including investment strategizing, estate planning, and insurance advice, and they usually attempt to influence their clients' investment decisions.

After deregulation, most full-service brokers began to target households with assets ranging from $100,000 into the millions. In addition, given that commissions were no longer fixed, discount brokerage firms began to appear that targeted price-sensitive, self-directed investors who did not require the level of service and high-priced advice offered by full-service firms. Discount brokerage firms made profit from margin balances and per-trade commissions; technology also enabled them to employ less-skilled labor. Fidelity and Charles Schwab, two of the dominant discounted brokerage firms in the mid-1990s, led the charge by introducing lower-cost investment services without advice at significantly lower commissions. Discount brokerage customers typically had assets ranging from $5,000 to $250,000. To execute trades, they could visit a branch office or they could call an "800" number to speak with a "live order taker," who would place their trade orders but was prohibited from giving any investment advice. Over time, discount brokers added touch-tone trading, which offered further commission reductions to investors who would key-in their trade orders.

By 1995, with the continued expansion of the Internet, technology offered another alternative with more convenience, lower costs, and easy access to investment information: online trading. Most online trading firms were offering customers numerous ways to access their accounts and place trades, including individual company Web sites, direct dial-up connections, online services (America Online, CompuServe, and Microsoft Network), interactive television, touch-tone telephone service, a broker on the telephone (as a situational alternative to online trading, for an additional fee), and 3Com Palm Pilots (available through selected online trading firms). With online trading, investors paid lower commissions—ranging from $10 to $30. They had full control over their investment decisions, with no one to blame but themselves—investors could enter trade orders any time of the day or night (Piper Jaffray, 1998d). Online brokerage accounts could be opened with as little as $1,000. While these firms first targeted frequent traders by offering low commissions, online trading evolved to support the needs of almost any individual investor.

History of the Company

E*Trade was a pioneer in online trading, a phenomenon that was rapidly changing the face of investing for both individuals and the firms that served them. The firm's growth mirrored that of the online trading industry as a whole. Trade*Plus, the company that would later become E*Trade, was founded as a service bureau in 1982 by Bill Porter, a physicist and inventor with more than a dozen patents to his credit. The company provided online quote and trading services to Fidelity, Charles Schwab, and Quick & Reilly. Using primitive information technology, Porter placed the first online trade on July 11, 1983. He imagined that someday everyone would own computers and "invest through them with unprecedented efficiency and control."[1] He spent most of the 1980s refining and adding to his vision without introducing his plan to the world.

In 1992, Porter founded E*Trade Securities, Inc. and began providing back-office, online processing services to discount brokerage firms and offering all-electronic investing through America Online and CompuServe. The minimum balance required by E*Trade to open an account was $1,000 ($2,000 for a margin account), well below industry standards at that time, and only a short, user-friendly application was required to set up an account. E*Trade began offering online trading through its company Web site in February 1996, and the demand flourished. To transact securities, a customer had only to log on to E*Trade via the Internet, a dial-up connection, or an online service such as America Online. However, for the first four years, E*Trade's trade processing, settlement, and custody of trades were provided by Herzog Heine Geduld, a third-party clearing and trading company.

In mid-1996, Porter handed E*Trade's reins over to Christos Cotsakos, a veteran of Federal Express and A.C. Nielsen. He immediately initiated in-house clearing activities to enable E*Trade to keep 100% of the revenue associated with its customers' margin and money market accounts (Piper Jaffray, 1997). This action proved crucial to the company's immediate success, since online investors, on average, carry margin balances three times those of traditional investors (CNN, 1998). On August 16, 1996, lead underwriter Robertson Stephens took E*Trade public at $10.50 per share. With the news spreading about E*Trade's capabilities, individual investors took notice. In 1992, E*Trade was processing barely 100 trades per day (Byron, 1997). By the end of 1996, that number had grown to almost 10,000 per day.

One of the keys to E*Trade's success was its stable and experienced management, consisting of technology, operations, finance, and marketing professionals who had a passion for the business. Figure 1 and Exhibit 1 present E*Trade's organizational chart and brief biographies of E*Trade's key leaders, respectively.

By 1997, the company had 650 employees and only three offices (located in Atlanta, Georgia; Sacramento, California; and Palo Alto, California). Thus, low overhead enabled it to offer low commissions that traditional brokerage firms could not afford to match.

With relation to information technology, E*Trade's computer system, fine-tuned over 15 years, permitted 85% of its transactions to be executed without human intervention (Piper Jaffray, 1997). Once a trade order was entered, E*Trade's computer system in Palo Alto took over. The computer system queried the prices available on at least four market makers, searching for the best executable price. Trades were usually executed in seconds, trading results were available shortly thereafter, and the customer's account balances were updated immediately.

SETTING THE STAGE

In 1997, E*Trade began to recognize that having low prices was not sufficient to compete with the discount brokerage firms that were moving into online trading. It

Figure 1. E*Trade organizational chart

*Exhibit 1: E*Trade's Management*

Christos M. Cotsakos, Chairman, President, Chief Executive Officer, and a
Director of E*Trade Group, Inc.

Before taking the reins at E*Trade, he was a senior executive at Federal Express, as well as AC Nielsen, Inc. He also serves on the boards of several leading-edge technology companies. He received a B.A. from William Paterson College, and an M.B.A. from Pepperdine University, and is currently pursuing a Ph.D. in economics at the University of London. Christos Cotsakos is also a decorated Vietnam War veteran.

Kathy Levinson, President and Chief Operating Officer.

Kathy Levinson came to E*Trade from Charles Schwab, where she served in a number of senior executive positions. She earned a B.A. in economics from Stanford University and a master's of human resources and organization development from the University of San Francisco, and completed the program for management development at Harvard.

Judy Balint, President and Chief Operating Officer, E*Trade's
International Division.

Judy Balint is responsible for building E*Trade's global financial network. Before joining E*Trade, she spent a number of years living and working abroad. She received a B.A. in journalism from the University of Wisconsin and an M.B.A. in international business from the Monterey Institute of International Studies in Monterey, California.

Debra Chrapaty, President and Chief Operating Officer,
E*Trade Technologies, and Chief Information Officer of E*Trade group.

Debra Chrapaty invents proprietary technology solutions for E*Trade. She came to E*Trade from the National Basketball Association, where she was vice president and chief technology officer. She has a bachelor in business administration and economics from Temple University and an M.B.A. in information systems from New York University. She often works around the clock and sleeps on a cot next to her desk. In 1998, she was named the chief information officer of the year by *InformationWeek*.

Leonard C. Purkis, Executive Vice President, Finance and Administration,
and Chief Financial Officer.

Len Purkis is responsible for building and managing E*Trade's financial architecture. Before joining E*Trade, he was chief financial officer for Iomega Corporation and senior vice president of finance for General Electric Capital Fleet Services. He is a graduate of the Institute of Chartered Accountants in England and Wales.

Jerry Gramaglia, Senior Vice President, Sales, Marketing, and
Communication.

Jerry Gramaglia is charged with creating innovative ways to build and expand global brands. Before joining E*Trade, he was vice president of Sprint's $3 billion consumer division and held senior management posts at Pepsico, Procter & Gamble, and Nestle. He earned B.A. in economics from Denison University.

Rebecca L. Patton, Senior Vice President, Advanced Products Group.

Rebecca Patton is responsible for designing E*Trade's new product strategies. Before joining E*Trade in September 1995, Ms. Patton served in a variety of management positions at Apple Computer. Ms. Patton received a B.A. in economics from Duke University and an M.B.A. from Stanford University.

Stephen C. Richards, Senior Vice President, Corporate Development and
New Ventures.

Stephen Richards's mission is to increase E*Trade's leadership position through strategic alliances, partnerships, mergers, and acquisitions. He previously served as E*Trade's senior vice president of finance and chief financial officer. Before joining E*Trade, he was managing director and CFO of correspondent clearing at Bear Stearns & Company. He has a B.A. in statistics and economics from University of California at Davis and an M.B.A. in finance from University of California at Los Angeles.

Connie Dotson, Senior Vice President, Service Quality.

Connie Dotson makes sure that everyone in E*Trade's customer service, operations, and trading areas provides end-to-end quality service. Before joining E*Trade in 1996, she served as senior vice president of operations for U.S. Computer Services/CableData, Inc.

needed to provide investors with a more comprehensive online service, including better research, charting, quotes, and stock screening. E*Trade began designing a new Web site, called "Destination E*Trade," which it hoped would become a financial portal, a one-stop shop for investors, customers, and non-customers. Breaking away from its competitors, E*Trade planned to open up 90 to 95% of its Web site to non-customers (Lipton, 1998). This first portal Web site within the online brokerage industry was originally slated for a launch date of January 1998.

CASE DESCRIPTION

The objective of E*Trade's expansion was to offer its customers the tools to handle all of their investment needs at one convenient, comprehensive, and secure online location. E*Trade CEO Christos Cotsakos reflected:

We are committed to offering independent investors the most comprehensive selection of financial services available in the online industry.... Our strategy is to be a financial full-service online provider. (E*Trade, 1998b)

Three general principles guided the firm's service expansion: (1) attract new investors and fortify existing customer loyalty, (2) develop multiple revenue streams to protect against an extended market correction, and (3) increase customers' switching costs in order to prevent them from jumping to another online brokerage firm. E*Trade embarked on a strategic initiative that began by restructuring the company into three business groups—technology, international operations, and brokerage. Debra Chrapaty, who was the chief information officer of E*Trade, was promoted to president and chief technology officer of the newly formed technology division. Fully half of E*Trade's 650 employees reported to Chrapaty. She controlled a budget of more than $130 million—a whopping 39% of E*Trade's $335.7 million revenue for the year ended September 30, 1998 (Dalton, 1998). The strategic initiative followed by E*Trade, however, included not only the expansion of technology but also a significant improvement of its marketing and advertising program. The initiative also included the development of new strategic alliances to increase its national and international reach.

Information Technology

Although technology had fueled the growth of the securities brokerage industry, some observers estimated that in 1995 the percentage of mishandled trades was as high as 45%. Many early entrants into the online trading segment were plagued by technological glitches, and as the existing problems were rectified, new problems appeared when online trading firms expanded their services. Industry-wide concerns related to technology included the following:

1. **System outage:** Online trading firms were continuously refining their systems to eliminate crippling glitches, such as lost e-mails, system overload, and system crashes, and to create backup systems and contingency plans. Many of these outages were caused by software and hardware upgrades that were intended to increase capacity.
2. **Web-based transaction glitches:** Trade orders could get lost after the customer had entered them, but well before the order reached the online brokerage. The problem could occur between the customer and his/her Internet service provider (ISP), between the ISP and the Internet backbone, or inside the Internet backbone itself. Although the Internet was a self-healing network and traffic was automatically routed around glitches, the rerouting process could take anywhere from seconds to 20 minutes. As Web traffic increased, the number of routing glitches was expected to increase. Many investors did not understand the technological side

of online trading, and often misunderstood who was at fault when trades went awry (Olmstead, 1998a).

3. **Removal of human intervention:** As an online investor explained, "I electronically entered a limit order to buy Zenith at $15, while the stock was trading around $16. The stock then rose to $22. While [I was] working, not paying attention to the market, negative news sent Zenith plummeting toward $5. When the stock fell, my order executed at $15, on the way down, and cost me thousands of dollars." The electronic system did what it was told: it executed the order at $15. A full-service brokerage firm might have called the customer, told him about the negative news, and suggested that he cancel the order or sell immediately after the purchase to cut his losses. By the time this investor realized that he owned the stock, it was trading at $6.

4. **Poor customer service:** Almost every online firm had been accused of poor customer service. Most customer service issues were handled via e-mail. However, often the responses did not provide a detailed response to every concern voiced by the customer. In particular, many customers felt slighted by the "canned" answers that firms used for frequently asked questions. Account holders who used telephone customer service commonly complained about extended hold times.

Chrapaty was well aware that in order to expand the firm's online investment services, she had to do more at E*Trade than simply implement technology. The expansion had to be done while continuing to support the level of online services—which meant paying special attention to accommodate the volatility of online trading marketplace, where trading volumes may soar and fall wildly. The rapid growth of the company also had to be supported—E*Trade was adding 2,000 customers a day to a base of 550,000 and the number of trades made daily, which averaged around 15,000 in July 1997, was running about 40,000 to 50,000 by the same time in 1998 (Dalton, 1998).

In August 1997, Chrapaty established daily 5:30 a.m. meetings—one hour before the opening of the stock markets in the United States—including all employees reporting to her. "Everyone needed to understand the changes and how they tentacle into their organizations," she explained (Dalton, 1998). These meetings, which Chrapaty referred to as change-management sessions, had an immediate impact—system errors dropped 75% during the next quarter. But that was the beginning. Over the next 12 months, she restructured the company's trading system and Web site. In 1998, $75 million was spent to upgrade these systems (Pettit, 1998). Much of this money was spent on the Destination E*Trade Web site and on E*Trade's proprietary information technology architecture. This technology enabled more than one million visitors to use the Web site simultaneously and allowed up to 150,000 customers to place orders simultaneously (E*Trade, 1998h). E*Trade's original computer system had used a common gateway interface (CGI) to link the servers of its Web pages to its databases (Stirland, 1998). The system was mainly coded in the computer language C++. The new system was based on BEA System's Tuxedo Architecture, which manages a distributed, component-based computing environment, and includes load balancing, distributed transaction processing, and security. Other elements of the new architecture include a Cisco Systems Local Director and several Netscape Version 2.0 Enterprise Servers. The BEA Tuxedo system manages transactions, while the Netscape servers manage user sessions.

Marketing and Advertising

E*Trade complemented its technology development efforts by further investigating who traded online and what attracted them. It was found that the original online investors tended to be active traders who jumped in and out of positions rapidly, looking to make a quick profit. They were especially concerned about commission rates and reliability of execution. Over time, however, the situation changed as investors began to give careful consideration to the types of services offered by each online brokerage firm. With the stabilization of commission rates, price became only one factor in investor choice. The breadth of products, services, and amenities became the critical deciding factors. The types of services required by online investors included electronic bill payment, free real-time quotes, low margin rates, quality of research reports, access to IPOs, and excellent customer service.

While there are many ways to describe online investors (see, for example, Exhibit 2 for typical demographics of online investors), three distinctive categories can be identified (Piper Jaffray, 1998a).

- **Straddlers:** Customers who occasionally invested online but still preferred traditional investment channels, such as branch offices and the telephone. These people were still hesitant about trading online and preferred conducting business with companies with established reputations.
- **Active investors:** Investors who used online trading only after conducting their own, self-directed research. These people were comfortable investing online. Their main needs were information and tools that would help them make better investment decisions.
- **Retail traders:** A new class of investors created by the low cost and speed of execution associated with online trading. These were short-term investors looking to take advantage of quick profits in the market. Retail traders, also known as "day traders," cared only about fast, cheap, and efficient execution of their orders.

Table 1 shows the key services required by each segment of the market and examples of the companies that met their needs.

E*Trade understood from its inception that establishing brand identity was critical in the online investment industry—customers are hesitant to deposit money with a firm

Exhibit 2. Demographics of typical online investors

(According to Forrester Research, Inc.)

- 75.7% of on-line investors are male.
- Age ranges between 25 and 44, mean is 39.
- Mean annual income is $69,000.
- Mean net worth is $144,177.
- 70% use a PC at work.
- 44% have completed college.
- Average investor places 7.86 trades per year.
- Online investors make 47% more trades than traditional investors.

Source: Pettit, 1998

Table 1. Online services required by type of customer (Source: Piper Jaffray, 1998a)

Type of Customer	Straddlers	Active Investors	Retail Traders
Commission Level	20-$30	$10-$20	Less than $10
Key Needs	Service & Reputation	Information & Tools	Price & Execution
Marquee Firms	Schwab & Fidelity	E*Trade & DLJ Direct	Datek & Ameritrade
The Firm's Key Attributes	Channels & Distribution	Partnerships & Brand	Execution & Technology

they have never heard of. Accordingly, the company has been an industry leader in marketing and advertising expenditures, and its campaigns can be described as aggressive, savvy, and eye-catching. In 1996, E*Trade was advertising in the *Wall Street Journal, Individual Investor, Smart Money*, and *Forbes*, but in 1997 it decided to increase its marketing and advertising program. E*Trade kicked off its first major campaign by spending $3.2 million on advertising during the NCAA basketball tournament. Since 1997, E*Trade has consistently spent four to five times more money on advertising per active account than its competitor Schwab (Piper Jaffray, 1997). By the end of 1997, E*Trade had spent $20+ million in advertising campaigns. The first half of 1998 was quiet, but E*Trade broke the calm by announcing a $100 million advertising campaign to coincide with the launch of its Destination E*Trade Web site.

While Cotsakos felt that this level of expenditure was necessary to transform E*Trade into "one of the blue-chip Internet companies for the 21st century" (Buckman, 1998), some analysts estimated that advertising had pushed E*Trade's account acquisition costs past $400 per account in 1998. The company began looking for cheaper ways to acquire accounts: direct mail, Web site sponsorships, and E*Mobile—a purple and green, 38-foot recreational vehicle that was to spend 200 days per year traveling to sporting events, college campuses, and trade shows. E*Mobile had nine demonstration suites on board and was projected to attract 15,000 visitors annually (Piper Jaffray, 1998a).

Strategic Alliances

To further increase its customer base and diversify its revenue steam, another key ingredient of E*Trade's expansion was seeking partnerships and alliances. Cotsakos explained:

*E*Trade has made a significant commitment to identify and ally with innovative organizations who are leaders in their fields, and who share our vision of providing the consumer with the convenience and control of Internet-based solutions.* (E*Trade, 1998b)

E*Trade established alliances and business agreements with leading technology, content, and distribution partners to provide relevant, insightful, and proprietary value-added investing and research information to its customers. Exhibit 3 provides a list of selected alliance partners.

At the same time, E*Trade began to pursue international licensing and partnership programs to reach new markets and to provide new capabilities to its users. E*Trade

Exhibit 3. E*Trade's partnerships, alliances, and acquisitions

The following is a list of selected alliance partners (in alphabetical order):

America Onlline (AOL)- E*Trade has provided on-line investing services to AOL users since 1992. As of January 1999, more than 14 million AOL members have access to E*Trade from the AOL Personal Finance Channel. In 1998, E*Trade agreed to pay America Online $25 million for two years of "premier placement" on the AOL service (Kane, 1998).

BancBoston Robertson Stephens - E*Trade's exclusive alliance with BancBoston Robertson Stephens provides Professional Edge subscribers with access to proprietary research and recommendations formerly available only to the largest investors and institutions.

BancOne - BancOne customers are able to manage their investments using E*Trade's on-line securities transaction, information, and portfolio management services. E*Trade customers, in turn, have on-line access to a range of integrated financial services, including checking and savings accounts, loans, and credit and debit cards.

Barclays Global Fund Advisors - Barclays has teamed up with E*Trade to offer a selection of index, enhanced index, and fund products that will be offered exclusively through E*Trade.

Bridgeway Capital Management - E*Trade is the exclusive no-transaction-fee outlet for the Bridgeway family of mutual funds. As a result of this agreement, no other brokerage firm will offer Bridgeway funds without charging transaction fees.

CNNfn - E*Trade has a significant branded presence on CNNfn, including the site's new Broker Center. That presence will be promoted on CNN, the cable network.

CompuServe - CompuServe users have had access to E*Trade on-line investing services since 1992. More than 5 million users have direct access to E*Trade from the CompuServe Personal Finance Center.

CUSO Financial Services - CUSO Financial Services credit union customers have the option of directing their own investments through E*Trade.

Critical Path - On July 14, 1998, E*Trade entered into an agreement to provide venture capital to Critical Path. Critical Path is an industry leader in providing outsourced e-mail services and infrastructure for Web portals such as Destination E*Trade. In addition, Critical Path became the exclusive host for E*Trade's web-based e-mail system. E*Trade hopes that an increasing number of account holders will access their trade confirmations via secure e-mail, thus reducing E*Trade's enormous postage expenses.

Data Broadcasting Corporation - Data Broadcasting Corporation, a leading on-line investment information service, provides millions of investors access to E*Trade from its on-line trading center at *http://www.dbc.com.*

Digital Island - E*Trade's investment in Digital Island, the first global IP applications network, allows it to leverage Digital Island's distributed star network to distribute E*Trade products around the globe.

E*Offering - E*Trade plans to invest in E*Offering, a full-service investment bank on the Internet. The deal will help provide E*Trade customers with greater access to subscribed public offerings. E*Trade will own 28% of E*Offering.

First USA - E*Trade has joined with First USA to offer Platinum and Classic Visa credit cards to E*Trade customers at competitive interest rates and no annual fees.

InsWeb - E*Trade assists customers with their personal insurance needs, allowing consumers to comparison shop for insurance on the E*Trade web site.

Microsoft Corporation - E*Trade's strategic partnership with Microsoft gives users of the popular Microsoft Investor service and MS Money application direct access to E*Trade's on-line investing services.

Novo/Ironlight - E*Trade has contracted with Novo/Ironlight to create and deploy its multilingual web sites in several international markets. The web sites will be culturally specific while building and maintaining the E*Trade brand and quality standards.

Omega Research, Inc. - E*Trade is the exclusive on-line investing sponsor of all of Omega Research's sales seminars.

OptionsLink - E*Trade's acquisition of the OptionsLink division of Hambrecht & Quist allows it to offer a Web-based and custom interactive voice response order entry system for employee stock option and stock purchase plan services to corporate stock plan participants.

Scudder Kemper Investments, Inc. - E*Trade's Mutual Fund Center offers more than 30 no-load Scudder Funds on-line.

Exhibit 3. E*Trade's partnerships, alliances, and acquisitions (cont.)

ShareData, Inc. - E*Trade has acquired ShareData, Inc., the leader in stock plan knowledge-based software and expertise for pre-IPO and public companies. ShareData, Inc. serves more than 2,500 companies and represents more than 2.5 million employee option holders worldwide (E*Trade, 1998c). The post-merger goal is for E*Trade to be able to offer plan sponsors and their employees a completely integrated and automated solution for stock plan management and company stock transaction capabilities. On the acquisition of ShareData, Cotsakos stated, "The acquisition of ShareData reinforces E*Trade's strategy of moving beyond transaction fees to increase the number of ways in which we generate revenue." E*Trade used stock to pay for the estimated $28 million acquisition (Piper Jaffray. 1998c).

Softbank - On July 13, 1998, Japan's Softbank Corp. agreed to buy 15.6 million shares of E*Trade stock for $400 million in cash (E*Trade, 1998f). Much of this cash will be used for acquisitions and to fund E*Trade's growth objectives. The agreement also includes a provision that prevents Softbank from selling its newly acquired shares for two years and prevents Softbank from purchasing additional shares for five years. At the time, Softbank also owned 31% of Yahoo!, 35% of GeoCities, and 71% of Ziff-Davis (Wettlaufer, 1998).

ThirdAge Media - ThirdAge.com, the most comprehensive source of content, community, and commerce on the Web for active older adults, has selected E*Trade to be its exclusive on-line securities trading partner. ThirdAge.com users will have convenient one-click access to E*Trade throughout the ThirdAge site.

United Airlines - E*Trade customers will have opportunities to earn frequent flier miles on United Airlines.

VeriSign - VeriSign's advanced digital identification technology will be used to simplify and enhance Internet security procedures for E*Trade customers.

VERSUS Technologies - VERSUS Brokerage Services offers on-line investing services in Canada under the E*Trade name.

WebTV Networks, Inc. - WebTV viewers are able to access E*Trade in the Investing and Brokerage sections of the WebTV Network.

Yahoo! - In August 1998, E*Trade entered into an agreement with Yahoo! Yahoo! has set the standard for Internet companies, and its site is the most trafficked site on the web. E*Trade's agreement with Yahoo! will substantially increase E*Trade's presence on banners, advertisements, and sponsorships throughout the Yahoo! network. Within the agreement, E*Trade also renews its status as one of Yahoo's premier merchants. E*Trade hopes its agreement with Yahoo! will help achieve its goal of becoming a leading branded, bookmarked financial destination site on the web.

Zurich Kemper Investments - Zurich Kemper Investments, E*Trade's money market fund provider, offers a combination of competitive current yields, service, pricing, and potential for new-service development to E*Trade customers.

sought to buy stakes in companies that advanced online trading and kept its brand name in the forefront to reinforce and leverage the E*Trade brand franchise worldwide. The following is a summary of E*Trade's international expansion efforts:

- **Canada:** E*Trade signed its first international license in January 1997. The license created an E*Trade franchise in Canada, where it became the first online firm to offer a broad mutual fund center.
- **Australia:** On April 22, 1998, E*Trade launched service in Australia after signing an agreement with Australia's Nova Pacific. Nova Pacific has since adopted the E*Trade name and also plans to launch online trading in New Zealand. As of October 1998, E*Trade had more than 3,000 active accounts in Australia (Olmstead, 1998b) and as of December 31, 1998, after nine months of operation, E*Trade Australia was handling 1% of the daily transaction volume on the Australian Securities Exchange.
- **Japan:** On June 4, 1998, E*Trade initiated two joint venture agreements with Japan's Softbank Corporation. One agreement established the E*Trade brand name in Japan, a key target of E*Trade's international expansion. Japan opened its

securities industry to foreign companies, and Japanese citizens have an estimated $10 trillion in individual savings.

- **Korea:** An agreement with Softbank helped in establishing E*Trade Korea. Korea's government has changed its stance and is now allowing foreign investment, especially in technology. As of July 1998, Korea had over 2.5 million Internet users (E*Trade, 1998d).
- **United Kingdom:** On June 11, 1998, E*Trade signed a joint venture agreement with Electronic Share Information, LTD., a leading financial services provider in the United Kingdom. The venture, called E*Trade UK, will give E*Trade access to Electronic Share Information's 170,000 customers (E*Trade, 1998a).
- **France:** On December 3, 1998, E*Trade announced a licensing agreement with CPR, a premier French investment and asset management bank. The new company, CPR E*Trade, had the exclusive right to use the E*Trade brand, technology, and services in France. As of December 1998, there were 1.5 million Internet users in France.

In addition to the countries mentioned above, E*Trade initiated service or was in the process of developing the E*Trade brand in Germany, Poland, Russia, and Israel (E*Trade, 1998a). Although international revenue accounted for only about 3% of its total revenue in 1998, E*Trade estimated that that percentage would increase to 30% by 2003 (Olmstead, 1998b). E*Trade also envisioned enabling investors in one country to trade stocks in several other countries, but this would require major changes in international legislation.

Launching "Destination E*Trade"

Although the opening was delayed several times, in September 1998 E*Trade launched the much anticipated "Destination E*Trade" with a celebrity-filled event including Bob Costas and Shaquille O'Neil. Destination E*Trade was intended to play a key role in helping E*Trade reach its ambitious goal of tripling its account base between 1998 and 2000. The new site offered features and content well beyond the reaches of E*Trade's previous site and beyond industry standards, as shown in Table 2.

Destination E*Trade allowed all visitors to view headline news, delayed stock quotes, and other widely available market information. Merely by registering, even without opening an E*Trade account, a visitor could get access to customizable tools, secure e-mail, investment chat rooms, and free real-time quotes. E*Trade targeted the estimated 20 million individual investors who accessed the Web for investment research and portfolio tracking but had yet to open an online investment account (E*Trade, 1998g). E*Trade used these freebies to convince some of its visitors to stick around and

*Table 2. Online investing services provided at destination E*Trade Web site*

Smart alerts based on price	Portfolio tracking	News updates from Reuters
Smart alerts based on volume	Watch lists	Earnings estimates from Zach's
Secure e-mail	Mutual fund information	A plethora of research report from Morningstar
Free real-time quotes	Company report	Java-based charting capabilities

open an account. Between September 1998 and January 1, 1999, more than 500,000 visitors became members (E*Trade, 1998i).

By early 1999, E*Trade had established a popular Web site offering self-directed investors the convenience and control of automated stock, options, and mutual fund order placement at low commission rates. In addition, E*Trade had a digital suite of value-added products and services that could be personalized, including portfolio tracking, real-time stock quotes, "smart" alerts, market commentary and analysis, news, investor community areas, and other information services. Exhibit 4 presents a comprehensive list of E*Trade's products, services, and features as of March 1999. Exhibit 5 highlights various measures of E*Trade's rapid growth.

CURRENT CHALLENGES/PROBLEMS FACING E*TRADE

In February 1999, Christos Cotsakos should have been one of the happiest men on the planet. As CEO of E*Trade, he had seen his company grow at an astounding pace, with 1998 revenues reaching $335.7 million and E*Trade's account base climbing to 676,000. (Exhibit 6 presents the company's financial data since 1995.) He had also watched the company's stock price increase 491% between September 30, 1998, and January 29, 1999. In 1998, his company became the first securities and financial services company to be awarded the CPA WebTrust Seal of Assurance by the American Institute of Certified Public Accountants. His efforts had earned him the honor of Ernst & Young as he was named the 1998 National Entrepreneur of the Year for Internet Products and Services Companies.

At the same time, Cotsakos must also have been terrified after watching E*Trade's computer systems shut down on three consecutive days during the week of February 8, 1999. Technological problems crashed E*Trade's entire online trading capacity for hours at a time and led to a class action lawsuit filed against E*Trade on February 9, 1999 (Glasgall, 1999). From February 2 to February 10, 1999, E*Trade's stock value plummeted 35%.

Cotsakos was pleased with the success of E*Trade so far, but he faced several challenges not only from the fiercer competition within an industry shifting toward online trading but also from emerging ethical and operational problems. While he wanted to push forward with international expansion, he wondered whether his company had grown too fast and could even handle its current customer base in the United States. Operating in the ever-changing world of online investing presented enormous challenges, gratification, and headaches for executives like Cotsakos, who were on the front lines of rewriting the rules of the investment world.

An Industry Shift Toward Online Trading

Competition in the online trading segment was fierce. (Exhibit 7 presents several measures of the online trading segment's rapid growth). What began in 1995 as a few firms competing for a small number of accounts turned into an industry segment with about 80 competitors vying for millions of accounts. In 1998, full-service brokerage firms still accounted for about 80% of dollar commissions generated in the retail brokerage

Exhibit 4. E*Trade's products (March 1999)

Comprehensive Trading - With an E*Trade account, customers can buy and sell stocks, options, bonds, and more than 4,300 mutual funds directly from their personal computer or by telephone.

Complete Account Management - E*Trade customers can review their portfolio holdings, balances, and outstanding orders on-line. E*Trade offers unlimited free checking, competitive interest rates on uninvested cash, on-line cash transfers, and an E*Trade Visa® card.

Free Real-Time Quotes - All E*Trade customers and members are offered free and unlimited real-time quotes.

Mutual Fund Center - Launched on November 3, 1997, E*Trade's Mutual Fund Center offers access to more than 4,300 mutual funds from many popular fund families, including American Century, Baron, Bridgeway, Invesco, Janus, and Vanguard. There are 900 no-load funds to choose from. Custom screening tools and research help guide customers to the funds that are right for them. E*Trade also provides direct access to on-line prospectuses for all the funds in the network.

Bond Center - Through E*Trade's comprehensive on-line bond trading capability, individual investors can place on-line orders for a wide range of fixed-income securities, including U.S. Treasury, corporate, and municipal bonds. The Bond Center also offers analytical tools, commentary, and credit rating information.

Investment Research - E*Trade offers access to investment research and analysis tools. Users can get breaking news, quotes, charts, earnings estimates, company fundamentals, and live market commentary 24 hours a day—all for free.

Power E*Trade - A powerful collection of free tools and services for the active trader. Customers who qualify can maximize their profit potential with ultra-fast order entry, NASDAQ Level II quotes, real-time streaming portfolios, and priority customer service.

Professional Edge - Customers can subscribe to get institutional research reports and real-time buy/sell recommendations before the market opens from the analysts at BancBoston Robertson Stephens. E*Trade expects premium content, such as the Professional Edge, to generate 2% of future revenue (Olmstead, 1998a).

Mortgages - E*Trade offers direct access to comprehensive information on mortgages. Users can compare market rates and apply for a home loan from their PC.

Insurance - Through E*Trade's Insurance Center, users can easily compare coverages and prices of different insurance carriers for policies that fit their individual needs.

Credit Cards - E*Trade offers Platinum and Classic Visa® credit cards at competitive interest rates and no annual fees.

Ideas and Tools - E*Trade provides free investing help and education, including mutual fund screening tools, tech stock analysis, options analysis, and retirement planning calculators.

Personal Market Watch - E*Trade customers can personalize their view of the markets with "My E*Trade," selecting Snapshot, Tech Spotlight, Trader, Portfolio, or Analyst views. The Portfolio Manager feature lets users follow the securities they own or track.

Smart Alerts - This free service allows customers to have stock price, volume, and P/E alerts delivered directly to their inbox on the Web and to any e-mail address or alphanumeric pager.

Discussion Groups - In Community @ E*Trade, members can exchange ideas and discuss hot stocks and investing strategies. E*Trade also offers live celebrity chat events.

E*Station - E*Trade's self-service information center lets customers find answers to their questions. It also allows customers to submit service requests on-line.

E*Trade Mail - E*Trade's free e-mail service provides customers the security, reliability, and speed to handle all of their e-mail needs free of charge.

Security - All E*Trade transactions over the Internet are secured by Netscape Secure Commerce Server (SSL), the industry's leading technology for web security. When customers access the E*Trade web site using either Netscape Navigator or Microsoft Internet Explorer, their communications are automatically protected through server authentication and data encryption.

Note: All these products were available through E*Trade's Destination web site.

Exhibit 5. Measures of E*Trade's growth

(a) E*Trade's account growth, 1996-1999 (in thousands)

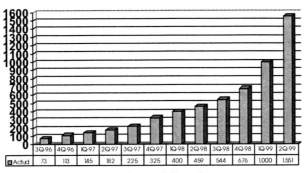

Account Growth

	3Q-96	4Q-96	1Q-97	2Q-97	3Q-97	4Q-97	1Q-98	2Q-98	3Q-98	4Q-98	1Q-99	2Q-99
Actual	73	113	145	182	225	325	400	459	544	676	1,000	1,551

Source: Forrester Research

(b) E*Trade's average number of on-line trades per day, 1996-1999

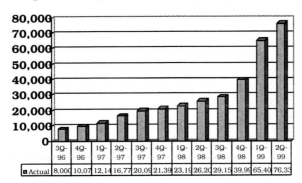

Trades per Day

	3Q-96	4Q-96	1Q-97	2Q-97	3Q-97	4Q-97	1Q-98	2Q-98	3Q-98	4Q-98	1Q-99	2Q-99
Actual	8,000	10,07	12,14	16,77	20,09	21,39	23,19	26,20	29,15	39,99	65,40	76,33

Source: Credit Suisse First Boston, Piper Jaffray, and E*Trade's 10K Reports

(c) E*Trade's fluctuations in market share, 1997-1999

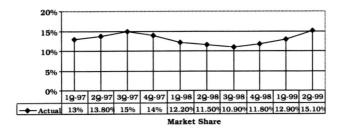

Market Share

	1Q-97	2Q-97	3Q-97	4Q-97	1Q-98	2Q-98	3Q-98	4Q-98	1Q-99	2Q-99
Actual	13%	13.80%	15%	14%	12.20%	11.50%	10.90%	11.80%	12.90%	15.10%

Source: Credit Suisse First Boston, Piper Jaffray, and E*Trade's 10K Reports

Exhibit 6. E*Trade's annual financial data

Years Ended September 30	1999 (Projected)	1998	1997	1996	1995
(in thousands, except transaction and per share amounts)					
Revenue	$621,402	335,756	$234,128	141,803	108,961
Pretax income	(91,536)	2,151	29,323	3,671	9,446
Net income (loss)	(54,438)	1,927	19,193	4,166	7,333
Income per share					
Basic	(0.23)	0.01	0.14	0.05	0.11
Diluted	(0.23)	0.01	0.13	0.03	0.07
Shares used in computation of income (loss) per share					
Basic	235,926	173,906	133,572	80,554	68,467
Diluted	235,926	185,479	147,833	121,863	111,427
Average transactions per day	68,484	27,620	16,382	6,148	2,335

Years Ended September 30	1999 (Projected)	1998	1997	1996	1995
(in thousands, except account, associate, and per share amounts)					
Active accounts	1,551,000	544,000	225,000	91,000	32,000
Number of associates	1,735	954	698	489	245
Working capital	319,634	615,968	270,778	74,041	22,257
Total assets	3,926,980	2,066,286	1,148,114	397,169	107,212
Shareowners' equity	913,667	734,410	303,694	89,785	27,908
Net book value per share	3.81	3.18	1.85	0.70	0.22

Exhibit 7. Measures of online trading growth

(a) U.S. online investment acount growth, 1996-2002 (in millions)

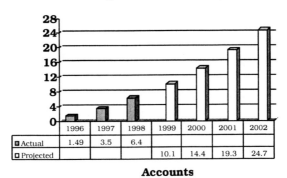

Accounts

Source: International Data Corporation, February 1999

(b) Average number of online trades per day, 1997-1999 (in thousands)

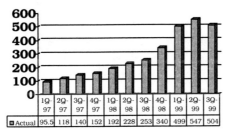

Trades per day

Source: Credit Suisse First Boston (1998a)

(c) Assets managed in online investment accounts, 1997-2002 (in billions)

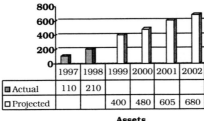

Assets

Source: Pettit (1998)

Exhibit 7. Measures of online trading growth (cont.)

(d) Online trading commissions generated, 1996-2001 (in millions)

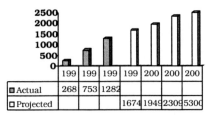

Commissions Generated

Source: Credit Suisse First Boston (1999a)

(e) Online trades as a percentage of all equity trades, 1997-1999

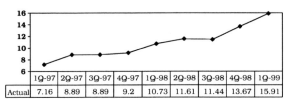

Percentage of Equity Trades

Source: Credit Suisse First Boston (1999a)

business (Credit Suisse First Boston, 1998b). But as some of their investors began to defect to online trading, full-service firms adjusted (Exhibit 8 depicts investors' primary reasons for trading online). By late 1998, several full-service brokerage firms began planning measures to offer select customers certain aspects of online investing without compromising the tradition of full-service investing. Instead of charging per transaction, the full-service firms began charging a flat percentage-of-assets fee similar to those charged by asset managers. For example, in early 1999, Morgan Stanley Dean Witter began offering online trading to 20,000 of its customers. Investors with $50,000 to $250,000 were charged 2.25% of their assets and were granted 56 trades per year (Glasgall, 1999). Prudential Securities was offering a rate of $24.95 per trade to account holders with more than $100,000 in addition to an annual fee of 1%. Merrill Lynch was planning to roll out similar services to 55,000 of its estimated 5 million account holders (*CBS*, 1999). Table 3 depicts the competitive breakdown as of September 2, 1999.

In 1999, Schwab had greater market share than its two nearest competitors combined. It also maintained a relatively high commission level ($29.95), while the average commission charged by the top 10 firms had steadily declined, as shown in Exhibit 9 (Credit Suisse First Boston, 1998b). Because of its well-established brand name, popular mutual fund supermarket, and huge existing account base, Schwab was able to grab an

Exhibit 8. Primary reasons for investing online (according to Jupiter Communications)

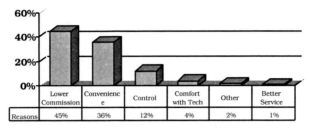

	Lower Commission	Convenience	Control	Comfort with Tech	Other	Better Service
Reasons	45%	36%	12%	4%	2%	1%

Reasons for Investing On-Lin

Source: International Data Corporation, February 1999

Table 3. Key players in the online trading industry

Company	Market Share	Assets Controlled	Number of Accounts	Ave. Trades per Day	Ave. Trades per Yr. (per customer)
Charles Schwab	23.3%	$263 billion	3,000,000	117,800	12.7
E*Trade	15.1%	$28 billion	1,551,000	76,333	16
Waterhouse	12.1%	$52.7 billion	877,000	61,031	21.6
Fidelity	11.9%	$202 billion	3,060,000	60,013	4.8
Datek	10.7%	$7 billion	290,000	53,840	59
Ameritrade	9.2%	$22.9 billion	560,000	46,199	26.4
DLJ Direct	3.8%	$14.2 billion	302,000	19,200	19.9

Source: Credit Suisse First Boston (1999b) and Piper Jaffray (1999a, 1999b)

Exhibit 9. Average commission charged by the top 10 online trading firms, 1996-1999 (in U.S. dollars)

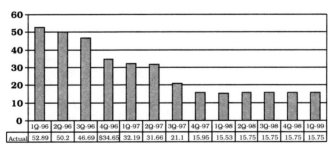

	1Q-96	2Q-96	3Q-96	4Q-96	1Q-97	2Q-97	3Q-97	4Q-97	1Q-98	2Q-98	3Q-98	4Q-98	1Q-99
Actual	52.89	50.2	46.69	$34.65	32.19	31.66	21.1	15.95	15.53	15.75	15.75	15.75	15.75

Average Commission

Source: Credit Suisse First Boston (1999a)

Table 4. Commissions charged by the top players in the online trading industry

Company	9/30/98	12/31/98	Notes
Schwab		$29.95	$29.95	For the first 1000 shares, $0.03 per share thereafter
E*Trade		$14.95	$14.95	$19.95 for limit and NASDAQ orders
Waterhouse		$12	$12	For the first 5000 shares, $0.01 per share thereafter
Fidelity Active Trader		$14.95	$14.95	To qualify, investor must place 36 trades per year
Datek		$9.99	$9.99	All trades up to 5000 shares
Ameritrade		$8	$8	$13 for limit and stop orders
DLJ Direct		$20	$20	For the first 1000 shares, $0.02 per share thereafter
Quick & Reilly		$14.95	$14.95	$19.95 for limit orders, $0.02 per share above 1000 shares
Typical Full-Service Broker		$300-$500		Varies by firm; often at the discretion of individual broker

(Source: Credit Suisse First Boston, 1998a)

early lead that it never relinquished. Table 4 lists the commissions charged by the top players in the online trading industry for a typical market order.

The growth in the online trading industry was driven by several key factors:

1. **Increased Internet usage:** In 1992, there were fewer than 10 million Internet users worldwide. By the end of 1999, that number was projected at 196.1 million (see Exhibit 10 for a chart of actual and projected worldwide Internet users from 1995 to 2003).
2. **Increased consumer comfort with electronic commerce:** For a while, people had been willing to "surf" the Web but unwilling to conduct business on it. Attitudes had begun to change and confidence was rising in the Internet as an alternate channel for conducting business.
3. **A roaring bull market:** With the strong market run since 1995, online trading emerged at an opportune time. Technology firms' stocks were rising faster than other stocks, and tech investors were predisposed to lead the movement toward online investing (Economist, 1999).

Exhibit 10. Actual and proejcted worldwide Internet users, 1995-2003 (in millions)

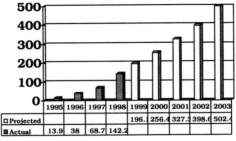

	1995	1996	1997	1998	1999	2000	2001	2002	2003
Projected					196.1	256.4	327.3	398.6	502.4
Actual	13.9	38	68.7	142.2					

Worldwide Internet Users

4. **Media attention:** The mass media had made online trading "chic." Articles in *Business Week*, the *Wall Street Journal*, and *Fortune* had raised awareness about online trading and hyped its potential.

5. **Baby boomers approaching retirement:** As the members of the baby boom generation approached retirement, they were pouring increasing amounts of their income into investments (Credit Suisse First Boston, 1998a). Many of them were shifting their investments toward online brokerage accounts.

6. **Continued international expansion:** E*Trade and Schwab had led the expansion, but others were ramping up their own efforts. Japan was a prime target as its securities industry was opening to foreign companies, and its citizens had low faith in local firms and high savings account balances.

7. **Partnering with investment banks:** Online brokerage firms were rushing to partner with investment banks in hopes of offering their account holders access to initial public offerings (IPOs). Critics charged that these arrangements were one-sided, guaranteeing the online firms very few shares of "hot" IPOs while using the online firms as a distribution outlet for the shares of "weak" IPOs. To mitigate this problem, online firms may begin to develop their own "limited" investment banking operations (Credit Suisse First Boston, 1999a).

8. **Large banks entering the online trading industry:** With the banking infrastructure created and refined over the last 100 years, banks felt that they could enter the online trading industry without major obstacles. Banks wanted to have online trading capabilities to help attract and keep customers. Initially, banks wanted to target high-end customers, not day traders. Many saw their advancement into the online trading industry as a defensive move (Piper Jaffray, 1998b).

Ethical Issues Within the Online Trading Industry

The following important ethical issues within the realm of online trading were emerging by the end of 1999.

1. **"Know thy customer":** Regulations by the Securities and Exchange Commission of the United States required full-service brokers to monitor their customers' investment activities and prevent them from entering into inappropriate transactions. Online trading firms were subject to the same regulations, but they "complied" by installing monitoring software that tracked their customers' transactions. It was not clear whether or not a software tracking system met the criteria of "know thy customer" (Piper Jaffray, 1998a).

2. **Access in high-volume periods:** When market volume was extremely high, access to online trading Web sites could become difficult, with so many users trying to logon at the same time. Several firms were considering buying or developing software that could distinguish whether the person trying to logon to its site had an account value of $5,000 or $10,000,000. The software could then block the $5,000 account holder and permit access to the $10,000,000 account holder. Would such a system be ethical? Would it be legal?

3. **Distribution of IPOs:** Access to IPOs had long been a point of controversy within the world of investing. Who should have access to the precious initial shares? Institutions always seemed to have access, and so did wealthy brokerage account

holders. As IPOs became available to online traders, how could firms decide who would have access? Would it be the wealthiest account holders, those who agreed not to "flip" the shares, or those who were first to request that particular IPO? With more and more IPOs available online, this issue was becoming increasingly important.

4.   **Registration:** Securities brokerage companies had to register in other countries before accepting or soliciting customers from there. These firms also had to respect the securities laws of these countries. Since online trading firms had sites on the Internet, and the Internet was available in virtually every country, did this mean online brokerage firms needed to register in every country?

E*Trade's Operational Problems

Some of the most critical problems that E*Trade was experiencing by the end of 1999 included:

1.   **Vague and broad investment agreement:** E*Trade customers had voiced concern about the "fine print" in E*Trade's investment agreement. To open an account at E*Trade, the customer had to agree to the terms of the E*Trade Customer Agreement, the introduction of which stated, "Please note that the information contained herein is subject to change without notice." Furthermore, the "General Provisions" section included the following sentence: "In consideration of E*Trade opening and maintaining one or more accounts, you agree to the terms and conditions contained in this Agreement, as amended from time to time."

This clause gave E*Trade wide latitude to change the terms of its customer agreement. Other agreement clauses allowed blame to be shifted from E*Trade to the market makers when confirmations moved slowly, granted E*Trade "Irrevocable Power of Attorney," and disclaimed liability regarding "losses resulting from a cause over which E*Trade or its affiliates do not have direct control."

2.   **Insufficient capacity:** In December 1997, a class action lawsuit was filed against E*Trade, claiming that customers had lost money because of E*Trade's failure to correctly handle the volatile trading days in October 1997. The complaint alleged that E*Trade knew that its communications systems could handle only 10,000 to 15,000 users, fewer than 7% of its accounts at that time (Iwata, 1997). A similar class action lawsuit was filed on February 9, 1999, after E*Trade's systems crashed three times during one week.

The 1998 launching of Destination E*Trade brought complaints about the new site's speed and accessibility. Investors continually complained that they could not access the Web site during peak trading periods and that the site loaded very slowly. Since E*Trade's decision to open the site to non-customers had contributed to the problem, customers suggested that E*Trade freeze new accounts until it could service existing accounts properly. Customers also found the new site difficult to navigate, and its error messages confusing.

3.   **Poor trade executions:** Given that E*Trade was selling its order flow to market makers who were executing orders with their own interests in mind, investors often complained that their "market" orders had been executed at unfavorable prices and at a very slow pace. Investors said that E*Trade shifted the blame over to its market

makers, who were looking to make money on each transaction. Unlike Datek, E*Trade did not have a one-minute market order fill guarantee. Customers reported that "market" orders placed at night were not executed until 11 a.m. the following day.[2] There were also complaints about long delays in confirming trade executions—from 10 minutes to 1.5 hours.[3]

4. **Questionable practices:** One of the investors interviewed, who tired of E*Trade's continual problems, elected to transfer his account to Fidelity. This investor held a risky position in the very volatile Amazon.com. The stock was trading at $135 in the summer of 1998 when E*Trade acted on the transfer order in the *middle* of the trading day. The investor was then blocked from selling his position later that day. Since the account was no longer accessible through the Web site, he had to wait a week until his new account was "live" at Fidelity. By then, the stock had fallen under $100. The investor, an attorney, considered E*Trade's decision to close his account in the middle of the day to be ludicrous and in bad faith. The matter was not resolved by several e-mail messages to customer service, and the investor ultimately sent a formal protest to E*Trade's compliance department. He was informed that the investment contract, in the fine print, gives E*Trade the right to close the account at its discretion. Furthermore, he was told that he could still have placed the trade using E*Trade's $35 broker-assisted trading through its "800" telephone number. The investor was further irritated by this response.

5. **Poor customer service:** E*Trade customers complained about "canned" e-mail responses that missed the point of their questions, long waits on calls to the "800" telephone numbers, a confusing telephone menu, waits of over a week for e-mail responses, and customer service representatives with poor attitudes.

During the summer of 1998, E*Trade ran a promotion offering an investor $50 if s/he placed five or more trades between June 16 and June 30. When one of the interviewees for this study complained via e-mail about not receiving his $50, an E*Trade customer service representative sent an e-mail apologizing and confirming that the $50 was being credited to his account. Two weeks later, the customer still had not received his credit and wrote back. The same customer service representative who had confirmed the credit two weeks earlier now explained that the previous e-mail was a mistake and that the customer did not qualify for the $50. (Actually, the customer did not qualify for the $50, but he still felt he deserved it because the customer service representative had confirmed that he would receive it).

Another customer had trouble with E*Trade's "tell-a-friend" program, which granted a free trade to a customer who referred a friend who ultimately opened an account. This customer recalled, "I referred about fifteen friends, seven of whom have opened an account. However, I had to send several e-mails to E*Trade's customer service to get the proper credit for my referrals. I have never received credit without having to chase E*Trade."

6. **Questionable security:** Perhaps most troubling of all were E*Trade's sloppy account set-up procedures. A customer from Colorado called several times regarding a trade. Each time, the representative could not find the trade request anywhere in the customer's account record. On the fifth call, the representative finally asked for more detailed information and inquired why the address associated with the account was in Massachusetts. It was revealed that E*Trade had mixed up the two

account numbers in its records, a dangerous error. The two customers involved happened not to be active traders, but they had had access to trade on each other's accounts.

REFERENCES

Buckman, R. (1998, July 30). E*Trade expects its stock price will benefit from losses but the market seems to disagree. *Wall Street Journal.*

Byron, C. (1997, May). Flame your broker! *Esquire.*

CBS. (1999, March 4). Merrill Lynch tiptoes into online trading. *CBS MarketWatch Report.*

CNN. (1998, August 22). *On-line trading—A special report.*

Credit Suisse First Boston. (1998a, August 20) *Online Trading Quarterly: June 1998.*

Credit Suisse First Boston. (1998b, November 11). *Online Trading Quarterly: 3rd Quarter 1998.*

Credit Suisse First Boston. (1999a, January 28). *Online Trading Quarterly: 4th Quarter 1998.*

Credit Suisse First Boston. (1999b, September 12). *Online Trading Quarterly: 4th Quarter 1999.*

Dalton, G. (1998, December 21/28). Chief information officer of the year: Debra Chrapaty. *InformationWeek.*

Economist. (1999, January 30). *When the bubble burst.* pp. 23-25.

E*Trade. (1998a, June 11). *E*Trade signs second international joint venture agreement in seven days* (Company Press Release).

E*Trade. (1998b, June 26). *E*Trade offers customers platinum and classic Visa card* (Company Press Release).

E*Trade. (1998c, July 6). *E*Trade to acquire ShareData, Inc.* (Company Press Release).

E*Trade. (1998d, July 9). *E*Trade enters Korean market as international expansion moves forward* (Company Press Release).

E*Trade. (1998e, July 14). *E*Trade makes strategic investments in high technology companies* (Company Press Release).

E*Trade. (1998f, July 21). *E*Trade reports third quarter earnings of 114 percent on revenue growth of 68 percent* (Company Press Release).

E*Trade. (1998g, August 6). *E*Trade expands marketing and commerce agreement with Yahoo!* (Company Press Release).

E*Trade. (1998h, September 10). *E*Trade launches new destination Web site and Stateless Architecture (SM) to empower individual investors* (Company Press Release).

E*Trade. (1998i, December 28). *E*Trade's new destination financial services Web site attracts more than 500,000 members since September* (Company Press Release).

Glasgall, W. (1999, February 22). Who needs a broker? *Business Week.*

Iwata, E. (1997, December 4). On-line brokerage sued for being slow; ads were deceptive, some customers say. *Seattle Post-Intelligencer.*

Kane, M. (1998, July 8). E*Trade to offer financial services. *Yahoo! News.*

Lipton, B. (1998, September 10). E*Trade launches portal site. *CNET News.*

Olmstead, A. (1998a, September 14). Investors have high hopers for E*Trade's new site. *On-line Broker*.

Olmstead, A. (1998b, October 22). Storming the borders. *On-line Broker*.

Pettit, D. (1998, September 8). Logged on. *Wall Street Journal*.

Piper Jaffray. (1997, August). E*Trade.

Piper Jaffray. (1998a, February). *Online trading update: Fourth quarter 1997*.

Piper Jaffray. (1998b, June). *Online trading update: First quarter 1998*.

Piper Jaffray. (1998c, August). *Online trading update: Second quarter 1998*.

Piper Jaffray. (1998d, October). *Online brokerage: industry at a critical inflection point*.

Piper Jaffray. (1999a, February 4). *Online brokerages explode in 1998*.

Piper Jaffray. (1999b, September). *Online trading update: Fourth quarter 1999*.

Stirland, S. (1998, April 1). Web balancing act. *Wall Street and Technology*.

Wettlaufer, D. (1998, July 13). An Investment Opinion. *The Motley Fool*.

FURTHER READING

Brown, S. A. (2000). *Customer relationship management: Linking people, process, and technology*. John Wiley & Sons.

Cotsakos, C. M. (2000). *It's your money: The E*Trade step-by-step guide to online investing*. HarperCollins.

Dutta, S., Kwan, S., & Segev, A. *Transforming business in the marketspace: Strategic marketing and customer relationships*. Retrieved from http://inside.insead.fr/rise/papers/tbmfull.pdf

Hagel, J., III, & Singer. M. (1999). *Net Worth: Shaping markets when customers make the rules*. Harvard Business School Press.

http://www.finpipe.com/

http://www.gomezadvisors.com

Johnson, D. (2000). *Discount commodity brokers ranked*. Retrieved February 8, 2000, from http://www.sonic.net/donaldj/futures.html

Prewitt, E. (1997, August). Coping with infoglut: What you can learn from the folks in financial services. *Harvard Management Update*.

Serwer, A. (1999, October 11). A nation of traders. *Fortune*, 116-120.

Shapiro, C., & Varian H. R. (1999). *Information rules*. Harvard Business School Press.

U.S. Securities and Exchange Commission. *Learn about investing*. Retrieved from http://www.sec.gov/consumer/jneton.htm

Adam T. Elegant graduated from Washington University (St. Louis) in 1995, with a BA in political science. After college he worked for American International Group (AIG) and Templeton Funds. In 1999, he earned his MBA from the University of Colorado at Boulder in finance and technology & innovation management. He currently works for Goldman Sachs in San Francisco, focusing on institutional on-line trading and venture investments related to financial services.

Ramiro Montealegre received his doctorate in vusiness administration from the Harvard Business School in the area of management information systems. His master's degree in computer science is from Carleton University, Canada. He holds a bachelor's in engineering degree from the Francisco Marroquin University, Guatemala. Currently, he is an assistant professor of information systems at the University of Colorado, Boulder. He is regularly Invited Lecturer at Case Western Reserve University, Instituto de Centro America de Administracion de Empresas (INCAE) in Costa Rica, the Instituto Tecnologico y de Estudios Superiores de Monterrey in Mexico, Instituto de Altos Estudios Empresariales (IAE) in Argentina, and Universidad Pablo Olavides in Spain. His research focuses on the interplay between information technology and organization transformation in highly uncertain environments. He has been involved in studying projects of organizational change in the United States, Canada, Mexico, and the Central and South American regions. His research has been published in MIS Quarterly, Sloan Management Review, Journal of Management Information Systems, IEEE Transactions on Communications, Information & Management, Information Technology & People, *and other journals.*

This case was previously published in M. Raisinghani (Ed)., *Cases on Worldwide E-Commerce: Theory in Action*, pp. 221-249, © 2002.

Chapter V

mVine Ltd:
A Case Study of a New Digital Music Label from Conception to Launch

Joanna Berry, University of Newcastle upon Tyne, UK

EXECUTIVE SUMMARY

This chapter analyzes a new digital music label—mVine.com—from conception in December 2003 to launch in March 2005. It discusses the turbulent context within which the company was launched and the particular individual strengths of the founding directors. The business model and specific revenue streams are described, and financial and marketing data are given to support the company's launch development. A full description of how mVine operated initially as a virtual organization provides a full understanding of the benefits and challenges that such a company faces and the opportunity to discuss the strategies that mVine employed to overcome this. Technical information is given that explains how open source software was used to address issues of security and cost while reinforcing the company's open and democratic ethic. An outline is given of the planned development of mVine from virtual startup to fully financed "clicks-and-mortar" corporation.

ORGANIZATION BACKGROUND

mVine Ltd (www.mVine.com) was an independent record label with an online A&R (Artist and Repertoire—i.e., talent spotting) process created over a period of two years, from December 2002 to its eventual launch in May 2005. Anyone could register for free to be a voter and/or artist. Music was not put into specific genres; the company believed that what voters felt was good music was, by definition, good music, without artificial genres being imposed. Voters would also hear a far wider variety of music than they would otherwise be exposed to and may even discover other music they enjoyed. Voters would vote on each track and offer qualitative comments; those artists who were consistently well thought of (statistically) would proceed to higher levels. Once they reached the top of this pyramid, mVine would approach and contract the "best" artists for development, production, release, and promotion. Artists who had been pre-voted to be popular could be developed, therefore, into commercially successful brands in a relatively short space of time with a modest investment.

The company believed that it could consistently attract at least 1,000 artists. If each provided three, three-and-a-half minute tracks, there would be almost 22 solid eight-hour days of listening without a single track repeating. While artists were given statistical feedback about their voting status, it was as a percentage rather than a statistic. They would know, for example, that the average vote for their song was 70% but not whether this was from 3, 30, 300 or 3,000 voters who had voted for them.

mVine was intended to counter what the founders felt was the sanitizing influence of the major music companies; it committed to offering artists a free and global platform for their work and to providing an environment within which consumers could listen to and vote on music of quality regardless of artificial genres, actively influencing the progress of each artist. It had been said (Peterson, 1975) that people who bought music neither got what they wanted nor wanted what they got; historically, the music industry had a top-down value chain. mVine set out to turn this on its head and create a bottom-up paradigm (similar to that of Leonhard, 2003).

FOUNDERS

Co-founder of mVine was Frank Joshi, a music aficionado and highly experienced, successful businessman, who already had built up and sold (for many millions of pounds) a very successful business-to-business dot-com company in 2000 (a time when a rapid succession of over-valued and under-performing dot-com companies was going out of business). After the sale of his company, he moved with his family from London to Brussels. Joshi ensured that financial, strategic and tactical issues were dealt with effectively.

Joshi's old school friend, Calum MacColl, got in touch with him through www.friendsreunited.com, and together, they became co-founders of mVine. MacColl lived in South London; he was the son of acclaimed folk musicians and songwriters, Ewan MacColl and Peggy Seeger, who were highly respected by the music industry and consumers worldwide. MacColl was a writer, producer, and guitarist who had worked with diverse artists, including The Backstreet Boys, Ronan Keating, Eddi Reader, Cathy Dennis, Latin Quarter, Brian Kennedy, and Sarah-Jane Morris. MacColl was responsible

Figure 1. Revenue streams, today and tomorrow (Leonhard, 2004)

for assessing the potential and quality of artists rising up through the mVine voting system. Once an artist had been voted up to a set level of success within the mVine system, MacColl's responsibility was to offer recording contracts and provide the detail of support offered within those contracts.

Raymond Field had known and worked with Joshi for more than two years. A database expert specializing in Oracle and SQL, he spent a decade working for large corporations, fine-tuning their databases. Before joining the mVine team, he spent five years personally developing InfoNow, the business intelligence system that underpinned mVine. Field was responsible for the smooth working of InfoNow, making sure that it was compatible with the external, visual aspects of mVine, ensuring that suitable data were collected and analyzed.

In keeping with the principle of partnership which MacColl and Joshi were determined should permeate the company from its inception, Kerry Harvey-Piper (MacColl's

Figure 2. Company structure: December 2003-December 2004

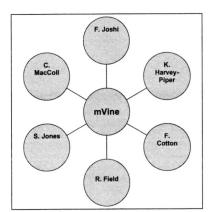

wife) also became part of the team. Harvey-Piper had worked as a freelance marketing and PR consultant for more than 15 years, assisting many small companies in the commercial and charity sectors to develop and sustain their visibility and growth strategies. Harvey-Piper ensured that all press, promotional, and marketing strategies were in place and coordinated communications among the various team members and outside suppliers, ensuring that everyone was as fully informed as possible about day-to-day developments in the lead up to launch.

Fran Cotton was a respected music industry lawyer, who had worked for 12 years for the two largest record companies in the world (WEA Records, Warner, and Mercury Records-Universal) as Director of Legal. Prior to that, Cotton had worked for five years in private practice in Australia. At the time of the study, she ran her own entertainment law practice representing artists, managers, producers, record labels, and film production companies. Cotton had managed artists for more than six years and was experienced in developing them from the grass-roots stage through recording albums and touring. She had her own artist management company; clients included legendary Irish singer/ songwriter Christie Hennessy, Irish rock group Macaboy, and Scottish songwriter Henry Gorman.

During his time working with Ronan Keating, MacColl met Steve Jones, a musician and multimedia artist from Belfast now living and working in London. Aside from time on stage, Steve had been working as a freelance graphic designer and Flash programmer for major clients such as BT, BAA, and Selfridges. MacColl had always enjoyed Jones' lateral approach to design and involved him in mVine from the outset. In particular, Jones devised a new voting mechanism using images and unusual value scales and continued this idea into other aspects of the site to give the user a more organic and personal experience.

Corporate development plans involved eventual recruitment of full-time staff to run day-to-day activities under the directors' supervision. Also planned was acquisition of office space (initially in London and then in other territories, as the company grew) to supplement the work of the founding directors. Both of these were to be implemented as soon as the company's financial position allowed.

mVine Business and Revenue Models

The company's business model evolved constantly over the startup period. For example, although it was initially intended that only unsigned artists would be accepted, the decision was made that any artist could register if they had their own label. Initial fears that mVine artists may be signed up by other labels (and, therefore, that a proportion of mVine's revenues that was expected to come from contractual deals would be lost) were discussed at length internally. Ultimately, it was decided that, consistent with the open philosophy of the company, if an artist was considered to be of value by another label, they were welcome to approach that artist with a view to signing them up. For mVine to be seen as a breeding ground for successful acts should only increase its audience of voters and artists.

In line with this philosophy, independent and major record labels were to be offered private screenings of particularly high-ranking artists (given only a reference number to identify them) to encourage this process. Once an artist was seen to be doing particularly well, an interim contract was offered to them; once they signed it, they were able to be

Figure 3. Developing business model

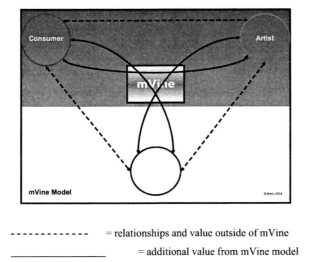

- - - - - - - - - - - - = relationships and value outside of mVine

_____ = additional value from mVine model

put forward in these private screenings. This interim contract (based on the presumption that the person putting the music up had the right to do so) required minimal commitment but was sufficient to ensure that mVine retained the right to a proportion of any subsequent deal that was done between that artist and another label, or an introduction fee, depending on each individual case.

To ensure that the listener had a good initial selection of music to listen to, mVine approached both artists and audience pre-launch. This resulted in a number of signed mVine artists, who already had a successful music career and a number of albums under their belts, which music voters could listen to and buy from launch.

Both revenue and non-revenue benefits were planned (represented by the solid lines in Figure 3) for artists and voters/consumers. These included better value music for the consumer; exposure to new audiences and fans, thus increasing sales for the artist; and loyalty scheme benefits, such as free tickets and signed merchandise for the voters. Alongside the revenues from musicians' union-approved contracts with signed artists were a variety of ways in which mVine proposed to make money:

- **Data sales from online artists' and voters' activities.** InfoNow (the software underpinning mVine) was a sophisticated data-collection engine that could track how, when, and how frequently individuals voted and the impact of the vote. It monitored the responses to individual artists' music and was fundamental in the elevation of tracks to higher levels. A clear and information-rich picture of each individual was available, which could be sold to other companies who wanted statistical (but not private, individual, or personal) information on the voting and purchasing patterns of all or specific groups of users for their own marketing purposes. It would also be intensively data-mined by mVine.

- **Sale of voters' written feedback to artists.** Once they were past a certain threshold of judging activity, users were able to give qualitative comments on any aspect of an artist's performance as well as simply voting on a scale of one to 10. These comments might cover anything that could guide artists in developing their acts. Once past a certain point in the voting process, artists could buy voters' qualitative feedback on their acts for a minimal fee to assist them in development.
- **Sale of downloads, compilation CDs, ring tones.** Downloading music onto a computer for personal use was an increasingly popular and acceptable activity. By September 2004, Radio One was producing a download chart show that reflected these activities, joining the traditional Radio One singles chart show, and in April 2005 downloads were finally incorporated with singles in one combined chart. It should be noted that the problem of illegal downloading was endemic throughout the music industry and an issue for all artists and music labels. While mVine (like all major and independent labels) could do little about this, it was felt that new, little known artists might perhaps benefit from increased interest in their work that the exposure any file sharing of their tracks could generate.
- **Sale of artists' CDs.** As mVine approached launch, it was already partnering with a number of very successful artists, as mentioned previously. These had agreed that their tracks could be on the site and their CDs could be sold in the mVine shop, thus increasing mVine's up-front revenues. In order to ensure that mVine helped individual artists as much as possible and attracted the widest variety and highest quality of music, it also was decided to offer them the facility to use mVine as a sales house. Many artists pressed their own CDs and had no natural mechanism to distribute them more widely than through friends, family, and their own live events. To keep the operation as simple as possible, it was decided simply to handle payments and receipts, letting the artist, who had the motivation to ensure that this happened swiftly and efficiently, pack and ship each CD.

Figure 4. The original revenue model

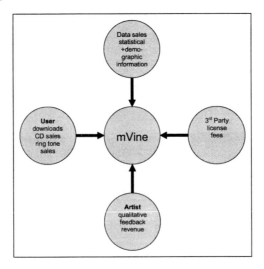

Figure 5. The revenue model: Planned phase two

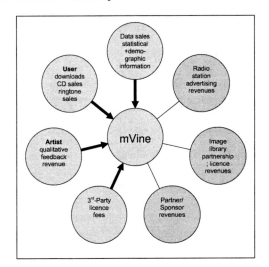

Although Web sites, such as CDBaby, offered an environment within which artists could sell their CDs for a fee, users tended to buy what they knew rather than music from artists that they had never heard of. With over 1.3 million CDs for sale (November 2004), CDBaby was not a very practical solution for the aspiring but unknown artist. mVine made it possible for them to reach a much wider audience by selling their CDs to mVine users for a small fee.

- **Licensing of unsigned artists to other labels.** Although artists may reach a high level within the mVine voting system, they may not be selected as candidates for further development through a formal contractual arrangement with mVine. In this case, the interim contract detailed previously allowed for their license to be offered to other record companies either for a split (from the label's proportion of the agreed 50%) of profits after costs or for a simple introduction fee, depending on the details of each case.

This wide range of revenue streams added to the company's initial investment income to reduce the requirements for startup capital.

Phase Two of mVine's development was planned for the spring of 2005 and was intended to cover a variety of additional revenue streams.

- **Sponsorships and partnerships.** As part of Phase Two, it was planned to recruit selected partners whose vision and operations matched those of mVine (Web sites such as iVillage.com, salon.com, and friendsreunited.com).
- **A digital radio/TV station.** In order to promote mVine artists, whether contracted or not, to the widest possible audience, Phase Two included plans to produce and advertise funded Internet-based radio stations and digital television stations. No voting

would be possible through these stations, but they would guide users to the Web site for more interaction and would be supported by cross sales of advertising.

- **Partnership with an image library.** The comprehensive data collection and reporting system inherent in InfoNow allowed for future plans to partner with an image library. By defining specific parameters such as style, content, and sound, mVine planned to offer music that could be matched with images licensed to such companies as advertising agencies, corporate video producers, and events management agencies.

Once the mVine team felt that they had proved the concept through the launch and second phases, future plans included a more global clicks-and-mortar (both digital and physical) presence for the company with offices to be set up in Asia, America, and Europe.

mVine proposed to engage consumers in the creation of a new music industry paradigm, changing the way that musical talent was identified, nurtured, and consumed, ultimately transforming the structure of the whole music industry.

Joshi (the managing director and a founding partner of mVine) stated in May 2004:

What we are proposing to do could in principle lay the foundation for an evolution in the way corporates and global brands communicate and interact with their consumers; the mVine model highlights the difference between corporates dictating and consumers creating.

SETTING THE STAGE

Technology Utilization and Advancements

During the course of developing the mVine model, it was agreed by all involved that the technology would need to be as user-friendly as possible in order to ensure that mVine was accessible to the widest audience. At the time, it was common for digital music to be distributed using a variety of incompatible, proprietary software. mVine went against this trend, distributing content using Open Source Software (OSS) (see Appendix 1) and providing a music player within the site rather than adopting one of the many competing and incompatible players available on the market at the time.

InfoNow

Where traditionally funded companies would have the money to buy hardware and software that did the job required at launch and then would have to pay to upgrade or adapt these systems in the face of change or growth, mVine chose to start from the very beginning with a solution that was able to handle any amount of change and development, requiring only additional hardware to grow with the success of the company. The software used for the development and maintenance of mVine was called InfoNow, scalable custom-built software created from OSS components.

Streaming Technologies

In line with the company's low cost, high-return, and open philosophy, music was streamed in 64K Ogg Vorbis rather than the more common 96K or 128K MP3 (a digital compression technology that allowed music tracks, videos, and albums to be stored and transmitted over landline and broadband Internet connections). This was because there was no license fee required for encoding files; it provided higher perceived sound quality, which mVine tested with expert listeners in a professional studio environment; and there was a lower bandwidth requirement (50% to 66% of the equivalent MP3/WMA bandwidth), thus saving on the largest expense.

Management Practices and Philosophies

We want unemployable employees who ask stupid questions. (MacColl, February 2003)

Neither of mVine's founders believed in traditional strategies of corporate hierarchy and authority. Joshi and MacColl were entrepreneurial managers, who believed that the sort of people they wanted to work with them (rather than for them) were those who would be classified more traditionally as bad employees. They chose unpredictable but clever, creative people, who perhaps worked odd hours, often at the same time as carrying on another job or profession, but who could get their jobs done on time, to budget, and to specification.

As long as basic strategy, finance deadlines, and meeting dates were met, the founders were fine that every person involved was independent. They had to be strong enough to question whatever was being taken for granted; able to contribute to the best of their ability; and comfortable joining in on the debates, brainstorming, and arguments that characterized the early days of the company, practicing a recognized focus on results rather than time (Cascio, 2000).

All of the initial members of the mVine team were known to each other (personally or professionally) and passionate about the company and its values of democracy, openness, creativity, and choice, which, they believed (along with others), were vital ingredients for the chances of mVine's success (Symon, 2000). At the startup stage, all team members except for Joshi also had other employment and contributed to the development of the mVine model for little or no money, although all of them were shareholders in the company to varying degrees and were happy to be involved in the formative stages of what they believed was going to be a very successful company.

Management Structure

This roundtable business arrangement echoed the attitude and beliefs of founding directors Joshi and MacColl, who did not want to set up a company with a fixed set of rules, regulations, time sheets, traditions, practices, and politics. Far from it, their plan was to set up a company as flat and virtual as possible, with each team member contributing (initially) what they could, when they could. All were encouraged to ask the so-called stupid questions that normally would not be asked, an unusual approach that only recently had been recognized as potentially effective (Gray, 2003; Kellaway, 2003). This set mVine on a path that looked very different from more conventional music companies of the time.

CASE DESCRIPTION

In 2004, the traditional popular music industry was in chaos. Record sales were down, companies were merging and downsizing, and the major record labels were threatened by rapidly advancing ICTs. The market changed very quickly as people's tastes changed, and even artists who showed signs of longevity always did not have a fan base large enough to justify the sort of expense required to keep them in the public eye. By May 2004, it could take as few as 25,000 sales to reach number one, whereas, in 1984, the figure was 107,700. In contrast, the Beatles sold 1.8 million with "She Loves You" in the 1960s, and Elton John's 1997 version of "Candle in the Wind" sold 4.8 million (McMonagle, 2004).

The Music Majors

There were four major record label conglomerates (controlling over 80% of American music and similar percentages in the rest of the world): Warner Music, EMI Group, Universal Music Group (UMG), and Sony BMG Music Entertainment. These four also owned distribution companies controlling over 80% of the wholesale market, and they were becoming a bigger presence in the retail sale of music. Their powerful positions were supported by the fact that, in 80% of cases, they owned the rights to the music that their artists wrote rather than the artists themselves (Hannaford, 2004).

1. **Warner Music Group** (aka WEA) included labels such as Atlantic, Elektra, London, Reprise, and Rhino.
2. **EMI Group** included labels such as Angel, Blue Note, Capitol, Odeon, Parlophone, and Virgin.
3. **Universal Music Group** included labels such as A&M, Decca/London, Deutsche Grammophon, Island, MCA, Motown, and PolyGram.
4. **Sony BMG Music Entertainment**, as of August 2004, consisted of the merger between Sony Music Entertainment and BMG entertainment and included labels such as Columbia, Epic, Arista, and RCA.

This oligopoly resulted in the production of music that pleased the greatest number of people and displeased the least, the narrowing and homogeneity of content forecast in Figure 6 (Butler, 2000; Parikh, 1999; Peterson, 1975).

The Impact of ICTs

In the late 1990s, the Internet's increasing ubiquity allowed other new (not always legal) technologies took hold. The music industry consistently has been resistant to technological change; even when MP3 arrived, the aggressive, well-financed, highly speculative corporations decided to fight rather than try to find a way to take advantage of this new technology (Reed, Heppard & Corbett, 2004).

Increasingly fast, cheap, and available bandwidth and digital compression techniques, like MP3, allowed any individual with a computer and an Internet connection to download and copy (at no cost and, therefore, no profit to the musician or label) any piece of music that they wanted using peer-to-peer file sharing engines, such as Napster and KaZaa. Combined with the high cost of CDs in the stores, the result was piracy of music

Figure 6. The cyclical nature of the music industry

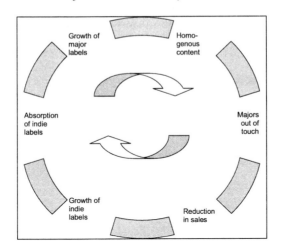

and videos at unprecedented and unforeseen levels. To add to the confusion, the traditional weekly singles charts were joined in August 2004 by BBC Radio One's new download chart (and a competitor, launched days before, from Virgin in conjunction with Napster) and ultimately, in April 2005, the two were combiend, giving an air of apparent legitimacy to the whole download process (Born, 2004).

The purpose of copyright is to encourage the creation and mass dissemination of a wide variety of works, which activities traditionally require a long distribution chain and heavy investment of capital (for such things as printing presses, transport, storage facilities, and so forth). Because of this, the law gave publishers and distributors the larger part of copyright income. The arrival of the Internet, digital compression, and peer-to-peer file sharing technologies provided an almost free route to market, turning this model on its head by shortening traditional distribution chains significantly and so reducing costs. This was a truly radical change (Jallat, 2001; Lam, 2001).

It was confirmed (Langenderfer, 2004) that, although the market environment prevailing at the time bore a great deal of similarity to previous crises, there were important differences that could dramatically and permanently alter the economic landscape for both content and copyright owners.

Dematerialization and Disintermediation

As Litman (2004) pointed out, this made a complete reconsideration of the assumptions underlying the conventional copyright model necessary. Music was in transition from a tangible CD or tape to intangible digital bits. This dematerialization of music concerned the big four companies, who worried that music would stop being a product from which they could make a profit and return to being a (much harder to charge for) service (Hannaford, 2004).

- Seventy-five percent of adults felt downloading music for personal use was an innocent act and should be legal (Harris Interactive, 2004).
- Seventy percent said that downloading music from the Internet would be much less common, if compact discs cost less (Zid, 2004).

2003 (Music on the Internet, 2003)

- Forecast that the value of global music sales in all forms via the Internet would reach $3.9 billion in 2008 (up 240% from 2002).
- Predicted that unauthorized music copies would rise from $2.4 billion to $4.7 billion in 2008.

However, in 2004, the IFPI reported that music piracy already was valued at $4.5 billion.

For traditional music companies, this disintermediation was seen as a real and dangerous threat to their existence. Marketing costs had increased, and sales had declined; the inevitable result being that only the major record labels could afford to support new talent. These companies prevented smaller independent labels from competing by using their superior purchasing power to buy up every part of the music production process. Habitually, they would sign up artists who showed any promise with meticulously drafted and restrictive long-term contracts. This was not necessarily to promote them, as most efforts were put into ensuring that the one or two top artists of the time were fully stretched, but to ensure that nobody else did.

They also tried to counter increasing levels of music piracy by implementing legislation like the EU Copyright Directive. However, attempts by copyright owners to sue a random selection of downloaders in the states resulted in nothing but bad publicity; it commonly was felt that litigation was not a viable business strategy (Mackie, 2003; Sherman, 2001). To confuse the issue for copyright holders, artists, and major labels alike, it also was reported that downloading music actually could be increasing the sales of CDs (Orlowski, 2002; Jardin, 2004).

Freedom for Major Artists

Combined with compression technologies, the Internet provided free access to the audiences of those artists who owned copyright in their work and had the back catalog and reputation to support it.

Freedom for Fans

For the music aficionado, ICTs allowed official and unofficial fan clubs to set up, threatening traditional music industry companies. The ability of artists and consumers to communicate directly (i.e., official music, merchandise, tickets, and information being transmitted easily, widely, and cheaply on the Internet) could be signaling the end of a very lucrative era for them.

Jumping on the Bandwagon

A number of companies tried to jump on the legitimate digital download bandwagon, including Apple's iTunes store, OD2, BuyMusic, My Coke Music, Bleep, eMusic, MusicMatch, MusicNow, RealPlayer, Rhapsody, Napster, and Wal-Mart. Oxfam sold downloads for charity, and computer companies, online service providers, and consumer electronics stores soon joined in.

Frustration for Unsigned Acts

However, for the new, original, and aspiring artist, there appeared to be little serious help on the road to the top. With no established fan base to support and promote them and very little chance of getting signed up by the short-term artist and repertoire (A&R) staff from the major record labels, they only could hope for discovery by a label with enough money and marketing power to promote them to success.

THE LAUNCH OF VINE

Funding

mVine was conceived in this turbulent and chaotic environment with initial funding of £250,000 from private investors and the debt equity of every director, which would support the company for its first 18 months. The intention at that point, once the model was proven, was to raise venture capital for future expansion. The founders had been in business for many years and had the ability to create maximum value for the least possible financial outlay. mVine was started with minimal costs; no salaries, and limited overheads; the only significant cost was bandwidth, which was increasingly cheap. However, the equivalent of 3.5 person years' work had been put in to the company up to the launch date, and the software itself represented another five person years' development work, for which the developer was given an increased shareholding. The sophisticated business intelligence and OSS tools and software underlying the site represented another £5m equivalent value.

Marketing

The marketing strategy of mVine at launch was planned carefully, as the music marketplace was increasingly complex (new entrants and developed offerings from current players created a noisy environment within which mVine needed its voice to be heard). The marketing director carried out intensive research, including the use of industry analysis from Mintel, Forrester, and similar organizations, focus groups, competitive analysis, interviews with industry experts, and thorough beta testing of the Web site to determine not only what mVine would offer but how best to present it and to determine the various target audiences to which the company had to appeal.

mVine's target audience was stated to be:

disenfranchised music lovers; pro-active consumers of all ages and sexes with eclectic musical taste. Sometimes described as the "sleeper" market, it is one which has considerable buying power but which has been traditionally difficult to identify demographically. (Harvey-Piper, 2004).

In order to narrow this down, thus making marketing and promotional activities more manageable, distinct, and quantifiable, Harvey-Piper settled on an age range of 17 to 55. This, in turn, was subdivided into the following subgroups for marketing purposes:

- 17-20
- 20-25
- 25-35
- 35-45
- 45-55

Individual strategies were put in place to ensure that each target age range was approached with relevant and timely messages over the course of the first six months of mVine's operation. Detailed analyses of each set of activities was put into place, so that effectiveness could be tracked and initial marketing strategies could be continually refined as the company developed.

The initial marketing strategy included promoting those successful artists who were with mVine at the launch; the CD sales, press, radio and live events, and other activities of these mVine artists were a very valuable contribution to initial marketing activities. Also planned was the use of music-related Web logs and forums to seed knowledge of mVine in communities of music lovers, to have direct contact with fan club proprietors to promote their artists on mVine and thus spread the word to all members, and to do a certain amount of advertising in carefully targeted trade and consumer publications.

The Web site was optimized to ensure that it ranked highly when searches were performed both for Web sites to which mVine was linked and for a variety of relevant keywords (specific methodology was kept strictly confidential to avoid any other company benefiting from mVine's expertise and experience). This activity was commonly known as search engine optimization (SEO) and was implemented to ensure that the results of online searches for music and music-related Web sites found mVine toward (if not at) the top of any search results. Online advertising was considered for later stages of mVine's promotion in order to allow initial assessment of the results of initial plans.

Although not built into the plan, significant spread by word of mouth was expected from the beta testing community. The post-launch strategy also incorporated public relations (PR), initially including the story around MacColl and his family with a view to creating additional publicity around successful artists as they were developed by mVine or other labels. Future marketing plans were fluid to allow for the turbulent environment but would continue to include both online and off-line PR, advertising, and promotional activities.

CURRENT CHALLENGES/PROBLEMS FACING THE ORGANIZATION

A number of different issues faced mVine in its startup phase.

1. Communication

The fact that all team members had other occupations, combined with the virtual nature of the company's initial configuration and the geographic distance between many team members sometimes could result in poor communication. For example, the results of conversations held between two people were not always transmitted to all other team members, leading to duplication of efforts or lack of follow through. The team found that face-to-face meetings fulfilled a variety of psychological and practical requirements that were not addressed in other ways of communicating.

The importance of teams in the virtual organization has been emphasized and identified as a basic building block of such a company. Important characteristics of a successful virtual team include good communication skills, sensitivity to different cultures, and the ability to network successfully and adapt to a variety of situations while being tolerant of ambiguity (Heneman & Greenberger, 2002). The likelihood of every member of the mVine team exhibiting all of these traits was remote and, in actuality, non-existent, which led to a variety of complexities.

Where most real-world, bricks-and-mortar companies work through face-to-face negotiations of the various issues and obstacles to corporate success, mVine's virtual negotiations went on largely through e-mail and by telephone. Although this had the effect of encouraging team members to take turns rather than talk over each other, they also could become less reserved than they may have been if talking face to face; equally, e-mails were occasionally misinterpreted because of this lack of non-verbal communication. The network of *To* and *cc* recipients, which varied from person to person, depending on how they set up their e-mail systems, also caused communication to be erratic at times.

By the time the company was ready for launch, communication and interpersonal relationships had improved. The team worked more consistently and shared areas of personal expertise when a fresh opinion or viewpoint was required. Conversations were more regular and communication was more effective.

2. InfoNow and Security

Security was a critical issue for mVine. Its initial revenue streams depended upon totally secure payment systems for sales of data, feedback, downloads, and licensing of artists. The data collected on the activities and preferences of users had to be kept completely secure, and, although voters' activities were recorded, it was imperative that no external person could access their details. The technical director was aware, as were all team members, that any breach of security would be considered extremely serious, not simply being a breach of trust with the voters and artists using the site, but, more importantly, in breach of the Data Protection Act of 1998. However, proprietary security software was both expensive and limited in its application to a bespoke piece of software such as the engine driving mVine.

At launch, the mVine technical director managed to create a most secure and stable system, which allowed a limitless number of users while retaining complete security of payments, protection of all data provided, and privacy regarding any activities they undertook while on site.

3. Naming the Baby

The lack of available dot-com names was a major factor in the delay of the company's incorporation, its logo, and all print and Web designs. Throughout debates, which started in earnest in February 2004, the inability of the team to decide on two issues also slowed down the launch process. First, they debated whether an alternative suffix (such as .net, .co.uk, or .biz) was worth investigating. By June 2004, this idea had been discounted, and a suitable, relevant, and available dot-com name had to be found, which caused its own particular set of problems. Those dot-com names that were available were irrelevant or overly expensive, and those names that the team all agreed on were not available (see Appendix 2).

The selection process was long and complex, involving many debates, conversations, and changes of direction. Many team members felt that the name should include some reference to music, notes, tune, or some similar word. Other team members felt that no reference to music was required or desirable. Over the course of three months, and particularly as it became apparent that the lack of a name was prohibiting development work on the logo, Web site, and corporate image as a whole, a name was determined.

4. Compatibility

Making the various OSS and paid-for software used in building mVine's interface collaborate, was complex and time consuming. A SOAP (Simple Object Access Protocol) interface, which allowed the server side components (i.e., the mVine Web server and the InfoNow server) to communicate, was used to ensure that the different layers of technology were as compatible as possible. However, this workaround for the problem was time consuming and difficult.

This situation was exacerbated by the conflicting and competitive operating systems mVine had to work with. Microsoft and Apple had an industrial-strength Mac/PC feud going back decades, the result being incompatible operating systems. The client side (i.e., interface) software communicated via a technology called LiveConnect, which was essentially broken on Macs (i.e., completely broken on IE for Macs rendering the site unavailable for that browser on that platform and partially broken for Safari and Firefox, allowing only the most limited communication between Java, Javascript, and Flash). Thus, standardizing software to work equally well on both was not simple, particularly as Flash elements were incorporated into the design of the mVine Web site from the start. This decision later was regretted, because it added a further layer of incompatibility that had to be dealt with.

5. Competition

The turbulence of the music industry at the time meant that many people were looking for opportunities to benefit from technologies and tactics similar to those being used by mVine. No direct competitor had emerged yet from the wide range of digital music business models adopted by companies on an almost daily basis. However, it would not be long before the model that mVine was constructing became evident to other companies that may have more upfront development capital; an established or distinguished name and attendant reputation; easily recognizable branding; and consistent, conventional, dedicated teams of staff in close daily contact with each other.

mVine launched into a marketplace without any direct competitors. It remains to be seen how long this situation prevails.

REFERENCES

Born, M. (2004). *Music industry backs download pop singles chart*. Retrieved August 25, 2004, from http://www.telegraph.co.uk/news/main.jhtml?xml=/news/2004/08/14/npop14.xml&sSheet=/news/2004/08/14/ixhome.html

Butler, P. D. (2000). *By popular demand: Marketing change in the arts*. B9f D.Phil., Ulster, 50-15455.

Cascio, W.F. (2000). Managing a virtual workplace. *Academy of Management Executive, 14*(3), 81.

Gray, D. (2003). Wanted: Chief ignorance officer. *Harvard Business Review, 2*.

Hannaford, S. (2004). Industry brief: Music recording. Retrieved August 19, 2004, from http://www.oligopolywatch.com/2003/06/28.html

Heneman, R. L., & Greenberger, D. B. (2002). *Human resource management in virtual organizations*. Information Age Publishing.

IFPI. (2004). *The recording industry commercial piracy report 2004*. London: International Federation of the Phonographic Industry.

Jallat, F., & Capek, M. J. (2001). Disintermediation in question: New economy, new networks, new middlemen. *Business Horizons, 44*(2), 55.

Jardin, X. (2004). *Music is not a loaf of bread*. Retrieved from http://www.wired.com/news/culture/0,1284,65688,00.html

Kellaway, L. (2003). Ignorance is the new knowledge. *Financial Times*.

Lam, C. K. M., & Tan, B. C. Y. (2001). The Internet is changing the music industry. *Communications of the ACM, 44*(8), 62-68.

Langenderfer, J., & Kopp, S. (2004). The digital technology revolution and its effect on the market for copyrighted works: Is history repeating itself? *Journal of Macromarketing, 24*(1), 17.

Leonhard, G. (2003). The future of music: Twice as large and twenty times as fair...?! Retrieved from http://gerdleonhard.typepad.com/the_future_of_music/files/ADEfutureofmusicgerdleonhard.pdf

Litman, J. (2004). Sharing and stealing. Retrieved from http://www.law.wayne.edu/litman/papers/sharing&stealing.pdf

Mackie, K. (2003). No innovation means no customers. *Communications of the ACM, 46*(11), 13.

McMonagle, M. (2004). Music industry crisis: Death of the single. Retrieved August 25, 2004, from http://www.sundaymail.co.uk/news/tm_objectid=14201810&method=full&siteid=86024&headline=music-industry-crisis—death-of-the-single-name_page.html

Music on the Internet. (2003). Informa Media.

Orlowski, A. (2002). *MP3s are good for music biz*. Retrieved from http://www.theregister.co.uk/2002/08/16/mp3s_are_good_for_music/

Parikh, M. (1999) The music industry in the digital world: Waves of change, putting the "e" in entertainment: E-music as a case in point. Retrieved from http://www.ite.poly.edu

Peterson, R. A., & Berger, D. G. (1975). Cycles in symbol production: The case of popular music. *American Sociological Review, 40*(2), 158-173.

Reed, T. S., Heppard, K. A., & Corbett, A. C. (2004). I get by with a little help from my friends. *Management Communication Quarterly, 17*(3), 452, 426.

Sherman, C. (2001). Music on the Internet: A new world is waiting. *The Brookings Review, 19*(1), 35-37.

Symon, G. (2000). Information and communication technologies and the network organization: A critical analysis. *Journal of Occupational and Organizational Psychology, 73*(4), 389.

Zid, L. A.-S. (2004). The beat goes on. *Marketing Management, 13*(3), 7.

APPENDIXES

Appendix 1: Technical Specifications

INITIALSETUP
Hardware: AMD Duron @ 750MHz, 512MB RAM, 20GB HDD
Operating System: RedHat9
Software: Apache 1.3.29, Perl 5.8.0, mod_perl 1.27
HTML: Mason (HTML templating tool)

DEVELOPMENT
Hardware: AMD Athlon @ 2.8GHz, 1536MB RAM, 320 GB HDD (SATA RAID0)
Operating System: Fedora Core 2
Software: Apache 1.3.31 Perl 5.8.5 mod_perl 1.29
HTML: Mason, InfoNow 4.2

PRODUCTION
Hardware: Intel Xeon 3GHz, 2GB RAM, 140GB HDD (RAID5) (with the option to double this capacity at short notice)
Operating System: Debian (Woody)
Software: Apache 1.3.31, Perl 5.8.5, mod_perl 1.27
HTML: Mason, InfoNow 4.3

Appendix 2: Naming the Baby

E-mail from MacColl to mVine Team
June 27, 2004

Hi Chaps,

So we haven't got a name yet, just bags under our eyes from waking up with names ranging from the sublime to the ridiculous.

I kno some of this is Department of Stating the Bleedin' Obvious but for my money, I think…..

- It doesn't have to be a .com. I think a .net is good, as it connotes the 'catch 'em' ethic we're trying to achieve. Besides, I reckon most people Google for things now anyway (who remembers URL's?). So the name is the game
- It doesn't necessarily have to have 'records', 'disc' or any keywords associated with the industry.
- No homophones (ie. Right/write/rite). They're confusing.
- Something one can drop into conversations without people gagging on their pizza.
- Rolls off the tongue, not too long.

Let's name that sucker.

(continued on next page)

Have a cigar	One of us	Dotted line
Broken line	Fineline	new direction
redirect	21st century	century21
favour the brave	solid gold	state of independence
green light	develop21	bands of gold.
Music talent	Beat	Inspired sounds
Survivor sounds	Exploration	Exploremusic
Xplore music	Tempo	Tone
Score	Majorminors	Groundsound
Pento	Smart	Tonic
Concept	Soundblock	Soundspeak
Musicplace	Soundsearch	Persue
Scour	Quest	Frontier
Rare Earth	Third Ear	Friday (people already know "the friday feeling")
Friday Music	First Music Corps Group (FMCG...geddit?)	Fateful (eg "A Fateful Recording")
Full Ashet Music (used in Iain Banks' Espedair Street book)	Gush	MJF
ME2	New Shoes Records	Bring It On Records
Jam Buttie Music	Diamond Records	Platinum Disks PLC (can we do that?)
C2H6O4 (chemical formula for ethanol/alcohol)	Geddit Recordings	Stream
Home Recordings	Blingo	Rattle Records
Cheese	Jiggy Music	Upfront
Out of the Box	Pie	lause Four
Newplay	Rethink	Reimagine
Opus21	Spirit 21	Discus
Spiritlevel	Label of Love	BON music (Best Of New Music)
Music Net Partners (musicnetpartners.com is available)	Music Partner (all but .com are available)	Grapevine Music (grapevinemusic.net available)
Mzuri.net (means "all right" in Swahili)	Music Mouth	Mouthmusic
The Body Music	Music Body	Kangura-blue (a large Japanese flute) kangura.com available
Sinawi (shamanist instrumental music)	Klar (means 'clear, distinct")	Musical Sand
Nebenstimme (means "next voice")	FAWAR ("feel all warm and runny")	Ardito (boldly)
Castanet (it needs two to play)	Carmen (means "song")	Sound Box
Sounding Board	Aurresku	Muta Music (means "change")
Quest	Level	alt - ie alt42
space ie kspace, ispace, zspace	stream	turningpoint
wildtruth	mih (making it happen)	qsc (quark, starangeness and charm) the last two are properties of quarks
sub atomic particles)	pojo	Thinking of x,y,z (z the third dim, and t the fourth)
42 = the meaning of life	Letter k in Phy refers to inverse space	Then apple with a t = Tapple
Music with a c = cmusic	Parallel	Mirror
base – tbase	create – icreate	creation
evolve	Zlevel - all available	alt42 - all available
mprosumer - all available	isumer - all available	klevel.net avail
mevolve - all available		

Joanna Berry is a PhD researcher at the University of Newcastle upon Tyne Business School. She obtained her MBA from the same institution and a BA in jurisprudence from St Anne's College, Oxford University. Her PhD research is focused on the introduction of a new e-music business model and the impact of this upon traditional value chains and networks within the music and related industries. Other research interests include the contrast between new and traditional broadcast technologies and business models, innovation in digital technologies and the impact of social and technological change on broadcast business models.

This case was previously published in the *International Journal of Cases on Electronic Commerce*, 1(3), pp. 1-20, © 2005.

Chapter VI

DataNaut Incorporated:
Growing Pains of a Small Company on the Verge of an Internet Revolution

Nancy C. Shaw, George Mason University, USA

Joan O'Reilly Fix, Citibank, N.A., USA

EXECUTIVE SUMMARY

At the end of 1999, a small software development company located on the outskirts of Washington, DC is faced with several strategic decisions regarding the marketing and financing of its high-tech products. The principals of the company must decide the type and dollar amount of financing they will try to secure, which of their two products should be the focus of their marketing efforts and how they should structure an equitable compensation plan for their existing and future employees. Cash flow has been an ongoing problem for this small company, which began as a one-person technical consulting company and has grown into a consulting and product development company with several full and part-time employees. While consulting has traditionally paid the bills, the CEO is interested in becoming a part of the "Internet Revolution" with the development of multimedia streaming applications. This case was written for the 8th annual Kogod School of Business Case Competition at American University. It discusses a small, locally run company that faced several strategic decisions at the end of 1999: marketing its new high-tech products, securing sufficient venture capital financing, and creating a profit-sharing plan for current and future employees. The case involves an actual corporation (although some of the employee names have been changed) and the issues that confronted the management team at the end of 1999. The case includes a complete description of the company's products, a glossary of terms, a list of Web sites summarizing existing radio market research, detailed operating expenses and pro-forma financial statements (numbers have been altered for confidentiality). This case combines new technology development, HR decisions, marketing and finance, which makes it a true cross-disciplinary case that can be used in several different courses.

BACKGROUND

On the evening of September 3, 1999, Mark Snuffin and his small staff sat around the living room of Mark's house, which also served as an office, and contemplated the future of their company, DataNaut Incorporated ("DataNaut").

DataNaut was at a critical stage in its development. The three-year-old consulting company had just completed a business plan for a new product idea and was in the early stages of developing a demonstration model (a "demo") that would be used to illustrate the product's features to potential investors. Although Mark and his team were confident that the new product would be a success in the marketplace, they were also aware that raising sufficient capital to finance the development of this product at such an early stage would be a challenge.

Since its inception, DataNaut had financed its daily operations with a steady flow of income from consulting work. Mark's goal in founding DataNaut was to create a company that would focus on developing next-generation technologies for the Internet. Mark started the company with an advanced concept for broadcasting audio and information, and the resulting product was extremely innovative. Mark had always been "ahead of the curve" with his inventions, and he was sensitive to timing issues with respect to Internet technologies. His team was also acutely aware of the importance of timing, and the product issue had become an increasingly important topic of discussion within DataNaut.

DataNaut's reputation for expert consulting services was growing, and Mark was involved with several simultaneous projects that consumed the majority of his time. The existing contracts were scheduled to last into the following year, and Mark remained busy planning his life around these contracts. Even though the consulting revenue was increasing steadily, DataNaut often found itself in a cash-crunch. The management of cash flow became a delicate issue in Mark's small company, as the receipt of payments for consulting services rendered did not always correspond to the payment of bills and payroll. In addition, Mark subcontracted much of his consulting work to individual software developers, and the cost of doing so was high (Exhibit 1). Mark often felt that the time spent on consulting was an opportunity cost to pursuing product development.

Mark knew that he could maintain his consulting practice and grow it steadily over time, but his passion was in product development. DataNaut's situation had changed

Exhibit 1. Distribution of time (hours per day) as of September 1999

Individual	Status	Consulting	Music Beam	Virtual Fan™	Admin	Salary ($per hour)
Mark	owner	12	2	0	2	30
Eric	full-time	10	0	0	0	20
Monique	part-time	0	7	0	3	15
Paul	part-time	0	8	1	1	10
George	consultant	10	0	0	0	100
Patrick	consultant	8	0	0	0	75
Chris	consultant	8	5	0	0	75
Mike	consultant	variable	variable	0	0	90
Sharon	consultant	variable	variable	0	0	95

dramatically over a period of four months, and Mark had recently hired a strategic consultant to help him sort out the various issues that confronted his company. It was time to make a decision.

SETTING THE STAGE

Prior to forming DataNaut in May 1996, Mark had worked for several years in prestigious consulting firms. By 1996, the Internet had exploded, becoming a legitimate environment in which to conduct business. Mark decided to venture out on his own and form a consulting company that would specialize in extending Microsoft technologies to the Internet, while maintaining a product business that would focus on the development of turnkey Internet applications called "Weblications."

For the past three years, DataNaut has operated as a virtual corporation, using an outsource model to support business operations. DataNaut has utilized outsourcing partners to assist with software development, telecommunications and visual imagery, as well as functional areas such as accounting and legal services.

In October 1998, Mark hired a full-time software engineer, Eric Lorenzo, to assist with the consulting practice. In May of 1999, Mark hired two MBA students, Monique LaChance and Paul Lee, to handle the business aspects of the company's operations, including marketing, business development and financial planning. In hiring the MBA students, Mark hoped to rekindle the product development side of his business, which had become a lower priority due to an increase in consulting work.

CASE DESCRIPTION

DataNaut is divided into two core businesses, one dedicated to Weblication (product) development and the other focused on consulting services for Microsoft BackOffice solutions.

As of September 1999, DataNaut outsourced a portion of its consulting and Weblication development to five different consultants, four of whom lived between Washington, DC and Baltimore. The fifth consultant lived in Australia and assisted mainly with highly technical graphic design work. Each consultant specialized in either software development or graphic design and had at least 10 years of work experience. Two of the local consultants, George and Chris, had been working exclusively for DataNaut for several months and planned to continue for the duration of the existing consulting contracts. Mark had often discussed the possibility of George and Chris joining the DataNaut team, as DataNaut would save money by hiring them full time. Consulting fees averaged $85.00 per hour per consultant. George and Chris, both entrepreneurs with their own start-up companies, were interested in DataNaut's product technology. However, they were hesitant to abandon their respective practices to join a company that had neither a capital investment nor a tested product.

Operating out of Mark's townhouse in Bethesda, Maryland, DataNaut is not unlike many start-up companies in the Washington, DC "technology corridor." Space is limited, and the software engineer, Eric, and the two business-oriented employees, Monique and Paul, share the three workstations that are located in the former living room of the townhouse. On a typical day, the full-time employees work anywhere from 8 to 16 hours. Each employee has the flexibility to determine his or her own work schedule, some preferring to arrive early, and others not arriving until well into the afternoon. Mark prefers to work into the early hours of the morning.

The Entrepreneur

Mark has many of the typical characteristics found in pioneers of the Internet. He has been writing software since he was 14 years old and has always been interested in technology. While he began his career in prestigious institutions, Mark always knew that he would one day work for himself.

Mark has spent the last three years building his business from scratch, working late into the night on consulting projects, while squeezing time in between client meetings during the day to work with his employees on new product development. He is dedicated to his work, and his entire life revolves around this endeavor. Mark, himself, is a study in contrasts. With his engaging personality and surfer looks, Mark is not the typical software developer. He is a former standout college wrestler, and his athletic discipline fuels a work ethic and determination that will not allow him to give up once his mind is set on a particular project or idea. He is very comfortable around people, as well as computers, and enjoys speaking about his industry in public.

Mark runs his company as he would a family. He cares about each employee's welfare, offering a solid insurance package, and in exchange, he expects each employee to exhibit similar enthusiasm, drive and dedication to the company and its ideas. Mark believes that his technology has true market potential, and he desperately wants his fledgling company to succeed. He has realized that, in order to maintain the momentum that has brought the company to this stage, he will need to give up full control and begin to offer equity shares to his employees, as the development effort and search for venture capital becomes more intense.

Consulting Services

Since its formation in 1996, DataNaut has provided consulting services to large organizations wishing to implement or extend Microsoft BackOffice technologies on the Internet. DataNaut's clients have included companies such as NASDAQ, Level 3 Communications, Sylvan Learning Systems and Microsoft Consulting Services. DataNaut

Exhibit 2. Projected statement of income—DataNaut consulting

	1999	2000	2001
Revenue			
Consulting	600,000	900,000	1,350,000
Total Revenue	**600,000**	**900,000**	**1,350,000**
Operating Expenses			
Employee Salaries	165,000	220,000	300,000
Consultant Fees	360,000	468,000	608,400
Telecommunications	20,000	13,000	13,000
Miscellaneous	10,000	10,000	10,000
Total Operating Expenses	**555,000**	**711,000**	**931,400**
EBIT	**45,000**	**189,000**	**$418,600**

has traditionally relied upon consulting services to offset internal Weblication development costs and to gain exposure to cutting-edge Microsoft technologies. Understanding and applying these technologies has allowed DataNaut to remain current with the evolution of Internet software, develop contacts and uncover potential applications for new software (see Exhibit 2). Through the knowledge and experience gained by consulting, DataNaut has been able to develop Weblications that meet real-world business needs.

Weblications

Product #1: virtualFan™

virtualFan™ is an enhancement to Internet broadcasting that allows users to receive real-time audio broadcasts of sports events synchronized with other media events such as live scoreboards, interactive interviews, action photos and video. The broadcasts can also be replayed at a later time with all of the live elements intact and synchronized with a television look and feel.

virtualFan™ is a content management service targeted to organizations, mainly universities that wish to broadcast their content but do not want the technical headaches associated with Internet broadcasting. In a typical client service contract, DataNaut would host a university sports Web site and provide the technical support to update information such as player profiles, schedules, or team rosters. Events would be broadcast from a customized Web site as a multimedia stream to Internet fans, who could view the event using a standard Web browser configured with a multimedia player. The eventual goal for virtualFan™ is to enable universities to manage their own Web sites through a licensing agreement, thereby empowering them with a Web-publishing tool to obtain jurisdiction over their content. As a former American University ("AU") athlete, Mark was able to sell this product to the AU Athletics Department and use AU as a prototype for the development of this multimedia streaming technology, as well as the content management system.

While Mark has spent a significant amount of time developing virtualFan™, he has recently become discouraged about the prospects of marketing and selling this product directly to university athletic departments. Within the last two years, the university sports market has become saturated with Internet companies offering similar services at no charge. For example, companies such as TotalSports and University Netcasting offer free Web sites to universities in exchange for a percentage of advertising revenues generated by the sites. In addition, companies, such as Rivals.com, generate revenues by consolidating university sports information on non-official sites, thereby capturing revenues that could otherwise have been gained by the universities themselves. By combining multiple universities' information on one site, the Rivals.com model presents a threat to universities, as recruiters and sports fans will be tempted to go to the "unofficial" site to read about their favorite teams. Advertisers are also more likely to pay for advertisements on such a site, as it would attract more viewers.

In pursuing the development and sale of virtualFan™, DataNaut is faced with the issue of whether to target companies that consolidate content (Rivals.com), or companies that host university sites (Total Sports, University Netcasting or Broadcast.com). Alternatively, DataNaut could sell its products and services directly to the universities at a cost, but the schools must be willing to pay this cost. DataNaut believes that universities will want a tool that allows them to maintain jurisdiction over their content and maximizes the Internet as an additional source of revenue without depending on an external provider. However, the initial costs to the university would be significant (see Exhibit 3), considering that many Web-hosting companies now provide free sites. Also, the costs associated with establishing a sales force to sell to each school and host the sites would be significant for DataNaut. Nevertheless, DataNaut is interested in this opportunity, as companies such as TotalSports have signed four-year agreements with universities for which they host Web sites. According to DataNaut's research, many of these contracts will expire within the next two years.

Product #2: MusicBeam

MusicBeam is a hardware and software solution for traditional radio stations that wish to broadcast their live signal and bring their brand equity to the Internet. MusicBeam is based on the virtualFan™ platform of multimedia streaming. Several years of development of streaming technologies in the university sports market led Mark to a broader application of the technology. Mark recognized an opportunity in Internet radio and created a turn-key solution that adapts to the popular multimedia players available (e.g., RealPlayer, Windows Media Player), allowing for the simultaneous streaming of audio and interactive content. The following are two key benefits of MusicBeam to radio stations:

1. The ability to add multiple, secondary channels, thereby promoting brand equity; and
2. The ability to manage content and gather demographic information on listeners, thereby facilitating targeted e-commerce and advertising.

Benefits to the Internet radio listener include the ability to interact with the radio station directly, via computer, without waiting for an open telephone line (including song voting, quizzes, purchasing of CDs, etc.) and the ability to receive a greater variety of information from a favorite radio station than would be possible through conventional radio transmission ("one-stop shopping").

Exhibit 3. virtualFan™ projected operating costs per university

Web Page Design Costs

1. virtualFan Web Features

Hours of Software Design:	15	
Software Design Hourly Rate:	$85	
Software Design Costs:	$1,275	
Hours of Creative Design:	15	
Creative Design Hourly Rate:	$75	
Creative Design Costs:	$1,125	
Total Design & Construction Costs		**$2,400**

2. Event Broadcast Costs

Number of Events:	70	
Average Event Duration (hrs.)	3	
Broadcasting Hours:	210	
Event Technician Hours:	42	
Event Technician Hourly Rate:	$10	
Event Technician Cost:	$420	
Technical Administrator Hours:	42	
Technical Administrator Hourly Rate:	$50	
Technical Administrator Cost:	$2,100	
Photographer Costs Per Event:	$240	
Number of Events Photographed:	70	
Photographer Cost:	$16,800	
Long Distance Charge per Hour Broadcast:	$10	
Total Long Distance Charge:	$2,100	
Total Broadcast Costs		**$21,420**

3. Network & Equipment Costs
Network

Contract Duration (yrs.)	1	
Space Dedicated to Web Site (Mb)	100	
Annual Cost of Mb on Network	$10	
Cost of Residing Web Site on Network	$1,000	

Equipment

MusicBeam will allow a radio station to quickly, easily and inexpensively add secondary channels to its Internet broadcast, in order to service a wide variety of listener tastes and manage mandatory programming requirements (see Exhibit 4). The content management feature of MusicBeam will place the radio station in charge of the content that is streamed over the Internet, and the "push" aspect of MusicBeam will create a "sticky" environment for the end user. Listeners will be compelled to stay on the site by the TV-like fashion in which information is presented to them. However, unlike television, MusicBeam will allow the end user to interact with the radio station and become a participant in the broadcast. For example, if a radio station uses MusicBeam to play a Rolling Stones CD, the end user, in addition to interacting with Rolling Stones trivia, quizzes, etc. will have an opportunity to submit additional content for a site that he or she has found which relates to the Rolling Stones. Additional content could include a unifrom resource locator (URL) that identifies the Web address of a site. The content manager, or program director, will consolidate and screen incoming URLs, monitoring listener habits, and be able to "push" applicable sites out in future Rolling Stone

Exhibit 4. MusicBeam projected operating costs per radio station

1. MusicBeam System Costs

System Software Cost	$5,000	
Hours of Software Design:	64	
Software Design Hourly Rate:	$60	
Software Design Costs:	$3,840	
Hours of Creative Design:	60	
Creative Design Hourly Rate:	$50	
Creative Design Costs:	$3,000	
Total Design & Construction Costs		**$11,840**
2. Station Broadcast Costs		
Number of Simultaneous Listeners:	500	
Bandwidth Cost/Year:	$30,000	
Technical Administrator Hours/Year:	260	
Technical Administrator Hourly Rate:	$40	
Technical Administrator Cost:	$10,400	
Total Station Broadcast Costs		**$40,400**
3. Hosting & Equipment Costs		
Hosting		
Contract Duration (yrs.)	1	
Site Resource Consumption (expressed in Mb)	1,000	
Annual Cost of Mb on Network	$6	
Cost of Site Residing on Network	$6,000	
Equipment		
Lease for Onsite Equipment	$1,000	
Total Network & Equipment Costs		**$7,000**
4. Summary		
Site Design & Construction Costs:	$11,840	
Broadcast Costs:	$40,400	
Network & Equipment Costs:	$7,000	
Total Operations Costs		**$59,240**
Mark Up Costs		$11,848
Cost to Customer		**$71,088**

broadcasts. In addition to attracting people to the site, the gathering of URLs will present a powerful information opportunity to the radio station that can be used for targeted e-commerce and advertising. The end user may also submit quizzes, photos and movies.

In May 1999, Mark hired an MBA student, Monique LaChance, to focus on business development for DataNaut. With an increase in consulting work in June, Mark was able to hire another MBA student, Paul Lee, to help out with technical as well as business issues. Mark intended for Monique and Paul to focus on the development of the virtualFan™ concept and the consulting practice. However, after seeing a demonstration of the MusicBeam concept, which was based on virtualFan™ technology, both Monique and Paul recognized the potential of this product to succeed in the market. The Internet Radio industry had become a "hot" area, and DataNaut would have a chance to take advantage of the current interest among radio stations for such a product. Only half of the 12,000 radio stations in the United States had an online presence (a Web site), and a fraction of those stations engaged in Internet broadcasting. Monique and Paul spent the summer working on a business plan to obtain capital investment so DataNaut would be able to produce, market and sell MusicBeam to radio station owners in America and Europe. Monique had connections in Paris that she was eager to explore, once the product was ready.

After two months of market research and a continuous evolution of the MusicBeam conceptual design (and back-end development from Mark), Monique and Paul completed the business plan. As of September, they were ready to begin contacting venture capital firms and "angel" investors. DataNaut estimated that it would require approximately $1,000,000 of initial investment to bring MusicBeam to market. Monique and Paul felt this money could come from a venture capitalist, a group of angel investors or a potential customer—a large radio station company who would absorb DataNaut and all of its technology.

Mark knew that raising this type of money would not be easy. DataNaut was a young company with no prior external financing, and the risks to the investor would be significant, given the early stage of product development. In addition, DataNaut was still heavily committed to consulting contracts, and Mark's time would be divided until a better solution could be reached.

CURRENT CHALLENGES FACING THE ORGANIZATION

On the evening of September 3, Mark gathered Eric, Monique and Paul into the conference room (previously known as Mark's living room) for an important staff meeting. Mark began by reflecting upon the last few months and all of the changes that had recently occurred at DataNaut. Within a period of three months, DataNaut's focus had changed from exploring market opportunities for virtualFan™ to searching for investment capital for MusicBeam. As MusicBeam technology was based on the virtualFan™ platform, Mark felt that both products were important and developments to one would enhance the other in the long run. The important issues were competition and the accessibility to customers in each distinct market. Both Paul and Monique felt that, given the company's current limitations with respect to resources, DataNaut should focus on the development and marketing of MusicBeam, as MusicBeam represented an immediate growth opportunity for DataNaut. However, Mark was hesitant to abandon his first development effort completely, believing that the university sports market would soon be ready for a quality product such as virtualFan™. The four-year contracts signed by many universities with other vendors would soon expire, and perhaps these universities would begin to seek alternative solutions to meet their Internet broadcasting needs.

In the meantime, Mark had to contend with cash-flow issues and the time constraints posed by the consulting contracts. Mark wanted to learn how to make the best use of his time—how to work smarter, rather than harder. He also wanted to make some internal adjustments by implementing an incentive system, whereby his employees would obtain equity shares in the company. However, Mark was uncertain as to the types of models that existed for structuring such internal equity.

Monique and Paul had begun to develop relationships with venture capital firms, and Mark was enthusiastic about the prospects of financing his product development. virtualFan™ and MusicBeam were two great opportunities in Mark's opinion, and market research indicated that both were feasible at the time. Mark's consulting practice was becoming increasingly lucrative, and his good reputation was spreading rapidly. Mark wondered how he should position DataNaut, with respect to strategy and product development, in order to obtain venture capital investment. Would micro-investment be a better option to solving short-term cash-flow issues? If so, how would DataNaut attract angel investors, and how would Mark determine the appropriate equity amounts to offer in exchange for investment dollars? Which product or combination of products should be the focus of DataNaut's marketing efforts? How many products would DataNaut have to sell in order to break even? If DataNaut focused on product development and marketing, could the company handle the loss of Mark's consulting revenues, which were fueling its day-to-day operations? Mark had many decisions to make, and he was hoping for some guidance from his staff.

The Alternatives

One week earlier Mark had engaged a strategic consulting firm for outside assistance, as the sudden changes within DataNaut and the tremendous market opportunities ahead prompted Mark to reevaluate his position. Mark felt that an outside perspective would assist him in making important decisions about capital investment, product development and operations. At tonight's meeting he wanted to outline the alternatives proposed by the consulting firm, and obtain a consensus from the team as to the direction in which they should move. The consulting firm had sketched out three courses of action for Mark.

Proposal One: As a first alternative, DataNaut would continue product development on MusicBeam, accompanied by heavy target marketing, and continue the consulting practice as a source of revenue. In this scenario, Mark would manage the consulting side of the business, and DataNaut would hire an experienced CEO to oversee daily operations and product development. The consultants suggested that Mark raise an initial $1 million in venture capital to finance ongoing operational costs and product development of MusicBeam, and recommended that Mark retain 20% of the company himself, offer 20% to the incoming CEO and allow no more than 30% to VC investors. The remaining 30% would be used for employee profit sharing.

Proposal Two: As a second alternative, DataNaut would phase out the consulting business and focus solely on the pursuit of funding with the intention of becoming a product-oriented company. The consultants felt that the MusicBeam demo, along with Mark's dynamic personality and confidence, would quickly sell the concept, and DataNaut would be able to secure financing (either VC or angel) within a period of four months, during which time the remaining consulting income would cover expenses. Under this aggressive plan, Mark would remain as CEO with 40% equity, allowing up to 40% for investors and 20% for employee profit sharing.

Proposal Three: As a third alternative, DataNaut would remain as a technical consulting company, but focus its efforts strategically towards clients that would offer the company the opportunity to engage in streaming application development. Under this scenario, DataNaut would grow gradually, acquiring knowledge and connections, and perhaps eventually be able to engage in a joint product venture with one of its partners. This alternative does not indicate a total abandonment of current product efforts but rather a strategic re-focusing of client targets. virtualFan™ and MusicBeam technology could be used as a part of a custom client solution. Mark would retain 60% ownership and use the remaining 40% to offer attractive compensation packages to its new and existing employees.

Mark and his team now had to choose between the three scenarios outlined by the consultants—or develop a new one of their own.

FURTHER READING

Further information on DataNaut can be found on the company Web site: http://www.datanaut.com.

An article from *The Industry Standard* by Maryann Jones Thompson contains an excellent summary of radio market research: http://www.thestandard.com/metrics/display/0,1902.9954.00.html.

The ultimate guide to streaming media can be found at http://www.streamingmedia.com.

Additional reading on similar products and companies that would compete with DataNaut can be found at the following two sites:

- http://www.spinner.com
  Spinner.com is the first and largest Internet music service, broadcasting over 22 million songs each week to listeners all over the world. With over 375,000+ songs in rotation on 150+ music channels, Spinner spans an extraordinarily diverse range of musical styles. The free Spinner Plus downloadable music player offers reliable, high-quality audio while providing dynamic links to comprehensive artist information and music purchase options. High-profile music downloads and promotional features with marquee artists are also available from the Spinner.com Web site.
  Based in San Francisco, CA, Spinner is dedicated to providing an exciting, interactive alternative to traditional broadcasting, effectively revolutionizing the Internet music listening experience with its breadth and depth of quality content. Spinner.com was acquired by America Online, Inc. in May 1999, and merged with Nullsoft, Inc., providing us with greater resources to produce innovative products and extend our reach. (http://www.spinner.com, April 19, 2001)
- http://www.totalsports.com
  The Revolution will not be televised. It will be streamed. Downloaded. Uploaded. Digitized, analyzed and customized. It will be synchronized. Layered. Played, replayed and emailed. It's taking place RIGHT NOW on the Southern Ocean. At the top of Everest. In stadiums and ballparks and the most god-forsaken, far-flung corners of the globe. But, most of all, this revolution is taking place in the hearts and minds of sports fans suddenly given powerful new tools. Suddenly given the ability to get inside their favorite sports. To understand what really goes on behind the screaming engines, the blasting windstorms, the sweaty grimaces of heroic exertion. To see what the athletes see. To hear what they hear. And to feel some of what they feel as they explore the boundaries of human ability.

It's all accessible through Quokka Sports. On the Internet. From your home or office. And the way the world experiences sport will never be the same.
In 1996, Quokka began bringing down the "old ways" of following sports by launching a whole new form of digital entertainment. It's called Quokka Sports Immersion and it's changing the face of sports coverage, as we know it (http://www.totalsport.com, April 19, 2001).

GLOSSARY OF TERMS

- **Angel Investors:** Wealthy individuals (usually successful entrepreneurs) who invest in start-up companies, usually taking an active role in the management of the company.
- **Internet Broadcasting:** See Multimedia Streaming
  Microinvestment: The receipt of small amounts of investment from individuals for a small equity stake in a company.
- **Microsoft BackOffice:** Suite of software applications written for the Windows NT platform (see http://www. microsoft.com/backoffice).
- **Multimedia Streaming:** The delivery of electronic data types—text, audio, video or spatial data (such as maps) over the Internet such that viewing begins instantly, without the need for downloading.
- **Sticky Web Site:** A site that attracts repeat visitors who stay longer.
- **Turnkey Solution:** A packaged solution with no customization required.
- **Weblication:** Turnkey Internet application.

Nancy C. Shaw received her PhD in information systems from the National University of Singapore. She holds an MBA and a BBA from the University of Kentucky. Dr. Shaw has been a practitioner and consultant in the information systems industry for over twenty years. She has worked for AT&T, General Electric and most recently as a senior systems analyst for the Central Intelligence Agency. She also served as a military intelligence officer in the U.S. Army Reserves during the Persian Gulf War. Currently she is an assistant professor of information systems at George Mason University in Fairfax, Virginia.

Joan O'Reilly Fix received her MBA in finance from American University ("AU") in May 2000. While studying at AU, she worked at DataNaut Inc. as the director of business development. Ms. O'Reilly Fix also co-founded a student investment club and served as the executive director of the 1999 Kogod Case Competition, for which this case was written. Prior to attending business school, Ms. O'Reilly Fix worked for six years as an international banker. She is currently a vice president in the Worldwide Securities Services area of Citibank, N.A. with a focus on product management.

This case was previously published in *Annals of Cases on Information Technology*, Volume 4/ 2002, pp. 1-11, © 2002.

Chapter VII

Building an Online Grocery Business:
The Case of ASDA.com

Irene Yousept, University of Newcastle upon Tyne Business School, UK

Feng Li, University of Newcastle upon Tyne Business School, UK

EXECUTIVE SUMMARY

This chapter uses the case of ASDA.com, ASDA's home-shopping arm, to demonstrate the challenges in building and developing an online grocery business in the UK. To set the stage, the initial implementation and learning from phone/catalogue home-shopping in ASDA is outlined to demonstrate why e-commerce was seen as most economically suitable to conduct a grocery home-shopping business. Then the chapter illustrates the development stages and critical aspects of ASDA.com's Web shop. Particularly, it delineates the operational aspects of B2C e-commerce in the grocery business: fulfillment center and fulfillment process. The case will also describe ASDA's efforts in overcoming problems with their home-shopping fulfillment model and present important elements of ASDA.com's virtual store and its operation. The chapter concludes with the challenges that ASDA.com has been facing, their current status, and future prospects.

ORGANIZATION BACKGROUND

ASDA Stores Ltd. (http://www.asda.co.uk) was Britain's second largest supermarket retailer, with a turnover of £13.2 billion (for fiscal year ending December 31, 2003). The company's trading activities involved the operation of food, clothing, home, and leisure superstores throughout Great Britain, mainly targeted at the British working class family. With its superstore format, the company had been very strong in non-food offerings. In January 2004, ASDA had 255 stores and 24 depots around UK with 122,000 employees and was a subsidiary of U.S.-based Wal-Mart Stores Incorporated (http://www.walmart.com), the biggest retailer in the world.

Wal-Mart Stores Inc., ASDA's parent, was founded by Sam Walton in Bentonville, Arkansas, United States (U.S.) in 1962. In the fiscal year ending January 31, 2004, the company was one of the biggest in the world, with a turnover of around $256.329 billion (£142.405 billion) under the lead of H. Lee Scott, Jr., the President and CEO. In total, Wal-Mart had nearly 5,000 stores and wholesale clubs across 10 countries and more than 1.3 million employees worldwide (which were referred to as the "associates" in Wal-Mart or "colleagues" in ASDA).

The ASDA headquarters were based in Leeds. Leeds is the premier city in Yorkshire, one of the northern counties in the United Kingdom. The company was founded by a group of Yorkshire farmers in 1965 as Associated Dairies. Its first store opened in the same year, and since then, it has specialized in bulk selling at low prices. ASDA then expanded into the South of England in the 1970s and 1980s. The company was acquired in June 1999 by Wal-Mart Stores Inc. In 2004, ASDA's management team was led by Tony Denuzio, CEO for ASDA, which reported to John Menzer, president and CEO of Wal-Mart's international division. ASDA acquired and retained customers by providing a broad assortment of quality merchandise and services at low prices. Wal-Mart's "Everyday Low Price" policy (EDLP) had gained ASDA the title of "British best value supermarket" for seven successive years. In 2004, it offered around 25,000 lines of food and non-food.

ASDA, as all other subsidiaries of Wal-Mart Stores Inc., was ruled by three basic beliefs: respect for individuals, service to customers, and striving for excellence. These rules were established by Sam Walton (1992). Walton also claimed that the success of building the company could be pinned down into 10 rules that were still true for the company in 2004. These rules were (for details of these rules, refer to http://www.walmart.com): (1) Commit to your business. Believe in it more than anybody else; (2) Share your profits with all your associates, and treat them as partners; (3) Motivate your partners; (4) Communicate everything you possibly can to your partners; (5) Appreciate everything your associates do for the business; (6) Celebrate your successes; (7) Listen to everyone in your company; (8) Exceed your customers' expectations; (9) Control your expenses better than your competition; and (10) Swim upstream. Go the other way.

IT at the Heart of Strategy

"People think we got big by putting big stores in small towns. Really, we got big by replacing inventory with information" (Walton as cited by Wal-Mart, 1999, p. 9).

IT played a major role in the success of Wal-Mart. It believed that IT was a key facilitator in staying focused on customers: getting customers what they want, at the

Figure 1. ASDA's ISD strategy

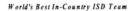

right place and the right time, and exceeding their expectations. The management of IT in ASDA was housed under the ISD (Information Services Division), led by Andy Haywood, who reported to Linda M. Dillman, Wal-Mart's CIO (chief information officer). Figure 1 describes ASDA's ISD strategy. The acquisition of ASDA by Wal-Mart meant that ASDA had access to the world's best IT infrastructure for a retailer. IT integration between ASDA and Wal-Mart was completed at the end of 2002.

In the long term, such integration would enable ASDA to grow without limitations, as was explained by Wal-Mart Europe ISD director in 2003: "...what we have done is to replicate to some extent the infrastructure we have in the rest of Wal-Mart to allow ASDA to expand in any way/shape/form they need to." In more immediate terms, such integration had enabled ASDA to leverage its supreme IT infrastructure to continuously maximize efficiency, lower prices, improve availability, increase the quality of goods provided, as well as widen variety.

At the heart of the IT infrastructure, a very powerful tool that allowed such improvement was Retail Link. Since the acquisition was completed in 1999, a lot of effort was put into adopting and developing the system to conform to ASDA's business practices. In 2003, Retail Link facilitated the daily trading practices between ASDA and more than 1,000 suppliers.

Retail Link was a proprietary Web-based exchange linking Wal-Mart (including ASDA) and their suppliers, or a private e-marketplace (Hoffman, Keedy & Roberts, 2002). In 2004, Retail Link was the biggest commercial data warehouse in the world (with 101 terabytes of capacity), which captured (among others) the point-of-sale figures—by item, by store, by day—enabling company and suppliers to track merchandise, study how the products sold, inventory information, and shipping deals. The system integrated Wal-Mart's EDI (Electronic Data Interchange) networks with an extranet used by the trading teams and some 10,000 suppliers. The sophistication of real-time data gathered from its network then helped the company to develop sophisticated data warehouse tools and computerized data exchanges with suppliers.

The impact of Retail Link on ASDA's business can be explained as follows:

1. Getting customers what they want:

    a. **Advanced data-mining for accurate merchandising.** The availability of historical data in Retail Link allowed sales from the past 10 years to be combined with variables such as weather, holidays, and school schedules to predict optimal product supply for specific stores under a range of situations.

2. In the price they want (even lower), when they want them:

    a. **Real-time data for minimized inventory cost.** Availability of real time data related to ASDA's business enabled the company to implement a just in time supply system, minimizing inventory costs. The level of buffer inventory could be minimized, whilst still ensuring goods were always available when customers want them by automatically alerting vendors whenever supply was needed using point of sales figures from Retail Link.

    b. **Perpetual inventory and collaborative planning, forecasting, and replenishment (CPFR) for optimized replenishment (for definition of CPFR, refer to http:// www.cpfr.org).** Instead of its previous systems of replenishment (store-driven ordering), with Retail Link ASDA imposed "perpetual inventory" using the timely information of sales, inventory, and so forth that were shared between the company and its suppliers. As such, the replenishment of goods could be continuously optimized. Retail Link also enabled ASDA and its suppliers to collaboratively conduct and analyze the planning and forecasting for related products. As a result, both parties could continuously advance their planning and forecasting techniques for optimum replenishment, further improve communication, and deepen the supplier-buyer relationship.

    c. **Global purchasing for improved bargaining power and quality of goods.** Retail Link allowed the aggregation of orders from different Wal-Mart divisions around the world into a single request to suppliers all over the world. By acquiring certain products from a single supplier, Wal-Mart was able to improve the quality of its goods as well as supply logistics and retail prices.

    d. **Improved logistics capability.** The timely information enabled by Retail Link allowed the logistics team to efficiently deliver goods from its hub-and-spoke systems to stores, to respond timely to customers' needs.

As can be gathered, Retail Link was an *important* source of ASDA's competitive advantage: low-cost leadership. This discussion is aimed to provide an understanding of the company's capability in continuously lowering prices, getting customers what they want when they want it, and exceeding their expectations. However, while it serves as an excellent background to the case, Retail Link is not the main focus of this case study. This chapter focuses on ASDA @t Home, the B2C e-commerce side of ASDA.

B2C E-Commerce: Strategic Role to ASDA and Major Developments

Before discussing the development of ASDA home-shopping initiatives, to enable readers to categorize major stages in ASDA's home-shopping development, an overall timeline was delineated in Table 1. Online home-shopping initiative in ASDA pursued a hybrid or brick-and-click model, which was the most widely adopted model for online supermarkets in the UK. Yousept and Li (2004) argued that in this model, existing players extended their off-line operations to include online offerings under the same brand name (e.g., ASDA @t Home, Sainsbury's To You, WaitroseDeliver, Tesco.com). The adopters did not believe that the future of the supermarket business was fully online, and the bulk of their business still came from the traditional channels. Nevertheless, they were seeking for growth from online customers. Such a strategic role of ASDA's B2C e-commerce was outlined by Wal-Mart Europe ISD director as an extension of the traditional branch-based business, as revealed below:

I think that we see the dot.com operation as an extension or another way of touching our customers. ... We have seen a growth in our business on the web. We continue to try to grow that business. It's important to us, because it's another means to talk to our customers. But we are not what you would call a web company by any means, the bulk of our business continue to be through our stores. ... Either through the web or ... the web and the stores – the combinations of both will continue to be our customers. So, that's what you see, a bit of the fusion of utilising the web or the brick and the click as a way to improve services to our customers. (Wal-Mart Europe ISD director)

The next section outlines the competitive situation in the UK supermarket industry to provide a background in understanding where ASDA was situated within the marketplace. Afterwards, the setting of the case study will be outlined, followed by the case study itself. This chapter concludes with the challenges and issues faced by ASDA @t Home at the time of writing.

Table 1. The timeline of major developments in ASDA home shopping

December 1998 – ASDA's home-shopping initiative piloted, called ASDA @t Home
January 1999 – ASDA @t Home launched via phone/catalogue with warehouse in Croydon, London
July 1999 – ASDA @t Home launched PC-based home-shopping using CD-Rom together with phone/catalogue; another warehouse was opened in Watford, London
November 2000 – ASDA @t Home online home-shopping was trialed
December 2000 – ASDA @t Home online home-shopping was launched
July 2001 – PC shopping with CD-Rom was terminated
August 2001 – ASDA @t Home embraced in-store picking model, running together with warehouses
January 2002 – ASDA home-shopping warehouses were closed and full in-store fulfillment was rolled out nationally from 32 stores; Web site development and maintenance were outsourced to third party
February 2002 – Digital TV shopping launched with Sky Digital
January 2003 – Digital TV shopping was terminated
August 2004 – Expansion of home-shopping to 21 more stores, covering 40% of UK population
End of 2004 – ASDA @t Home changed to ASDA.com

Supermarket Industry in the UK

In 2003, UK grocery market was predicted to be worth £115.0 billion (Institute for Grocery Distribution, IGD, 2004). Within this figure, TNS industry group Superpanel indicated that more than 75% of the market share was owned by the "Big Four" supermarket multiples, with composition as follows: Tesco with 27%, ASDA with 17%, J. Sainsbury's with 16.2%, Morrisons (including Safeway) with 15.2% (BBC, 2003). Other supermarket players included the fifth competitor within the top five, Sommerfield, as well as those targeting more upmarket segments of the UK population, Marks & Spencer and Waitrose (owned by John Lewis Partnership).

The competition between players within the Big Four had always been very intense with Tesco leading the pack since 1995. Soon after the takeover of ASDA by Wal-Mart, both J. Sainsbury's and ASDA started competing for the second place, which was finally won by ASDA in 2003. Indeed, in 2004, J. Sainsbury's were struggling with internal problems and strategic directions. Following a major restructure in the company, the company still suffered from a static sales growth. Its interim results for 2004/2005 showed 50.5% decline in profit from the previous year. The fourth player, Morrisons, had only emerged to the table following its takeover of Safeway in 2003.

Among the Big Four, ASDA, Morrisons, and Tesco had been positioned as low-cost or value providers, with ASDA targeting a slightly lower level market than Tesco, while Morrisons was more or less similar to ASDA. J. Sainsbury's, on the other hand, had been trying to reach a slightly higher end of the market, yet was "caught in the middle" when competing with the likes of Marks & Spencer or Waitrose. Its loss of market share against ASDA illustrates that price was still a key factor for customers (Michaels, 2004).

The distribution of power between supplier-retailer-consumer in the grocery industry had evolved in the last few decades. While in 1970s most power was held by producers that supplied grocery retailers, between the 1980s to mid-1990s, the power had shifted to the retailers. Nonetheless, since the late 1990s, consumers were claimed to possess the most power (as revealed by ASDA's head of ISD infrastructure during an interview) along with their changing lifestyles and demographics. As such, there had been a transformation in the UK supermarket industry marked by intense competition and tighter profit margin to players. This development had then forced retailers to pursue better partnerships with their suppliers (Zairi, 1998). At the same time, physical expansion got harder along with increased population and market saturation. Such a situation had made customer acquisition and retention difficult. More than ever, retailers were forced to experiment with creative innovations (e.g., product, store format, service) and adoption of advanced new technology to achieve the optimal rate of operational efficiency as well as customers' shopping experience.

SETTING THE STAGE
FOR ONLINE SHOPPING

In the face of difficulties in the grocery market since late 1990s, as outlined above, home shopping was seen as an attractive option for supermarket players. The UK grocery market was oligopolistic with high utilization of average store space. Therefore, it was arguably very suitable for the grocery home-shopping business (Boyer & Frohlich,

2002). In fact, the need for a grocery home-shopping service had been identified for decades.

Nevertheless, in the UK there had not been a mechanism of rolling it out profitably. This was due to the efficiency of the self-service model in grocery retailing, coupled with a tiny profit margin related to the business. The economical offering of home-shopping services was not possible without charging customers excessively due to the expensive labor and logistics costs.

The year of 1990 marked the beginning of the UK grocery home-shopping era with the launch of The Food Ferry (http://www.thefoodferry.co.uk), the world's oldest operating grocery home-shopping company. This company used a catalogue home-shopping model and outsourced its goods to local suppliers targeting a small area of customer households around central London. Later on in the mid-1990s, some of ASDA's strong competitors, Tesco and J. Sainsbury, had entered the online shopping market (1995 for Tesco and 1996 for J. Sainsbury). Inspired by the development of online grocery supermarket in the U.S. as well as the aspiration to capture competitors' market shares, both players started investing in building the online grocery market. They were also followed by several other supermarket players. During this time, both Tesco and J. Sainsbury had been fulfilling customers' orders from their stores. (In 1999, J. Sainsbury started investing in a warehouse for home-shopping purposes).

ASDA took a "wait and see" stance for their e-commerce launch and opted for a phone/fax catalogue-based shopping to start with (Faragher, 2002). In order to bring ASDA's offering to a whole new audience, ASDA's first ever home-shopping initiative was piloted in December 1998. The business, called "ASDA @t Home," initially sold groceries. After a two-month pilot, ASDA @t Home went live in the form of catalogue home shopping, adding paper-based catalogues to the existing online catalogue, offering next day delivery. Orders were taken by several phone operators or by fax via a small third-party call center with links to ASDA's home-shopping systems. Figure 2 explains how the shopping process was conducted during these days. The business offered a full product mix with 5,000 lines of grocery products from its dedicated home-shopping warehouse. This service charged £3.50 (free delivery charge for order over £50.00). ASDA @t Home was then led by Angela Morrison, the Head of Home-Shopping, who reported to ASDA trading director, Mike Coupe.

In contrast to its traditional market segment, the home-shopping arm had been cherry-picking south London's most affluent neighborhoods during its first roll-out. Traditionally, the company had a stronger presence in the northern part of England and focused on middle to lower economic classes. At the end of its two-month pilot, the service was extended to reach as many as 450,000 upmarket households within the radius of 15 miles from its first home-shopping warehouse in Croydon, South London.

After less than a year of running the business, supporting existing home-shopping systems with a third-party call center had proved very expensive for ASDA. A lot of it had to do with the cost of phone operators, which facilitated the main channel of getting the business. As seen in Figure 2, the customer ordering process was very tedious. It took on average 30 minutes per order (Whalley, 1999) plus 15 to 20 minutes of keying in orders to the system, which added up to only 1.14 to 1.235 orders per hour (taking into consideration 5% tolerance, e.g., for operator's personal needs and changeover time between one order to another). Rough calculations tell us that the £3.50 delivery charge

Figure 2. Phone-based catalogue shopping ordering process for ASDA @t Home

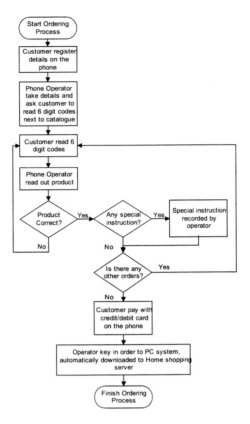

per order would barely cover the operators' wages, assuming standard minimum pay of £4.80 in 1999 (DTI, 1999, http://www.dti.gov.uk/er/nmw/nmwhist.htm). Furthermore, low profit margins of the grocery business would have to cover fix and variable costs inherent in the home-shopping service (such as driver costs, petrol, depreciation costs for vans, warehouse operation costs, labor costs for picking and packing customer orders, and others).

July 1999 marked the gradual changeover from phone/fax to include PC-based home shopping. It was Octavia Morley, ASDA's director of home and online home shopping who was directly responsible for the venture. Trials of PC-based shopping were conducted in August that year. Customers used a CD-Rom, which allowed them to order the whole range of products available from the catalogue. PC-based orders would be created off-line, and then customers would connect to the home-shopping servers using the Internet to transfer their orders. At about the same time, the company started its second warehouse in Watford, expanding their reach to another 250,000 households; they also had planned another 13 to 15 depots nationwide in 2003. The trial was successful; Morley reported that it was a significantly cheaper channel to conduct a home-shopping business (compared to phone/fax) (Mugan, 1999).

PC-based home shopping acted as a trial for a seamless multi-channel home-shopping offering that was seen as the preferred choice by ASDA's management since the year of 2000. The completion of Wal-Mart's acquisition of ASDA promised big developments for ASDA @t Home. In total, it had been around two years since ASDA had started piloting its home-shopping operation to the point at which www.asda.com "went live" to take customer orders. During this time, the company had learned from its competitors' mistakes and perfected its warehouse operation. After it was launched in November 2000, the company started expanding its services until yet another major changeover in 2001 for ASDA @t Home's operation. This fact showed how complicated the implementation of an e-commerce application was, even for a company with such vast resources. The next section provides a discussion on the development of ASDA @t Home online, the problems it faced, how it overcame them, and its vision forward.

CASE DESCRIPTION: ASDA @T HOME WEB SITE

In summer 2000, a team of 20 people was put together to start the ASDA @t Home e-commerce project (Spence, 2002b). This was the starting point of ASDA @t Home's migration to a higher level of home-shopping operation. For over six months, the team conducted the design, coding, testing, and deployment of the ASDA.com Web site. They identified several critical aspects for the Web site, among all: techniques for finding products, checkout mechanism, shopping basket facility, delivery booking, security, customer help/guidance, account information, and registration.

In November 2000, ASDA @t Home launched their Web site for a closed community. For this, a team of developers was put together to support the launch of the Web site in Bentonville (Wal-Mart's head office). The project team rapidly ironed out initial glitches using feedback from the initial users of the site, ready for the full launch in December 2000. When the Web site was finally launched, ASDA @t Home allowed customers to be able to hop between the Web and telephone, at the time offering 6,000 lines of products. Customers could even "mix and match" between different ways of accessing ASDA @t Home to place an order. The business had also launched its Interactive Digital TV shopping in 2002. This, however, was closed down after approximately a year in operation.

Customers' Orders Fulfillment

A key element of online grocery was how fulfillment was handled (Boyer, Hult, Splinder, & Santoni, 2003; Ellis, 2003). There were two basic models available (Tanskanen, Yrjola, & Holmstrom, 2002). The first was to piggy-back on an existing supermarket or cash and carry (this will be referred to as *in-store picking*). Online grocer could either pick goods from its existing supermarkets/cash and carries or, in the case of pure plays, from others' stores. The second alternative was to serve the online grocery customers by building a dedicated picking center, either automated or not.

In comparing both models, according to Delaney-Klinger, Boyer, and Frohlich (2003), the in-store picking model would minimize cost when sales were limited by sacrificing some degree of picking efficiencies. Furthermore, this model would enhance existing customers' shopping experience as goods were delivered from their local stores (Seybold, 2001). Nonetheless, in-store fulfillment bore the risk of cannibalization to the existing stores, as shoppers needed to compete with in-store pickers; it would also be inefficient for huge volumes (Boyer & Frohlich, 2002).

With a dedicated fulfillment model, a company could serve much more orders than with an in-store model. The order fulfillment process could be optimized, and the cost of picking could be minimized with this model. Furthermore, food quality as well as availability could be ensured by having a dedicated center (Roberts, Xu, & Mettos, 2003). Customers could benefit from almost real-time visibility to the availability of goods when ordering from companies using this model (Yousept & Li, 2004). Nevertheless, this model required a significant upfront investment; Webvan, for example, spent $25 million (£13.8 million) for each of its automated warehouses (http://www.cnbc.com). Furthermore, it also entailed more logistics cost compared to the in-store picking model, as warehouses were usually built relatively far from customer residence (Roberts et al., 2003). Table 2 compares the limitations and benefits of both approaches.

Rather than implementing any of the fulfillment models in their purest form, companies could also implement a hybrid model, an operational option between in-store picking and a dedicated fulfillment center (Yrjola, 2001). This way, players were trying to combine the benefits of both worlds. In practice, there was no best way of implementing a hybrid model. In the UK, due to the emerging development of the online grocery business, in 2004, a lot of experiments were still conducted to find the best way for each player to optimize fulfillment.

For example, Tesco in the UK had different combinations of its online shopping fulfillment model:

Table 2. In-store picking vs. dedicated picking center

In-store Picking	Dedicated Picking Centre
Benefits	*Limitations*
Negligible start-up cost	Significant start-up cost
Instant coverage of service to wide audience using supermarkets network nationwide	Only covering areas surrounding the warehouse (even though each warehouse can cover a much wider area than a store), therefore slow coverage to wider audience
Little extra to current operational cost	Significant additional operational cost, wastage, overhead and other cost related to running a warehouse
Wide range of products offered (following the store's range)	Smaller range of products offered
Limitations	*Benefits*
Limited home-shopping fulfilment capacity	High home-shopping fulfilment capacity
Inefficient picking process – high cost	Optimised picking process – low cost
No visibility of goods availability	Near real-time visibility of goods availability
Risk of error in goods replacement	Limited chance of the need to replace goods
Big risk of product error in general	Less risk of product error in general
Disturbance to offline customers	No disturbance to offline customers
Lower assurance over food quality in online order fulfilment	Better assurance of food quality in online order fulfilment

1. In-store picking for grocery goods.
2. Combination of dedicated/in-store for wines: Cases of goods were picked in a central depot, they were then sent through to stores. In the designated store, wines were then being cross-stocked (i.e., they did not go the store's stock). Finally, they were shipped to customers.
3. Outsourcing for items, such as CDs, DVDs, white goods, and general merchandise, to a third party (where the company used the supplier's warehouse).

Nevertheless, embracing hybrid models usually involved different customer ordering systems, back-end systems as well as fulfillment processes. In some instances, players might decide to adopt hybrid methods for different geographical areas with varying levels of demand and population density. This might sometimes result in twice the effort of designing work practices and investment in different systems.

The problem of home delivery service also represented a big challenge in online grocery shopping (Punakivi, Yrjola, & Holmstrom, 2001). One of the most important factors that affects the cost for home delivery was sales per area (sales per mile^2 or km^2) (Yrjola, 2001). The more sales there were until a certain point, the lower the cost of home delivery. This represented a challenge for a dedicated fulfillment center. Other important aspects were related to the delivery time window offered to customer as well as when the delivery was in comparison to the order. Different combinations included one-hour delivery window, two-hour delivery window, either next delivery or longer (Punakivi & Saranen, 2001; Punakivi, Yrjola, & Holmstrom, 2001).

ASDA @t Home fulfilled its customers' home-shopping orders using a dedicated warehouse. This model was chosen for ASDA @t Home's operation instead of the in-store picking model to avoid the cannibalization of their existing stores. It was believed that a bespoke dedicated fulfillment model would be more efficient than an equivalent store operation, which was designed to ensure maximum shopping enjoyment, impulse buying, and ease of finding based on consumption habits. Arguably, the traditional supermarket store design could not produce the optimal process to fulfill customers' home-shopping orders. The dedicated warehouse model would also be able to handle a greater volume of orders (Spence, 2002a) and enabled ASDA @t Home to reach areas where it did not have a strong presence at the time.

The Changeover

ASDA @t Home had been operating for 18 months when it became apparent that the dedicated fulfillment center was not suitable to support the growth of the business. Roundabout the time of introduction to a new multi-channel platform, Iain Spence was conducting a feasibility analysis to compare in-store fulfillment and ASDA's warehouse model; he concluded that in-store picking was more commercially viable. This was confirmed by ASDA's general manager for e-commerce in 2003.

There were several reasons why a dedicated fulfillment center would not be suitable for ASDA @t Home:

1. **Low customer uptake for online grocery home shopping while it was very expensive to run the warehouse.** ASDA @t Home was experiencing problems in achieving breakeven on the warehouse operations costs on a daily basis. Both existing ware-

houses had problems reaching the breakeven point of 500 orders a day. The short shelf life of much food led to a massive amount of wastage, while no steady income was definite. In addition to wastage, other aspects (e.g., rent, depreciation, labor) also added to the expensive cost of warehouse operation. Some unconfirmed reports quoted warehouse operational losses as large as £7 million (e-logistics, 2002).

2. **Small coverage of ASDA @t Home's current warehouses.** In August 2001, ASDA @t Home only covered around 3 million households, equal to only 12.29% of the whole UK population (the UK had around 24.4 million households at the time, http://www.nua.com). As such, the business was only exposed to around £35 million of UK annual online grocery market at the time around £285 million annually. Coupled with competition with other online grocery providers, some which had a better "grip" on the market, this only left ASDA @t Home with a small slice of the pie.

3. **It took a lot of investment to expand the business further with the current model.** Building new warehouses to enable national roll-out (13 to 15 as planned) would have cost ASDA around £26 to £30 million of investment (£4 million for each of the warehouses, according to Goddard, 2002).

4. **Smaller variety of product offerings with dedicated fulfillment center.** With their current warehouses, ASDA could only offer 6,000 lines of products (in comparison to some 11,000 lines of products when they started the in-store picking model). This number represented their most popular products in-store to ensure that wastage was minimized. Customers who were used to consuming certain brands or certain flavors of products might not be able to purchase it at ASDA @t Home and had to do it elsewhere. This could result in loss of business or even reduction in customer satisfaction and less repeat purchases.

In March 2002, a big project was conducted to migrate ASDA @t Home's fulfillment model to a full in-store picking model. (The different stages of fulfillment centre migration were constructed based on Spence, 2002a, under written permission). To ensure that customers only experienced minimal disruption, in January 2002, ASDA @t Home stabilized their warehouse systems as a short-term tactical initiative to keep them operational during the migration period (Spence, 2002a).

Meanwhile, manual in-store picking operations were trialed in-store to perfect the process design: ensuring optimal picking, packing, and delivery of customer orders. At this stage, a minimal system was built to be thrown away quickly. At the back-end of the Web site operation, a "smoke-and-mirror" approach was used: instead of automated electronic transfer of customer shopping orders and automated devices for picking process, orders were printed out in-store, and paper-based picking sheets were used to pick products.

This stage proved successful, which then led the company to the development of in-store picking technology. An out-of-the-box system was chosen from Excel's retail services division. It downloaded orders from ASDA @t Home's Web site and transmitted the details via WAN (wireless area network) to handheld terminals carried by pickers (e-logistics, 2001). After orders were picked and packed, drivers (who carried the same devices) would deliver the goods to customers' doors. The palm-based system provided picking support, product tracking and tracing, matched deliveries to the corresponding address, and accepted doorstep credit card payment and electronic signing (Grocer, 2004).

Following this, to facilitate ASDA @t Home's particular business requirements and to optimize processes and service levels, customization of the technology was conducted along with its integration into the multi-channel platforms. A full store trial then went live, shortly before it was launched in 20 stores within eight weeks. The pilot had proved successful with satisfying process design and highly acceptable implementation methodology. As such, the in-store picking model was ready for roll-out. In the middle of 2001, ASDA @t Home started to embrace an in-store picking model nationally. At this stage, both in-store and dedicated picking centers were running side by side. In January 2002, 22 stores were already serving ASDA @t Home's customers using these systems. They were scattered all over the UK: the Midlands, Yorkshire, Lancashire, Wales, the South, and the Southwest of England.

ASDA announced the closure of its home-shopping warehouses in January 2002, after pursuing all efforts to minimize the negative impact on their business. Three hundred thirty of ASDA's employees (colleagues) affected by the closure were mostly redeployed in other parts of the company. In March 2002, a temporary service shutdown was experienced by ASDA @t Home's customers who had previously been served by Croydon/Watford warehouses. Since then, ASDA @t Home's service had been wholly fulfilled from 32 stores reaching around 30% of the UK population.

Although the company planned to roll-out to cover 60% of the population by the end of 2002, ASDA @t Home chose to stay with only 32 stores (30% of the population) until the end of July 2004. This was a decision from the management who were not prepared to rush into expansion while they were perfecting the systems and processes to make the business operationally profitable, as was claimed by ASDA's general manager for e-commerce in 2003.

In January 2004, ASDA @t Home was run by a dedicated team that reported to Paul Mancey. From ISD, Doug Cliffe, general manager for e-commerce, was responsible for the systems side of e-commerce to facilitate requirements of the home-shopping team. A team of 30 was assigned to deal with the ASDA @t Home operations, including marketing and merchandising. For day-to-day operations, the in-store operational level was dealt with by a separate home-shopping team in each store made up of pickers, van drivers, and managers of the Home-Shopping Department. In Bentonville, around 12 people were assigned to deal with Web site development and maintenance. This function was taken over from a third party in 2002. In the end of 2004, the business name of ASDA @t Home was changed to "ASDA.com."

The Virtual Store and Fulfillment Processes

ASDA.com's online home shopping was ruled by four values: convenience, range of products, price, and service delivered (Fox, 2004). In August 2004, ASDA charged a fee of £3.50 for delivery, with free delivery for shopping over £99.00. This was the cheapest in the market. Products were sold online at the same price as those in-store, and around 15,000 lines were offered. At the time, the role of the call center was fully advisory and for receiving complaints. The call center was gradually decreasing, evolving into a support mechanism for the online channel. To get a better understanding of ASDA.com, the virtual store, shopping process, and order fulfillment will be explained in this section. Table 3 summarizes the Web site's features while Figure 3 shows ASDA.com's virtual store. On the other hand, Figures 4 and 5 outline the main customer shopping process as well as order fulfillment and delivery. For delivery, each store was divided into one or more zones to enable delivery planning. Pickers used several totes (crates used to place groceries) in the picking process, each comprised of a particular department (e.g., frozen) and corresponded with customer orders. By the end of the process, the numbers of totes already filled with orders were manually handled and "ticked off" from the list. The procedure was then copied into a delivery manifest for loading to vans (Fox, 2004). Ambient products (products that were stored in room

Table 3. ASDA.com: Important aspects of online suprmarket's Web site structure

Aspects	Asda @t Home's Web site features
Techniques for finding products	"Search" facility, shop by aisles, previous 3 orders, personal shopping list, and enter few details from the receipts of ASDA's supermarket tills.
Checkout mechanism	Involved 3 steps: check delivery & order details, make secure payments & submit orders, as well as check receipts.
Shopping basket facility	Appear in every page, summarising delivery details, goods in the basket and total spending so far. The amount of each item could be amended at any time.
Delivery booking	Delivery booking could be conducted anytime before, during, after shopping. Asda @t Home had 2 hour delivery window (everyday from 10 am – 10 pm). Customers should choose a day and a delivery slot.
Security	The website was 100% secure, using 128 bit of encryption for payment.
Customer help/guidance	2 types: Frequently Asked Questions page as well as customer call centre (phone and email).
Account information	Account information was protected by password and user number. This could be amended in a separate page.
Registration	Account registration should be done before shopping was conducted. Customers should enter a postcode, after the systems were sure that Asda @t Home delivered to that area, then customers should register their names, contact details and delivery addresses.

Figure 3. ASDA.com virtual store

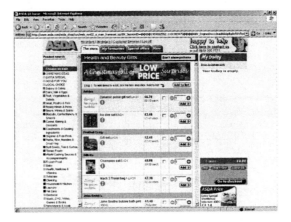

Figure 4. Customer online shopping process at ASDA.com

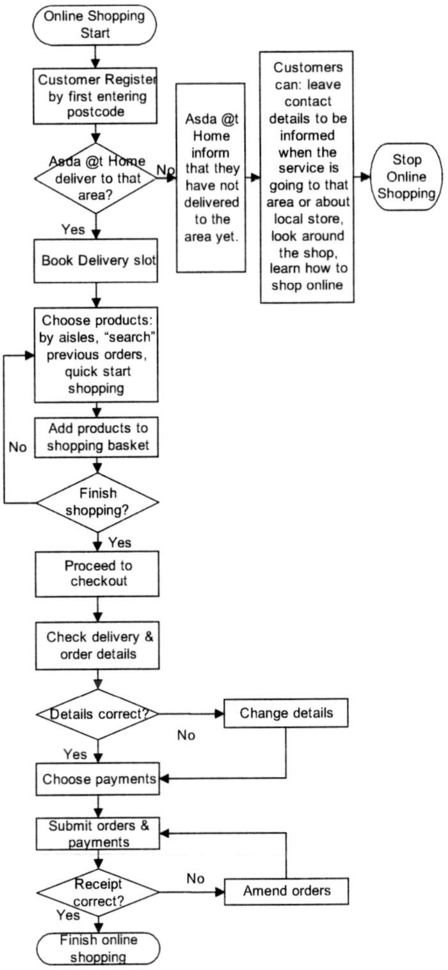

temperature, e.g., cereals) were mainly picked by night shift pickers, while chilled and frozen products were picked two hours before loading (Fox, 2004).

In Table 3, readers can learn how ASDA designed the important aspects for online shopping as identified by Spence (2002b), which was previously outlined (see http://www.asda.com). First, to find products, customers could perform a search, browse by aisles (e.g., dairy, milk, eggs), generate an automatic shopping list from one's previous three orders, or create shopping lists from scratch. ASDA also allowed customers to enter a few details from till receipt to automatically generate a shopping list. Second, virtual shopping basket appeared in every page to inform customers about the goods that they had chosen to purchase. Third, to assist shopping, customers could access the help page

Figure 5. ASDA.com in-store fulfillment process

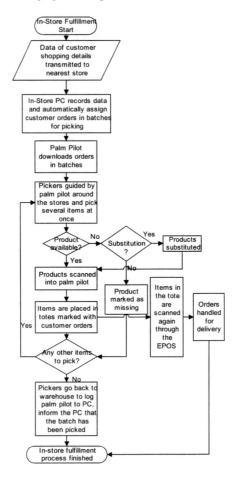

(that provides FAQ-type information) or call/e-mail the contact center. Other aspects of the virtual store in Table 3 are self-explanatory and therefore will not be discussed further.

ASDA.com Today: Opportunities and Visions Forward

The growing online home-shopping market in the UK in general and online grocery in particular potentially presented a big opportunity for ASDA.com (around £1 billion in 2004 according to Hayward, 2004). As has already been discussed, with Retail Link, ASDA owned a powerful source of low-cost leadership ability. As the company perfected the service levels, operational efficiencies, and the performance of the Web site, its low-cost leadership ability should have allowed the company to attract online customers that were otherwise—by default—less loyal than traditional customers. In the long run, ASDA aspires to have the ASDA.com division dissolved into its main business and seamlessly integrate the "brick" and "click" parts of the business.

In the virtual world, customers were no longer limited by the physical establishment and could easily switch between different shops. The increasing convergence of online supermarket shopping sites (in terms of shopping processes and facilities) also made price one of the most powerful differentiating mechanisms. Therefore, there was a real opportunity for ASDA.com becoming an engine of growth. This was explained by the general manager for e-commerce in 2003:

...our aim is to win a lot of regular (competitors') shoppers. ...if we're getting the delivery and the service that customers require...we can deliver it in much less cost than (competitors). Then, we hope to have an Internet shopping operation which will not be existing ASDA shoppers. (ASDA's general manager for e-commerce)

For this to materialize, however, there was a lot of work still to be done by the ASDA.com team. One issue was operational efficiency, which could be gained from the synergy of different Wal-Mart subsidiaries. To enable global leverage of all Wal-Mart's subsidiaries' online home-shopping systems and processes, a team of Wal-Mart staff from all over the world was founded, called "lowcost.com." It included representatives from ASDA.com in the UK, superhour.mx in Mexico, walmart.com in the U.S., and a Wal-Mart technical team from Bentonville. This committee regularly discussed strategic direction, current initiatives for e-commerce solutions and the sharing of best practices.

In January 2004, lowcost.com was working to achieve what they referred to as the "85/15 principle," where 85% of e-commerce development would be conducted globally, and the remaining 15% would be conducted in-store/in-country specific. For ASDA.com itself, a global in-store pick solution instead of packaged-based solution was seen as the key method to gain operational benefits. Doug Cliffe claimed, "a global in-store pick system will actually introduce a lot more efficiencies on our current picking fulfillment model." The ISD team expected to complete the global in-store solution toward the end of 2004, when ASDA.com could then accelerate its growth.

CURRENT CHALLENGES FACING ASDA.COM

Customer Uptake for Online Grocery Shopping

Despite the growing market of UK online grocery shopping, a lot of customers were still uncomfortable buying food online. Issues included security, shopping habits, difficulties conducting online shopping, the customer's lack of control in making a choice, and delivery charges. ASDA.com and all online supermarket players were faced with the challenge of "educating customers" to change the grocery shopping habit of their lifetime (Boyer & Frohlich, 2002) and build their trust to adopt online grocery shopping.

For ASDA.com, challenges also lie in capturing a bigger slice of the market share (currently still less than its overall market share of 16.5%). The small number of online grocery players (only six in the UK) meant that direct competitors were few, and the company should expect to have bigger market share than its off-line operation. ASDA.com faced the challenge of increasing its business as well as providing the capacity to meet such an increase. In early 2004, Fox (2004) conducted an investigation of one of the 32 stores that conducted ASDA.com in-store fulfillment and reported that the store was planning to increase its daily transactions to 1,000.

Increasing Churn Rate, Repeated Purchases, and Profitable Basket Sizes

Ellis (2003) argued that one of the biggest challenges for online grocery retailers was to take customers quickly through their learning stage to become a comfortable user of online grocery shopping. Until the fifth purchase, the likelihood that a customer would leave the business was still fairly high, as revealed by ASDA's general manager for e-commerce. Also, until this level of repeat purchase was reached, customers usually only had small basket sizes. ASDA.com was trying to encourage customers to purchase more than a £74 basket size on average. Another major problem was that a lot of the customers had a tendency to "dip-in," shop once and never come back. Doug Cliffe, General Manager for E-Commerce at ASDA in 2003, explained:

It could be that they dip in to try it out, it was fine but I'm just as easy to get in the car and nip to the supermarket rather than spending 40 min trying to build a shopping list, it's equivalent to a day out. (ASDA's general manager for e-commerce)

Enhancing the Efficiency of the Picking Process and Increasing Service Levels

As explained by a contact at ASDA.com, one of the biggest resource utilizations in conducting online home-shopping business was related to the in-store operation of fulfilling customer orders. Tied into this issue were two problems with ASDA's in-store fulfillment systems and processes. First was lack of integration between shop-floor systems and the picking operation. This meant that double scanning was necessary during the picking process, first to the palm pilot to ensure that the goods were correct and second to the EPOS (electronic point of sales or cashier) to connect to the shop's SMART system. This was very wasteful of time and efficiency (an extra 15 minutes was wasted per order). Second, the handheld terminals held by pickers worked with batch processes, where pickers needed to go back into the warehouse every time to connect the palm pilot to the PC to download the completed picking task and get the next batch of orders. These trips back and forth from the shop floor to the warehouse were time consuming and inefficient. Therefore, in 2004, the company was planning some initiatives which will help increase the efficiency of in-store fulfillment.

Online Propositions

ASDA.com has proved strengths in non-food offerings, especially white goods and general merchandise, but was facing challenges to transfer these strengths online. Picking practices and supporting fulfillment devices (such as the tote and vans) were not geared up to deliver large white goods. The company had the ability to offer them cheaper than other retailers, and the Internet was an appropriate medium for the sale of these types of products. Therefore, if the company could create an efficient way of delivering them, they would capture a better online market share. In addition, the company also faced the challenge of expanding its current range of online offering (a competitor could offer 30,000 to 40,000 lines of grocery goods plus many non-food goods). In building its online proposition, the company also faced the problem of providing information content for its food products as consumers were increasingly critical and wanted better knowledge of what they were eating.

Geographical Expansion

An important problem faced by ASDA.com was geographical coverage. With its latest expansion costing £3 million in August 2004, the service only covered 40% of the UK population (based on 53 stores nationwide). Therefore, 60% of the population was not reached. Nevertheless, as explained before, ASDA.com wanted to ensure that the existing in-store operations could achieve operational benefit before it expanded nationally.

ACKNOWLEDGMENTS

This case would not have been possible without the cooperation of the Information Services Division of ASDA Stores Ltd. Interviews were conducted in 2003 with Wal-Mart Europe ISD director, general manager for e-commerce, head of ISD infrastructure, and ISD systems manager for MIS. The authors would also like to express their gratitude to Andy Haywood, ASDA's ISD Director, for the permission to publish this case and Andrew Pattinson, ASDA's ISD Project Manager, for facilitating it.

REFERENCES

BBC. (2003). *ASDA overtakes Sainsbury's*. Retrieved January 2, 2005, from http://news.bbc.co.uk/1/hi/business/3112689.stm

Boyer, K. K., & Frohlich, M. (2002). Ocado: An alternative way to bridge the last mile in grocery home delivery. In *European Case Clearing House collection* (Vol. 602-057-1, pp. 1-19). MI: Michigan State University.

Boyer, K. K., Hult, T., Splinder, M., & Santoni, R. (2003). *Bridging the last mile: Online shopping in UK and US*. MIT Sloan School of Management.

Delaney-Klinger, K., Boyer, K., & Frohlich, M. (2003). The return of online grocery shopping: A comparative analysis of Webvan and Tesco's operational methods. *The TQM Magazine, 15*(3), 187-196.

DTI. (1999). *A guide to national minimum wage* (No. Pub/5642/50K/9/01/AR). London: Department of Trade and Industry.

Ellis, C. (2003). Lessons from online groceries. *MIT Sloan Management Review, 44*(2), 8.

e-logistics. (2001, July-August). ASDA equips for home delivery roll-out. *e-logistics Magazine, 13*. Retrieved January 2, 2005, from http://www.elogmag.com/magazine/13/asda.shtml

Faragher, J. (2002, February). The information age interview—ASDA @t Home. *Information Age, 6*. Retrieved January 2, 2005, from http://www.infoconomy.com/pages/search/group47275.adp

Fox, H. (2004). *Investigation into the developing market with regards to the food sector.* Unpublished BSc Thesis, University of Newcastle upon Tyne, Newcastle upon Tyne.

Goddard, C. (2002, February 6). *Store to door.* Retrieved January 2, 2005, from http://www.revolution.com

Grocer. (2004). From the shop floor to the front door: How Exel's technical innovation helps ASDA makes its customers feel @home with its online shopping service. *The Grocer, 227,* 18.

Hayward, S. (2004, March 7). Net shopping is really clicking. *The Sunday Mirror*, 40.

Hoffman, W., Keedy, J., & Roberts, K. (2002). The unexpected return of B2B. *The McKinsey Quarterly, 3.*

IGD. (2004). *Retail market overview factsheet.* London: Institute of Grocery Distribution.

Michaels, L. (2004). *What's wrong with supermarkets.* Oxford: Corporate Watch.

Mugan, C. (1999, July 9). ASDA online takes off. *Super Marketing, 8.*

Punakivi, M., & Saranen, J. (2001). Identifying the success factors in e-grocery home delivery. *International Journal of Retail & Distribution Management, 29*(4), 156-163.

Punakivi, M., Yrjola, H., & Holmstrom, J. (2001). Solving the last mile issue: Reception box or delivery box. *International Journal of Physical Distribution & Logistics, 31*(6), 427-239.

Roberts, M., Xu, X. M., & Mettos, N. (2003). Internet shopping: Supermarket model and customer perceptions. *Journal of Electronic Commerce in Organisations, 1*(2), 32-43.

Seybold, P. B. (2001). Get inside the lives of your customers. *Harvard Business Review, 79*(5), 80-89.

Spence, I. (2002a). *Case study: ASDA @t Home e-commerce fulfilment.* Retrieved January 2, 2005, from http://www.spenceco.com/Casestudy_Fulfilment.html

Spence, I. (2002b). *Case study: ASDA.com development.* Retrieved January 2, 2005, from http://www.spenceco.com/Casestudy_Asdadotcom.html

Tanskanen, K., Yrjola, H., & Holmstrom, J. (2002). The way to profitable Internet grocery retailing—Six lessons learned. *International Journal of Retail & Distribution Management, 30*(2), 169-178.

Wal-Mart (1999). Annual Report. Bentonville: Wal-Mart Stores Inc.

Walton, S. (1992). *Made in America: My story.* New York: Bantam Books.

Whalley, S. (1999, January 15). ASDA @t Home trial is ready for rollout. *Super Marketing, 1.*

Yousept, I., & Li, F. (2004, June 21-23). Online supermarkets: Emerging strategies and business models. *Proceedings of the 17th Bled E-Commerce Conference*, Bled, Slovenia.

Yrjola, H. (2001). Physical distribution consideratios for electronic home shopping. *International Journal of Physical Distribution & Logistics, 31*(10), 746-761.

Zairi, M. (1998). Best practice in supply chain management: The experience of the retail sector. *European Journal of Innovation Management, 1*(2), 58-66.

Irene Yousept is currently a full-time PhD researcher at the University of Newcastle upon Tyne Business School, UK, funded by the Overseas Research Scholarship. She holds a BEng (Honors) with cum laude in industrial engineering from the University of Trisakti, Indonesia, and an MSc with distinction in business IT systems from the

University of Strathclyde, UK. She was a teaching assistant for e-business module. Her research interests include emerging business models and strategies in the information economy, particularly in retail banking and supermarkets. Miss Yousept has worked closely with UK leading companies in banking and retailing. She has been a reviewer for a number of journals and conferences. Her recent work in Internet banking has won the best paper prize in e-business and technology management in British Academy of Management (BAM) Conference.

Feng Li is chair of e-business at the University of Newcastle upon Tyne Business School, UK. His research has focused on the interactions between information systems and emerging strategies, business models, and organizational designs. He is the author of two books and numerous journal articles, and he speaks regularly at international conferences and to business executives from both the private and public sectors. Professor Li is a member of several programs on ICTs, e-commerce/e-business, supply chain/value chain, and virtual teams. He has worked closely with companies in banking, telecommunications, manufacturing, retailing, electronics as well as the public sectors. He is the e-business SIG chair in British Academy of Management (BAM). His recent works on Internet banking and on telecommunications pricing models and value networks have been extensively reported by the media.

This case was previously published in the *International Journal of Cases on Electronic Commerce*, 1(2), p. 57, © 2005.

Chapter VIII

Developing Inter-Organizational Trust in Business-to-Business E-Commerce Participation:
Case Studies in the Automotive Industry

Pauline Ratnasingam, University of Vermont, USA

EXECUTIVE SUMMARY

Inter-organizational-systems such as EDI have been the main form of business-to business e-commerce participation in the automotive industry for the last two decades. Previous studies in EDI adoption mostly examined environmental, organizational and technological factors. This study draws insights developed within the sociology of technology, in which innovation is not simply a technical-rational process of solving problems, but involves economic, behavioral and political processes required for building inter-organizational trust. The transition to cooperative relationships between buyers and suppliers may be more difficult for automotive companies because of complexity, compatibility, long lead times and ingrained adversarial supplier relationships (Langfield-Smith & Greenwood, 1998). Therefore, trust is important as organizations need to cooperate, collaborate and communicate timely and relevant information, in order to facilitate EDI that entails not only technological proficiencies, but also trust between trading parties, so that business transactions are sent and received in an orderly fashion.

An analysis of the trust behaviors that influence EDI adoption will be useful for evaluating EDI participation. The aim of this study is to address the following intriguing questions:

- *How does trading partner trust impact EDI participation?*
- *How do issues relating to coercive power among trading partners impact inter-organizational trust? and*
- *What is the importance of trust within an inter-organizational dyad?*

Ford has been using EDI since the electronic data transmissions commenced in 1988. The aim of EDI is to communicate production requirements of five car manufacturers (namely, Ford, General Motors Holden, Toyota, Mitsubishi, and Nissan), to their component suppliers in order to meet the demands of the Australian and overseas motor vehicle markets. The automotive industry had more experience than other industries in developing inter-organizational relationships. Ford Australia was nationally and internationally popular because motor vehicles were exported to New Zealand and the Asia Pacific region.

BACKGROUND

EDI implementation at Ford started with the Button Car Plan in the mid-1980s. The objectives of the Button Car Plan included:

- Creating a timeframe to restructure and modernize (1985-1992);
- Increasing the industry's efficiency;
- Holding down vehicle price rises to no more than raises in the consumer price index;
- Minimizing disruption during restructuring; and
- Reducing job losses and providing job stability (Mackay & Rosier, 1996).

In 1984, the Federation Chamber Automotive Industries (FCAI) was formed to set up a standard procedure for adopting EDI. FCAI committee members discussed business issues, ramifications, and operations before negotiating with General Electrics in Information Services (GEIS) and Telstra Tradelink to create an EDI Value-Added-Network (VAN) system.

Ford was one of the earliest innovators of EDI inter-organizational network technology. In late 1987 and early 1988, the company conducted acceptance testing of EDI business transactions was carried out. Telstra developed the Tradelink software in 1988. EDI messages such as materials requirements schedule (MRS) and advanced shipping notice (ASN) were initially implemented followed by other documents. Thus, by 1997, EDI use at Ford was in a mature stage. Ford aimed to streamline its business processes and optimize its supply chain management activities. Ford implemented two EDI systems and many application systems across its five branches: Parts and Accessories, Original Equipment, Non-production, Purchasing, Ford Credit and Finance. Ford's parent company in America was two to three years ahead of their Australian counterparts and supervised EDI implementation in Australia.

The automotive industry remains a major segment of the Australian manufacturing sector, despite a general decline in the manufacturing output in Australia. It is particularly important in Victoria, where Ford Australia, General Motors Holden, and Toyota have their headquarters and principal assembly plants. Although it is only a small part of the global motor vehicle industry, the Australian automotive industry makes an important contribution to the gross domestic product of Australia. In this research, the original manufacturers are subsidiaries of large transnational corporations based in the USA or Japan.

Figure 1 demonstrates the flow of EDI transactions between Ford and Toyota (the manufacturers) and their first tier supplier (Patent Brakes and Replacement Ltd). For example, the supplier sends an advanced shipping notice (ASN) to the manufacturer before supplying the parts. At the same time, a copy of the ASN is sent to the Transport Company for the truck driver to deliver the right quantity. The truck driver also brings a copy of the ASN that was sent electronically to the manufacturer. The completed motor vehicle is sent to the finance company and they collaborate with motor vehicle dealers and arrange credit terms for selling the motor vehicles.

SETTING THE STAGE

EDI is one form of business-to-business e-commerce inter-organizational system (IOS) which transmits standard business documents electronically among trading partners. EDI allows firms' to fundamentally change the way they do business, thereby improving the firm's performance and enhancing its competitive advantages (Emmelhainz, 1990). While EDI clearly provides economic benefits, it may be costly to implement, particularly when an organization lacks hardware or software compatibility. Security becomes an important issue because EDI systems do not operate unilaterally. Organi-

Figure 1. EDI implementation at Ford and Patent, Brakes and Replacement Ltd.

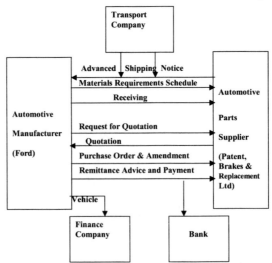

zations motivated to adopt EDI must either find similarly motivated trading partners or persuade and/or coerce their existing trading partners to adopt EDI (Hart & Saunders, 1998; Webster, 1995). One key barrier to this is the lack of trading partner trust derived from uncertainties, lack of open communications and information sharing (Cummings & Bromiley, 1996; Doney & Cannon, 1997; Ganesan, 1994; Gulati, 1995). Despite the assurances of technological security mechanisms, trading partners in business-to-business e-commerce do not seem to trust the "people side" of the transactions because of uncertainties. Uncertainties reduce confidence both in the reliability of business-to-business transactions transmitted electronically and, more importantly, in the trading parties themselves. For example, Scala and McGrath (1993), in their broad assessment of advantages and disadvantages of EDI, identified social and organizational issues that impact organizational culture, structure and low levels of adoption. The objective of this study is to investigate the importance of trading partner trust in EDI participation (adoption, integration and use).

The automotive industry provides an interesting focus for studying this topic because of the following reasons:

- The automotive industry has a well-developed supplier strategy, because it was the first Australian industry to introduce EDI on a coordinated industry-wide basis. For example, the automotive industry has been using EDI since electronic data transmissions commenced in 1988. Therefore, the automotive industry had more experience than other industries in developing trading partner relationships (Helper, 1991; Mackay & Rosier, 1996).
- It has been suggested that the transition to cooperative relationships between buyers and suppliers may be more difficult for automotive companies, due to high levels of complexity, compatibility, long lead times and ingrained adversarial supplier relationships of the past (Langfield-Smith & Greenwood, 1998). Japanese automotive companies have a long established history of developing relationships with suppliers based on dependence and cooperation. Unlike the Japanese, in western countries like Australia and the U.S. recognizing cooperative partnerships is a relatively recent phenomenon, and may be a distinct contrast to the adhoc relationships of the past (Helper, 1991). Choosing two automotive organizations namely, Ford Motor Company of Australia Limited, and their first tier supplier, Patent Brakes and Replacement Automotive Proprietary Limited in Australia, provides a better understanding of cooperative trading partner relationships and trust in EDI implementation.

CASE DESCRIPTION

The Ford Motor Company of Australia Limited (Ford Australia), located in Melbourne, Australia, is a subsidiary of the Ford Motor Company at Dearborn, Michigan, USA. Employing 9,000 workers, Ford Australia is the second largest manufacturing enterprise in Australia. Ford produces about 125,000 motor vehicles per year. It uses approximately 8,000 local parts and 250 imported parts from their 220 parts suppliers. Ford is the largest consumer of locally manufactured parts. It is currently running an inventory of about 10 days stock (although the stock level of some components replenished by JIT is smaller than this). Ford's main objective is to increase productivity and profitability by reducing costs.

Patent Brakes Replacement (PBR Ltd) is a large company with 1,100 employees and is a major supplier, principally supplying original equipment (OE) to Ford and Toyota. PBR in aggregate supplies up to 92% of component parts to the passenger motor vehicle (PMV) lines and/or spare parts divisions. PBR has two branches, namely Original Equipment (OE) and After Marketing Company (AMC).

PBR started adopting EDI when their manufacturers (Ford and Toyota) demanded high efficiencies in EDI operations. Table 1 presents a summary of the background information of the two cases Ford and Patent, Brakes and Replacement Ltd.

Driving Factors for Adopting EDI

Ford's objective for adopting EDI is to streamline its business processes and contribute to more efficient transactions across the supply chain. Implementing EDI and electronic trading was expected to bring about a number of benefits in the automotive industry. The benefits include improvements in general logistics, increased productivity, improved product quality, enhanced customer service and lower inventory requirements. The automotive organizations were able to eliminate manual re-keying of data, thus reaping economics of scale in time and labor savings.

Table 1. Background information of Ford, and Patent, Brakes and Replacement Ltd.

Background Information	Ford – Buyer	PBR Ltd First–Tier Supplier
Year Implemented EDI	Mid 1980s - 1989	1987
Type of EDI Technology	EDI/VANs	EDI/VANs
Type of Translation Software	Telstra Tradelink Software	Telstra Tradelink Software
Number of EDI Systems	2	3
Number of Staff Operating EDI Systems	2	6
Volume of Transactions	40-60 daily	5-10 daily
Types Transactions	Purchase Orders Advance Shipping Notice Remittance Advice Acknowledgment	Purchase Orders Advance Shipping Notice Monthly Statements
Number of Trading Partners	350	150
Number of Branches	5	2
Number of Employees	9000	1100
Size of Organization	Large	Large
Stage of IT Growth	Mature	Mature

EDI was seen as a tool to transmit standard structured messages electronically from a computer application in one location to another computer application in another location. Therefore, EDI is an enabling technology which allowed Ford to meet their business goals, and the analogy is the same as if one wishes to purchase a mobile telephone or a fax machine, EDI gave us competitive advantage. (Ford's EDI Project Leader)

The driving factors that led to EDI adoption include:

- Time was saved from a faster trading cycle, because trading partners do not have to re-key the information. Seventy percent of the output was treated as input into the receiving trading partner's system, contributing to savings in time and cost.
- Simplification of the business processes (via automation) eliminated the use of paper.
- Speed from savings in time derived from the standardized routines and structured EDI messages, increased productivity and thus profitability.

Table 2 presents a list of respondents who participated in the exploratory case study. Although, most of them were not directly involved in EDI adoption, they were employed for at least a decade and attended most of the meetings related to EDI implementation. The participants agreed that trust was important for EDI participation because business transactions had to be sent and received in an orderly fashion.

Table 2. Interview participants from the two case studies

Title of Participants	Name of Organization	Years of EDI Experience	Directly Involved in EDI Implementation	Number of Interview Sessions	Is Trust Important for EDI?
Project Leader Communications Operations Process Leadership	Ford Motor Co	15	Yes	5	Yes
Auditor	Ford Motor Co	10	No	2	Yes
General Accounting Manager	Ford Motor Co	12	Yes	3	Yes
IT Manager	Ford Motor Co	12	No	3	Yes
Supply Chain Management, Materials Planning and Logistics Core Group Management Manager	Ford Motor Co	10	No	2	Yes
FCAI Chairman and EDI Coordinator	PBR Ltd	15	Yes	5	Yes

CURRENT CHALLENGES FACING FORD AUSTRALIA AND PBR LTD

Technological Issues

Issues relating to streamlining advancedshipping notices (ASNs) with the actual physical shipment of goods were identified in EDI adoption. Ford currently requires about 95% of its part suppliers to send an advanced shipping notice (ASN) in advance of the actual physical shipment accompanying a printed delivery docket. The ASN pre-loads the receiving system, prints a "receipt list" and uses it to check the physical shipment. The ASN identifies the physical shipment with the delivery truck registration number, and uses it as a reference. Discussions with Ford materials management staff revealed the following technical problems with its current EDI systems.

- Use of the truck registration number effectively limits the system to parts that are delivered no more than once per day, and also causes problems when several suppliers' shipments are consolidated onto one truck;
- Ford's leading position in the Australian automotive industry and its increasing insistence on JIT deliveries, forced Ford's suppliers to be positioned less than 10 minutes drive away from the Ford plant. Ford currently polls its EDI/VAN service every 10 minutes, in order to retrieve the ASN data. As a result with parts that are being called by JIT, there is no guarantee that the ASN arrives before the physical shipments, thus causing delays and congestion in the production line; and
- The EDI/ASN process is dependent on computers at the supplier's site, and the VAN service at Ford.

Given the computer-dependent nature of the automotive industry operations, the first problem can be solved by using a unique identifier for the shipment bar coded on the delivery docket or cartons. The second problem can only be solved within the existing framework by polling the VANS more frequently, and imposing an expensive option at a cost of $A0.50 upwards per call.

Political Issues—Power Among Trading Partners

Power was seen as an important contextual factor in EDI adoption, because it was an important influence in the adoption of e-commerce and in building trust among trading partners. Power is "the capability of a firm to exert influence on another firm to act in a prescribed manner."

Ford applied power when its EDI network was introduced. Ford made it clear to its established suppliers that they should use EDI. Ford did provide its suppliers with initial training and software to run on IBM machines. Suppliers with incompatible systems or with no systems were requested to find appropriate solutions as quickly as possible. Clearly, this was a situation where coercive power exercised by Ford was seen in establishing connections that involved the expense of the suppliers buying new equipment (Ratnasingam, 2000). Dependence can arise due to limited supply alternatives or from an imbalance of power between suppliers and car manufacturers. Furthermore, the inconvenience of having to use Ford's system in addition to other systems for trading with other customers was another issue, especially at a time when the smaller suppliers were unaware of EDI's potential.

Similarly, Hart and Saunders (1997) suggested that in most cases the adoption of EDI is due to pressure from the more powerful trading partners, usually buyers. Their findings indicated that power was negatively related to the volume of EDI transactions, reflecting that while electronic networks may facilitate easier exchanges, they may not necessarily lead to increases in the frequency of business transactions. EDI not only affects the efficiency of coordination, but also power dependency and structural aspects of inter-organizational relationships. Thus, power exists on two levels: (1) as a motive, and (2) as a behavior.

It is quite clear from both the design and implementation of Telstra Tradelink, that Ford does not regard their trading partners as if they were partnerships made on equal basis, but relationships involving domination and their subordination. Companies who supply to Ford find their trading relationship coercive and the strictness of using their EDI system caused unnecessarily expense and inconvenience. The findings relating to power in the automotive industry reported that doing EDI with Ford has increased the costs of their trading relationship and has not reduced expenses in any way. Similarly, Ford's attitude towards their trading partners was revealingly expressed by the reactions of their suppliers across Europe. "The Spanish were extremely obedient. Ford is their bread and butter. When we say 'Jump,' they jump. The Germans gave us the most trouble. Among other things, they didn't like the dedicated network." (Webster, 1995, p. 34).

Ford's main objective was to gain competitive advantage by locking their suppliers into their system, and their competitors out of them.

We felt that we were coerced to adopt EDI, although initial support and directions via software for our IBM machines was given by Ford. (PBR Ltd EDI Coordinator)

Hence, the way power was used to influence trading partners determined the extent to which trust was built during EDI implementation.

Behavioral Issues—Performance Assessment

Ford possessed a set of punishments they used when their suppliers did not cooperate. A check on their suppliers' competencies, product quality, timeliness of delivery, service quality and how they resolved disputes were observed. The supplier performance checklist determined whether to renew the contracts of their suppliers.

Our suppliers do have to meet the standards outlined in the Suppliers' Performance Assessment. Although, our suppliers have been trading with us for a long time, we usually undertake a screening test to examine their credibility, technical ability and skills. A standard of 85% and above was expected in their performance. (Ford EDI Coordinator)

Trust Issues: Lack of Cooperation Among Trading Partners

The more likely they are perceived to use these punishments, the stronger will be their coercive sources of power. Examples of coercive sources of power an automotive manufacturer may exercise include slow delivery on vehicles, slow payment on warranty work, unfair distribution of vehicles, turndowns on warranty work, threat of termination and bureaucratic red tape. There is considerable evidence of coercion by large manufacturers to smaller suppliers to move to EDI, in order to suit information technology and business strategies of manufacturers. It is here where trust develops. Ford can either choose to see it proactively and renew their suppliers' contract or choose to punish their suppliers by terminating their contracts. The absence of collaboration or prior consensus about the structure, function, and design of these networks provided suppliers with little opportunities to develop their knowledge and expertise in EDI use. In the EDI user community, this practice has been associated with the catch phrase "EDI or die" meaning that suppliers are required to use the system or the manufacturer (Ford) will not trade with them at all. It is a practice that has been particularly prevalent among large retail outlets in United Kingdom (Webster, 1995).

Trading Partner Trust—Key Findings

The findings indicate that trust was embedded in the EDI adoption procedures, and was seen as an implicit factor, because trading partners were expected to behave in a rationale manner. Trading partner trust was rated high because trading partner performance significantly impacts EDI operations and system. For instance, the EDI via Value-Added-Network mailbox was shared by all trading partners, thus demanding confidentiality and integrity measures to be taken by all trading partners who were registered to use it. In some cases, the participants indicated that their status of trust was based on their management representation of knowledge of EDI implementation.

Trading Partner Trust at Ford

Mayer, Davis and Schoorman (1995, p. 712) defined trust as "the willingness of a party to be vulnerable to the actions of another party based on the expectation that the other will perform a particular action important to the trustor, irrespective of their ability to monitor or control that other party."

Trust is important for EDI operations and the participants agreed that trading partner trust is essential.

We define trust as a level of confidence we have in our suppliers in being honest, reliable, having integrity and not taking actions that is detrimental to our business. (Ford Communications and Operations Manager)

Two Types of Trading Partner Trust

Two types of trading partner trust were identified in this study. The first type of trust "soft trust or relationship trust," focuses on the trading partner relationship (that is between a manufacturer and a supplier).

We do not only communicate using EDI, but other means such as telephone, fax and email when there is a discrepancy. This related to communication openness as in high trust derived from information sharing and concern. We do not check the delivery of goods, due to consistency in the quality service provided by our suppliers. (Ford Supply Chain Management Materials Planning and Logistics Core Group Manager)

Prior history of trading partner relationships enabled Ford to make predictions about their suppliers' performance.

The second level of trust, "hard trust or technology trust," focuses on integrity issues with IT departments, and EDI/VANs infrastructure. Thus technology compatibility and organizational readiness were seen as important in EDI participation.

In addition, the following interactions led to trading partner trust:

* Increased communication during initial EDI adoption.

Although EDI was established in the 1980s, to reflect back on our initial implementing procedures, we would still print off the order, and fax the same order again. After sending the order via EDI we would call our suppliers to check if they have received it. (Ford Accounting Manager)

During the early stages of EDI implementation Ford relied heavily on the daily audit trail, and other feedback mechanisms such as fax and telephone:

* Information sharing on the potential use of EDI. The Advanced Shipping Notice is sent before the actual delivery of the parts arrive;
* Reliability of the trading partners, (that they did what they said they will do). Prior history of trading experiences enabled trading partners to depend on each other;
* Belief in trading partners' ability to perform the required task; and
* Maintaining confidentiality and privacy of business information. Functional acknowledgments with unique identifiers and authorized mechanisms (user IDs and passwords) were implemented.

Hence, beyond the apparent need for a cooperative relationship, trading partners formed a governance structure that brought about repeated encounters and used the passage of time to their advantage to build trust. These trust mechanisms, although coming from EDI, had a lot to do with trading partner interactions in the form of open communications and timely sharing of information that contributed to the smooth flow of EDI operations.

Therefore, trust plays a very important role in EDI for two main reasons:

* It encourages organizations to make investments necessary for electronic information exchange, which includes technical investments needed for supporting greater information exchange across organizational boundaries. This in turn contributes to improving inter-organizational coordination, in particular for EDI use and information-sharing requiring investments in computer integration at the time of EDI adoption. It is therefore important to reinforce trust during the EDI adoption process so that trading partners will be encouraged to make investments in computer integration, and over time will support expanded EDI use and information sharing; and
* It discourages opportunistic behavior, which clearly reduces the opportunity for greater information sharing over time. Here trust is important because it reduces the probability of a firm behaving in an opportunistic way. Hence, trust mitigates risks and by reducing risks it reinforces the opportunity to expand information sharing over time.

This study explored the impact of inter-organizational trust in EDI adoption between Ford Australia and their first tier supplier Patent, Brakes and Replacement Limited. The two case studies formed an inter-organizational-dyad between (a manufacturer and a supplier) in EDI participation paved the way to increased awareness and importance of trading partner trust in EDI. Implicit factors such as power among trading partners were found to impact trust among trading partners. Most of the participants agreed that their service-level agreements need to be amended in order to include trading partner trust development guidelines that will promote open communications, sharing of knowledge and information (that is accurate, timely, complete and relevant), thereby preventing privacy issues and encouraging good business practices. For example, trading partner agreements should encourage good business practices that will prevent trading partners from opportunistic behaviors.

The Future of the Australian Automotive Industry

Australia's automotive industry is moving closer to developing one of the largest industry-wide extranets seen in this country until now (in 1999). According to the new development, the Australian Automotive Network Exchange (AANX) project will specify and begin implementing a common TCP/IP network infrastructure for the Australian automotive industry. The FCAI committee manages the AANX project, with members including nominees of the four Australian care manufacturers—Ford, Holden, Mitsubishi and Toyota. The Federation of Automotive Product Manufacturers (FAPM), importers and suppliers were also involved in this project. Telstra and Optus have been invited to participate in the initiative, but both were unable to meet the industry's requirements. In addition, Telstra, with its X.400-based Tradelink network service is the current supplier of EDI, and links the Australian automotive industry. The decision to exclude Telstra will then raise a question on the future of the industry. The mission of the committee is to establish and govern a reliable and secure communication network capable of hosting applications of e-commerce and business-to-business transactions for the Australian automotive industry.

The supplier (PBR Executive) describes the AANX project as an auto industry intranet and indicated that it is the next development of the industry's EDI system. It will solve the main problems with doing EDI over the Internet, namely security and reliability. We are trying to duplicate precisely what they have in America and it looks like this is the way the rest of the world is going too (i.e., Japan and Europe). EDI is now becoming tired, and both it and our various other supply-chain links need to be brought into a Web-enabled e-commerce system.

REFERENCES

Cummings, L. L., & Bromiley, P (1996). The organizational trust inventory (OTI): Development and validation. In R. M. Kramer, & T. R. Tyler (Eds.), *Trust in organizations: Frontiers of theory and research* (pp. 302-220). Thousand Oaks, CA: Sage Publications.

Doney, P. M., & Cannon, J. P. (1997, April). An examination of the nature of trust in buyer-seller relationships. *Journal of Marketing*, 35-51.

Ganesan, S. (1994). Determinants of long-term orientation in buyer-seller relationships. *Journal of Marketing, 58,* 1-19.

Gulati, R. (1995). Does familiarity breed trust? The implications of repeated ties for contractual choice in alliances. *Academy of Management Journal, 38*(1), 85-112.

Hart, P., & Saunders, C. (1997). Power and trust: Critical factors in the adoption and use of electronic data interchange. *Organization Science, 8*(1), 23-42.

Helper, S. (1991). How much has really changed between U.S. automakers and their suppliers? *Sloan Management Review, 32*(4), 15-28.

Langfield-Smith, K., & Greenwood, M. R. (1998) Developing co-operative buyer-supplier relationships: A case study of Toyota. *Journal of Management Studies, 35*(3), 331-353.

Mackay, D., & Rosier, M. (1996). Measuring organizational benefits of EDI diffusion. *International Journal of Physical Distribution & Logistics Management, 26*(10), 60-78.

Mayer, R. C., Davis, J. H., & Schoorman, F. D. (1995). An integrative model of organizational trust. *Academy of Management Review, 20*(3), 709-734.

Ratnasingam, P. (2000). The influence of power on trading partner trust in electronic commerce. *Internet Research: Electronic Networking Applications and Policy, 10*(1), 56-62.

Scala, S., & McGrath, R., Jr. (1993). Advantages and disadvantages of electronic data interchange: An industry perspective. *Information & Management, 25*(2), 85-91.

Webster, J. (1995) Networks of collaboration or conflict? Electronic data interchange and power in the supply chain. *Journal of Strategic Information Systems, 4*(1), 31-42.

FURTHER READINGS

Emmelhainz, M. A. (1990). *A total management guide.* NCC Blackwell.

Frey, S. C., & Schlosser, M. M. (1993, Fall) ABB and Ford: Creating value through cooperation. *Sloan Management Review,* 65-72.

Raman, D. (1997). The Internet and EDI, What is EDI's place on the information superhighway? *Tenth International Bled Electronic Commerce Conference* (pp. 66-73).

Ratnasingam, P. (2000). The influence of power on trading partner trust in electronic commerce. *Internet Research: Electronic Networking Applications and Policy, 10*(1), 56-62.

Rayport, J. F., & Jaworski, B. J. (2001). *Electronic commerce.* McGraw-Hill/Irwin.

Ring, P. S., & Van de Ven, A. H. (1994). Developing processes of cooperative inter-organizational relationships. *Academy of Management Review, 19,* 90-118.

Saunders, C., & Clark, S. (1992). EDI adoption and implementation: A focus on inter-organizational linkages. *Information Resources Management Journal, 5*(1), 9-19.

Senn, J. A. (1996, Summer). Capitalizing on electronic commerce—The role of the Internet in electronic markets, getting on board the Internet. *Information Systems Management,* 15-25.

Senn, J. A. (1998). Expanding the reach of e-commerce, The Internet-EDI alternative. *Information Systems Management.*

Sullivan, J., Peterson, R. B., Kameda, N., & Shimada, J. (1981) The relationship between conflict resolution approaches and trust—A cross cultural study. *Academy of Management Journal, 24* (4), 803-815.

Sydow, J. (1998) Understanding the constitution of inter-organizational-trust. In C. Lane, & R. Bachmann (Eds.), *Trust within and between organizations, conceptual issues and empirical applications.*

GLOSSARY

- **EDI:** The computer-to-computer (application-to-application) exchange of standard formatted business documents transmitted over computer networks (Senn, 1996, p. 17).

- **EDI:** The structured exchange of information between applications in different companies (Raman, 1997, p. 67).

- **IOS:** Inter-Organizational-Systems (IOSs) is simply "an automated information system shared by two or more companies" implemented for efficient exchange of business transactions (Cash & Konsynski, 1985, p. 134).

- **B2B EC:** Refers to the full spectrum of electronic commerce that can occur between two organizations. Activities include purchasing and procurement, supplier management, inventory management, channel management, sales activities, payment management and service and support (Rayport & Jaworski, 2001).

- **TRUST:** Mayer, Davis, and Schoorman (1995) defined trust as "the willingness of a party to be vulnerable to the actions of another party based on the expectation that the other will perform a particular action important to the trustor, irrespective of the ability to monitor or control that other party."

- **IOT:** Inter-Organizational Trust is "the confidence of an organization in the reliability of other organizations regarding a given set of outcomes or events" (Sydow, 1997, p. 35). This study defines IOT as "the confidence in the reliability of two organizations in a possibly risky situation that all trading partners involved in the action will act competently and dutifully."

Pauline Ratnasingam is an assistant professor in the School of Business Administration, The University of Vermont, Burlington, Vermont. Before that she was a lecturer at Victoria University of Wellington, New Zealand. Her PhD dissertation examined the importance of inter-organizational trust in electronic commerce participation (extent of e-commerce adoption and integration). Her research interests include business risk management, electronic data interchange, electronic commerce, organizational behavior, inter-organizational relationships and trust. She has published several articles related to this area in conferences and refereed journals. She is an associate member of Association of Information Systems (AIS).

This case was previously published in *Annals of Cases on Information Technology*, Volume 4/ 2002, pp. 184-194, © 2002.

Chapter IX

Office Depot's
E-Commerce Evolution

In Lee, Western Illinois University, USA

EXECUTIVE SUMMARY

Office Depot Inc., founded in 1986, is currently known as one of the leaders in the office supplies industry. Office Depot's distribution channels include stores, direct mail, contract delivery, and electronic commerce. In the mid-1990s, three major office supplies retailers (Office Depot, Staples, and Office Max) dominated the office supplies market. The entry barriers to the new entrants were extremely high due to the three retailers' extensive distribution networks and physical stores. The competition among these retailers was also fierce in cities where all three stores existed. In 1997, Office Depot first introduced B2B e-commerce for larger corporate customers and realized that OfficeMax had already launched B2C e-commerce for the general public. In 1997, the executive committee of Office Depot worked with retail analysts and concluded that a full-scale move to e-commerce was an opportunity it must seize. To maintain the lead in the e-retailing race, Office Depot quickly launched B2C e-commerce in January of 1998. This case study investigates critical factors managers should take into consideration in adopting new e-commerce strategies and technologies that will leverage corporate resources.

COMPANY BACKGROUND

Office Depot is known as one of the leaders in the office supplies industry. Office Depot sells business machines, computers, computer software, and office furniture, while its business services include copying, printing, document reproduction, mailing, and shipping (http://www.vikingdirect.com/eu_content/eucorp/content/comp_history.htm). Office Depot's customers include individual customers, small office/home offices (SOHO), and medium-/large-sized businesses located in the U.S. and in 20 other countries around the world. Office Depot sells its products through multiple distribution channels, including more than 1,000 office supply stores, direct mail, global Internet sites, B2B e-commerce, and sales forces. Office Depot operates under the Office Depot®, The Office Place®, Viking Office Products®, Viking Direct®, and 4sure.com brand names.

While Office Depot is one of the leaders in the office supplies industry today, its beginnings were quite modest. Office Depot was founded in Delray Beach, Florida in 1986 and opened its first store in Fort Lauderdale. By the end of 1990, Office Depot had 173 stores in 27 states. That same year, Office Depot merged with The Office Club, Inc., becoming the largest office products retailer in North America. Domestic growth, however, was only one aspect of Office Depot's expansion in the early years. Office Depot expanded international markets as well. In early 1992, Office Depot acquired H.Q. Office International, Inc., which included the Great Canadian Office Supplies Warehouse chain in western Canada. Expanding steadily, Office Depot also opened new retail stores in Israel and Colombia under international licensing agreements.

As Office Depot expanded internationally, it also began to extend beyond its traditional markets. In 1993, Office Depot entered the contract stationer business by acquiring two market leaders: Wilson Stationary & Printing Company and Eastman Office Products Corporation. The merger of six additional contract stationers followed these acquisitions during 1994. Office Depot continued its steady international growth between 1995 and 1998. In 1998, Office Depot merged with Viking Office Products, a public company and the world's leading direct mail marketer of office products. The addition of Viking to the Office Depot organization not only vastly expanded Office Depot's international presence, but also made the company the leading provider of office products and services in the world.

In 1998, Office Depot began to leverage e-commerce aggressively, launching the first of a number of new public Web sites, www.officedepot.com. The Web site established Office Depot as the industry's e-retail leader, expanded its domestic e-commerce capabilities, and extended the range of products and services the company could offer its customers. In 1999, the company launched its first European e-commerce site, www.viking-direct.co.uk, in the UK.

In 2000, chief executive officer David Fuente stepped down, and Bruce Nelson was appointed the new chief executive officer. Nelson immediately undertook several new management initiatives geared to make Office Depot a more compelling place to work, shop, and invest. With a deliberate focus on improving the company's U.S. retail operations, expanding its international business, and growing its world-class e-commerce business, Office Depot made dramatic improvements in the management of its supply chain, inventory, and warehouse operations. Office Depot's timeline, recent financial performances, and management structure are included in the Appendices at the end of this case.

SETTING THE STAGE: EMERGENCE OF E-COMMERCE

In the mid-1990s, three major office supplies retailers (Office Depot, Staples, and Office Max) dominated the office supplies market. Staples, Inc. launched the office supplies superstore with the opening of its first store in Brighton (Boston), Massachusetts in May 1986. Office Depot and Staples were two of the three largest office supplies superstores in the country, competing in approximately 40 metropolitan areas. Office supplies superstores, unlike any other retail stores in the United States, offer consumers the convenience of one-stop shopping for a wide variety of office supplies, computers and computer-related products, and office furniture at discount prices. The typical superstores also offer a Copy Center that provides on-site copying, printing, and binding services.

The entry barriers to the new entrants were extremely high due to the three retailers' extensive distribution networks, brand name recognition, and physical stores. Office Depot tried unsuccessfully to merge with Staples in 1997. Office Depot had hoped that by joining forces it could fight off competitors like Wal-Mart (Stires, 2001). But the Federal Trade Commission voted 4-1 to block the proposed merger, charging that combining the two leading office supplies superstores would be anticompetitive and bring higher consumer prices. The ruling was damaging to Office Depot, which recently lost a significant market share to both Staples and OfficeMax.

Furthermore, e-commerce was rapidly shifting the balance of powers among competitive forces in the office supplies industry. In early 1997, Office Depot realized that online sales would explode soon and felt that it was running behind. Traditional competitors, Staples and OfficeMax, had also been serious about e-commerce. Staples was planning to launch its B2C e-commerce Web site in 1998. OfficeMax already launched an e-commerce Web site in 1995. A growing number of customers became comfortable with the use of the Internet applications and were willing to buy online.

In addition to the potential entry into the office supplies market by Amazon.com, a number of small-sized e-retailers, such as Opivotal.com and BuyOnlineNow.com, had entered or planned to enter into the office supplies market. E-commerce was especially suitable in the office supplies industry since most office supplies products are commodity-type and standardized. These types of products include computer accessories, printer cartridges, office paper, and transparency films. The demand for office supplies came from offices, schools, universities, and individual customers, with the largest demand coming from offices.

CASE DESCRIPTION

B2B and B2C E-Commerce

Office Depot's e-commerce venture evolved from a 1994 pilot study at Massachusetts Institute of Technology (MIT) to full-scale B2C e-commerce over four years. In 1994, Office Depot took part in an experiment initiated by MIT in which a group of MIT's suppliers would build Web sites that MIT would make purchases from (Berkman, 2001). This experiment was an opportunity to test an e-commerce potential as a new distribution channel well ahead of other competitors.

In the 1997, Office Depot first introduced private B2B e-commerce for large corporate customers. When Office Depot decided in 1997 to launch a B2C e-commerce for individual customers and small businesses, it decided not to use a return-on-investment (ROI) analysis, which is one of the most popular methods in a large project evaluation. Instead, Office Depot's executive committee made a strategic decision on the e-commerce investment. The committee worked with industry analysts and concluded that a move to the B2B e-commerce was an opportunity it could not lose. The committee believed that the benefits of B2C e-commerce could be both strategic and operational: low order processing costs; brand recognition; business efficiency and economy of scale; improved customer service; market extension to locations where no office supplies stores exist; reduced labor cost due to streamlined internal process; and improved information systems integration. To keep the lead in the e-commerce race, Office Depot quickly launched B2C e-commerce in January 1998 (Sharon, 1998).

In 1997, Office Depot already had the technology infrastructure in place to make an e-commerce venture move fast. Bill Seltzer, Office Depot's executive vice president and CIO in 1997, believed that B2B and B2C e-commerce would fit Office Depot's business model very well because Office Depot already had a strong distribution network and a technology infrastructure. Bill Seltzer identified that the order-fulfillment and back-end processes of its existing catalog business would be the same for the e-commerce processes. Therefore, the e-commerce systems would be easily integrated with the back-end information systems and database that supported the catalog channel. However, since there was no solid infrastructure for the front-end side e-commerce, significant resources were needed for the development of the e-commerce systems, tools, and procedures.

E-Commerce Organization Structure

Traditional retailers have two options on an e-commerce organizational structure: an online division and a spin-off. Some arguments for creating an online division include use of complementary assets, sharing of technological resources, and ease of channel coordination. On the other hand, advantages of the spin-off strategy include new culture, independent organizational structure, and flexible reward systems that are suitable to the e-commerce environment.

Evidence showed that a misdirected e-commerce strategy led to costly and frequent revisions of e-commerce organizational structure. Kmart and Wal-Mart experienced a costly revision of their e-commerce organizational structure. Kmart initially created a spin-off entity, BlueLight.com, in December 1999 as a joint venture between Kmart and

Softbank Venture Capital. After Kmart withdrew from a planned initial public offering (IPO) for BlueLight.com in 2000 due to the e-commerce shakeout, it acquired all of the interests of BlueLight.com in 2001.

Walmart.com is another example of the costly revision of an e-commerce organizational structure. Walmart.com was established in January 2000 as an independent company operating as a joint venture between Wal-Mart and Accel Partners. In 2001, Wal-Mart acquired all the minority interest in Walmart.com in order to establish the tight integration between its e-commerce entity and physical stores. These costly reorganizations could have been avoided if they had adequately analyzed the external environment and internal organization before the e-commerce strategy development.

To the contrary of the spin-off approach that most major retailers adopted in the late 1990s, Office Depot created an online division that could leverage its internal resources to the largest extent. Office Depot viewed the e-commerce as the backbone of the company's supply chain (Landau, 2002). According to Monica Luechtefeld, Executive Vice President of E-Commerce at Office Depot, Office Depot decided early on that its e-commerce channel would not be an independent entity but a gateway into all of Office Depot's other sales channels. To minimize channel conflicts, strong coordination mechanisms were installed and business process redesign was initiated. Office Depot's e-commerce did not undercut store prices. Office Depot believed that the advantages of the e-commerce were not the cheapest price but service and convenience (Warner et al., 1999). Web-based transactions were also built into compensation plans for the sales representatives, instantly resolving conflicts over who would get credit for which orders (Tischler, 2002).

E-Commerce Technology Infrastructure

In 1997, Office Depot had a highly centralized IT group where IT professionals collaborated closely (Berkman, 2001). All sales channels were tied together with a sophisticated multi-tiered management process. Bill Seltzer, who led a 500-person IT staff, led the channel integration initiative built around Web connectivity and data warehouse. Office Depot deliberately managed its technology investment to deliver seamless multi-channel experience to customers. Bruce Nelson said "If the customer sees it and touches it, we're going to develop it ourselves, and cost is not a consideration." The heavy investment in in-house application development was easily justified when the newly developed systems could retain customers and encourage them to interact with the company through the multiple channels. On the other hand, Office Depot was willing to use commercial application software for standardized internal business processes, such as data warehouse and other back-end systems.

Development of an e-commerce technology infrastructure created a significant challenge for the seven-person information technology team that developed the e-commerce Web site. Office Depot's IT infrastructure was a balanced combination of object-oriented technology (Java), data warehouse, extranet for suppliers, intranet, commercial software, in-house developed information systems, communications network for Internet, and the e-commerce applications. Office Depot had consciously developed its IT infrastructure to deliver consistency and convenience to customers (Carr, 2001). Office Depot's hardware included three clustered IBM MVS mainframes, AS/400 servers, and custom-developed components running fully integrated accounting, inventory management, financial management, and sales management systems. Data warehouse and data mining systems were developed to measure business performance and to analyze customers' purchase behaviors.

Bill Seltzer developed the IT strategy around flexibility that was based on the enterprise-wide data architecture. Office Depot used Microsoft's COM-plus as a component platform as well as a messaging technology to move data among legacy systems. Object-oriented languages and component technologies offered methods and tools for achieving code reuse. By centralizing the development of most core business components, Office Depot was able to incorporate them into different front-end systems for stores, call centers, and e-commerce Web sites.

Office Depot also emphasized scalability because it would be easier to add new features onto a simple clean system. Due to these enterprise-wide data architecture and scalability, Office Depot's e-commerce channel was able to quickly integrate with the company's various sales and distribution channels and its back-end systems that did not distinguish between channels. All front-end systems, regardless of the channels, were integrated with the back-end systems, and the information was consistent throughout no matter what data was accessed.

E-Commerce Implementation

To keep the lead in the e-retailing race, Office Depot quickly launched a B2C e-commerce Web site in January 1998, 11 months ahead of the Staples.com debut (Joachim, 1998). Office Depot outsourced the design of the Web site to Studio Verso in San Francisco after determining it did not have the expertise to pursue in-house development. Officedepot.com ran on IBM AS/400 computers and Microsoft software, including Internet Information Server, Transaction Server, and SQL Server. The Web site allowed users to find specific products by keyword or numbers as well as by browsing the catalog.

The new B2C e-commerce Web site took advantage of capital investment in general corporate information systems. Office Depot's Web site tied the e-commerce front-end to the company's inventory and order management systems, and conducted real-time inventory checks to ensure stock was available nearby. Office Depot's customer-centric e-commerce systems were intended to make customers so satisfied with their online shopping experience that they would not bother looking elsewhere on the Internet to save a few pennies. Customers were able to check warehouse inventory in real-time, place orders online, pay for orders online, and arrange for returns at a local store.

Although Office Depot did not reveal how much it had spent for the e-commerce promotion in 1998, analysts estimated that Office Depot invested nearly $10 million in efforts to encourage customers to place orders online. Since the beginning of 1998, Office Depot consistently drove more business to the e-commerce than its competitors. While many retailers had difficulty in transforming their traditional brick-and-mortar businesses into profitable click-and-mortar businesses, Office Depot was one of the few profitable e-retailers. Office Depot was the most successful at e-commerce among the office superstores (Troy, 1999). Office Depot owed much of its success in the e-commerce to its nationwide network of 750 superstores, 30 warehouses, and $1.3 billion in goods (Rocks, 1999).

Office Depot benchmarked key competitors in terms of Web performance through Keynote Systems' performance monitoring service to rate its site availability, download times, and transaction speeds against 40 other companies, including competitors, such as Staples and OfficeMax everyday (Wilder, 2000). Office Depot fully integrated its e-commerce systems with its existing distribution centers. Online orders were filled from the same distribution centers that supported physical stores and call centers. Office Depot's internal research showed that customers who bought through multiple channels (catalog and store; or catalog and Web) tended to be more loyal and buy about 30% more products.

Office Depot decided to launch a product and service differentiation strategy in an effort to reduce price sensitivity of the commodity-type office supplies. Office Depot's e-commerce channel did not undercut store prices by ensuring that prices are the same across channels. Office Depot created e-commerce partnerships with major suppliers to keep them from disintermediating. Office Depot set up customized Web pages for 37,000 corporate customers with parameters that provided different customers with various degrees of freedom to buy supplies.

Office Depot also used Web technology to speed internal processes (Violino, 1999). Its intranet, which let employees access a variety of human resources information, e-mail, and applications from desktops, had been reducing paperwork and cutting process time. An online training program, called Office Depot University, reduced cycle times for management and employee training. Unlike the vast majority of pure-play e-commerce companies, Office Depot had been widely considered to be the leader in the online office supplies market (Boyler & Olson, 2002).

CHALLENGES FACING OFFICE DEPOT

Though Office Depot took the initiative in e-commerce and started toward achieving its goals, it had been struggling with the declining profit in 2000. "Our overall financial results were disappointing in 2000," said Bruce Nelson. Total company sales increased 13% to $11.6 billion from $10.3 billion in the year-earlier period. Worldwide store sales increased 7%, but earnings per share, including one-time charges and credits, decreased to $0.16 from $0.69 in 1999. Net income decreased to $49.3 million from $257.6 million in 1999.

One of the 2001 goals for Office Depot was to expand the company's e-commerce business. Implementing the right e-commerce strategy and technology was of the utmost importance for Office Depot, and Bruce Nelson reviewed several options including investments in emerging e-commerce technologies, strategic partnerships, and business process re-engineering. He believed that a constant innovation in technology and management practice was needed to maintain their leadership in e-commerce.

Strategic Alliance

In the early 2000s, many traditional retailers struggling to develop an e-commerce application sought out the expertise of Amazon.com which had baffled retailers with its best-of-breed technology, brand reputation, and built-in traffic. Some of the successful strategic alliances with Amazon.com include Toys "R" Us and Borders Group. In August 2000, Toys "R" Us created a strategic partnership with Amazon. Amazon took over the order fulfillment and Web operations for the online store of Toys "R" Us. The Toysrus.com

Copyright © 2006, Idea Group Inc. Copying or distributing in print or electronic forms without written permission of Idea Group Inc. is prohibited.

and Amazon.com alliance was created to maximize operating efficiencies and provide meaningful benefits to consumers. Borders Group, struggling to keep pace with competitor Barnes & Noble, created a partnership with Amazon.com in April 2001. This deal marked the second time that Amazon has teamed with a traditional retailer. The alliance brought together the highly complementary corporate resources—one in brick-and-mortar retailing, the other in e-commerce—to create a better shopping experience.

The strategic partnership was also an important initiative for Office Depot. Office Depot created a lot of strategic partnerships with other companies. These companies include consumer magazine *PC World*, Stamps.com, PurchasePro.com, and America Online Inc. Under the agreement, these companies formed a cobranded business site, offering online office products to small-business customers. To expand the office supplies market, Office Depot was considering the creation of a strategic alliance with Amazon.com. The nature of the strategic alliance with Amazon.com would be quite different from the strategic alliances Office Depot had created in the past because Amazon.com was a general purpose e-retailer. Amazon.com was also aggressively looking to expand selection for their customers and expanding the strategic alliance with other major retailers.

Re-Engineering the Business Processes Toward a Web-Enabled Company

By the end of 2000, Office Depot had 1,020 office supply stores in the United States, Canada, and nine other countries. Web sites were also established in nine countries. Office Depot was the leader in office supplies in 2000 sales, but it was struggling with both stores and inventory that were performing poorly. Because Office Depot simply ventured into markets that were already saturated with competitors, a lot of its stores had been either losing money to an unacceptable level or earning sub-par returns on investment. The surviving stores also needed to improve financial performance. "We're getting out of markets we never had a chance of getting any return on," says Bruce Nelson.

Office Depot had been taking orders through virtually every channel including stores, catalogs, phone, fax, direct sales, and the Web. In 2000, its national delivery network included over 2,000 trucks, 25 domestic delivery centers, more than 60 local sales offices, 8 regional call centers, a state-of-the-art public Web site, and a customized Web site for corporate customers. The challenge was keeping up with ever-increasing transaction volume from the corporate customers and the general public. Tracking all its inventories, invoices, outstanding bills, and custom sales arrangements was a time-consuming but critical task. In order to turn around the disappointing financial performance, Bill Seltzer began looking for ways to internalize the power of the Internet in order to redesign the complex web of the entire business processes.

The Business Services Group at Office Depot was tasked with the responsibility for redesigning the downstream supply chain (webMethods, 2003). A major task was enabling the corporate customers to view product catalogs, check inventory and prices, and submit purchase orders electronically. All transactions were previously completed using the proprietary electronic data interchange (EDI) technology, which was not only a cumbersome process, but also required expensive connections to value added networks (VANs). While EDI was acceptable for large corporate customers with sophisticated IT capabilities, Office Depot was unable to extend its solution to small- and medium-sized corporate customers that lacked financial resources to invest in the proprietary EDI technology.

The most significant challenge in redesigning the downstream supply chain was that the purchase orders received from different corporate customers differed in format, requiring complicated transformations and manual intervention to convert every purchase order into formats compatible with Office Depot's internal systems. Moreover, transactions were not completed in real-time, thereby impeding Office Depot's ability to provide immediate details on product availability and pricing.

Office Depot has had a tradition of fostering an environment where recognition, innovation, communication, and the entrepreneurial spirit of each employee are encouraged and rewarded (Cisco, 2001). To support this environment, Office Depot needed a way to disseminate timely and accurate information to its more than 48,000 employees worldwide. Office Depot wanted a technology solution to truly empower its workforce while at the same time increasing accountability and ownership. Bruce Nelson explained:

Through technology we can give our employees access to more comprehensive information more quickly than we could in the past. And we can deliver it at a lower cost. Technology provides the power to make better decisions more quickly and cost-effectively by eliminating the steps and reducing the errors that are inevitable with all paper-based, manual processes. Our ultimate goal is to streamline our entire business and rededicate the savings to improve customer service.

Due to the complex and intensive re-engineering requirements, Bill Seltzer recognized the need to identify critical success factors for the achievement of re-engineering the business processes toward a Web-enabled company. Bill Seltzer was interested in a scalable technology infrastructure for the future with the goal of becoming a totally integrated Web-enabled organization, completely connected via networked systems. At the time of declining corporate performance, he became very concerned with the justification of the investment in the re-engineering process to Bruce Nelson.

REFERENCES

Berkman, E. (2001, February 1). Clicklayer. *CIO Magazine*, 92-100.

Boyler, K. K., & Olson, J. R. (2002). Drivers of Internet purchasing success. *Production & Operations Management, 11*(4), 480-498.

Carr, D. F. (2001, December 10). *Case 007: Office Depot—Making liquid code.* Retrieved January 2, 2005, from http://www.baselinemag.com/article2/0,3959,656620,00.asp

Cisco success stories: Office Depot. (2001). Retrieved on January 2, 2005, from http://www.cisco.com/en/US/about/success-stories/industry/retail.html

Joachim, D. (1998). Office Depot moves to Web sales. *InternetWeek.com*. Retrieved January 2, 2005, from http://www.internetweek.com/news/news0114-3.htm

Landau, M. D. (2002, May). Sweet revenge. *Chief Executive, 178*, 58-62.

Office Depot history. Retrieved January 2, 2005, from http://www.vikingdirect.com/eu_content/eucorp/content/comp_history.htm

Rocks, D. (1999, September). Why Office Depot loves the net. *Business Week, 3648,* EB66-EB68.

Sharon, M. (1998, January 16). *Office Depot leverages corporate e-commerce effort with online storefront.* Retrieved on January 2, 2005, from http://www.computer world.com/news/1998/story/0,11280,19613,00.html

Stires, D. (2001, February 19). Office Depot finds an e-business that works. *Fortune, 143*(4), 232.

Tischler, L. (2002, November). Monica Luechtefeld makes the net click. *Fast Company, 64,* 122-128.

Troy, M. (1999, December 13). Office supplies: Clicks-and-mortar dominates—For now. *Discount Store News, 38*(23), 57.

Violino, B. (1999, December 13). Office depot builds winning strategy on the Web. *Informationweek, 765,* 84-86.

Warner, M., Roth, D., Schonfeld, E., et al. (1999, November 8). 10 companies that get it. *Fortune, 140*(9), 115-117.

webMethods success stories: Office Depot. (2003). Retrieved on January 2, 2005, from http://www.webmethods.com/PDF/Office_Depot_ss.pdf

Wilder, C. (2000, September 11). Profile: Office Depot Inc.—E-commerce pays off for Office Depot. *Informationweek, 803,* 360.

APPENDIXES

Appendix 1: Timeline

1986	Office Depot, Inc. founded in Florida by Pat Sher, Jack Kopkin and Stephen Dougherty. Opened our first store in Fort Lauderdale, Florida.
1988	Initial public offering of common stock. Introduced full service Copy & Print Center in our stores.
1990	Opened, under the Viking brand, our first distribution center in the United Kingdom.
1991	Acquisition of The Office Club, Inc.
1992	Acquisition of H.Q. Office International, Inc., including the Great Canadian Office Supplies Warehouse stores, in western Canada.
1993	Entrance into the contract stationer business via the acquisition of two leading Contract stationers: Wilson Stationary & Printing Company and Eastman Office Products Corporation. Opened, under the Viking brand, our first call center and distribution center in Australia.
1994	Opened, through separate international licensing agreements, first Office Depot stores in Israel and Colombia.
1995	Opened, through an international licensing agreement, first Office Depot store in Poland. Opened, through a joint venture agreement, first Office Depot store in Mexico. Opened, under the Viking brand, our first distribution center in Germany and Ireland and first call center in The Netherlands.
1996	Opened, through a joint venture agreement, first Office Depot store in France. Opened, under the Viking brand, our first distribution center in The Netherlands.
1997	Opened, through separate international licensing agreements, first Office Depot stores in Hungary and Thailand. Opened, through a joint venture agreement, first Office Depot store in Japan. Opened, under the Viking brand, our first call center in Austria.
1998	Launched www.officedepot.com public web site. Viking Office Products becomes wholly owned subsidiary of Office Depot. Acquired remaining 50% of our French joint venture operations. Marketing alliance with Telepost, Inc. to offer Web based teleconferencing, presentation and messaging services on OfficeDepot.com Opened, under the Viking brand, our first call center and distribution center in Italy.
1999	Acquired remaining 50% of our Japanese joint venture operations. Join forces with UPS to offer shipping services in our stores. Viking launched its first European e-commerce Web site, www.viking-direct.uk.co, in the United Kingdom. Viking began business in Japan and opened our first call center and distribution center.
2000	Viking launched e-commerce sites in Germany, www.viking.de, The Netherlands, www.vikingdirect.nl, Italy, www.vikingop.it, Japan, www.vikingop.co.jp, Australia, www.vikingop.com.au, and France, www.vikingdirect.fr . Office Depot launched e-commerce site in Japan, www.officedepot.co.jp and France, www.officedepot.fr. European Business Services Division is created to better service medium to large sized corporate accounts in Europe through specialized sales forces, individualized pricing for key corporate accounts, and overnight order fulfillment. Office Depot launched Vendor Extranet to provide Office Depot suppliers with a secured Internet access to monitor critical business information between both parties.

Appendix 2: Financial Highlights

	1999	1998	1997	1996	1995
Income Statement Data:					
(In thousands, except per share data)					
Sales	**\$10,263,280**	\$8,997,738	\$8,100,319	\$7,250,931	\$6,233,985
Operating Profit[1]	**413,373**	404,759	398,881	343,060	328,669
Net Earnings	**257,638**	233,196	234,861	196,218	185,060
Diluted Earnings Per Share[2]	**0.69**	0.61	0.62	0.53	0.50
Shares Outstanding for Diluted EPS	**393,657**	402,319	394,930	393,855	388,461
Balance Sheet Data:					
(In thousands)					
Working Capital[1]	**\$ 687,007**	\$1,293,370	\$1,093,463	\$ 860,280	\$ 836,761
Total Asset[1]	**4,276,183**	4,025,283	3,498,891	3,186,630	2,891,390
Common Stockholders' Equity	**1,907,720**	2,028,879	1,717,638	1,469,110	1,238,820

(1) We have reclassified certain amounts in our prior year financial statements to conform with our current year presentation. (2) Earnings per share previously reported for 1995 through 1998 have been restated to reflect the three-for-two stock split declared on February 24, 1999. Source: Office Depot 1999 Annual Report. Retrieved January 9, 2004, from http://www.of

Appendix 3: Managerial Structure

Corporate Directors and Officers

Directors

DAVID I. FUENTE[3]	**NEIL AUSTRIAN**[2]	**JAMES L. HESKETT**[1,3]
Chairman of the Board	Chairman	Professor Emeritus
Chief Executive Officer	iWon.com	Harvard Business School
Office Depot, Inc.	**LEE A. AULT, III**[1]	**MICHAEL J. MYERS**[1]
IRWIN HELFORD	Chairman of the Board	President
Vice Chairman – Office Depot, Inc.	In-Q-Tel, Inc.	First Century Partners
Chairman Emeritus – Viking Office	**CYNTHIA R. COHEN**[2,3]	**FRANK P. SCRUGGS, JR.**[1]
Products	President	Shareholder
BRUCE NELSON	Strategic Mindshare	Greenberg Traurig
President – Office Depot	**W. SCOTT HEDRICK**[2]	**PETER J. SOLOMON**[3]
International	General Partner	Chairman of the Board
President, CEO – Viking Office	InterWest Partners	Chief Executive Officer
Products		Peter J. Solomon Company

1. Member of Audit Committee
2. Member of Compensation Committee
3. Member of Governance Committee

(continued on next page)

Corporate Officers

DAVID I. FUENTE Chairman and Chief Executive Officer **SHAWN McGHEE** President, North America **BRUCE NELSON** President – Office Depot International President, CEO – Viking Office Products	**BARRY GOLDSTEIN** Executive Vice President, Finance & Chief Financial Officer **THOMAS KROEGER** Executive Vice President Human Resources **WILLIAM SELTZER** Executive Vice President Chief Information Officer	**CHARLES BROWN** Sr. Vice President, Finance Controller **DAVID FANNIN** Sr. Vice President, General Counsel & Secretary

Operating Officers

STEVEN EMBREE Executive Vice President Merchandising **ROBERT KELLER** Executive Vice President Business Services Division **KEVIN PHILLIPS** Executive Vice President Stores **THOMAS SHORTT** Executive Vice President Supply Chain Management **ROLF VAN KALDEKERKEN** Executive Vice President Europe **FRED ABT** Sr. Vice President Marketing – Asia, Australia & Latin America	**GAYLE AERTKER** Sr. Vice President Real Estate **JEFF AIKEN** Sr. Vice President Tax **KEITH BIBELHAUSEN** Sr. Vice President Stores – Eastern Division **ROBERT CONKLIN** Sr. Vice President MIS Operations **GRAHAM CUNDICK** Sr. Vice President Marketing – Europe	**DAVID GUZMAN** Sr. Vice President MIS Development **MARK HOLIFIELD** Sr. Vice President Supply Chain Management **MARY HULTGREN** Sr. Vice President Stores – Western Division **MONICA LUECHTEFELD** Sr. Vice President Electronic Commerce **TIM TOEWS** Sr. Vice President International Systems Development

Source: 1999 Office Depot Annual Report

In Lee is an associate professor in the Department of Information Management and Decision Sciences in the College of Business and Technology at Western Illinois University. He received an MBA from the University of Texas at Austin and a PhD from the University of Illinois at Urbana - Champaign. His current research interests include e-commerce technology development and management, agent-oriented enterprise modeling, and intelligent simulation systems. He has published his research in such journals as IEEE Transactions on Systems, Man, and Cybernetics, Computers and Operations Research, Computers and Industrial Engineering, Business Process Management Journal, Journal of Applied Systems Studies, International Journal of Simulation and Process Modeling, *and* Journal of Electronic Commerce in Organizations.

This case was previously published in *International Journal of Cases on Electronic Commerce*, 1(2), pp. 44-56, © 2005.

Chapter X

Implementation Management of an E-Commerce-Enabled Enterprise Information System:
A Case Study at Texas Instruments

R. P. Sundarraj, Clark University, USA

Joseph Sarkis, Clark University, USA

EXECUTIVE SUMMARY

This chapter presents a case study of an overview of the efforts of Texas Instrument's (TI's) internal and external ERP implementation, with a focus on linking its ERP system in a global e-commerce setting. This linkage is especially important since it had been stated in TI's strategic plan as an objective of this project to provide visibility of the ERP system to external constituents via Web linkages along with the objective of standardizing internal processes and important information technology systems to support market needs. Thus, its ERP system is central to managing its supply chain and B2B e-commerce linkages from both a customer and supplier perspective. Issues faced by TI are clearly outlined with future questions also posed in the final section.

INTRODUCTION

The integration of enterprise systems and the supply chain to an organization is becoming more critical in an ever-changing, globally competitive environment. As markets mature and customer preferences become more diverse and specific, quick response to those needs is required to maintain competitive advantage. This quick response will require close relationships, especially communications and information sharing among integrated internal functional groups, as well as the suppliers and customers of an organization. Texas Instruments (TI), headquartered in Dallas, Texas, is one organization that has come to realize this requirement for building and maintaining its competitive edge. One strategic decision made by the organization was to implement an enterprise resource planning (ERP) system with a focus on linking it with a global electronic commerce (e-commerce) setting.

This case study provides an overview of the efforts of TI's internal and external ERP implementation that led to over 70% of the transactions being conducted in a global e-commerce setting. TI's strategic goals include providing visibility of the ERP system to external constituents via Web linkages and standardizing internal processes and information technology to support market need. The e-commerce linkage is especially important in achieving these goals. Thus, TI's ERP system is central to managing its supply chain and Web e-commerce linkages from both a customer and supplier perspective.

In this situation there were a number of major players, including project management direction from Andersen Consulting Services, software vendors such as SAP and i2 Technologies, hardware vendors such as Sun Microsystems, and various suppliers and customers of TI. Part of the process involved outsourcing some of TI's internal information systems capabilities to these vendors, especially Andersen Consulting.

The various stages of implementation from adoption to preparation and operation are detailed as separate sections. At each stage of the implementation TI used performance metrics to manage the process. We also provide an overview of how these performance metrics played a role in the implementation.

STRATEGIC SYSTEMS IMPLEMENTATION BACKGROUND

Much research has been undertaken to develop a better understanding of IT implementation and to assess its contribution to improving organizational efficiency. A meta-analysis of IT implementation research (Lai & Mahapatra, 1997) indicates that there is shift in emphasis from studying individual IT to organizational and inter-organizational systems. Since an ERP system has long-term and broad organizational implications, strategic planning is key to the successful management of such systems. There is an extensive body of literature related to strategic planning. Critical antecedents to developing a successful strategic plan are (Lederer & Salmela, 1996; Lederer & Sethi, 1992):

1.   External and internal environments,
2.   Planning resources and processes, and
3.   An information plan that actually gets implemented.

Figure 1. Timeline of TI's ERP implementation

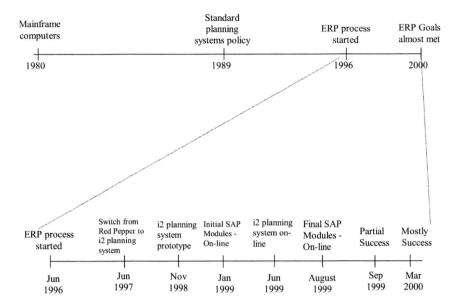

These constructs provide a theory of strategic information systems planning and are important to both researchers and practitioners involved with planning.

By borrowing from the literature on the management of advanced manufacturing technologies (Meredith, 1987; Sarkis & Lin, 1994; Small & Yasin, 1997), a process-oriented framework for ERP management is presented (see Figure 1). As indicated in the figure, the process suggested by this framework is iterative, in the sense that it allows for higher level strategies and processes to be reformulated when they are discovered to be incompatible with lower level systems and configurations, and vice versa.

Strategy Formulation and Integration

Strategic justification frameworks should begin at the upper levels of management. The technology selected should fit within the vision, goals and strategic objectives of the organization. An organization should undergo a SWOT-MOSP process in which it assesses its Strengths and Weaknesses in the light of environmental Opportunities and Threats, then develops its Missions, Objectives, Strategies and Policies. One of the results of this step in the process is determination of an organization's core competencies that need specific technology support.

Process Planning and Systems Design

At the next level is the initiation of process plans that support the organizational competencies identified earlier and that in turn get supported by the chosen system (ERP or otherwise). Also known as the reengineering phase, three studies are usually undertaken at this stage, and they are named AS-IS, SHOULD-BE and TO-BE.

The AS-IS study provides baseline measures for later justification purposes and provides measures for post-implementation auditing. The SHOULD-BE study tries to exhibit how the current system should function after non-automation/non-hard technology improvements (e.g., total quality management) are instituted; a currently disordered system will lead to a disordered ERP system as well. The TO-BE study is used to define the system necessary to meet the objectives set forth by the strategic units.

System Evaluation and Justification

Here, analysis focuses on the economic, technical, and operational feasibility and justification of the system. The justification step should consider many different types of factors—tangible, intangible, financial, quantitative, and qualitative. Since the analysis of tangible factors (e.g., financial) is well-studied using methods such as Return on Investment (ROI), our focus will be on the evaluation of intangible factors.

System Configuration

An ERP system has some of the characteristics of packaged software such as Microsoft Excel and some of those of custom-built ones. It certainly is not designed and programmed for the exclusive use of one organization nor is its implementation and management as easy as that of packaged software. Each ERP software company is likely to have its own business model in the design of its package. As a packaged software system, there are likely to be discrepancies (at the detailed level) between the needs of an organization and the features of the software (Lucas, Walton, & Ginzburg, 1988). Hence, a significant amount of effort can be expected to configure the system or the organizational processes in order to produce an alignment between them.

System Implementation

The implementation stage can be classified into: startup, project management and a migration handling the switchover from the old to the new system. ERP systems force large-scale overhaul of business processes and, therefore, their implementation needs to be supported by appropriate change management approaches (Markus and Benjamin, 1996). Another key concern of implementation is that of systems integration, in which multiple types of subsystems, platforms and interfaces must be integrated over diverse and dispersed geographic locations. Systems implementation involves:

- **Acquisition and procurement:** Actual purchase of software, hardware and supporting equipment, and personnel.
- **Operational planning:** The project plan necessary to bring up the system.
- **Implementation and installation:** This is the actual implementation and startup step.
- **Integration:** Linking the systems to each other and other organizational systems.

Post-Implementation Audit

This last "feedback" stage, although very important from a continuous improvement perspective, is one of the more neglected steps. According to Gulliver (1987), for example, auditing should:

- Encourage realistic preparation of investment proposals;
- Help improve the evaluation of future projects as well as the performance of current Projects that are not proceeding as planned;
- call attention to projects that should be discontinued.

As can be seen, the process suggested above can be arduous, but this necessary effort must be anticipated for the successful integration of complex and strategic systems into an organization.

IMPLEMENTING A GLOBAL ERP SYSTEM AT TI

Company Background

Texas Instruments Incorporated (TI) is a global semiconductor company and the world's leading designer and supplier of digital signal processing (DSP) solutions and analog technologies (semiconductors represent 84% of TI's revenue base). Headquartered in Dallas, Texas, the company's businesses also include materials and controls, educational and productivity solutions, and digital imaging. The company has manufacturing or sales operations in more than 25 countries and, in 1999, derived in excess of 67% of its revenues from sales to locations outside the United States. In the past few years, TI has sold several non-core businesses to focus on DSP solutions and analog technologies, where TI is the world leader. DSP and analog devices have more than 30,000 customers in commercial, industrial and consumer markets. TI faces intense technological and pricing competition in the markets in which it operates. TI's expectations are that the level of this competition will increase in the future from large, established semiconductor and related product companies, as well as from emerging companies serving niche markets. Prior to the implementation of ERP, TI had a complex suite of stand-alone nonintegrated marketing, sales, logistics and planning systems consisting of thousands of programs that were based on many independent databases and running on proprietary mainframe systems.

Overview

Since the 1980s, TI had used a highly centralized infrastructure utilizing proprietary mainframe computers for meeting its IT requirement. As the first step toward global business processes, certain planning processes and systems were standardized in 1989. However, the systems were independent of one another, and were, therefore, inadequate to meet changing customer demands. Market conditions dictated that TI must operate as a global DSP business, with greater flexibility, shorter lead times and increased productivity to meet customer demand. The company determined the need for dramatic changes in its technological infrastructure and its end-to-end business processes, in order to achieve these business goals. Starting in 1996, TI underwent a company-wide reengineering effort that led to the implementation of a four-year, $250 million ERP system using Sun Microsystems' hardware platform, SAP AG's ERP software, i2's advanced planning tools and Andersen Consulting's implementation process (see Figure 1 for a summarized timeline).

In 1998, Texas Instruments implemented the first release of the ERP system, which primarily consisted of a prototype implementation of the i2 system running on a Sun E10000 platform. This was the first step toward migrating the manufacturing and planning of TI's orders. In early 1999, TI began rolling out the second release. The initial deployment included the SAP Procurement and Materials Management module and the Financial Management and Reporting module. In the middle of 1999, TI completed the i2 Technologies software implementation as part of the third release. Finally, TI turned on the remaining financials, and new field sales, sales and distribution modules. Included in this release were the first Web-clients to be used with SAP and a next-generation, distributor-reseller management system, both developed in conjunction with SAP.

A high-level architecture of TI's pioneering ERP implementation consists of SAP, and the i2 system for advanced planning and optimization (see Figure 2). The system is a pioneering large-scale global single-instance implementation of seven modules (finance, procurement and materials management, logistics, planning, field sales, and marketing) for all of TI's divisions, and it is in use by 10,000 TI employees to handle 45,000 semiconductor devices and 120,000 orders per month. As shown in the figure, this solution also enabled global Web access to information for TI's 3,000 external users at

Figure 2. A conceptual model of ERP system, linkages

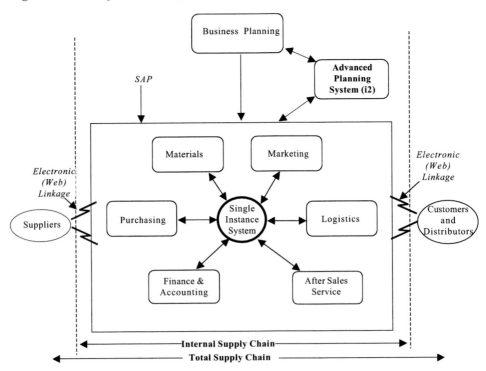

customer's, distributor's, and supplier's sites. In total, over 70% of the business transactions conducted with TI by all customers and partners are now via the Web or electronic data interchange (EDI). In summary, the implementation:

- Institutes standardized process to support the market trend of order-anywhere/ship-anywhere services;
- Provides global visibility of the system to customers and suppliers, permitting them to conduct many activities via the Web; and
- Standardizes key information technology systems so as to support business goals.

The next two sections describe some of the activities involved in the substages of this large-scale implementation.

STAGES IN MANAGING THE GLOBAL ERP SYSTEM IMPLEMENTATION

We now describe TI's activities in each of the stages of the strategic framework that was generally described earlier in this case.

Strategy Formulation

Traditionally, TI was primarily running what was called a "commodity" business, wherein orders were received, manufactured and shipped as a batch. Throughout the 1980s and 1990s markets evolved from the one-size-fits-all status to one in which customers started demanding customized products. This mass customization phenomenon, combined with the maturity of TI's business, caused it to reexamine its goals and strategies. TI started its shift towards a more customized product environment.

Within this new customized product environment, TI had a number of customer needs that could not be met easily. For example, a customer in Taiwan wanted to place all orders in California and then allocate a worldwide destination for the ordered products only at the time of shipping. This was difficult for TI to coordinate, because each of the regions was on a separate system. Other customers wanted to place orders for complete sets of devices that all worked together. Since its existing system could not handle such orders, TI had to enter the order for each device separately. The delivery of each of the devices was done at different times, implying that the customer will have to carry inventory while waiting for the remainder of the set. Manual workarounds and interventions were needed to handle these kinds of demands. Thus, the goal was to determine the appropriate processes and information systems that had to be put in place in order to support such agile design and manufacturing strategies (see, for example, Peters & Saidin, 2000, who describe the use of IT for supporting mass customization).

Another goal was a move toward supplier-managed inventory and customer-managed orders. Going beyond EDI and extending e-commerce meant that TI decided that leveraging the capabilities of the Internet to provide visibility of its systems to its customers and suppliers would be necessary. Finally, standardizing systems was another integrative corporate goal. TI's strategy was to ensure standardization of its systems as much as possible. Specific areas such as factory automation were left to use custom solutions, but other areas such as planning were required to be on standardized open systems in order to support the other goals.

TI makes extensive use of metrics. Strategic goals are translated into tactical and operational quantifiable objectives. Key metrics are developed and used as a fact-based management approach that keep clarity in the project direction and manage the scope of the project. The metrics include standard operationally and organizationally strategic ones, such as Time, Cost, Flexibility and Quality. In addition, since TI's manufacturing equipment is very expensive, its management made it clear that it was also concerned with level of use—Utilization—of the organizational equipment.

Process Planning and Systems Design

TI conducted a massive reengineering effort for the whole organization with the goal of setting standard processes globally. The major result of this effort was to declare that all inventory and manufacturing management be done globally. This process change caused the practice of earmarking a production lot for specific customers to be discontinued. There were thousands of programs in use at that time, and this proliferation of stand-alone systems inhibited the implementation of global processes. Thus, a proposal to implement an ERP system was made to the president and other strategic business unit managers.

Many organizations find multiple-instance implementations more flexible and sometimes easier to implement. Yet TI decided to implement a single-instance ERP system so as to fully leverage the system's capabilities to support the flexibility and standardization demanded by global processes. After site visits by major ERP vendors, TI selected SAP, mostly because of its scalability to handle voluminous amounts of data. Yet, the actual selection and justification included the evaluation of a number of systems by TI. These systems were evaluated through a questionnaire that contained hundreds of detailed questions pertaining to capabilities, ranging from user friendliness to support of major functions. Many of these same questions were used in aiding in the system justification.

System Justification

A budget of approximately $250 million was set for the implementation. The justification of the system was done using a combination of tangible and intangible factors at both the enterprise and business-unit levels. Standard hard-justification measures such as ROI and IRR were used to ensure the financial viability of the project. In fact, if these were the only measures to be used, then the system would have been justified. Yet, the data for these measures were still forecasts and estimates. Strengthening the financial justification by evaluating other measures and factors helped to provide stronger foundation for managerial acceptance. In estimating financial measures, global capacity utilization as a result of the ERP system was also projected. The project managers kept in mind that such projections were only guidelines that could get offset or boosted as a result of other continuous-improvement activities that were ongoing in the company. These estimates ranged from 3-5% output improvements based on current assets, which although seemingly small, amounted to increased cost savings of several hundred million dollars. Some additional intangible and tangible factors included:

- TI's proprietary-mainframe-based ordering was incompatible with the goal of moving toward a Web-based e-commerce model.
- TI had thousands of programs that incurred huge maintenance costs such as integration among these software systems.
- Accurate global inventory was not possible without a "single-instance" ERP system.
- An ERP system would facilitate in cycle-time reduction, which would help TI compete effectively in the custom DSP market.

Through this business case justification, acceptable financial returns, along with strategic factors such as competing effectively within a given niche market, and operational factors, such as global inventory management, all played a role in ERP's justification at TI.

System Configuration

The goals and processes described above entailed a number of changes at the detailed level. Many of the changes are difficult to manage because of drastic changes needed to the ways of doing business (e.g., the business rules). The processes used to address the arising conflicts range from top-management-enabled dialogue among the participants to top-management-backed decisions that laid down the policy for TI. A few examples follow:

- All inventory is global. For example, inventory in Europe must ship, if needed, to any part of the globe, rather than be held for European orders that can potentially come at some time in the future.
- The number of levels of approval on a purchase order was standardized at four (there were some countries that had fifteen levels).
- Authorization amounts were standardized according to the level of the concerned person in the organization.
- An 18-character, globally accepted part number became an agreed upon standard. This standardization involved a huge IS and business effort because changes had to be made to the databases, programs supported by them, and some manufacturing procedures, in addition to having to communicate the changes to the customers.
- All systems were mandated to be in English except for customer-specific information such as addresses, etc., used for external communication with them. In general, English was used when information was to be shared among multinational facilities, while local data, specific to a facility, could be in the local language.

Implementation

In this phase, concepts and goals are translated into tangible action, and as a result, it is perhaps one of most difficult phases of the project. General principles such as global processes and standard systems need to be backed up by convincing and deploying the right people to implement the processes.

We briefly describe TI's implementation phase in the following categories, startup, project management, and "going live." This description contains the manner by which problems were addressed in each category.

- **Startup:** A number of key personnel, along with their families, were expatriated to the U.S. and stationed in Dallas for a few years. About 250 people were transitioned from TI to Andersen Consulting (i.e., put on Andersen's payroll) which became the main provisioner of services with respect to the ERP system. IT outsourcing in this case involved Andersen Consulting taking over the employment and management of former TI people.
- **Project management:** Change management played a large role in this stage. The roles of training, planning, and communicating were of equal importance. All management levels were involved in this process, as were various vendors and suppliers. Some of the practices included:

    - On-site experts were made available to new users of the system.
    - A help desk was set up to handle problems that could not be addressed by these experts.
    - A ticketing system for managing and prioritizing problems was also established (e.g., a system stop was a high-priority ticket that would get round-the-clock attention).

- **Handling go-live:** To get prepared for "go-live," the key managers who were stationed in Dallas were sent back to their territories for educating the next level of users. Using selected experts, user-acceptance scripts were defined and tested, with problems, if any, being resolved as per one of the schemes outlined above. Daily conference calls were set up for thirty days prior to go-live to obtain status checks on progress and on the tickets.

    Based on the results of these checks, a risk analysis was conducted weekly to determine the effects of various potential failures. The implementation plan was to have a few go-live dates one after another, but in relatively quick succession. Except for the planning system, in all the other stages, in this case a direct conversion was employed. That is, with a downtime of about two to three hours during a weekend, the old system was turned off and the new one turned on.

Post-Implementation Status

The system met most of its goals nine months after the complete implementation. Response time for the system has exceeded expectations, with 90% of the transactions worldwide getting a response within three seconds. There are around 13,000 users (10,000 TI + 3,000 outside) on the system, with concurrent users ranging from 300 to 1,700. The integrated system allowed TI to better manufacture and deliver its 120,000 orders per month involving 45,000 devices.

Some of the key performance measures and parameters evaluated were:

- **Productivity dip:** There was a period of reduced productivity. Given the voluminous changes involved, this was to be expected. TI expected this and discussed with Andersen methods to ameliorate this problem.
- **On-time delivery:** TI was not hitting its goal of on-time delivery. In addition to the new system, market conditions caused more orders than they could deliver. They were falling short of capacity.

- **Single-instance, global system:** The single-instance, integrated, global model was successful, fundamentally transforming how business is conducted at TI.
- **Better response:** Because of its Web capability, the system is used by TI's external constituents as well, namely, distributors, customers, suppliers, and field sales people worldwide. This Web capability allowed easier-to-use order management systems for customers. Customers no longer had to use TI-specific software applications and/or costly point-to-point connections.
- **Inventory reduction:** Some TI factories reported output increases of 5-10%, and up to 15% reduction in work-in-process inventory.

MANAGERIAL IMPLICATIONS

This case study of a successful ERP/e-commerce implementation offers and reiterates a number of lessons for the management of these systems. The following lessons are summarized:

- **Conduct a thorough strategic plan:** The case illustrated how market forces had compelled the company to make radical shifts in its organizational environment and culture.
- **Align IT plans with business plans:** Conduct reengineering studies and develop strategic IT plans to align key IT needs with those of the business.
- **Get top management support:** The prescription of top management support has been made ever since early IT implementations (O'Toole & O'Toole, 1966) to the present. Strangely enough, as stated by Jarvenpaa and Ives (1991), it also remains to be one of the prescriptions that have been regularly ignored. In this case, TI's president and the Chairman of TI's Board communicated the importance and status in their quarterly satellite broadcasts to the company. The president sat in on quarterly meetings, and even stipulated that if anyone wished to "customize" aspects of the system that they would have to personally explain it to him and show why TI would get more profit out of this change.
- **Change management:** Set realistic user expectations such as the initial productivity dips. User involvement is critical. Andersen Consulting's process helped to ensure that such was the case. Make sure that the user is supported to help improve user satisfaction.
- **Strong champion characteristics:** In TI's situation, the manager of the ERP project had over two decades of experience in various levels of the organization. This manager had broad knowledge of Corporate operations since he was in charge of the previous business process reengineering programs that formed the foundation of the new ERP system. Previously he was a vice president of one of TI's divisions.
- **Rationalize business models and processes:** Make sure the business models and processes fit within the strategic direction and goals of the organization. Time, mass customization, and flexibility concerns led to a global model. Part of this rationalization was also completed after the SAP system was agreed upon, since SAP required business processes to be completed as specified by them or significant customization of the system would be required.

- **Manage external enterprises:** Appropriate and well-planned involvement of consultants is important for keeping the project on a tight schedule. Further, with the advent of e-commerce, companies are more likely to ship and order goods on the basis of Web-based inputs (Kalakota & Whinston, 1996). A training program must encompass such constituents as well, an aspect that seems to be ignored in the research literature. Managing external enterprise relationships (and systems) is not something that many organizations have had experience completing. This makes the e-commerce setting more complex, especially when organizations seek to integrate inter-organizational systems.
- **Manage using metrics:** TI and Andersen Consulting have a corporate culture and policy that requires the stringent and formal use of metrics in the management and evaluation of projects. They attribute this policy adherence as one of the key reasons for success of the ERP implementation.

CONCLUSION

Traditional information systems are often implemented with the goal of improving the internal productivity of an organization. In contrast, modern enterprise and inter-enterprise systems have supply chain integration as an additional and an increasingly critical goal. This makes their management and implementation a very time-consuming and difficult task. TI's ERP implementation with an e-commerce perspective compounded these inherent difficulties by requiring additional features.

- It is a single-instance system, providing access to the same data, irrespective of the geographic location of the user.
- It provides access to 3,000 external users (customers and suppliers), thereby enabling 70% of the transactions to be conducted electronically.

Management did see some problems in this implementation process and tried to address the issues. Some of the major problems included:

1. The software for supply chain management (Red Pepper) that was initially chosen did not meet expectations of TI. This system had to be scrapped; this resulted in a multimillion dollar cost. The i2 system was then implemented.
2. A productivity dip did occur. The implementation had to address this issue for all managers throughout the organization who had some stake in the performance of the system. The expectations that this would occur were communicated through newsletters and messages. Consistent and continuous communication helped to mitigate a situation that could have caused a major project failure.
3. Getting buy-in from internal functions not directly associated with the implementation process was difficult. This occurred with the marketing function. This function needed to be on board for the e-commerce linkage with customers to work effectively. Training and pressures from upper level management helped to ease the transition for the global marketing group.
4. Engineering is still not fully integrated into the ERP system. The e-commerce linkage incorporating product design with the ERP system was not feasible for

management. For such a technology driven organization, the lack of engineering function integration with the ERP system may need to be investigated.

Key questions to consider:

1. Can a large multinational organization implement a single instance global ERP system without the aid of an outside consultant? Could they manage this process even after implementation? Is outsourcing the IS function for ERP a good idea?
2. Which functions are critical within a global ERP system? Why would engineering not be considered a central function for E-commerce? Why should it be?
3. What metrics could be considered for system selection, system implementation, system auditing? Would these be the same metrics? Can e-commerce based metrics be used? What type of e-commerce based metrics may exist?
4. What lessons could be learned from TI's implementation process that could be used for future module integration? How much inter-organizational system integration is required for TI in the ERP/e-commerce system linkage?

REFERENCES

Gulliver, F. (1987). Post-project appraisals pay. *Harvard Business Review, 65*, 128-132.

Jarvenpaa, S., & Ives, B. (1991). Executive involvement in the management of information technology. *MIS Quarterly*, 205-224.

Kalakota, R., & Whinston, A. (1996). *Frontiers of electronic commerce*. Reading MA: Addison Wesley.

Lai, V., & Mahapatra, R. (1997). Exploring the research in information technology implementation. *Information and Management, 32*, 187-201.

Lederer, A., & Salmela, H. (1996). Toward a theory of strategic information systems planning. *Journal of Strategic Information Systems, 5*, 237-253.

Lederer, A., & Sethi, V. (1992). Root causes of strategic information systems planning implementation problems. *Journal of Management Information Systems, 9*, 25-45.

Lucas, H., Walton, E., & Ginzberg, M. (1988). Implementing packaged software. *MIS Quarterly*, 537-549.

Markus, M., & Benjamin, R. (1996). Change agentry—The next frontier. *MIS Quarterly*, 385-407.

Meredith, J. (1987). Manufacturing factory automation projects. *Journal of Manufacturing Systems, 6*, 75-91.

O'Toole, R., & O'Toole, E. (1966, June). Top executive involvement in EDP function. *PMM and Co-management Controls*, 125-127.

Peters, L., & Saidin, H. (2000). IT and the mass customization of services: The challenge of implementation. *International Journal of Information Management, 20*, 103.

Sarkis, J., & Lin, L. (1994). A general IDEF0 model for the strategic implementation of CIM systems. *International Journal of Computer Integrated Manufacturing, 7*, 100-115.

Small, M., & Yasin, M. (1997). Developing a framework for the effective planning and implementation of advanced manufacturing technology. *International Journal of Operations and Production Management, 17*, 468-489.

R. P. Sundarraj is an associate professor of information systems at Clark University in Worcester, MA. He obtained his bachelor's in electrical engineering from the University of Madras, India, and his MS and PhD in management science from the University of Tennessee, Knoxville. Professor Sundarraj's research encompasses the development of methodologies for the efficient design and management of emerging information systems, as well as the use of massively parallel computing for solving large-scale problems. His research has been accepted in journals such as Information Systems Management, IEEE Transactions, ACM Transactions, *and* Mathemtical Programming. *In addition, he has consulted with Fortune 100 companies on the development of decision support and other software systems for materials and marketing management.*

Joseph Sarkis is currently an associate professor at the Graduate School of Management at Clark University. He earned his PhD from the State University of New York at Buffalo. His research interests include manufacturing strategy and management, with a specific emphasis on performance management, justification issues, enterprise modeling and environmentally conscious operations and logisitics. He has published over 120 articles in a number of peer reviewed academic journals and conferences. He is a member of the American Production and Inventory Control Society (APICS), Institute for Operations Research and Management Sciences (INFORMS), the Decision Sciences Institute (DSI), and the Production and Operations Management Society (POMS). He is also a certified production and inventory manager (CPIM).

This case was previously published in L. Hossain, J. D. Patrick, & M. A. Rashid (Eds.), *Enterprise Resource Planning: Global Opportunities and Challenges*, pp. 133-148, © 2002.

Chapter XI

From Catalogs to the Web:
The Evolution of Airgun Products, Inc.*

Michael K. Shearn, Drake University, USA

Chip E. Miller, Drake University, USA

Troy J. Strader, Drake University, USA

EXECUTIVE SUMMARY

Airgun Products, Inc. (API) is a small firm that sells airguns and related products directly to consumers. From their founding in 1989 through the mid-1990s, they sold their products through a catalog-based phone order sales channel, and in 1995, they introduced their first Web site. Since the introduction of the online channel, they have struggled with how to best utilize their complementary channels and produce a profit. API is in a common retail scenario—a small firm in a niche market with an off-line and online channel with limited monetary and human resources that wishes to effectively use both channels, minimize their costs, increase sales, and become profitable. Their current challenges are to identify which of their customers prefer which channel (market segmentation), identify and take advantage of the relative advantages of their two channels (paper vs. online catalogs), and identify opportunities for enhancing the value provided by their Web site.

ORGANIZATION BACKGROUND

History, Products, and Human Resources

Airgun Products, Inc. (API) is primarily a micro direct marketing firm that sells airguns and airgun-related products directly to consumers. The company was founded in 1989 in the basement of the owner's home as a mail order business, and they are currently headquartered in a town in the midwestern United States. By 2004, API had developed a broad product mix, including 5,600 stock keeping units (SKUs). Examples of the products they sell include air rifles, pistols, scopes, mounts, pellets, targets, accessories, and other airgun-related items. Airguns can fire either steel BBs or lead pellets of various diameters, depending on the design of the gun. BB guns are less expensive, tend to be less accurate, and are commonly viewed as toys for younger shooters. BB guns use coiled springs, compressed air, or CO_2 as power sources. Pellet guns are generally more powerful than BB guns and can range from inexpensive models that shoot either BBs or pellets up to very expensive models with special sights and beautiful woodstocks. Pellet guns are most often spring powered, although some use CO_2 also. Airguns can be used for informal target shooting, field shooting, hunting, or competition. API now carries airguns for all pursuits, although it originally focused only on higher priced models for serious shooters, eschewing BB guns entirely.

Some of their suppliers include companies such as Beeman, Beretta, Crosman, Gamo, RWS, Smith & Wesson, Walther, Webley & Scott, and Winchester. None of these firms has granted API exclusive distribution rights to their products, and all suppliers provide identical products to API's competitors. API enjoys a highly workable relationship with their suppliers. This is reflected in the amount of inventory that API maintains. The average inventory level maintained during the period of this study was $355,000 with $1.8 million in sales—approximately five inventory turns per year. The majority of this amount is held in the most current inventory from API's eight main suppliers, which are the major manufacturers of airguns and accessories. Any dead inventory or slow selling items are discounted and sold out quickly. Overall, API has 47 different suppliers. Gross margins run from a low of 22% to a high of 46%. Every effort is made to purchase in as effective and efficient manner as possible taking advantage of seasonal discounts and early buy programs. Maintaining viable gross margins helps keep payments for inventory to suppliers current. In turn, staying current with suppliers helps keep overall costs lower. Several larger suppliers seek out API when they have excess inventory to liquidate at more favorable prices because, within this niche market, API is known to be dependable with their accounts payable.

API had one employee during its first year and two employees during its second year. As sales increased during the early years, additional employees, primarily phone sales representatives, were added although the business continued to be managed by two individuals—the owner, Will Smith, and one senior manager, Liz Brennan. By August 2003, API had 10 full-time employees and two part-time employees, with business, sales, and orders growing steadily. An organizational chart for the period prior to the hiring of the marketing manager is shown in the Appendix in Figure 1. The current organizational chart is found in Figure 2.

Airgun Products Market

The airgun products market is a niche market that actually is a niche within a niche, that is, a small offshoot within the larger firearms market. Total U.S. market size is estimated to be no larger than $51 million although verifiable market figures are difficult to pinpoint because the U.S. Department of Commerce statistics do not track the airgun market separately from the firearms market. Although the airgun products market is relatively small, API does have four direct competitors that sell similar products. The United States and United Kingdom are the largest marketplaces for these products. The majority of airguns produced each year are manufactured in Germany, China, the United States, Korea, the Czech Republic, Mexico, and England. In 2001, the last year that figures are available, importation of airguns into the U.S. reached 1.5 million units with domestic production figures estimated to be about the same. Retail cost can be as low as $25 to as high as $2,500. The average cost of a rifle alone, without any accessories, is $180. Sales by API are conducted in the U.S. and its territories. No attempt has been made by API to export airguns simply because many countries classify airguns as firearms and therefore subject to severe restrictions and licensing requirements. In the U.S., airguns are not classified as firearms and are not subject to the same laws that control firearms sales, but no attempt is made by the U.S. Department of Commerce to separate the two very distinct markets.

There are four major competitors of API that perform the same functions in its niche. Competitor #1 has a new ASP Web site that was upgraded from a static site. The firm does 100% of its business from its Web site and does not offer a catalog. Their approach has been to attempt to take the position of low-cost leader in the market with margins as low as 10%. Typical loss leaders are free shipping on any order higher than $149.00 and one tin of pellets free with the purchase of four tins which equates to a reduction in margin of 25%. Competitor #1 does not offer any after-sales service, technical advice, or mounting of scopes purchased as a combination.

The owner seems intent on buying the market by offering the lowest advertised price except for items that have a manufacturer mandated minimum advertised price. Although it attempts to "buy 'em cheap and stack 'em deep," it often fails to carry a very deep inventory in many lines. API won against Competitor #1 on a number of competitive bids for educational facilities that offer marksmanship programs simply because API had the product in inventory and could ship immediately where the competitor could not.

The next biggest competitor is #2, which offers a catalog and a static Web site. They concentrate on selling very low cost airguns manufactured and imported from Asia. They offer very few accessories. Because the imported airguns are poor in quality and lack available repair parts or companies willing to work on them, Competitor #2 does not enjoy many repeat buyers. This necessitates their spending a large amount of advertising dollars on prospecting for new customers in the major gun publications. They do not offer any warranty repair, after-sales services, or technical help. Their catalog is a four-color production printed on slick paper distributed free of charge. In product lines where they compete with API, they sell at approximately 10% lower price than API. One major drawback is their Web site is poorly designed and difficult to navigate.

Competitor #3 has only a static Web site and no catalog. Its product mix is a very similar product mix to API, but they have a different marketing approach. They attempt to sell all products coupled together with related products in what they term *Combos*. An example of this would be a particular air rifle coupled with the correct scope mount and scope, set up, sighted-in, and shipped ready to shoot as soon as the customer opens the box. This marketing approach was actually begun by API approximately six years ago but unfortunately was bypassed for less effective methods of increasing sales. The Combo approach works very well in this niche because the products themselves require special tools and some specific expertise to set up properly. Competitor #3 has capitalized on this approach and managed to take some market share from API in past years. API has been able to recapture most of the lost market share by having a better Web site with an online shopping cart, offering a catalog, and by stressing after-sales service and warranty repair.

The last major challenger is Competitor #4, which has a static Web site only, no catalog, and no online shopping cart. This competitor fills a very odd niche within a niche. Number 4 acts as a primary importer for several brands of very high-end airguns and accessories from Europe. The company then attempts to offer these imports for sale at two different price levels, dealer and retail. API actually purchases two lines of airguns from #4 at the dealer level. The company maintains separate pricing structures for imported and domestic guns. To protect their dealers, they maintain a minimum advertised price on their imported lines of airguns and accessories. On all domestically produced airguns, where they compete directly with other distributors, they have assumed the role of low-cost seller offering products at gross margins of below 15%.

The company's Web site is poorly constructed and very difficult to navigate. They have only two incoming phone lines, so at peak hours, their phone lines are often busy, and the lack of an online shopping cart prevents customers from purchasing online. The firm must rely heavily on their dealer sales to help offset their cost of advertising in several popular gun press publications.

Customers

The original target market for API was the airgun purchaser who was fairly knowledgeable about airguns and who sought a higher quality airgun. These are typically the group that one sees featured in articles about "adult airgunning" in most magazines. API sold only pellet guns and carried no entry level products. Over time, they have continually stretched their lines downward to reach more price-sensitive or entry level consumers.

There are no apparent regional segmentation variables. The two factors that do matter are price and the manner in which the guns are used. The former is most evident in the sales jump that was experienced when lower priced lines were added. It is also compounded by the fact that identical products are available from many sources, and low price often sways the buyer.

End use as a segmentation variable yields the following categories: field shooters and hunters, competition shooters and target shooters, and plinkers (people who shoot at random targets). All groups are well served by the variety of products available from API.

Financial Status

API's sales in fiscal 2001-2002 were $1.2 million. Unfortunately these sales figures came at a price. Since its inception, API consistently failed to generate a profit despite ongoing, although sometimes misdirected and costly, marketing attempts. In August 2002, Arnold Zimmerman was hired as marketing director and given the challenge of reorganizing API's marketing policies, designing and implementing a marketing plan, as well as finishing production of the company-specific catalog which had been in various stages of production since 2000 but remained largely unfinished. By the end of fiscal 2003, gross sales had increased to $1.4 million, but API found itself approximately $80,000 dollars in debt with Will Smith and Liz Brennan at a loss as to what to do to change that status. Smith then made the decision that if API could not be placed in a profitable status by the end of fiscal 2003-2004, the company would close its doors. The firm's recent financial data for 2002 through early 2004 is included in the Appendix. Table 1 shows the percent sales volume by category for the company's products. Table 2 shows the monthly sales data for each channel (phone and Internet) as well as the total sales figures. A breakdown of the various contributions by product line is in Figure 3. Figure 3 provides a graph of API's gross monthly sales for the 27 months and the trend line. As shown in the figure and table, sales for the past several years have been steadily increasing, but there are a number of issues that need to be addressed to improve overall profitability. How can the online sales channel be successfully implemented in this niche market by a small firm during a time when so many other firms' e-commerce initiatives failed? And related to this, how can a catalog-based phone sales company evolve into a successful synergy of catalog and online sales? What issues are most important to improving the company's bottom line? And can the organization continue to be managed by its owner and one senior manager, or are changes necessary in the leadership and organizational structure?

SETTING THE STAGE

Gun Shows and Catalog Sales

Attending gun shows in the Midwest and soliciting names from the retail attendees gained API their first mailing lists. Initial advertisement was conducted in firearms-related publications. In API's early years of operation, there were no magazines published in the U.S. that exclusively focused on airguns, and even by 2004, there were still no domestic titles in print despite several attempts by three different publishers. This fact may provide some insight regarding the limited width of this market and its very narrow appeal. The advertisements run by API often featured a variety of specific models offered at sale prices and requested that customers write or call for free catalogs. Catalogs for distribution to API customers were furnished free of charge from API's two major suppliers, RWS and Beeman, Inc., both importers of European-made airguns.

After the third year of business, attendance at gun shows was halted in favor of expanded marketing efforts through mailings and increased emphasis on providing airgun products strictly via mail order. A database in the form of a transaction processing system was added, and API became an official direct marketer that the U.S. Small Business Association (SBA) refers to as a microbusiness. A repair shop and the offer to perform repair work were added in 1993 to increase business flow and offer installation of telescopic sighting devices on air rifles that were sold. This service work offer allowed increased sales in other accessories as well. Also, based on their ability to service and repair airguns, in 1995, API became the RWS Warranty Repair Center for the entire United States, and repair parts were imported directly from Germany. Additional repair personnel were added to staff this appointment. The business continued to be managed by Will Smith and Liz Brennan, who doubled her function as a buyer.

Web Site Introduction

In June 1995, a static information-only Web site was developed for API by an outside contractor using MS FrontPage. The Web site listed products and services offered by API and general information articles on airguns. No provision was made for online ordering. Customers could call the toll-free phone lines or place an order via e-mail. By 1999, API had moved to a new custom-developed Access 97 database which served as a transaction processing and inventory control system. While Access 97 is a cost effective and robust platform for this type of application, API found that significant cost savings could have been garnered by having an in-house employee cross train to write the many queries that inevitably were required for ongoing marketing and management purposes.

Newsletter

Sales have continued to increase since the company's inception. In 2000, the company moved to a 5,400 square foot facility that now houses offices, a warehouse, and a repair facility. A marketing and informational newsletter was implemented in 1992, and this became API's primary marketing focus and list building tool until 1999. The newsletter was written and developed out-of-house. By 1999, the newsletter grew too large to be mailed at a cost-effective rate. In that year, desktop publishing software was purchased and an employee with some desktop publishing experience, Ray Watson, was taken from sales and retrained. Ray was then given the job of producing a single-page letter-folded flyer that was substituted for the informational newsletter. Ray also composed product ads for magazines and began work on a company-specific catalog.

Issues Associated With Multi-Channel (Off-Line and Online) Customer Interaction

For more than a decade, API has used a plethora of methods to interact with customers, including attendance at gun shows, supplier-furnished catalogs, their own Web site, and an informational newsletter. With these channels comes a varying degree of control over the information included, distribution cost, and resulting effectiveness (translation into actual sales) (Malaga, 2001; Strader & Shaw, 1999). There is also the potential for channel conflict (Lee, Lee, & Larsen, 2003). In the following section, the primary focus for this case will be on how to best utilize API's advertising and sales channel options given the technological, competitive, and economic climate of 2004. The case description begins with the hiring of Arnold Zimmerman as marketing director. From 2002 to 2004, a number of initiatives were implemented with varying degrees of success and failure leading to lessons learned and identification of the current challenges facing API in mid-2004.

CASE DESCRIPTION

Shortly after being hired, Arnold was successful in developing and presenting a viable marketing plan to the ownership by the end of calendar year 2002. Also, due to an extensive background in desktop publishing, Arnold was able to send the first API catalog to press in September 2002, with initial distribution accomplished by the first week in November of that year. The API catalog was very well received by the customers, and the first issue helped push holiday sales well ahead of expectations by the end of 2002. Nonetheless, as previously stated, they were still far from the figure that was required to show a profit. It was during this time that requested changes to the report generation module in the Access database revealed that API's static Web site was, despite its shortcomings, generating a consistent 15% to 18% of the overall business. Simply designating and separating which orders were gained from the shopping cart and which orders were taken over the phone accomplished this task. Also, many of the new products that had been added at the end of the summer were starting to sell as API headed toward its usual holiday sales increase.

By November 2002, Arnold requested and received additional funding for enhanced report generation from the database. The focus of the reports was to dissect the makeup of API's sales and determine if changing the company's basic offer would help stimulate sales. Also, a Web analysis tool was purchased, Web Log 1.2. For the first time since the site's inception, log files were downloaded from the host's server, and statistical information on the site's performance was collected and analyzed. The results of the Web Log reports detailing the gradual increases in Web traffic and the attendant gradual increases in sales are shown in Figure 4.

The overall management of the Web site was still another problem that required a fix. The decision to outsource the Web site development and management is a common problem for small businesses (Al-Qirim, 2004; Cullen & Willcocks, 2003; Sparrow, 2003). An outside contractor had done a redesign and an update of the original FrontPage generated site in 2001 using FrontPage 99. Due to the contractor's limited knowledge of Web site development, the navigation bar that appeared on the left hand side of the page was incorrectly generated. This programming defect in essence stalled later attempts to modify the site. If the included navigation bar was altered or changed in any way, such as adding another product category, it required opening up and resaving all 1,000 pages of the site one page at a time.

On the plus side, a shopping cart feature was added during this redesign. The shopping cart was provided by an off-site entity, while credit card processing was still done in-house. Web buyers did not have access to real time inventory, which for a micro-business is not a real problem. Maintenance of the Web site had been handed over to a slowly changing list of part-time employees, all of them adding their own varying degrees of style and embellishments to the individual pages. Header text, body copy text, and page title text point sizes were not uniform. No alt tags had been assigned to the graphics. There were at least two broken internal links on every page, some pages having up to four. The file hierarchy of the site was inconsistent and somewhat of a shambles; there had been no attempts to standardize use of upper or lower case text in folder, subfolder, or file names. The overall look and feel of the Web site was disconnected and lacked uniformity. Amazingly, even though site navigation was difficult, it was accurate.

To Arnold's dismay, some of API's most requested and highly profitable products could not be ordered online simply because it would present some degree of difficulty in making site updates. Essentially, due to the somewhat uncertain and constantly changing inventory levels of these highly profitable products, the decision was made by Liz and Ray to simply leave these products off of the site because the list of the products might have to be checked and updated on a daily basis. Also, adding this entire category of products would require changing the navigation bar. Repeated attempts to convince Liz and Ray of the importance of having those highly profitable and popular products available to the Web-based customers essentially went unheeded. Their continual and predictive responses to Arnold's requests were "It can't be done." It was a good example of technology driving strategy rather than vice versa.

In an attempt to increase Web site traffic, two different outside firms hired over the phone had done a limited amount of search engine optimization on a very sporadic basis. However, search engine results for most of the site's content remained poor. Keyword search engine results conducted through Google showed no listing in the first three pages. Despite this, the results for specific products carried by API ranged from acceptable to outstanding in the top three search engines at the time: Google, MSN, and Yahoo!. This meant that if potential customers conducted a specific airgun product search and did not simply enter keywords, API stood a good chance of having them find that product on API's Web site. While 35% of customers find a Web site through a specific product search, Arnold knew that a higher percentage generally access the company's URL directly (Jupiter Media Metrix, 2001).

It seemed obvious to Arnold that a change had to be made if advances in product sales were to take place. A recommendation to discharge Ray and Ernie, one of the full-time shop employees who was also highly resistant to change, was made to and accepted by Will. A full-time better-trained employee, Jill Weber, was hired to oversee the Web site. By May 2003, Liz, who had been the company's first employee and was currently acting as overall manager, head buyer, and bookkeeper, decided that this amount of change was not conducive to good business. She tendered her resignation and was gone one and a half weeks later.

Arnold was keenly aware that change, if properly implemented in a micro-business, can provide highly substantial outcomes (Futrell, 2000). The result of the rather drastic employee replacements caused the following other changes to take place. Arnold was promoted to general manager. He in turn promoted two other longstanding and well-qualified employees, George Williams and Amy Beckwith, to buyer/warehouse manager and office manager, respectively. Arnold believed strongly in a well-developed management hierarchy that provides each manager the freedom to manage and the proper tools to manage effectively. The company's books, which were kept in QuickBooks, were sent outside of the company to a local CPA. The CPA delivered weekly reports to management. These reports included a weekly profit and loss statement, YTD profit and loss statement, a weekly and YTD balance sheet, outstanding payables report, and biweekly paycheck report.

The accounting firm also took over all disbursements, including payroll on the approval of ownership and posted all expenses and income. Will and Arnold reviewed the reports on a weekly basis in addition to weekly Web log reports and an itemized breakdown of individual products sold during that week separated by source of the sale, either Web site or phone. For 2002 through early 2004, a breakdown of monthly total sales is shown in Figure 5, and a comparison of monthly phone vs. Internet sales is shown in Figure 6.

Arnold was then free to go about effectively measuring and implementing the desired changes that were needed to bring about a drastic but much needed change in API's overall market performance. Will was firm in his commitment to close the doors at the end of fiscal 2003-2004 if a cure for the red ink could not be found. To make matters worse, an additional $40,000 of unposted and unpaid invoices from one of API's major suppliers were found in Liz's top desk drawer. The red ink was worse than first believed.

Despite the bad news, Arnold, with the new tools at his disposal, created a plan to alter and upgrade the Web site. It was decided to promote and implement a two-pronged attack designed to recapture market share through the use of the complementary marketing channels, print generated phone sales, and Internet-driven sales. The previous marketing plan approved by Will was modified to include small but increasingly graduated expenditures for Web site improvement that included the following:

- Hiring a *local* outside firm to monitor and track search engine performance as well as make recommendations to improve that performance.
- Hiring a new more highly trained graphic artist that had an extensive background in Web site development (a Web master) and, with the proper Web site development software, was able to make all Web site updates in house.
- Making the commitment to place all products that were currently available from API on the Web site and available for sale through the shopping cart regardless of how difficult the updating might become.
- Updating and changing the overall look of the Web site while at the same time standardizing the text size for all individual page attributes.
- Improving and standardizing the look and feel of the navigation menus so products would be easier to find.
- Increasing outside links to the API Web site.
- Assigning alt-tags to all graphics.
- Repairing all broken internal links.
- Recreating and/or reclipping all existing graphics.
- Adding a "Special Offers" page, a "New Products" page, and a catalog sign-up page.
- Changing Web hosting companies to improve Web log access.
- Instituting a regular daily back-up regime that required downloading a copy of the Web site to a local hard drive and burning a copy to a CD kept in a fireproof safe.

In addition to the upgrades to the Web site, the following changes were made to the existing advertising campaign:

- All individual product advertisements were halted. New ads were designed that prompted consumers to either call or go online to sign up for a free copy of the API catalog.
- Ads in marginal publications were halted, and the money was redirected to placing a small ad in the marketplace index of the *American Rifleman*, the primary publication of the National Rifle Association. This publication enjoys the widest readership among all firearms publications—over 5 million households.

- Ray, who was responsible for producing the revolving content ads and the flyer, was let go. Responsibility for producing monthly flyers was given to Jill, who appreciated the change of pace from doing Web-based updates.

Also, the following changes to infrastructure were needed to improve inventory control and unify the ordering process. API was saddled with a woefully outdated and non-uniform stockkeeping system. A year-long plan was drawn up that would reassign a uniform nine digit stockkeeping numbering system to all SKUs. This new system included a unique supplier identifier and a category code that would allow quick visual identification for all products. Order takers and sales personnel would also benefit from this new system by not having to remove their fingers from the number keypad while taking orders or doing order entry. This plan also included the stock numbering of heretofore unnumbered SKUs that consisted mainly of airgun repair parts that had been imported from Germany. After implementing this stockkeeping system, an additional $42,000 of paid inventory was placed on the books near the end of fiscal 2003-2004.

Implementing the Web Site Changes

The changes to the Web site were implemented on an ongoing basis with measurement reporting done on a weekly basis. Web site expenses for 2002-2003 totaled $45,090. This included $10,870 for advertising, $32,720 for development ($25,920 for the Webmaster salary and $6,800 for search engine fees), and $1,500 for maintenance ($600 for hosting, $300 for the shopping cart, and $600 for software).

It soon became clear that the improvements being made to the Web site were beginning to make a difference in sales. By the middle of May 2003, the CPA was greatly encouraged by the sales numbers he was now able to put together for Q4 of 2002-2003. In fact, the usual robust holiday season carried well over into the fourth quarter, and a previously moribund business began the new year posting an overall 12% increase in YTD sales. The end of fiscal year 2002-2003 saw an average 8% increase overall in sales to $1.4 million, but the red ink was still there.

One of the biggest hurdles to overcome was how to set priorities on which changes to the Web site would be made first. After consultation with two separate Web site-building services it was determined that the site's rather dismal functionality must be addressed first. This decision was made because improving how the site functions would help achieve two important goals. First, Web sites that suffer from poor functionality will never rate highly with any search engine. Arnold had seen that broken internal and external links are the kisses of death for any Web site. Second, improving the functionality made it easier for customers to navigate and find the product they were searching for which should help generate more sales. Keeping these two directives in mind, Jill went about refining the functionality of the site without completely redesigning it. The original ambiance and flavor of the site had to be kept intact.

The other major obstacle to increasing sales was poor quality or non-existent graphics. To illustrate the importance of this issue, think about the situation where you went to a store that advertised that it sold only first quality merchandise and the entire group of products in that store looked as though they were beat up and used. You would immediately call into question the veracity of the seller's claim. It is no different for a microfirm's Web site. If all of the graphics are dark, show no detail, are out of focus, taken at obtuse angles, or look grainy and poorly prepared, the reaction by the Web site visitor would be no different than the customer in the store. A Web merchandiser must make their products appear even more presentable than the local fruit merchant running a small roadside stand. The lesson is simple—polish those apples if you want to sell more fruit. On the Internet, the customer controls the sale. "If the customer doesn't like what they see it only takes one click and they are gone" (Novo, 2002).

Arnold quickly determined that most suppliers were a very questionable source of high-quality graphics that could be used for both print and Web use. Many, if not most, of the graphics that had been placed on the site were improperly prepared for Web use. They were too small, the resolution was too low, and they had not had the backgrounds removed. API purchased a good quality digital camera, a broad selection of inexpensive lighting equipment, and a photographic cove to set up their products. Arnold and Jill then spent the next eight months retaking almost every graphic API needed to post on the Web site or use in print. The results were worth the expense—having a first quality graphic image library at their disposal helped API enhance its competitive advantage.

Figure 7 shows the average page views per visitor for November 2002 through March 2004, the time when the Web site functionality was being improved. There was a steady increase in the number of pages viewed by visitors during this time period. When Web site customers like what they see, they stay longer and open up more pages. Analysis of reports during this period showed that (excluding the index page) the rifles main page was viewed 29% of the time, pistols main page 18%, specials main page 9%, demos main page 8%, pellets main page 6%, used guns main page 5%, optics main page 4%, cash and carry main page 4%, and all other pages 17%.

Project Results

Prior to Q4 of fiscal 2003-2004, the online sales were seen by Arnold and Will more as an extension of the entire business that was incidental to the focus of the main operation—pursuing phone sales generated by print advertising. It was never viewed as a revenue source that had both the potential and the capability to greatly expand API's entire retail sales base. After sales began to increase, Will was impressed enough to begin budgeting increased amounts of capital to expand and improve the Web site's operation. In essence, the Web site's success caused a rethinking of what value API offered to its customers as an intermediary between airgun product producers and the consumers.

The new emphasis on the enhanced importance of the Web site brought about many changes. Now that it had been clearly demonstrated that the Web site could generate enough income to make a meaningful change in the bottom line, new Web site-specific offers were developed and tried first on the online customers. If they were successful, the offer was enlarged and also offered to the print-generated customers. Also, through careful tracking of those Web offers, new information was acquired on customer preferences, and this information led to a further refinement of the product mix and new product selection.

Here is an example. Through careful tracking of the products sold, it was clearly demonstrated that a meaningful cross section of the customer base had a preference for air rifles in the $120 and below category. These were primarily first time buyers. Two new suppliers were brought on that offered an abundance of models in that price category. It was a very simple decision to feature those models on the home page and add more models in this price category from those two suppliers. Sales in that price category doubled. In years past, there had been tremendous resistance to even adding a limited number of products from those suppliers simply because their lower cost products were not deemed to be worthy. Many other changes to the Web site actually helped implement changes to how API selected and added new products. Products began to be added to the line if customers simply requested them, instead of being based on certain employees' preconceived ideas of inherent value or quality.

Simply put, API began to pay more attention to what their new customers were telling them. This fact helped generate more new customers. With the lifetime value of today's direct market customers being measured in minutes instead of days or months, a constant supply of new customers is an absolute necessity. API had proven to itself the immediate value of the Internet and how quickly it adds relevant customer feedback (Novo, 2002).

The Web site also helped generate changes in the print offers. Internet customers are essentially contacted all the time, not just once a month as print customers are. Previously, a single page, four color, letter-folded flyer that featured monthly specials and introduced new products was sent to API's "A" list customers once a month. The primary list sort criterion was recency. The mailing was sent on or very close to the first of the month to all customers that had made a purchase regardless of size in the previous twelve months or had requested catalogs be sent to them. The increase in overall business from that mailing came primarily within the first two weeks of the month with the last two weeks trailing off and substantially diminishing.

In August 2002, a mistake made by the printer and mailing agency prompted a second mailing on the 15th of that month. This mistake was brought to light because API received e-mails from their print-based customers complaining that their sales flyers had not arrived. The mailing was made to the same audience with the new offers that had previously been given only to the Web customers. The results were phenomenal. That month was the first time sales broke $120,000 for a single month. This is a primary example of what Lester Wunderman meant when he said, "Direct marketing advertising must become a strategic rather than a tactical tool. Direct marketing must learn to intercept and affect the behavior of consumers no matter how and where they shop" (Wunderman, 1996, p. 281).

This idea was reverse tested in November of the same year. A decision made by Arnold and Will curtailed the regular mailing of the sales flyer in an attempt to save money, and the new catalog was mailed on the first of the month instead. The hope was that pent-up demand for the catalog would help generate sales. The result was a disaster for sales. For the first time in four months, sales dipped below $105,000. While Web sales were virtually unchanged, the lack of relevant contact with the print-generated customers caused them to forget about API. The first and second mailing was then instituted as a regular monthly occurrence. The message was clear—regular and repeated contact through a Web site or mail is an absolute must for the direct marketing firm searching for success.

CURRENT CHALLENGES/PROBLEMS FACING THE ORGANIZATION

As of early 2004, API had learned a number of lessons on how to best utilize their online and off-line channels for interacting with their customers and increasing sales. Having gotten the operation in the black, the next step was to identify important issues and an overall future direction that would enable API to continue toward improved overall profitability. Three examples of current challenges they must face are:

1. **Market segmentation.** What are the characteristics of their off-line customers and their online customers? Are the two groups of customers distinctly different? Or, are all of their customers buying through both channels?
2. **Identifying advantages and disadvantages for paper vs. online catalogs.** Are online catalogs always better, or would the elimination of the paper catalogs result in losing some customers and their orders?
3. **Creating value as an online intermediary (also known as a cybermediary)** (Jin & Robey, 1999). How can API, a small intermediary firm that has a Web site, add value for their customers that the customers cannot obtain through direct purchase from a single supplier?

If these questions can be answered, then API can fully utilize their advertising and sales channels, reduce their costs, be efficient in identifying customers who prefer the off-line or online channels, and create a competitive advantage by providing valuable services not available elsewhere in the industry.

REFERENCES

Al-Qirim, N. (2004). *Electronic commerce in small to medium-sized enterprises: Frameworks, issues and implications.* Hershey, PA: Idea Group Publishing.

Cullen, S., & Willcocks, L. (2003). *Intelligent IT outsourcing: Eight building blocks to success.* Oxford: Butterworth-Heinemann.

Futrell, C. (2000). *ABC's of relationship selling.* Dubuque, IA: Irwin McGraw-Hill.

Jin, L., & Robey, D. (1999). Explaining cybermediation: An organizational analysis of electronic retailing. *International Journal of Electronic Commerce, 3*(4), 47-65.

Jupiter Media Metrix. (2001). Access, activities and transactions of the online user. *The Jupiter Online Consumer Survey, 6.*

Lee, Y., Lee, Z., & Larsen, K. (2003). Coping with Internet channel conflict. *Communications of the ACM, 46*(7), 137-142.

Malaga, R. (2001). Consumer costs in electronic commerce: An empirical explanation of electronic versus traditional markets. *Journal of Organizational Computing and Electronic Commerce, 11*(1), 47-58.

Novo, J. (2002). *Drilling down, turning customer data into profits with a spreadsheet.* St. Petersburg, FL: Deep South Publishing.

Sparrow, E. (2003). *Successful IT outsourcing: From choosing a provider to managing the project.* New York: Springer-Verlag Telos.

Strader, T., & Shaw, M. (1999). Consumer cost differences for traditional and Internet markets. *Journal of Internet Research, 9*(2), 82-92.

Wunderman, L. (1996). *Being direct.* New York: Random House.

ENDNOTE

*   Airgun Products, Inc. (API) is a pseudonym used to protect the anonymity of the actual company and its proprietary data that is the basis for this case study.

APPENDIX

Table 1. Breakdown of sales by category (FY 2003-2004)

Rifles	35%
Pistols	19%
Accessories	11%
Parts & Warranty Labor	10%
Optics	6%
Pellets	6%
Mounting Systems	5%
Targets & Traps	2%
Maintenance Items	2%
Other Non-Shooting Items	2%
(Gross sales for period were $1.8 million)	

Table 2. Monthly sales data (January 2002 through March 2004)

API Gross Sales Data				
2002	**Phone**	**Internet**		**Total**
Jan				$112,119
Feb				$104,525
Mar				$84,316
Apr				$115,417
May				$104,046
Jun				$101,010
Jul				$109,399
Aug				$127,194
Sep	$115,021	$5,860		$120,881
Oct	$81,768	$30,638		$112,406
Nov	$72,788	$29,491		$102,279
Dec	$117,331	$50,669		$168,000
			Total	$1,361,592
2003				
Jan	$103,934	$33,970		$137,904
Feb	$87,571	$21,176		$108,747
Mar	$97,888	$31,730		$129,618
Apr	$97,572	$40,271		$137,843
May	$98,368	$44,469		$142,837
Jun	$103,717	$39,633		$143,350
Jul	$119,955	$40,973		$160,928
Aug	$94,158	$44,117		$138,275
Sep	$91,033	$43,382		$134,415
Oct	$115,697	$46,380		$162,077
Nov	$93,707	$36,082		$129,789
Dec	$130,054	$75,906		$205,960
			Total	$1,731,743
2004				
Jan	$92,729	$49,528		$142,257
Feb	$105,639	$43,931		$149,570
Mar	$122,625	$55,018		$177,643
			Total YTD	$469,470

Figure 1. Organization chart prior to marketing manager

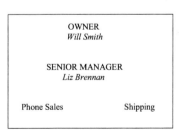

Figure 2. Current organization chart

Figure 3. Monthly sales totals and trend

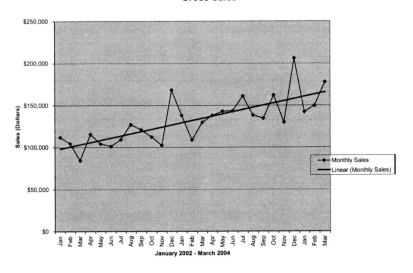

Figure 4. Monthly Web site hits and total sales

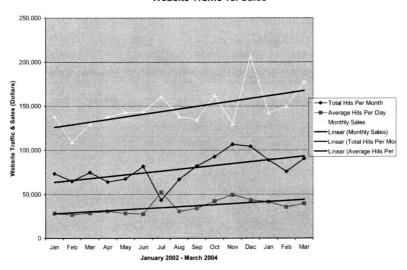

Figure 5. Breakdown of total monthly sales

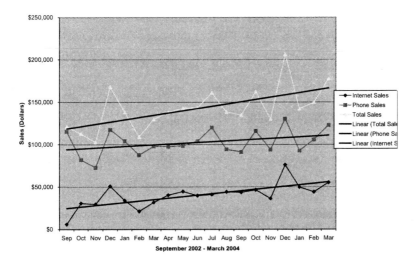

Figure 6. Comparison of phone vs. Internet monthly total sales

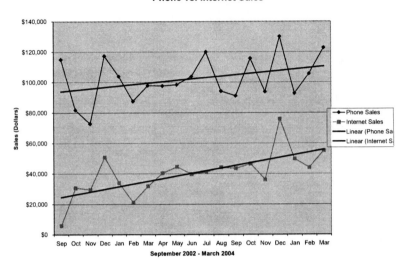

Figure 7. Average page views per visitor

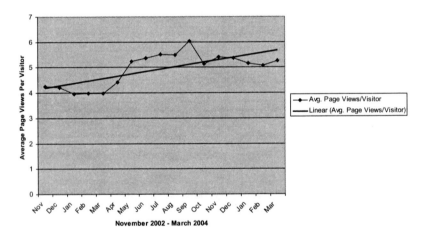

Michael K. Shearn is general manager and marketing director of the company used as the basis for this case. He received his BSBA in marketing from Drake University. He has 18 years of managerial experience performing direct marketing, copy writing, desktop publishing, catalog production, and product and publication promotions in the firearms and firearms-related industries. His specialties are highly focused Web and print marketing campaigns conducted in niche markets.

Chip E. Miller is associate professor of marketing at the Drake University College of Business & Public Administration. He received his PhD in marketing from the University of Washington in 1990. Dr. Miller has published in the Journal of Marketing, Marketing Theory, Journal of Marketing Theory and Practice, *and other journals. His research interests include international marketing, professional selling, and information processing.*

Troy J. Strader is associate professor of information systems at the Drake University College of Business & Public Administration. He received his PhD in business administration (information systems) from the University of Illinois at Urbana-Champaign (1997). Dr. Strader has co-edited two books on mobile commerce and e-commerce and has published in Communications of the ACM, *the* International Journal of Electronic Commerce, Decision Support Systems, *the* Journal of the AIS, Electronic Commerce Research, Electronic Markets, *and several other academic journals. His research interests include mobile commerce, online investment banking, consumer behavior in online markets, and communication technology adoption.*

This case was previously published in the International *Journal of Cases on Electronic Commerce*, 1(2), pp. 133-148, © 2005.

Chapter XII

Growth and Consolidation in the Spanish-Speaking E-Commerce Market

Roberto Vinaja, University of Texas-Pan American, USA

EXECUTIVE SUMMARY

This case aims to analyze, in some detail, the major challenges in the widespread adoption of electronic commerce in the Spanish-speaking population. The case also provides a general overview of related issues in global e-commerce, specifically: language, localization, currency, cultural difference, export controls, payment methods, taxation issues, consumer protection, and legal issues. The case includes a description of the strategies followed by companies entering the Latin American market in order to illustrate some of the major cross-border issues. The case clearly exemplifies how localization involves a considerable financial investment and commitment. The chapter illustrates that while Latin America initially attracted many investors by offering one of the world's fastest growing online populations, the market was not large enough to accommodate all the new entrants.

A GROWING MARKET

Analyst studies in 1999 pictured Latin America as one of the world's fastest growing online populations; Internet access was growing faster in Latin America than in other regions of the world (Vidueira, 1999). The number of new Web sites in Spanish was rapidly increasing. This explosive growth rate was attracting investors and newcomers into the online Spanish-speaking market (Vidueira, 1999).

All new entrants were looking after a share of the "potentially" huge Latin American market (Fattah, 2000b). Latin America seemed an attractive market with huge growth potential (Anonymous, 2000c). More and more U.S. e-tailers were offering Spanish versions of their own Web sites, while others were establishing alliances with companies with existing Web sites in Spanish in an effort to reach the online Spanish-speaking market.

Many U.S. companies, especially those run by U.S. Latinos, were targeting Spanish speakers. Forrester predicted the development of more ethnic portals from expatriates who retain ties to the motherland, Americans who opt out of using English as their primary language, and residents of emerging Internet markets (Mand, 1999).

Many U.S. e-tailers were realizing the revenue potential from Latin American markets (Slover, 2000). Many U.S. companies were implementing dynamic plans to direct their e-commerce efforts to reach Hispanic or Latin-American Internet users (Anonymous, 2000e; Oldham, 2000; Werner, 2000). 1-800-Flowers.com inaugurated a Spanish version of its site called 1800-LasFlores.com. Sears was also pursuing the Spanish-speaking community and opened its Spanish-language site in early 2000 (Rutledge, 2000).

According to *eMarketer*, the overall Internet Hispanic population is around 14 million, and almost half of those are Hispanics in the U.S. (Zoltak, 2000; Azios, 2000). StarMedia estimated the worldwide online Hispanic community at 20 million, about 5% of the overall potential market.

THE HISPANIC POPULATION IN THE U.S.

According to the 2000 census data, there were approximately 34 million Hispanics in the U.S. In addition:

- The Hispanic group was the fastest growing group in the U.S. growing at a yearly rate of 2%.
- The Hispanic population was expected to double by 2025 (Trujillo, 1998).
- Hispanics would become the largest minority in the U.S. by 2010.
- Hispanic youth would be the largest non-white population in the U.S. by 2025.
- In 1998, the Hispanic purchasing power within the United States was over $383 billion.
- There was a 50% gap in home computer ownership between the general population and middle-class Hispanics (Trujillo, 1998).
- 19.4% of Hispanic households owned a PC, compared to 40.8% of White households (Anonymous, 1998).
- 27% of Hispanics were planning to buy a computer in the short term.
- 20% of U.S. Hispanics had Internet access at work.

- 75% of U.S. Hispanic households with incomes above $75,000 owned computers, of which half had Internet access.
- About half of households with incomes between $35,000-$74,999 owned computers, and a quarter had Internet access (Trujillo, 1998).
- In 1999, Internet access among U.S. Hispanics was around 4.5 million users.
- 50% access the Internet (includes any location).
- 23.4% of Hispanics not accessing the Internet cited monthly service costs as the major obstacle.
- From the bilingual Hispanic group, 47% of those who own a computer also had Internet access.
- The estimated PC purchases by U.S. Hispanics in 2000 were more than 1.5 million, equivalent to the whole U.S. college student market (Rutledge, 2000).
- Approximately 61% of U.S. Hispanics online made a purchase in 1999, and 74% of those purchasers accessed the Internet on a daily basis (Rutledge, 2000).
- 12% of U.S. Hispanics have bought something over the Internet (Zbar, 1999).
- U.S. Hispanic shoppers were predominately male; the average age was 32, and the average annual income was $51,600.
- Younger Hispanics (13-17) tend to use the Internet more for chatting, music, etc., while those age 18-35-plus use the Internet for information and news, etc. (Anonymous, 2000d).
- The average shopper bought six items and spent an average of $547 during 1999.
- 86% of the shoppers bought music and 45% bought books (Rutledge, 2000).

CAG (Cultural Access Group) claimed, based on a study conducted in 2000, that the Hispanic Internet was becoming as important as Spanish language TV, radio, and print as an advertising medium.

THE HISPANIC POPULATION IN LATIN AMERICA

- The Latin American market as a whole had 500 million potential Internet users and $2 trillion in GDP (Shetty, 2000).
- Internet use in Latin America was growing at a fast rate. The number of Latin America Internet users grew from 4.8 million in 1998 to 10.6 million in 2000 (2% of the population) and was expected to grow up to 19.1 million users by 2003 (Disabatino, 2000) or up to 38 million in 2003 according to the most optimistic estimates (Oberndorf, 2000).
- Jupiter forecasted up to 66.6 million (12% of the population) in 2005 (Ebenkamp, 2000). Jupiter report was based on number of Internet users, not households, because Latin Americans were more likely to access the Web at kiosks, a friend's house, at Internet cafes or at computer rental shops.
- The e-commerce market in Latin America was expected to grow from $167 million in 1998, up to $8 billion by 2003 (Oberndorf, 2000; Disabatino, 2000) of which more than $6 billion would be business-to-business e-commerce. More optimistic estimates forecasted $82 billion by 2004, out of a global Internet economy that

would reach nearly $7 trillion by 2004. Brazil will register $64 billion in online sales, and Argentina, $10 billion (Anonymous, 2000c).

- According to Jupiter Communications, Latin America's online sales would reach $8.3 billion by 2005 (Ebenkamp, 2000). This was an optimistic estimate that assumed that companies would find solutions to current impediments.
- The majority of Internet users were in Brazil, Argentina, and Mexico.
- Internet penetration in Latin America was only about 2 to 3% (Fattah, 2000b).
- The number of Internet users in Mexico was 500,000 and 350,000 for Colombia (Zoltak, 2000).

ANALYSIS OF CHALLENGES

As electronic commerce in the region was growing in popularity, cross-border issues in Latin America were critical factors in the success of online ventures. Despite the expected growth, entrants faced many obstacles. Some of the obstacles for the expansion of Internet access in Latin America were:

- Poor PC penetration and low Internet usage (Graves & Nucete, 2000);
- A nascent and not highly reliable delivery infrastructure;
- Low credit card ownership among consumers (Ebenkamp, 2000);
- Weak credit card processing infrastructure;
- High costs of access;
- Antiquated back-office computer systems;
- Inefficient distribution networks;
- Expensive phone charges;
- Widespread credit card fraud (Petersen, 2000a);
- Tariff barriers;
- High shipping costs;
- Distrust of mail-order shopping;
- Preference to pay cash (Ebenkamp, 2000);
- Distrust of online transactions; and
- The need to handle multiple currency payments.

In the U.S. the major barriers for Hispanic widespread use of the Internet were the price of computers, high monthly Internet access fees, and lack of familiarity by the less acculturated Hispanics

Making e-commerce happen in Latin America would require overcoming some serious obstacles (Petersen, 2000c). Major challenges needed to be addressed before the Latin American market potential could be capitalized. Computer ownership and Internet usage was highly correlated with income. However in Latin America, relatively few people own computers. Although a growing number of Hispanics were online, only a small percentage was purchasing online (Ebenkamp, 2000).

Financial-related Web sites were facing the challenge that access to financial information had always been restricted (Schmerken, 2000). The logistics infrastructure and the postal service were less than 100% efficient, and order fulfillment was really challenging. Just as in the U.S. the most successful players would likely be retailers that use the Web as an extension of their stores (Ebenkamp, 2000).

Given the current obstacles, Internet companies moving into the Latin American online market had to implement several strategies in order to be successful. Some of the strategies included adapting Web sites to cultural differences, the use of localization services for translation of Web sites into new languages (instead of using machine language translation) (Dodd & Graves, 1999), protecting brands via local domain registration, understanding local business customs, and implementing payment mechanisms in multiple currencies.

Language

Some companies mistakenly thought of Latin America as a homogeneous region; nothing was so far from the truth. Although all countries (but Brazil) shared a common language, Spanish was spoken in so many different ways across the continent. The Latin America population was composed of many nations with different backgrounds and cultural values. Some U.S. retailers had committed the big mistake of just mimicking their English Web sites and were offering a translated carbon copy of their English language Web sites. The Latin American market had very unique characteristics, and in order to conquer the market, companies needed to implement new strategies and creative business models. There was no cookie cutter solution for the region. Indeed, Latin America was not one country and one language, but many countries and two languages (Schmerken, 2000). A report by CAG showed that English was the preferred language for U.S. Hispanics, Spanish was preferred only when U.S. Hispanics visited Latin American Web sites. However, older U.S. Hispanics were more concerned about content in Spanish, and they thought that more Web sites in Spanish were needed. By 2000, only about 2% of the Internet content was in Spanish (Shetty, 2000). The same reports showed that U.S. Hispanics teenagers tended to use the Internet more for chatting, and music, while the rest of the U.S. Hispanic population used the Internet for information and news. Recent studies showed that U.S. Hispanics refer to Web sites from their home country when accessing information in Spanish. Web portals such as StarMedia and Terra were taking this fact into account when offering content. Web sites were targeting audiences of each nation and culture.

Companies entering the Latin American online market were aware of language differences when building their Web sites. Many businesses today are involved in Electronic Commerce. It is important to understand that communication can be a major barrier in regards to cross-border negotiations among countries. It is also very important to provide information in the local language. Although, English is the major language of business communication in the world, many local Latin American customers would not understand any other language than that of their native country (Fridman, 2000). Web sites offering information in the local language were having a selling edge over the competition not using the local language. Consumers were more likely to buy from a Web site with content in the local language. Every nation in Latin America had special characteristics and had to be considered individually. The Latin American market was culturally rich and diverse; in addition to Spanish many dialects were still in use. Winning the battle for the Latin American market meant winning a series of battles in each country.

A multilingual Web site with icons that feature different language options would cater to more markets.

However, offering multiple versions of the same Web site was an expensive alternative. Major problems experienced by startups were the costs of creating multiple Web sites, and customizing/adapting to different cultural tastes and suit language variances. Latin American startups were very expensive to run because they were organized as micro-multinationals. The cost involved with maintaining multiple regional offices and developing separate flavors of a Web site was tremendous.

Legal Issues

Economic activities need regulations and laws; however, most legislation was only applicable within the borders of every specific country (Mosquera, 1999). There are many legal issues that needed to be considered (Engler, 1999). Some of the legal issues included customs, laws and regulations, privacy, copyrights, jurisdiction issues, export/import regulations, and compliance with intellectual property, cryptography and security contracts (Drake, 1998). Only a few countries had established committees or initiatives for the development of domestic and global legislation to facilitate global electronic commerce.

Currency

Currency varied from country to country. Local currency included pesos, bolivares, quetzales, cruceiros and sucres, to name a few. Because of currency devaluation, some country's currency may be of a higher rate or lower rate than the hosting Web site's currency. Because currency exchange rates were different, the value of the currency could increase or decrease in different countries. Purchasing in different Latin American currencies was a potential barrier, as exchange rates could literally change every minute. However, major credit card companies operating in the region provided their customer with automatic currency exchange services for multiple currencies.

Infrastructure

The region's IT infrastructure varied from nonexistent to rudimentary to adequate. Many regions in Latin America were still lagging behind in terms of infrastructure. However, major telecommunications providers were reluctant to invest in less profitable parts of the continent and preferred to focus on closed loops to selected cities. For example, 70% of the overall connectivity market constituted traffic between Brazil and Argentina, and many companies were focusing their efforts in this region.

International connectivity was a critical factor to provide Internet access for the nascent Latin America's e-commerce economy. However, a major hindering block in Latin America was the high cost of international half circuits. Telecom Argentina charged $71,351 per month for 2Mbps leased lines. Chile's Entel charged $26,600 and Brazilian Embratel charged $20,109 per month. One of the reasons for these high tariffs was that while many new ISPs had been entering the region, the supply market was highly concentrated (Shetty, 2000).

There were several obstacles to achieving universal coverage for businesses all over Latin America. An alternate solution to the current obstacles was the use of the wireless application protocol (WAP) to enable Internet access through wireless devices.

Cultural Differences

Companies entering a new market must get to know the culture of that country. Countries may have diverse views on e-commerce regulations. A few countries in Latin America did not have defined electronic commerce initiatives, and therefore they lacked a established body of regulations. Credit card penetration was extremely low. The estimated card ownership was as low as 10% in some regions. Concerns over credit fraud and a cultural preference for price haggling and face-to-face transactions were prevalent (Pereiera, 1999). According to Francisco Ramirez, sales director with Mexico City reseller Getronics: "Mexicans do not even make purchases by phone because merchants insist on verifying credit card signatures. It's not a technology issue, it's a cultural issue."

Building customer loyalty and trust in the region would require additional efforts. Many Latin American customers were not used to catalog shopping, store returns or exchanges. Many Latin Americans were also distrustful about the security of online transactions and were reluctant to buy products they had never seen or touched. In order to overcome this attitude, many companies were exploring alternative payment methods and others were implementing alternative Web currencies and extensions of their traditional services (Ebenkamp, 2000).

In the Latin culture, community features such as chat rooms, personal pages, e-mail and shopping were strongly emphasized. The average Latin American user spent a considerable amount of time chatting or sending e-mails (Fattah, 2000a). According to Fernando Espuelas, founder of StarMedia, there is a difference in Internet utilization in Latin America. Whereas the U.S. user has a greater focus on information retrieval, the Latin American users places more emphasis on communication.

New Initiatives

Many obstacles had hindered e-commerce in Latin America; however, the situation was beginning to improve. Many countries in Latin America, such as Mexico, Brazil and Argentina, were opening their economies and markets to the new globalization trend and facilitating the development of global e-commerce.

Electronic commerce in Latin America was expected to rise after a slow start. Although Latin America was still lagging behind North America in technology, many Internet trading partners were investing in the region in key technologies, such as phone lines, computers, Internet hosts, and cell phones.

The trend of increasing local content and regulatory cooperation would pave the way for economies of scale that would drive the growth of e-commerce in the region. Optimistic forecasts expected a continuous drop in computer prices, the proliferation of satellite and wireless technology, a growing number of free Internet service providers, the issuance of new e-commerce legislation, and new developments in telecommunications (Gower, 2000). One of the benefits of Latin America as an emerging market was that entrants were able to learn from success and failure stories from their experienced counterparts in more mature markets.

Many analysts expected the index of PCs per head of population to grow. Many ISP were trying to provide alternative and affordable options for Internet cccess. The number of Web-based applications was also increasing at a fast rate (Shetty, 2000).

There were many projects underway. Approximately, 15 new fiber projects were close to completion. Major projects totaling 170,000 kms of cable were under construction. The new improvements in infrastructure would likely decrease the price of Internet connectivity.

According to the Americas Telecommunications Indicators 2000, released by the ITU, in some of the large markets, the incumbent carriers had anticipated the Internet growth and captured a large share of Internet subscribers. For example, in Argentina, Telecom Argentina's Arnet and Telefonica Argentina's Advance shared 43% of the Internet subscribers in the country. In Chile, incumbents CTC's and Entel's Internet service had left only a 5% market share to independent ISPs. Likewise, in Mexico, Uninet, the official ISP of Telmex had taken 50% of the access market and in Venezuela, CANTV Servicios had 35% of the market.

Many local governments were encouraging Internet service providers and telecommunications companies to offer Internet access at affordable prices and, if possible, offer free access (Oberndorf, 2000). The Chilean government mandated interconnection among Internet service providers and a national peering exchange was established so that Chile's bound Internet traffic would stay within the country, rather than traveling through outside networks before reaching a neighboring city. Other countries were implementing innovative measures to provide Internet access to the general population. Colombia's Minister of Communications, Claudia de Francisco Zambrano became a champion of universal Internet access through an elaborate program called Comparatel. Plans were to take the Internet to all Colombian municipalities, the poorest of which would receive free access. In addition, the Colombian Ministry of Education was planning to wire 2,000 schools. The plan was ambitious and many analysts were skeptical about the cooperation of the national carrier, EBT (Shetty, 2000).

Despite the major challenges, many improvements, mostly resulting from the ongoing privatization of telecommunications were underway (Pereiera, 1999). The number of Spanish language Internet sites was constantly growing, and the number of Spanish-speaking users was also increasing.

MAJOR PLAYERS AT THE END OF 2000

Many Web portals were offering localized content and local Web brands for every specific country. Some portals were targeting the U.S. Hispanic population, others focused on the Latin American population and still others were trying to reach both groups. Each company was trying to target Latin America in many different ways. Many sites were targeting specific niches among U.S. Hispanic Internet users and those in Latin America (Zoltak, 2000). Each Web site was trying to differentiate their style and offerings, both in terms of content and community. Some portals specialized in content, while others were emphasizing community.

Table 1 lists the major players and whether they were targeting the U.S. Hispanic population, the Latin American population or both. Table 2 indicates which sites emphasized content versus those emphasizing community features.

Starmedia.com

StarMedia was founded in 1996 by Fernando Espuelas, a former AT&T executive and Jack Chen, a securities analyst (Katz, 1999). Starmedia was one of the first pioneer Latin portals (Malkin, 1999). Based in New York, StarMedia Network started with $80

Table 1. Major players who targeted the U.S. Hispanic population, the Latin American population, or both

STRATEGY	COMPANIES	DESCRIPTION
OPENING A SUBSIDIARY	YAHOO!	Yahoo! entered the market by opening a subsidiary.
ACQUISITIONS	STARMEDIA TERRA	Starmedia made a series of strategic acquisitions. Terra also acquired local companies in several countries
JOINT VENTURE	AOL	AOL formed a 50-50 joint venture with Venezuelan Cisneros group.
MERGERS	TERRA	Terra merged with U.S. Lycos.
PARTNERSHIPS	MICROSOFT TELMEX	Microsoft and Telmex joined efforts to launch T1MSN
NICHE	QUE PASA	Que Pasa was mainly focused on the U.S. Hispanic population.
GROWING OVERSEA CUSTOMERS	EL SITIO YUPI	El Sitio was entering the U.S. market Yupi was gradually targeting the Latin American population.

Table 2. Content vs. those emphasizing community features

COMPANIES	Emphasis on U.S. market	Emphasis on Latin America	Emphasis on content	Emphasis on community
AOL	X	X	X	
EL SITIO		X		X
QUE PASA	X		X	
STARMEDIA	X	X		X
T1MSN		X	X	
TERRA		X	X	
YAHOO!		X	X	
YUPI				

million in private financing. The company's IPO in May 1999 raised $110 million. The company had over 750 employees and operations in Argentina, Brazil, Chile, Colombia, Mexico, Puerto Rico, Spain, Uruguay, Venezuela and the United States. Starmedia was mainly a portal with a few incursions in the ISP business. The traffic at Starmedia.com was estimated at 2.1 billion page views in the first quarter of 2000. StarMedia had a Pan-regional approach, targeting Spanish and Portuguese speakers worldwide. The company operated a network of sites in virtually all Latin American countries, including several in Brazil. The main focus of Starmedia was the Latin American market, but it was also targeting the U.S. Hispanic market. Starmedia was one of the pioneers and offered community features both in Spanish and Portuguese. Starmedia specifically targeted users in major population capitals in Latin America and the U.S. The content was customized to every country.

Partnerships with advertisers and merchants was an important factor of Starmedia's business model (Fattah, 2000a). Most revenues at Starmedia came from advertisement. The site had about 150 advertisers, including Ford, Chrysler, General Motors, Intercontinental Hotels and Lufthansa (Mand, 1999). Starmedia acquired several local companies in 1999, including LatinRed, one of the largest Spanish-language online communities, OpenChile, a Chilean portal, Zeek!, a Portuguese site directory, and AdNet, a Mexican portal. Starmedia also owned several other media properties, such as Pidemasonline.com, launched in conjunction with Pepsi-Cola, Cade, Guia SP, and Paisas.com. Starmedia also operated StarMedia Mobile, its wireless division, and StarMedia broadband, its broadband services arm. Starmedia had strategic partnerships with several companies, including Netscape Communications, RealNetworks, Billboard, Dell, Reuters, eBay, NBC, Hearst Communications and Fininvest (Fattah 2000a).

StarMedia was recently faced with a major challenge to its position in the U.S. as Spain-based Terra Networks made a strategic move by acquiring the U.S. portal, Lycos.

Terra.com

Terra Networks S.A. was a publicly traded company and its major stockholder was Telefonica de Madrid, Spain, with portals and ISPs around Latin America. Terra's Web site, opened in 1997, was offering a balanced combination of customized content and connectivity features. Terra's Web site offered links to customized pages for every country it served. An audit conducted in the fourth quarter of 1999 estimated Terra's traffic at 1.2 billion page views.

Terra built a strong position in 1999, thanks to 2 million ISP customers in the region and to a $100 million IPO in late 1999 (Fattah, 2000a). Terra was expanding its market share in Latin America by acquiring Internet service providers in Brazil and Mexico (Ewing, 2000). Terra bought Infosel, its Mexico unit for $280 million.

Terra had just acquired Lycos in May 2000 for $12.5 billion. Lycos was the fourth-largest portal in the U.S. and is a portal in 25 countries, through 65 sites in 13 languages. The combination Terra-Lycos would potentially reach 91 million users in 40 countries. (Disabatino, 2000). Terra was attracted to Lycos because of Latin America's proximity to the U.S. and the large Spanish-speaking U.S. population. The Lycos purchase would help Terra reach 30 million U.S. Hispanics (Fattah, 2000a). Terra-Lycos would be based in the U.S. and Bob Davis, former Lycos CEO would continue performing the same function.

Yupi.com

Yupi was a private company based on Miami Beach, Florida founded in 1996 by Colombian-American Carlos Cardona (Vidueira, 1999). Yupi started as a Spanish-language search engine on the AltaVista network (Robinson, 1999). Yupi was a leading search engine in Spanish offering community links and related content. Yupi's traffic was estimated at about 143 million page views in February 2000. Yupi featured special separate Web sites focused on health, kids, and auctions.

QuePasa.com

The Hispanic portal QuePasa was initiated in 1998 and was based in Phoenix, Arizona. QuePasa raised $48 million and surged from $12 to $19.75 a share on its first day of trading (Vidueira, 1999). It achieved 30 million visits at the end of 1999. QuePasa was targeting specifically the U.S. Hispanic population. The Web site provided two versions, one in English and one in Spanish. Content was focused on Hispanic pop starts and leaders in the U.S. and news generated in the U.S. QuePasa emphasized content over community options.

QuePasa.com launched in 2000 its own shopping pages targeting the U.S. Hispanic consumer market. The shopping site, available in both English and Spanish, featured merchandise from popular sites such as Amazon.com, eToys, Dell Computer, Barnes and Noble, Staples, JCPenney and other merchants in 13 product categories. QuePasa also entered a partnership with MapQuest to offer maps and door-to-door driving directions in both Spanish and English. This strategy was intended to drive traffic to the brick-and-mortar stores of QuePasa's online partners. QuePasa had also recently signed famous pop star Gloria Estefan as its spokesperson (Zoltak, 2000).

El Sitio

El Sitio, established in 1997, was based in Buenos Aires, Argentina. El Sitio was the first company from Argentina to go public on the Nasdaq. El Sitio started as a content provider, but gradually offered Internet features after acquiring several fiber network companies in Brazil, Argentina and Colombia (Fattah, 2000a). Nevertheless, the ISP unit was not considered the core function. El Sitio reached 300 million page views in the last quarter of 1999. El Sitio offered content in both Spanish and Portuguese. El Sitio focused on community aspects rather than content. El Sitio also bought DeCompras, a privately held Mexican online retailer for $44.7 million in stock and cash. El Sitio's increased its efforts to appeal to the U.S. Hispanic population. El Sitio signed on Sammy Sossa, a famous major league baseball player, as its spokesperson in the U.S. and developed a new site: Sammysossa.com targeting U.S. Hispanic sports fans.

T1MSN

The richest man in the world, Bill Gates, joined efforts with Carlos Slim, president and CEO of Latin America's largest telecommunications company, Telmex, to develop a Web portal in Latin America (Fineren, 2000). Telmex and Microsoft combined their expertise into a Spanish-language Internet portal aimed at Latin Americans. Telmex and Microsoft were equal partners in the venture and according to the agreement, Microsoft would offer Spanish-language content through its MSN Web service. In addition, MSN would give Spanish-speaking subscribers bundled software services: free e-mail through Hot Mail, instant messaging and Web publishing services. All 1.8 million Hot Mail registered users in Mexico were turned into users of T1MSN. The portal got a guaranteed captive audience because Spanish-language subscribers to Telmex's Prodigy and Microsoft's MSN.com were automatically forced into the portal. The site reached 2.3 million unique users only two months after launch (Fattah, 2000a). The portal also included online shopping and access to other Microsoft services (Rutledge, 2000).

AOL

Internet service providers such as America Online (Willoughby, 2000) were also beginning to target Hispanic Americans (Gonzales, 1999). AOL offered $575 million of stock to the public to feed its expansion in the Latin American Internet market (Goldsmith et. al., 2000). AOL took its first big step into the Latin American market by launching a Brazilian portal in partnership with the Cisneros Group, a Venezuelan media conglomerate (Fritsch, 1999). The Cisneros Group invested $100 million to fund a 50-50 joint venture with AOL to bring AOL to Latin America.

Yahoo!

Yahoo! was also offering local guides. For example, Yahoo! Argentina was designed specifically for users in Argentina and individuals with special interest in the country. Yahoo! also developed an agreement with Hispanic Television Network, a Hispanic television media company. Yahoo! would provide Internet broadcasting solutions for Hispanic Television Network through Yahoo! Broadcast. Yahoo! also unveiled Camp Yahoo! in Spanish, a Spanish-language Internet education initiative.

THE FUTURE

The projected growth in Latin America initially attracted many investors, but the market was not accommodating all the companies looking for business. Despite the projected growth, pioneer companies had not posted a profit yet. The Latin American market was fragmented and overcrowded, and shares prices were dropping. Analysts expected that the numerous ISP players would consolidate to only a few major players via mergers, acquisitions and strategic partnerships, a trend that would gradually change the current landscape as foreign Internet competitors came to the Latin American market (Shetty, 2000). Many analysts predicted that troubled companies would become takeover targets (Druckerman, 2000a). Rumors about acquisitions were generated on a daily basis, followed by denials of the companies involved.

According to analysts, after the drop of the NASDAQ index in the U.S., the volume of investments in Latin American Internet companies was expected to dramatically decrease (Reuters, 2000). The plummeting NASDAQ index and the subsequent tightening of funds for Internet ventures were accelerating the pace of consolidation in the market. Many start-up ventures, including Yupi, had delayed their plans for initial public offerings.

Luis Mario Bilenky became president of StarMedia. Francisco Alberto Loureiro, formerly with AOL, became its chief operating officer (Petersen, 2000a). StarMedia posted losses in the first and 44 million for the second quarter of 2000 because of increased product development costs and marketing expenses. Star Media's shares dropped from a high of $70 in July 1999 to $15 in August 2000 (Petersen, 2000c). In the last quarter of 2000, StarMedia announced it was cutting 125 of its 850 positions, in a company-wide restructuring (Rewick, 2000). This was called a proactive cost-cutting measure aimed at making the company profitable once more. There were some rumors that StarMedia would not rule out the possibility of a merger with larger U.S. Internet players. Terra had just established a stronghold in the U.S. Hispanic market after acquiring Lycos (Palatnik, 2000). El Sitio was hit by the collapse in the stock market and was facing major problems in its acquisition and expansion efforts (Fattah, 2000a).

QuePasa's stock was recently being traded at 33% below its first-day closing price. QuePasa.com laid off two-thirds of its staff as it recorded disappointing third-quarter results. Its shares fell 24%. QuePasa, Phoenix said it was firing 38 of 58 employees in an effort to reduce spending, as it continues its search for a buyer. It also posted a third-quarter loss of $7.9 million, down from $8.3 million a year ago, and disclosed that at the end of September it had only $9.5 million in cash.

The chaotic situation implied that only a few companies would survive—the ones with the most resources to support the initial losses, and those patient enough to wait the years it would take to make a profit. Although industry forecasts indicated an expected growth, the future of the Spanish-speaking e-commerce market was still uncertain.

REFERENCES

Anonymous. (2000a, March). El Sitio expands by acquiring Mexican online retailer. *New York Times*, C4.

Anonymous. (2000b, January). AOL Latin America plans stock offering of up to $575 million. *The Wall Street Journal*, B8.

Anonymous. (2000c). Hypergrowth for e-commerce? *Futurist, 34*(5), 15.

Anonymous. (2000d). The wired Hispanic market. *Direct Marketing, 63*(2), 54-56.

Anonymous. (2000e, December 19). MasterCard continues tradition of innovation with first Spanish-language Web site by major payment card brand. *Business Wire*.

Anonymous. (1998). Blacks, Hispanics still own far fewer PCs than Whites: Study. *Jet, 94*(12), 39.

Azios, D. A. T. (2000). Hi-tech Latinos. *Hispanic, 13*(4), 60.

Disabatino, J. (2000). U.S., Latin America blending e-commerce. *Computerworld, 34*(22), 45.

Dodd, P., & Graves, L. (1999, February). Globalization, overcoming challenges of geography and language (Vision Report). *Jupiter Communications*. Retrieved from http://www.jup.com/sps/research/reportoverview.jsp?doc=sos99-14.

Drake, W. J. (1998, August 23). Toward sustainable competition in global telecommunications: From principle to practice. *International Lawyer*.

Druckerman, P. (2000a, April). Latin Web firms venture out to markets in Spain, US-Hispanics abroad offer quick route to retail revenue. *The Wall Street Journal*, A23.

Druckerman, P. (2000b, October 9). Latin American Web concerns struggle to stay in business. *The Wall Street Journal*.

Ebenkamp, B. (2000). Manana's opportunities. *Brandweek, 41*(9) 26.

Engler, N. (1999, October 4). Global e-commerce, how products and services help sites expand worldwide. *Information Week*. Retrieved from http://www.informationweek.com/755/global.htm.

Ewing, T. (2000, January). Deals & deal makers: Softbank aiming at online market in South America. *The Wall Street Journal*, C18.

Fattah, H. (2000a). Livin' e-vida. *Brandweek, 41*(27), IQ46-IQ54.

Fattah, H. (2000b). Latin crowd. *Mc Technology Marketing Intelligence, 20*(8), 36-44.

Fineren, D. (2000, March). Microsoft and Telmex plan a latin region Web portal. *New York Times*, C4.

Fridman, S. (2000, January). *Global e-commerce requires more than a foreign language Web site*. Retrieved from http://www.bizreport.com/news/2000/01/20000124-11.htm

Fritsch, P. (1999, November). AOL takes major step in Latin America—U.S. firm joins local group to launch Web site aimed at Brazilian users. *The Wall Street Journal*, A24.

Goldsmith, C., Boston, W., & Druckerman, P. (2000, January). You've got time Warner!—World looks much smaller from abroad-foreign media, Web firms see AOL deal sparking copycat acquisitions. *The Wall Street Journal*, B13.

Gonzales, E. J. (1999). Latinoamerica.com. *Hispanic, 12*(3), 34-38.

Gower, M. (2000). Helping emerging markets thrive in the digital age. *Business Mexico, 10*(9), 54.

Graves, L., & Nucete, V. (2000, March 15). No easy victories in Latin America's projected $8.3 billion online commerce market (Concept Report). *Jupiter Communications.*

Katz, I. (1999). La vida loca of a latin Web star. *Business Week, 3653,* 196.

Malkin, E. (1999). The Web's southern frontier. *Business Week, 3661,* 120.

Mand, A. (1999). Missing the target. *Brandweek, 40*(5), 65-68.

Mosquera, M. (1999, May). Lawmakers offer bills to spur e-commerce. *TechWebNews.* Retrieved from http://www.techweb.com/wire/story/TWB19990506S0024

Oberndorf, S. (2000). Going worldwide via the Web. *Catalog Age, 17*(2), 41-42.

Oldham, C. (2000, November 29). Internet marketers search for way to reach latino audience on Web. *The Dallas Morning News.*

Palatnik, M. (2000, May 12). Nasdaq composite's drop speeds Latin American Internet M&As. *Dow Jones Newswires.*

Pereiera, P. (1999). E-business washes into Latin America. *Computer Reseller News, 873,* 5, 12.

Petersen, A. (2000a, January). Opening a portal: E-commerce apostles target Latin America, but it's a tough sell-limited use of the Internet, lack of venture capital stymie effort in Mexico-Big US players take aim. *The Wall Street Journal,* A1.

Petersen, A. (2000b, January). StarMedia lures executives, including one from AOL, to lead its operations. *The Wall Street Journal,* B23.

Petersen, A. (2000c, August 8). StarMedia net loss widened in quarter, but beat estimates. *The Wall Street Journal.*

Reuters. (2000, February 7). *Internet en A. Latina no atraera grandes inversiones en 2001.*

Rewick, J. (2000, September 14). Starmedia sets layoffs in effort to reach profitability by 2002. *The Wall Street Journal.*

Robinson, E. (1999). Salsa beat: Meet Latin America's Net bets. *Fortune, 140*(7), 346-348.

Rutledge, K. (2000). Increased interest speaks well for Spanish language Web sites. *Discount Store News, 39*(9), 25-27.

Schmerken, I. (2000). Financial site serves up a Latin beat. *Wall Street & Technology, 18*(2), 52.

Shetty, V. (2000). Latin lessons. *Communications International (London), 27*(5), 42-45.

Slover, P. (2000, September 28). Web companies cater to Hispanic market with Spanish-language site. *The Dallas Morning News.*

Trujillo, S. D. (1998). Opportunity in the new information economy: Technology, the great equalizer. *Vital Speeches of the Day, 64*(16), 490-492.

Vidueira, J. (1999, July-August). Rocketing to cyberspace. *Hispanic Magazine.*

Werner, H. M. (2000, June). International: Bank of America equity builds IT services co. for Latin America. *Venture Capital Journal,* 39-40.

Willoughby, J. (2000). Offerings in the offing: AOL ole? *Barrons, 80*(31), 31.

Zbar, J. D. (1999). Powering up Internet en Español. *Advertising Age, 70*(49), S2.

Zoltak, J. (2000). The Web goes south. *Billboard, 112*(25), LM1-LM3.

Roberto Vinaja is assistant professor of computer information systems at the University of Texas-Pan American and has a PhD from the University of Texas at Arlington. He has published in the Handbook of IS Management, *presented at international/national conferences, and developed software for EDS, Mattel Toys and AETNA.*

This case was previously published in F. B. Tan (Ed.), *Global Perspective of Information Technology Management*, pp. 145-162, © 2002.

Chapter XIII

From Edison to MP3:
A Struggle for the Future of the Music Recording Industry

Conrad Shayo, California State University, San Bernardino, USA

Ruth Guthrie, California Polytechnic University, Pomona, USA

EXECUTIVE SUMMARY

This case discusses the challenges facing the music recording industry through the eyes of two of its most influential trade associations: the RIAA and the IFPI. First, readers of the case will learn about (a) the history of the music recording industry and how new emerging and innovative technologies can impact individual organizations or entire industries and (b) the music industry value chain and its various stakeholders, for example, record labels, artists, composers, distributors, and retailers. Second, they will learn about (a) the strategic opportunities and business models being unleashed by the new emerging technologies, for example, MP3 and peer-to-peer networks, and (b) the challenges facing music industry trade associations, such as the RIAA and the IFPI in protecting copyright in a digital age, reconciling conflicting goals of its members, and implementing new business models.

INTRODUCTION

The music recording industry is at a crossroads. Internet technologies have disturbed the traditional distribution channels. Music sales are dwindling, as consumers continue to use peer-to-peer (P2P) and MP3 technology to illegally share copyrighted music on the Internet. Some consumers think there is such thing as free shareable online music! Traditional music industry associations, such as the International Federation for Phonograph Industries (IFPI) and the Recording Industry Association of America (RIAA), have responded by tracking and taking the online piracy copyright violators to court. This includes a 12-year-old elementary school girl!

The barriers to entry into the music recording industry have been lowered, as new artists may now produce, market, and distribute their work on the Internet without the involvement of major record companies. In turn, record companies can undercut wholesalers or retailers on price by selling directly to consumers. Additionally, new competitors with new business models, such as aggregators and infomediaries, are entering the recording industry and are jockeying for position. Potentially, we are now witnessing the demise of some parts of the music industry value chain as we know it today. The big companies in the music recording industry may have seen the red light at the end of the tunnel.

This case discusses the challenges facing the music recording industry through the eyes of two of its most influential trade associations: the RIAA and the IFPI. First, readers of the case will learn about (a) the history of the music recording industry and how new emerging and innovative technologies can impact individual organizations or entire industries and (b) the music industry value chain and its various stakeholders, for example, record labels, artists, composers, distributors, and retailers. Second, they will learn about (a) the strategic opportunities and business models being unleashed by the new emerging technologies, for example, MP3 and peer-to-peer networks and (b) the challenges facing music industry trade associations, such as the RIAA and the IFPI in protecting copyright in a digital age, reconciling conflicting goals of its members, and implementing new business models.

ORGANIZATION BACKGROUND

Over 100 years ago on December 4, 1877, Thomas Edison invented the phonograph. He was the first person ever to record and play back his own voice. He recited *Mary Had a Little Lamb* to an astounded audience. This early invention was not without controversy; some insisted it was a hoax and many people attended demonstrations to see what they could not believe was possible. A world that enjoyed only live music was soon able to buy Long Plays (LPs) and hear music in their own homes on phonographs playing vinyl records at speeds of 78, 33, and 45 rpm. In the 1980s, record stores thrived with huge sales and huge profits. In 1985, music CDs and CD players became available. By 1990, only five years after their introduction, record stores had fully transitioned into CD stores. Today, CD sales are in decline in favor of MP3s, a music format that allows people to download, copy, and store music on many different devices, including cell phones, cameras, and MP3 players. The music industry is struggling to change because they cannot control the copying and distribution of downloaded music. Technological discontinuities (also called disruptive technologies) have been the staple of the music recording industry since its conception. Companies that have been unable to adjust and adopt the new technologies, including Thomas Edison's own company—Edison Diamond Discs, have most certainly fallen along the wayside.

Technological Discontinuities and the Music Industry

What are Technological Discontinuities?

Technological discontinuities are breakthrough innovations that significantly improve the technological state of the art of entire industries. Such technological discontinuities may threaten to upset the mode of doing business in the industry (Ehrnberg & Jacobsson, 1997). According to Anderson and Tushman (1990) and Utterback (1994), technological innovations tend to have a life cycle of their own.

As shown in Figure 1, the cycle begins with a new technological invention or the arrival of a newer technology that is a substantial improvement of the state-of-the-art technology of an industry. The onset of an era of turmoil then occurs as the new technology replaces its predecessor. In this era, entrepreneurs and innovators experiment with alternative designs and compete for market share. Finally, a dominant design emerges as the industry default standard. The industry default standard wins by offering a combination of features and services that allow customers to make productive use of the design at a reasonable price. Then the technological innovation cycle enters an era of incremental change. The incremental changes focus on market segmentation and lowering costs. This era continues until the arrival of the next technological discontinuity. Schumpeter (1942) argues in favor of technological discontinuities and states that unprofitable methods, firms, and industries must be liquidated to release resources for new enterprises.

Technology Innovation Life Cycle in the Music Recording Industry

The technology innovation life cycle in the music industry can be divided into five periods: (1) the technology introduction period (1877-1919) with industry turmoil and experimentation; (2) the competition and emergence of an industry standard period (1920-

Figure 1. Technology innovation life cycle

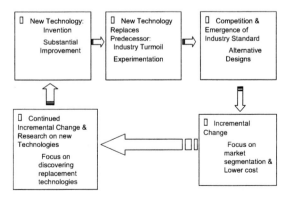

1950) where innovators experimented with alternative designs and tried to establish an industry standard; (3) the incremental change period (1950-1970) where the focus was on market segmentation and lower cost; (4) the search for new technologies period (1970 to early 1990s) where we saw the growth of the Internet and digital storage; and (5) the technological discontinuity period (mid-1990s-2003) where we saw the convergence of the Internet, P2P, and MP3 technologies.

New Technology Introduction Period (1877-1919)

The first two stages of the technological innovation cycle in the music recording industry seem to have occurred between 1887 and 1919. Entrepreneurs concentrated on experimenting with alternative designs of Edison's tin-foiled cylinder phonograph. For example, instead of using tin foil, Frank Lambert experimented with a lead cylinder, while Augustus Stroh in England experimented with a brass cylinder. In 1885, Chichester Bell and Charles Tainter invented an alternative design of a phonograph, a machine they called the "Graphophone" that used wax-coated cylinders incised with vertical-cut grooves. In 1887, Emile Berliner using a nonwax disc photo engraved with a lateral-cut groove and invented a third alternative design of phonograph called a "Gramophone." In the same year, Thomas Edison responded by developing an improved phonograph that used a battery-powered electrical motor and wax cylinder. However, neither Edison nor Berliner were able to mass produce copies of their new inventions for commercialization.

Columbia Phonograph Company (formed in 1889), Victor Talking Machine Company (formed in 1904), and Edison Diamond Discs Company concentrated on producing phonograph machines and records to satisfy consumer demand. At the time, the first main business of the budding music industry was to sell phonograph machines, but the companies soon found recording and selling music was more profitable in its own right. They accordingly shifted their focus to records, thus creating the music recording industry.

In 1909, the United States Congress passed the Copyright Act. In 1914, the American Society of Composers, Authors, and Publishers (ASCAP) was formed to enforce the Copyright Act. The 1909 Copyright Act allowed a copyright owner to enjoy a 28-year renewable entitlement for royalties after first publication.

Competition and Emergence of Industry Standard (1920-1950)

The third stage of the life cycle seems to have occurred between 1920 and 1950. Although record sales declined in the early 1920s due to the growing popularity of the radio, sales rebounded again in the mid-1920s because the radio popularized a lot of songs that people wanted to purchase.[1] From 1920 to 1950, innovators continued to develop alternative designs that culminated in the introduction of the jukebox, low cost electric-powered gramophones, the long play (LP), and higher quality HiFi speakers. They also experimented with alternative materials for the recording cylinders, including celluloid, gold, and condensate plastic, to improve sound and reduce cost. Competition soared, and new recoding companies, such as Radio Corporation of America (RCA), EMI, CBS Records, Broadcast Music Incorporated (BMI), BMG, Universal, and Warner, were started. Also, Capital Records, Decca, MGM, and Sony were started during this period.

In 1948, Columbia Phonograph Company introduced the vinyl 33 1/3 rpm, 12-inch LP disk that held over 20 minutes of music per side to compete with the existing 78-rpm disc that could only hold four minutes of music. In 1949, RCA responded by introducing the 45-rpm, seven-inch "single" disc album. The two types of discs represented a compatibility problem since consumers had to choose the record player they should buy. The problem was resolved when Capital Records manufactured record players that could play 78, 45, and 331/3 rpm. That became the industry default standard.

Incremental Change: Market Segmentation and Lower Cost Period (1950-1970)

In the early 1950s, it was inevitable that companies found better ways to predict and influence consumer demand. It was difficult to know how many songs they should produce, and overproduction became costly. Record companies started to target the youth who could now earn income while in high school or got an allowance from their parents. Research indicated that teenagers preferred to play the same songs at jukeboxes. Radio programmers took the hint and started playing top hits only. This way, they were able to influence demand.

The invention of the TV enabled music consumers to see their favorite stars performing live. This drove sales higher. The music recording industry became very profitable at this time. Some companies concentrated on mainstream music, while others published non-mainstream music, such as country, rhythm and blues, and gospel. Record companies that did not foresee the growth potential of emerging music, such as rock and roll, died off. Other companies merged. For example, in the 1960s, six major record companies emerged: RCA/Victor, Columbia/CBS, Warner Communications, Capital-EMI, MCA, and United Artists - MGM. The six controlled 80% of record sales in the USA. Small independent record labels concentrated on new music, such as disco, reggae, and funk.

Incremental developments during this period included:

- 1951—Development of the tape recorder by Stefan Kudelski in Switzerland.
- 1963—Philips demonstrated its first compact audio cassette.
- 1966—U.S. cars were equipped with stereo cartilage tape players.
- 1969—Dolby Noise Reduction introduced for prerecorded tapes.

Continued Incremental Change and Research on New Technologies (1970-Early 1990)

This period prepared the ground for the technological discontinuities that are experienced today. The early 1970s saw the introduction of the videocassette recorder to the consumer market. People could now tape their favorite TV shows or music performances at home. In 1975, Sony introduced the Betamax consumer VCR to the U.S. market. In 1979, Sony introduced the TPS-L2 Walkman portable audio cassette player where people could listen to music while walking or in private.

During this period, discoveries made in computing technology also found wide application in the music recording industry. It was now possible to store music in analog as well as digital form. In 1982, the first digital audio five-inch CD discs were marketed. By 1988, for the first time, CD sales surpassed LP sales, leaving CDs and cassette tapes as the two dominant consumer formats for recorded music. Since CDs are more durable and cheaper, they have become the medium of choice for recorded music. In 1994, the recorded music industry grew to $30 billion worldwide. The six major players were Philips (owns PolyGram, A&M, Mercury, and Island), Sony (owns CBS Records), Matsushita (owns MCA and Geffen), Thorn-EMI (owns Capitol and Virgin), Time Warner, and Bertelsmann (owns RCA Records).

New Technology: Substantial Improvement and Legal Wars (Mid-1990s-2004)

By the mid-1990s, computers became cheaper and faster with massive memory and storage capabilities. The networked economy was taking shape, and the convergence of the Internet, P2P technology, and MP3 led to substantial improvements in music recording (Goldberg, 2004). In 1995, the MPEG-Audio Layer 3 (MP3) was invented, and a patent (5,579,430) was granted in 1996. In 1997, Michael Robertson founded MP3.com with 3,000 songs available for download. Today, CD sales are in decline in favor of MP3s, a music format that allows people to download, copy, and store music on many different devices, including cell phones, cameras, and MP3 players.

Market Share

The global market share for music sales worldwide for 2002 was (1) Universal (part of Vivendi) with 25.9%; (2) Sony with 14.1%; (3) EMI with 12.0%; (4) Warner (part of AOL/Time Warner) with 11.9%; (5) BMG (Bertelsmann) with 11.1%; and (6) Independents with 25%. Figure 2 shows the global market share of the major record companies. From 1993 to 2002, the first top five companies accounted for about 75% to 80% of music sales worldwide. The remaining 20% to 25% of sales came from independent specialized record label companies. The major challenge facing independents is to raise enough money to market artists worldwide. They also do not have enough resources to provide local artists with the technology they need to produce and compete with artists affiliated with the big five. What independents have going for them is that they can provide more flexible music contracts and also expose and popularize new music styles more quickly.

Sixty percent of all worldwide recorded sales come from new releases (called *front catalogue*) and the remaining 40% from old material (called *back catalogue*). The main drivers for profitability are:

- Number of physical products sold per release.
- Diversity of artists to keep a continuous flow of new releases.
- Size and variety of music catalogue.
- Profit margins that the market can bear.

Figure 2. Global market share of major record companies in 2002 (Source: IFPI)

Forecast of technology infrastructure growth: In the next 10 years, it is expected that greater bandwidth will be available to music consumers, especially in North America, Europe, and Japan. The spread of broadband technologies, such as WiFi, cable modems, and DSL, will make it possible for people to have faster Internet connection and downloading capabilities.

Forecast of consumer needs in the USA market: Surveys show that American music consumers want the flexibility to copy downloaded music and create their own libraries and also be able to listen to that music on any device. A survey conducted in the USA by John Barrett (2003) of Park Associates indicated that 60% of listeners spend most of their time enjoying music in their cars, 26% at home, 12% at work, and 2% in other places. Thirty-eight percent of those surveyed indicated that it was important for them to have the ability to download music directly to a CD, 33% to a PC, and 28% to a portable device.

Key Players in the Music Recording Industry

Organization of the IFPI and RIAA

Companies in the music recording industry are represented by two main trade organizations: the IFPI and RIAA. The IFPI is a trade organization that operates at the international level, and the RIAA operates in the USA. The RIAA represents the five major music recording companies in the world and is affiliated with the IFPI.

The International Federation for Phonograph Industries (IFPI)

The IFPI was founded in 1993, and it comprises a membership of 1,500 record producers and distributors in 76 countries. It also has national groups in 46 countries. IFPI's International Secretariat is based in London and is linked to regional offices in Brussels, Hong Kong, Miami, and Moscow. Members range from the major international record companies (BMG, EMI, Sony, Universal, and Warner) to small independent producers.

Information provided on the IFPI Web site describes its organization as follows:

- IFPI represents its members at three levels—international, regional and national. Internationally, IFPI's Secretariat in London reports to the Main Board of Directors, and works directly with industry committees in areas such as legal policy, performing rights and technology.
- At the regional level, the organization's work is split between IFPI Europe, IFPI South East Asia and, as from January 2000, IFPI Latin America (formerly FLAPF). IFPI's regional offices are based respectively in Brussels, Hong Kong, Moscow, and Miami. They report to a regional Board of Directors comprising the heads of multinational and independent record companies. Representatives of the regional boards, both multinationals and independents, also sit on IFPI's Main Board.

Figure 3 shows an organizational chart for IFPI reconstructed from the information on their Web site. For more information about the IFPI, visit http://www.ifpi.org.

Figure 3. IFPI's international structure, reconstructed from IFPI's Web site http://www.ifpi.org/site-content/about/structure.html

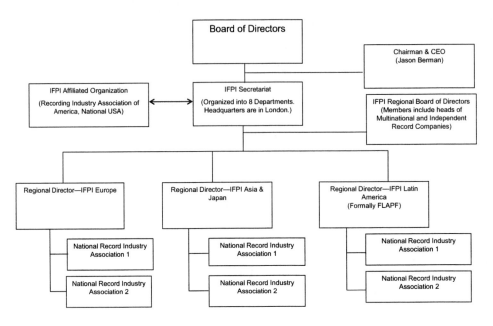

The Recording Industry Association of America (RIAA)

The RIAA is a trade association that was founded in 1952 to promote intellectual property protection and prevention against piracy of music produced by its members. RIAA members create, manufacture, or distribute approximately 90% of all legal sound recordings produced and sold in the USA. Its 250 members include the major record label companies in the world, such as Warner Brothers Records, Columbia, Motown, RCA, Geffen, and Capitol. The USA remains the number one market for music sales in the world. According to the data we assembled from the RIAA Web site and other sources on the Internet,[2] the RIAA chairman and CEO reports to the RIAA board and is assisted by a president who has two executive vice presidents—one in charge of antipiracy and copyright, the other international affairs. There are five senior vice presidents: international affairs, antipiracy and copyright, public affairs, communications, and marketing, respectively. Figure 4 shows an organizational chart for the RIAA that was reconstructed using information on the RIAA Web site. For more information about the RIAA, visit http://www.riaa.com.

The Music Industry Value Chain and Its Main Stakeholders

Figure 5 shows the music industry value chain. Support activities include infrastructure, information, human resource management, finance, and technology develop-

Figure 4. RIAA organizational structure, reconstructed from riaa.com Web site and various other Web sites

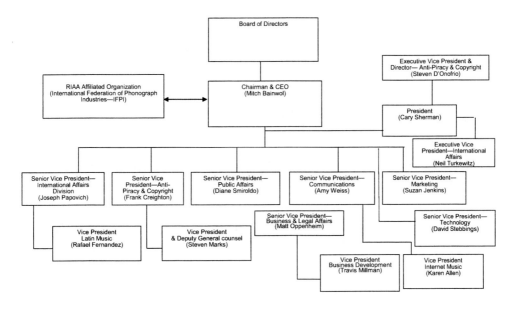

Figure 5. Current music industry value chain

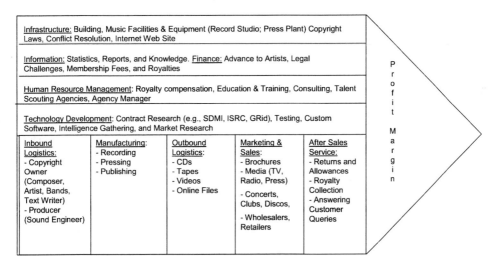

ment. Primary activities include music composers and producers, recording and pressing (CDs, cassette and video tapes, online files), marketing, advertising, and distributing the songs; and providing after-sales service.

Main Stakeholders

Composers/Songwriters: The originators of the music. They could be artists, bands, individuals, or companies. They stake a claim on royalties. There are three types of royalties: (1) mechanical royalties that come from record sales, (2) performance royalties that come from live performances or playing a song on another medium, and (3) synchronization royalties that come from using a composition or song to accompany visual images on television, in films, advertising, or videos.

Artists/Bands: Individuals who perform the compositions or songs. Most of them sign contracts with record label companies. They receive a share of revenues from record sales and certain fees from the record label companies.

- **Publishers:** Composers/songwriters sign contracts with publishers. Publishers enforce the copyright of compositions and songs on behalf of the composers/songwriters. They collect mechanical, performance, or synchronization royalties from licensees using the compositions or songs.
- **Manufacturers:** Mainly record label companies who own record-pressing facilities. They also design the artwork and packaging for the record sleeves.
- **Distributors:** Mainly the record label companies. They mostly sell the records to wholesalers or retailers.
- **Marketers:** Clubs, discos, radio stations, TV stations, concert organizers, and other public relations agencies that promote the artists/bands and their music.
- **Retailers:** Brick and mortar companies or online companies that sell the music to consumers. They buy the music from wholesalers or directly from the record label companies. They may also purchase licenses from record labels to allow customers to download music online into MP3 devices.
- **Consumers:** Individuals who buy the music for personal enjoyment. They may also attend live performances.

SETTING THE STAGE

In early September 2003, as Mitch Bainwol, newly appointed Chairman and CEO of the RIAA, drove to his plush office located at 1330 Connecticut Ave. NW, Washington, DC, he was thinking about a report he would present at the RIAA's e-board meeting, his first such presentation. He had spent the last few months trying to learn the dynamic forces in the music industry—past, present, and future—and the role technology has played to shape it. He realized that future music consumers are looking for the ability to legally bundle the music they enjoy in a fashion unique to each individual, and emerging technologies, such as MP3 and P2P networks, will provide this capability. He believed that the music industry could do the best job of providing the consumer empowerment that new technologies make possible. Not only will the new technologies have a profound effect on traditional music production and distribution networks and in the hardware and software industries; but they may also pose a threat to the existing music recording industry business model, especially if the music recording industry chose to downplay the significance of the emerging Internet technologies. As he sat at his office desk, his thoughts focused on four main questions:

1. Given the role technology has played to shape the music industry, has the RIAA and its affiliated organizations taken actions they should not have taken, or have they omitted taking other actions?
2. How can the key players in the music industry best utilize the emerging forms of value creation to facilitate legal downloads or uploads of music on the Internet?
3. Is the current music recording industry business model viable? If not, how should it be changed?
4. How do you reconcile the differing goals of various stakeholders in the music industry, such as consumer electronics manufacturers, information technology developers, music companies, and music consumers?

Advantages of Utilizing Internet Technologies

The Internet offers an opportunity for a variety of stakeholders to sell music to anyone with a computer, worldwide. There are virtually no aspects of the current music industry that will be untouched from this change (Fisher, 2000).

- **Shelf space:** Online music will allow retail shops to have access to an infinite number of titles and artists than they currently have. The limitation of having to keep only physical copies of best selling music will disappear. The music market will be more diverse since new artists can be included more easily.
- **Economies of scale:** The amount of music one can burn on a CD is usually limited. By using digital distribution, the fixed costs required to set up press masters, packaging, and printing will be avoided. Also the costs of storage and transmission of the music is minimal.
- **Music screening:** Users can screen and sample music on their own time and download what they deem interesting. This means no more need to buy "unwanted music" on a CD when one is actually interested in only one song.
- **Disintermediation:** All intermediaries (including CD burners, packagers, printers, wholesalers, retailers, and distributors) who depend on physical production or storage of music will be in danger of going out of business.
- **New entrants:** New companies will emerge to facilitate the digital distribution and selection of music on demand. There will also emerge companies that perform as aggregators or infomediaries. Music aggregators will provide information on available music and services being offered by others in the value chain. Potential customers will then use the aggregator service to locate the best music sources and services. The revenue model for aggregators will mostly be based on referrals and advertising. MusicNet, a new company formed by Warner, EMI, BMG, and Sony is an example of an aggregator. Infomediaries collect information about the music interests of customers and provide the customers with the information they may need to make music purchase decisions. They may also provide updates on new releases or music analysis information. The revenue model for infomediaries will mostly be based on a subscription fee or advertising.

- **Portals:** These could be established by the existing record label trade associations or by new entrants. Three different types of portals may emerge: horizontal, vertical or affinity. Horizontal portals will help members to locate music information, including current scheduled events and news, financial performance, and trends in the industry. These portals will also help members locate other Web sites where they can find the music they are looking for. The revenue model for horizontal portals will mostly be based on member subscription fees and advertisements. Vertical portals will provide deeper analysis about trends in the music industry and educate members on available business opportunities, nationally and internationally. The revenue model for a vertical portal includes referral fees, subscription fees, and advertising. Affinity portals will provide specialized information to specific music market segments. Such segments may include gospel music community, blue music community, concert community, or classical music community. Revenue may come from subscription and advertisement fees.

Disadvantages Utilizing Internet Technologies

As well noted by Dr. William Fisher (2000), there are disadvantages of using the Internet as the new distribution channel.

Problems with MP3:

1. *First, MP3 files are unsecured: that is, nothing prevents a person who has acquired (with or without permission) an MP3 file to make an unlimited number of copies of it. This definitely undermines the ability of music creators to earn money.*
2. *Unlike the copies of musical works made using analog technology (such as ordinary cassette tape recorders), the copies made using digital technology are perfect. In other words, each copy is identical to the original. The result is that unauthorized perfect MP3 copies of copyrighted recordings are widely available on the Internet for free.*
3. *Therefore, Internet distribution of digital music may result, not in an increase in the amount and variety of music available to the public but in a decrease.*

According to a survey conducted in April 2003, digital music formats (including CD-Rs and digital music/MP3 files stored on a PC) account for 16% of American music collections, with this proportion jumping to 34% among teens aged 12 to 17 and 30% among Americans aged 18 to 24. The survey also found that by April 2003, 80 million Americans had listened to digital music files that were stored on a PC, and 65 million had downloaded music or an MP3 file from the Internet. The proportion of overall U.S. downloaders who have paid for digital music doubled from 8% in December 2002 to 16% in June of 2003. (Kleinschmit, 2003). However, a significant proportion of music consumers continue to share and/or download music from the Internet illegally.

According to Cary Sherman, President and General Counsel of the RIAA, any copying of music to a CD performed on one's computer is deemed copyright infringement. It does not matter whether the source is digital or analog; a copy of a CD, tape, or LP that you own, or a compilation of songs from various sources that you own. The RIAA considers making such a copy to be a violation of the right of reproduction granted to copyright holders by the Copyright Act of 1976.

CASE DESCRIPTION

Since its creation, the music recording industry has been technology driven. The technology life cycle started in 1877 with the introduction of the phonograph. Thanks to Internet, P2P, and MP3 technologies, we are now witnessing a technological discontinuity in the music recording industry. Between 1877 and the mid-1990s, most inventions either improved existing products and services (sustaining technologies) or helped to build on the skills and technologies existing in the music recording industry (competence enhancing). The recent technologies threaten to destroy the skills and technologies embodied in the industry (competence destroying) and may bring in new competitors who will champion the creation of entirely new ways of producing and distributing music products and services. Furthermore, these new competitors may unseat current industry leaders.

MP3.com

In November 1997, Michael Robertson founded MP3.com in San Diego, California. To use MP3.com services, members had to furnish proof of ownership of a particular CD in order to get a copy of that CD in MP3 format. Proof of ownership was provided in one of two ways: (1) ordering the CD online through MP3.com or (2) placing the CD in one's computer CD-ROM drive so that MP3.com could verify it.[3] MP3.com used its own library of CDs to make the actual MP3 recordings for its members. By 2000, MP3.com had created a library of more than 40,000 CDs and had over 10 million registered members.

The RIAA took notice, and in January 2000, sued MP3.com for copyright infringement. MP3.com contended that their service was legal because it just provided music lovers a way to copy music they already own in another format, something that is allowed under the "fair use" doctrine in the U.S. Copyright Act. The act allowed a people to copy music from CDs they own into a cassette or vice versa for personal use. In April 2000, a U.S. District Court ruled that a part of the download service from MP3.com, called "my.mp3.com," violated copyright law by allowing songs from commercial CDs to be downloaded. The problem was that MP3.com did the copying rather than the consumer and that the company was not copying the music for its own use. In November 2000, MP3.com agreed to pay $53.4 million to end its copyright infringement suite with Seagram's Universal Music Group. In August 2001, Michael Robertson sold MP3.com to Universal Records (owned by Vivendi) for $372 million.

Napster

In 1999, Shawn Fanning, who was 18 years old then, created Napster. When using a music file sharing application like Napster, you can create a folder in your computer in which the MP3 files you want to share are stored. When you connect to Napster, your computer becomes a server that allows other Napster users to download your MP3 files. When one uses a computer to search for a song, a list of songs in your folder is sent to

Napster's central servers. As shown in Figure 6a, when there is a song match, the Napster server links the IP addresses of the two users and allows download to take place. Unlike MP3.com, Napster did not store the music on its servers; it was just a hub. Also, no proof of ownership of the music was required.

In December 2000, the RIAA filed a suit against Napster alleging that the company was operating as a haven for music piracy on the Internet and promoting copyright infringement. In July 2000, Napster was ordered to remain off-line until it met court demands of blocking trade in copyrighted music. Napster argued that its intention was to bring artists and their fans together and never to allow users to illegally swap copied songs, that is, allow small independent bands to make their music available to be downloaded without having to go through companies, such as MP3.com.

The problem is that Napster's service opened itself up to liability for its users' actions by actively playing a role in connecting people who were downloading and uploading songs—a little like a physical swap meet that provides the facilities for people exchanging illegal material. In February 2001, Napster was shut down.

Other "Baby Napsters" Technologies

Once the RIAA succeeded in closing MP3.com and Napster, other file-sharing technologies emerged, with each one figuring out ways to avoid responsibility and accountability for copyright infringement. One example is Grokster.

Grokster

Grokster is similar to Napster, in that when using its music files sharing application, you will create a folder in which the MP3 files you want shared are stored. However, unlike Napster, you do not use a central server where the individual files are sent and accessed. By contrast to Napster, Grokster provides the software that allows any user computer to become a central server. For example, as shown in Figure 6b, when users search for a song and initiate transfer of an MP3 file using the Grokster client, they do so without any information being transmitted to or through any computers owned or controlled by Grokster. Grokster does not provide the site and facilities for direct copyright infringement. Once one gets the software, there is no additional connection with the company. This eliminates some of the accountability issues of Napster. Many companies that use a similar P2P technology have emerged: Aimster, Streamcast Networks, KaZaA, BitTorrent, Earthstation, Edonkey, FileNavigator, mlMac, and Soulseek. Others include Scour, Gnutella, Freenet, Spinner.com, eMule, FastTrack, Winmx, BearShare, and Morpheus from StreamCast Networks. Hybrid distributed variations are also emerging (Oberholzer & Strumpf, 2004). The main revenue source for these companies is advertisement. In October 2001, the RIAA and the Music Publishers Association of America (MPAA) jointly filed a suit against Morpheus (whose parent company is StreamCast), Grokster, and KaZaA in Los Angeles. KaZaA, which is a Dutch company, did not join Grokster and Morpheus in requesting for a summary judgment. To the surprise of many analysts in the music recording industry, the RIAA and the MPAA lost. Judge Stephen Wilson ruled that these companies did not have control over their users' actions and therefore did not contribute to copyright infringement. Citing the 1984 Sony Betamax decision of the United States Supreme Court, Judge Wilson stated:

Figure 6.

(a) Centralized P2P (Napster) (Adapted from Oberholzer & Strumpf, 2004)

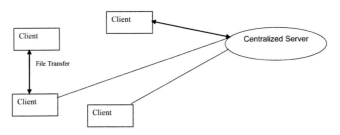

(b) Centralized P2P (Grokster) (Adapted from Oberholzer & Strumpf, 2004)

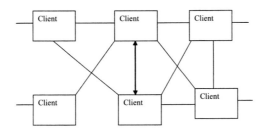

Neither Grokster nor StreamCast (the parent company of Morpheus) provides the site and facilities.... If either defendant closed their doors and deactivated all computers within their control, users of their products could continue sharing files with little or no interruption.

The RIAA and the MPAA have since appealed Judge Wilson's ruling.

RIAA Goes After Individual Music Downloaders

In September 2003 the RIAA filed a suite against four college students who run what the RIAA called "Napster-like internal campus networks" that aid in the theft of copyrighted songs. In September 2003, the RIAA filed a suite against 261 individuals, including a 12-year-old girl who had always thought that downloading music from the Internet was fun. The girl's parents settled the case for $2,000. "I am sorry for what I have done. I love music and don't want to hurt the artists I love," the girl said after the settlement.

A report on the settlement filed by the Associated Press appeared in the *Los Angeles Times* issue of September 10, 2003. In October 2003, the RIAA sent individual letters to file swappers requesting them to settle out of court or else they would be sued.

Reaction to RIAA Litigation

Decline in Music Downloads

A phone survey by Pew Internet & American Life Project, conducted between November 18 and December 14, 2003, showed indications that the percentage of music downloading had declined from 29% in February 2001 to 14%. Also during the same period, downloading by users 18 to 29 years old declined from 52% to 28%, 30 to 49 years old declined from 27% to 13%, and 50 years and above from 15% to 6%.

Men had the largest decline (36% to 18%) compared to women (26% to 11%). Users with household incomes under $30,000 reported higher download percentage (22%) in December 2003 compared to higher household income earners (16% for household income above $75,000).

Some analysts have cautioned that this data may mean that people are more apprehensive to tell the truth about their Internet use activities. The best data should come from the P2P companies offering such services. However, it is difficult to get this type of data since most of the "Baby Napsters" do not allow connections through their servers.

Society's Ambivalence

Those in defense for the current practice of illegal downloading of music from the Internet have argued that the violations of copyright are so rampant in society that it will be impossible to enforce the laws behind them. People have been making copies of songs from the radio or friend tapes for a long time. You can make back-up copies of your CDs, and even loan them to your friends so that they can listen to them. Resources needed to regulate home audio and video recording are similar to those needed to enforce driving speed. "The speed limit on American motorways had to be changed because of general disobedience. Alcohol prohibition had to be abolished too. And copyright is more difficult to enforce than the consumption and production of alcoholic beverages" (Bergmann, p. 5). Industry analysts, like Wade (2002), think it is unfair for the IFPI or RIAA to come down so tough on individuals who infringe copyright through file sharing. She contends:

Everyday there are people ripping CDs, copying from the radio to the cassette and previously copying form one cassette to another. How many people have bought a CD from a shop copied it and returned it? I could name countless. Are the police now going to enforce each and every copyright infringement like that and make the copier pay damager? Surely the copyright laws are there to prevent mass unauthorized reproduction of other artists work? Evidently not.

The file sharing community has also argued that CDs are too expensive, and most of the money goes to the big recording label oligopolies represented by the RIAA and the IFPI and not to the music composers or artists.

CURRENT CHALLENGES/PROBLEMS FACING THE INDUSTRY

Some of the current challenges facing the music recording industry fall in four main areas: (1) preventing piracy, (2) better public relations, (3) developing a viable business model, and (4) government legislation.

- **Preventing piracy:** Piracy still remains the big problem. The RIAA and IFPI have acknowledged that the music industry was slow in responding to the P2P downloading problem started by Napster (Singh & Zook, 2001). Although the music industry has since stopped Napster, P2P companies—"Baby Napsters" such as Morpheus, KazaA, Winmx, Aimster and others—have emerged. These "Baby Napsters" are set up to circumvent copyright law.

  - *Scorpion/Frog Tale:* Some analysts have used the well-known tale to explain away the inevitability of piracy on the Internet:

A scorpion, waiting to cross a river, meets a frog. "Would you mind carrying me across the river?" he asks. "You must be joking," replies the frog, "you'll sting me." "Of course I won't sting you," says the scorpion. "If I did that, we'd both drown, wouldn't we?" Eventually, the frog agrees to carry the scorpion over the water. Half way across, of course, the scorpion stings the frog. As they sink beneath the water, the frog asks, "Why did you do that?" "I'm sorry," says the scorpion, "it's just my nature." (Parker, 2001)

  - *Digital Rights Management (DRM) Systems:* DRM systems restrict illegal use of digital files, thus protecting the interests of copyright holders. DRM technologies can control file access (number of views, length of views), printing, sharing, saving, altering, and copying. These technologies may be embedded within the program software, operating system, or in the firmware. The problem is that available DRM systems tend to inconvenience both legal and illegal users. A copy-protected DVD is a nuisance for someone who wants to legally make a back-up copy. Most users tend to avoid buying DRM-enabled content or use available free software to disable the protection. Efforts by the RIAA and IFPI through the Secure Digital Music Initiative (SDMI) to oversee development of a Digital Rights Management (DRM) System for digital music failed because the interests of consumer electronics manufacturers, information technology developers, and music companies were incompatible. The music companies wanted hardware manufacturers to develop firmware that will protect their music. The hardware manufacturers did not want to compromise the usability of their products, since the firmware would have made their product less functional. This left the software vendors whose DRM products have been cracked as soon as they are released (Felten, 2001).

After some lobbying by the music industry, the 1998 Digital Millennium Copyright Act (DMCA) was passed by congress to protect copyright holders' rights. The law provides civil and criminal penalties for the creation or distribution of DRM circumvention tools. Consequently, a user attempting to circumvent copyright protection, even for legitimate reasons, may violate federal law.[4]

- **Public relations:** The industry legal action (especially from the RIAA) against individuals downloading music from P2P networks on the Internet has been a public relations disaster; especially when one of the targeted individuals was a 12-year-old elementary school girl. There are efforts to boycott music licensed by the big five—companies represented by the RIAA—and "Boycott the RIAA" Web sites have been launched. The IFPI initially tried to avoid going for individuals and focused on music pirate manufacturing companies on public education campaigns instead. However, the IFPI has recently started to go for individuals (Bryne, 2004).

- **Declining sales:** The music industry has claimed that the downloading of music over the Internet using P2P and MP3 technologies caused the recent decline in record sales. They also claim that file-swapping technologies have discouraged new artists and songwriters from entering the music profession. But music industry analysts have noted that there was a 15% decline in sales during the 1980 to 1981 recession. They also report a 9% decline in sales during the 2001 recession. The analysts contend that the impact of the early 1990's recession was abated by the introduction of the CD as people upgraded their old record collections for new versions on CDs. Appendix 2 provides the 1993 to 2002 Year End Statistics of Manufacturers' Unit Shipments and Dollar Value in the USA. It seems the noted decline in music sales may be attributed to national and global economic factors in addition to free downloading. Individual music purchases come from discretionary income that is normally squeezed during lean times. Also, just because an individual has downloaded a free song from the Internet does not necessarily mean that the person would not have bought the song (Oberholzer & Strumpf, 2004). According to Merrill Lynch analysts, global music sales were unlikely to recover before 2005, after which there will be an expected growth of about 6.5% a year for the following five years. It is also predicted that by 2006, about 40% of online music sales will come from digital downloads compared to about 5% in 2004.

- **Business model:** The key players in the music industry are still searching for viable business models that will embrace P2P technology (Lindstrom, 2003). Early new entrants who are currently providing industry-licensed digital music services include Wal-Mart Stores Inc., the revamped Napster, Apple Computer Inc.'s iTunes Music Store, and iPod digital player. Also, record label companies are now considering making much of their music catalog available for digital sale. Moreover, a few artists are succeeding in selling their music directly to consumers (Goldberg, 2004).

- **Government legislation:** A global enforceable copyright legislation may be difficult to attain. Even when a country is a signatory of the General Agreement on Tariffs and Trade (GATT) that requires all signatories to conform to the international norms of copyright protection, there is a danger that national governments may implement legislation "unsympathetic" to the copyright community.[5] It is not far fetched but in some countries:

...the idealistic (mostly) young people who believe they are fighting for a just cause when they trade music for free—have been completely turned off by what they perceive as the big bad corporations stepping in and ruining their party. As history has shown,

the collective power of people who believe strongly enough in any cause can make governments topple... (Music Business International, 2001)

REFERENCES

Anderson, P. C., & Tushman, M. L. (1990). Technological discontinuities and dominant designs: A cyclical model of technological change. *Administrative Science Quarterly, 35,* 604-633.

Anderson, P. C., & Tushman, M. L. (1997). Managing through cycles of technological change. In M. L. Tushman, & P. Anderson (Eds.), *Managing strategic innovation and change* (pp. 45-52). New York: Oxford University Press.

Angle, H. L., & Van de Ven, A. H. (2000). Suggestions for managing the innovation journey. In A. H. Van de Ven, H. L. Angle, & M. S. Poole (Eds.), *Research on the management of innovation: The Minnesota studies.* New York: Oxford University Press.

Barrett, J. (2003). *Thinking outside the disk: Piracy, digital music and the future of the recording industry.* Dallas, TX: Parks Associates.

Byrne, S. (2004). *247 file swappers across Europe & Canada face legal action.* Retrieved January 1, 2005, from http://www.cdfreaks.com/news/9432

Champ, H. (2001). Internet concerns dominate industry plans. *Music Business International, Supplement, 11*(5), 52-53.

Champ, H. (2003). RIAA to sue over file sharing. *Music & Media, 21*(28), 1-2.

Christensen, C. M. (1997). *The innovator's dilemma: When new technologies cause great firms to fail.* Boston: Harvard Business School Press.

Christensen, C. M., & Ovedorf, M. (2000). Meeting the challenge of disruptive change. *Harvard Business Review, 78*(2), 67-76.

D'Angelo, J. (2003). *Morpheus, Grokster are a-ok, judge says.* Retrieved January 1, 2005, from http://www.mtv.com/news/articles/1471561/20030428/story.jhtml

Dougherty, D., & Heller, T. (1994). The illegitimacy of successful product innovations in established firms. *Organization Science, 5*(2), 200-218.

Ehrnberg, E., & Jacobsson, S. (1997). Technological discontinuities and incumbents' performance: An analytical framework. In C. Edquist (Ed.), *Systems of innovation technologies, institutions, and organizations.* London: Pinter.

Electronic commerce in the music industry and steel industry in Sweden. Retrieved January 1, 2005, from http://www.oecd.org/dataoecd/31/61/2669241.pdf

Felten, E. (2001). Hacking in public. *Music Business International, 11*(4), 7.

Fisher, W. (2000). *Digital music: Problems and possibilities.* Retrieved January 1, 2005, from http://www.business.com/directory/media_and_entertainment/music/reference/

Foster, R. N. (1986). *Innovation: The attacker's advantage.* New York: Summit Books.

Goldberg, J. (2004). *The ultimate survival guide to the new music industry: A handbook from hell.* Hollywood, CA: Lone Eagle Publishing.

How much does a band earn? (n.d.). *New York Daily News.* Retrieved January 1, 2005, from http://www.nydailynews.com/entertainment/v-pfriendly/story/60991p-57008c.html

Lindstrom, J. (2003). Embrace P2P services. *Music & Media, 21*(15), 4.

Kleinschmit, M. (2004). *The hype is back! Online music and the rise of the empowered music consumer*. Retrieved January 1, 2005, from http://www.ipsos-ideas.com/articles/vol5-2.cfm

Music and motion picture groups move for ruling in case against MusicCity and others. (n.d.). Retrieved January 1, 2005, from http://www.nmpa.org/pr/MusicCityPressRelease.pdf

Music industry settles first case—With 12-year-old. (2003, September 10). *Los Angeles Times*. Retrieved January 1, 2005, from http://www.theage.com.au/articles/2003/09/10/1062902092627.html

Napster and the music industry. (n.d.). Retrieved January 1, 2005, from http://www.fraber.de/gem/Napster%20and%20the%20Music%20Industry%20010617.pdf

Oberholzer, F., & Strumpf, K. (2004, March). *The effect of file sharing on record sales: An empirical analysis*. Retrieved January 1, 2005, from http://www.unc.edu/~cigar/papers/FileSharing_March2004.pdf

Parker, N. (2001). The sting in the copyright tale. *Music Business International, 11*(4), 62.

Rainie, L., Madden, M., Hess, D., & Mudd, G. (2004). *Pew Internet project and Comscore Media Metrix Data demo*. Retrieved from http://www.pewinternet.org/reports/pdfs/PIP_File_Swapping_Memo_0104.pdf

Recording industry goes after students on music sharing. (n.d.). Retrieved January 1, 2005, from http://msl1.mit.edu/furdlog/docs/nytimes/nytimes_industry_student_file_sharing_apr_23_2003.pdf

Singh, A., & Zook, C. (2001). Fear is never a substituted for strategy. *Music Business International, 11*(3), 58.

Striking the right balance. (2001). *Music Business International, 11*(2), 11.

The music industry in the new millennium: Global and local perspectives. (n.d.). Retrieved January 1, 2005, from http://portal.unesco.org/culture/en/file_download.php/7c68835ea9cfe0cdf220441af9494fa0The+Music+Industry+in+the+new+Millenium.pdf

Top ten file sharing sites. (n.d.). Retrieved January 1, 2005, from http://www.p2p-page.de/napster_history.htm

Tushman, M. L., & Anderson, P. C. (1986). Technological discontinuities and organizational environments. *Administrative Science Quarterly, 31*, 439-465.

ENDNOTES

[1]   Note that the same phenomenon occurred when the television was introduced in late 1940s and early 1950s. Record labels started to promote their high selling music on TV, just as they did on radio.

[2]   Please note that despite a number of requests, it was not possible to obtain an organizational chart from the RIAA. What we provide is the best reconstruction based on public data.

[3]   The problem is that a person could borrow someone else's CD and place it in his/her computer's CD-ROM.

[4]   Visit, for example, http://www.epic.org/privacy/drm/.

[5]   Those norms were set out in the Berne Convention for the protection of literary and artistic works. The United States signed the Berne Convention in 1978.

DEFINITIONS

- **Competence-Enhancing Discontinuities:** These build on the skills and technologies embodied in the firm and enhance the firms' know-how in the new technology. It may increase barriers to entry.
- **Competence-Destroying Discontinuities:** These render obsolete the skills and technologies embodied in the firm. It may reduce barriers to entry and allow new competitors, firms with know-how in the new technology. These new competitors may unseat industry leaders.
- **Disruptive Technologies:** The ones that create entirely new markets through the introduction of new products or services. These offer a different value proposition to the market and tend to appeal to new categories of customers who have different perceptions of product value. Well-managed firms that do not listen carefully to their customers may not invest in these new technologies, for example, Kodak.
- **International Federation of the Phonographic Industry (IFPI):** IFPI is the organization representing the international recording industry. It comprises a membership of 1,500 record producers and distributors in 76 countries. It also has national groups in 46 countries. IFPI's International Secretariat is based in London and is linked to regional offices in Brussels, Hong Kong, Miami, and Moscow.
- **Piracy:** The term is generally used to describe the deliberate infringement of copyright on a commercial scale. In relation to the music industry, it refers to unauthorized copying and, in this context, falls into three categories:

    - *Simple piracy* is the unauthorized duplication of an original recording for commercial gain without the consent of the rights owner. The packaging of pirate copies is different from the original. Pirate copies are often compilations, such as the greatest hits of a specific artist or a collection of a specific genre like dance tracks.
    - *Counterfeits* are copied and packaged to resemble the original as closely as possible. The original producer's trademarks and logos are reproduced in order to mislead the consumer into believing that they are buying an original product.
    - *Bootlegs* are the unauthorized recordings of live or broadcast performances. They are duplicated and sold—often at a premium price—without the permission of the record label company, artist, or composer.

- **Secure Digital Music Initiative (SDMI):** An initiative sponsored by the IFPI and others to bring together the recoding industry, consumer electronics, and technology companies to develop a secure and legal trading environment for music over the Internet.
- **Sustaining Technologies:** The ones that improve the performance of existing products and services. They are based on measures of performance that current customers value and tend to reinforce the current models that firms are using to bring products to the market.

APPENDIX 1: 2002 YEAR END STATISTICS

The Recording Industry Association of America

(Manufacturers' Unit Shipments & Dollar Value)
(In Millions, Net after Returns)

	1993	1994	1995	1996	1997	1998	1999	2000	2001	2002
CD (Units Shipped)	495.40	662.10	722.90	778.90	753.10	847.00	938.90	942.50	881.90	803.30
CD (Dollar Value)	6511.40	8464.50	9377.40	9934.70	9915.10	11416.00	12816.30	13214.50	12909.40	12044.10
CD Single	7.80	9.30	21.50	43.20	66.70	56.00	55.90	34.20	17.30	4.50
CD Single	45.80	56.10	110.90	184.10	272.70	312.20	222.40	142.70	79.40	19.60
Cassette	339.50	345.40	272.60	222.50	172.60	158.50	123.60	76.00	45.00	31.10
Cassette	2915.80	2976.40	2303.60	1905.30	1522.70	1419.90	1061.60	626.00	363.40	209.80
Cassette Single	85.60	81.10	70.70	59.90	42.20	26.40	14.20	1.30	-1.50	-0.50
Cassette Single	298.50	274.90	236.30	189.30	133.50	94.40	48.00	4.60	-5.30	-1.60
LP/EP	1.20	1.90	2.20	2.90	2.70	3.40	2.90	2.20	2.30	1.70
LP/EP	10.60	17.80	25.10	36.80	33.30	34.00	31.80	27.70	27.40	20.50
Vinyl Single	15.10	11.70	10.20	10.10	7.50	5.40	5.30	4.80	5.50	4.40
Vinyl Single	51.20	47.20	46.70	47.50	35.60	25.70	27.90	26.30	31.40	24.90
Music Video	11.00	11.20	12.60	16.90	18.60	27.20	19.80	18.20	17.70	14.70
Music Video	213.30	231.10	220.30	236.10	323.90	508.00	376.70	281.90	329.20	288.40
DVD Audio	0.00	0.00	0.00	0.00	0.00	0.00	0.00	0.00	0.30	0.40
DVD Audio	0.00	0.00	0.00	0.00	0.00	0.00	0.00	0.00	6.00	8.50
DVD Video*	0.00	0.00	0.00	0.00	0.00	0.50	2.50	3.30	7.90	10.70
DVD Video*	0.00	0.00	0.00	0.00	0.00	12.20	66.30	80.30	190.70	236.30
Total Units	955.60	1122.70	1112.70	1134.40	1063.40	1123.90	1160.60	1079.20	968.50	859.60
Total Value	10,046.60	12,068.00	12,320.30	12,533.80	12,236.80	13,810.20	14,584.70	14,323.70	13,740.90	12,614.20
Total Retail Units					817.50	850.00	869.70	788.60	733.10	675.70
Total Retail Value					10,785.80	12165.4	13048	12,705.00	12,388.80	11,549.00

* While broken out for this chart, DVD Video Product is included in the Music Video totals.

Conrad Shayo is a professor of information science at California State University, San Bernardino. Over the last 23 years he has worked in various capacities as a university professor, consultant, and manager. He holds a Doctor of Philosophy and a Master of Science in information science from Claremont Graduate University. He also holds an MBA in management science from the University of Nairobi, Kenya, and a Bachelor of Commerce in finance from the University of Dar-Es-Salaam, Tanzania. His research interests are in the areas of IT assimilation, performance measurement, distributed learning, end-user computing, organizational memory, instructional design, organizational learning assessment, reusable learning objects, IT strategy, and "virtual societies." Dr. Shayo has published these and other topics in various books and journals. Currently, he is involved in developing reusable learning objects and Web based learning game simulations. He is also a co-editor (with Dr. Magid Igbaria) of the book Strategies for Managing IS/IT Personnel.

Ruth Guthrie is a professor of computer information systems at California Polytechnic University, Pomona. She has experience in systems engineering, software test and program management of space based IR sensor programs. Ruth has a PhD from Claremont Graduate University, an MS in statistics from the University of Southern California, and a BA in mathematics from Claremont McKenna College. Her research interests are user interface design and computer ethics. She has authored several papers in a variety of areas including two books on Web development. Currently, she is associate director for AACSB for the College of Business at Cal Poly and is involved in several Web development efforts using Video Embedded Flash.

This case was previously published in the *International Journal of Cases on Electronic Commerce*, 1(2), pp. 1-25, © 2005.

Chapter XIV

Student Advantage Captures the College Market Through an Integration of Their Off- and Online Businesses

Margaret T. O'Hara, East Carolina University, USA

Hugh J. Watson, University of Georgia, USA

EXECUTIVE SUMMARY

This chapter describes how Student Advantage successfully transformed itself from a brick-and-mortar company to the leading online portal to the higher education community. The company has followed a business strategy that includes creating Web sites that appeal to college students and forming partnerships with businesses and universities. Through its activities, Student Advantage has assembled a wealth of information about college students, all organized around a common student identifier. This information is important to Student Advantage and to its partners who are willing to pay for the insights that Student Advantage can provide about the college market. Interestingly, Student Advantage only recently developed a strong in-house information technology capability. This capability is now allowing Student Advantage to implement a variety of e-marketing applications. Lessons learned from Student Advantage's experiences are discussed.

INTRODUCTION

In what many people call "the new economy," there are three kinds of businesses. There are the traditional "brick and mortar" companies that sell their products through physical retail outlets. Then there are the "pure plays" that operate only electronically and have no physical stores. And finally, there are the "bricks and clicks" that operate in both the electronic and physical worlds.

Each kind of company faces challenges. The brick and mortars are at potential risk, at least for lost sales opportunities, if they do not have electronic channels. The pure plays have the cost savings of not operating physical stores, but frequently experience serious order fulfillment problems that can lead to their demise. The bricks and clicks are normally the result of brick and mortar companies establishing a presence on the Internet, but they often have a difficult time adding an electronic business to their existing ones. There are several reasons for this:

- The need to change the mindsets of existing organizational personnel;
- The need to change organization structures and reward systems;
- The need to manage off-line and online businesses in an integrated manner;
- The need to integrate disparate systems using a common customer identifier;
- The need to create a stable, scalable architecture; and
- The need to present a "single face" to the customer.

These are difficult challenges and not all companies have handled them well. One that has is Student Advantage. In 2000, The Data Warehousing Institute selected Student Advantage for inclusion in its study "Harnessing Customer Information for Strategic Advantage: Technical Challenges and Business Solutions." The companies included in this study had demonstrated "best practices" in their use of customer information. Student Advantage was selected, in part, for its successful integration of its physical and electronic businesses. This chapter presents the Study Advantage case study and provides you with valuable insights about how to successfully create and operate bricks and clicks companies. It also describes how contemporary information technology can be used to support electronic marketing.

ABOUT STUDENT ADVANTAGE

In 1992, Student Advantage started as a traditional brick and mortar company. At that time, its only product was a card that college students used with participating merchants to obtain a discount on their purchases. Over the last five years, Student Advantage has successfully transformed itself and moved online with a variety of new products and services. It has become the leading media and commerce connection for students and the businesses and universities that serve them.

Student Advantage's mission is to help students save money, work smarter, and make more informed life decisions. In carrying out its mission, Student Advantage has developed relationships with universities and business partners. It helps universities provide services to their students at little or no cost. It helps business partners increase sales and better understand the college market. Information, in general, and information about the college market, in particular, is a large part of Student Advantage's business.

Student Advantage's position in the marketplace has been hard won. For its college student members, it has continued to be fresh and relevant with the products, services, and content provided. Equally important, Student Advantage has developed long-term relationships with universities and business partners built on trust and performance. This two-prong strategy has been the source of a sustainable competitive advantage.

Student Advantage's creative, constantly evolving business strategy—enabled by information technology—has allowed Student Advantage to:

- Develop an estimated membership base of nearly 2 million college students at the end of the fall 2000 semester, in over 125 local markets;
- Become the leading provider of online and off-line content, products, and services for the college market;
- Develop proprietary business relationships with over 15,000 business partners; and
- Position itself for success in the networked economy.

In this case, the history and evolving business strategy of Student Advantage are described. Of importance is how the company has changed while still capitalizing on its previous strengths. Critical to the successful evolution have been the fundamental beliefs about how Student Advantage should responsibly handle its interactions with students, universities, and business partners. Next, Student Advantage's various products and services are described, followed by a description of the technology that makes it all possible. Several applications are described that illustrate how Student Advantage uses data and technology to understand and develop relationships with college students. The case concludes with a discussion of Student Advantage's business model, the lessons learned, and future directions.

COMPANY HISTORY

As a college student, Student Advantage founder Ray Sozzi wondered why no one had successfully organized the purchasing power of college students at a national level, as the American Association for Retired People (AARP) had done for senior citizens. After all, college students represent the most sought-after demographic group by marketers everywhere—first-time heads of household, destined to join the most educated, high-income segment of the economy. Faced with new decisions to be made every day–from simple to complex, from choosing a telecommunications provider to selecting soap—college students' good experiences stay with them, often for a lifetime.

For most businesses, recognizing the significance of the college market was easy; however, targeting marketing campaigns was more problematic. Although much generic information was known about the group, specifics were tough to come by. Businesses knew their average age–could even segment them into specific groups based on class year, and knew they lived predominantly in towns in which universities were located. However, college students are among the most transient population group; the typical college student moves twice every year. The college population has significant turnover, and students neither read the same publications nor watch similar television shows across their demographic group. Thus, the issue becomes, how does a firm really locate this easy-to-find population?

Following up on his idea, Sozzi started Student Advantage in 1992. The initial business model was to provide college students with a discount card that they could use with participating merchants. The idea was simple and inherently appealing on two fronts: (1) students did not have much money, and retailers felt good about cutting them a break, and (2) students were receptive to the discounts. For the next two years, Student Advantage systematically increased its reach to more college campuses and businesses. In the early years, the Student Advantage Membership Card was simply shown at the local retailer when a purchase was made. No data were captured beyond the initial membership application from the student.

In 1994, Student Advantage signed an agreement with American Express that made the Student Advantage Card available to student American Express cardholders. Continuing to go national, in 1996 Student Advantage struck an agreement with AT&T that resulted in the offering of an AT&T/Student Advantage Card that functioned both as a discount and a calling card. The agreement was a major turning point that extended AT&T's and Student Advantage's presence in the college market, and almost overnight, Student Advantage increased its membership to 1.3 million students in 80 local college markets. As part of the relationship, Student Advantage also provided AT&T with information about the college market based on analyses of the Student Advantage student database.

Next, Student Advantage aggressively signed agreements with national, best of breed companies like Amtrak, Barnes & Noble, Greyhound, and Foot Locker that serve the college market but tend to not compete with one another. Once again, part of the agreement was to provide the participating companies with information about how college students use their products.

By 1996, the Internet had become important to interacting with customers and Student Advantage took its business to the Web. The initial motivation was to reduce the cost of servicing members by providing information on the Web rather than through the mail. This began the movement from an off-line, bricks-and-mortar business to one with most of its activities online. This was a turning point for Student Advantage and created both challenges and opportunities. As with most dot.coms, the challenge was to grow market share by offering an increasing set of online products and services in order to create an electronic "community." To do this required in-house application development, the acquisition of competing companies, and the further development of relationships with business partners and universities.

On the university side, Student Advantage worked to become a trusted partner. For example, its acquisition of Campus Direct allowed students to access their grades online and to have a cash card that could be used on and off campus. The business model was to help universities better provide their students with an enhanced set of services but at little or no cost to the schools.

As a result of these efforts, Student Advantage's network of Web sites (e.g., studentadvantage.com, CollegeClub.com, uwire.com, FANSonly.com and estudentloan.com) offers a variety of products, services, and information—discounts on products, news from college campuses nationwide, entertainment, sports information, scholarship information, and help with term papers—all things that appeal to college students. In June 1999, Student Advantage went public and is traded on the Nasdaq as STAD. Student Advantage's corporate offices are located in Boston, Massachusetts. A series of acquisitions, most notably of FANSonly, a popular college sports destination, and CollegeClub.com, a leading integrated communications and media Internet company, has taken the size of the company's workforce to approximately 450 full-time employees.

THE COLLEGE MARKET BUSINESS STRATEGY

Student Advantage's objective is to enhance its position as the leading media and commerce connection for college students and the businesses and universities that serve them. It intends to increase the breadth and depth of its relationships with students by continuing to serve the needs of its three constituencies: students, businesses, and universities. The key elements of their strategy include:

- Strengthen the online destination for students. By extending its already comprehensive network of Web sites, Student Advantage through studentadvantage.com and CollegeClub.com, will offer students e-commerce services, content, and community, all targeted specifically to their demographic group. Toward this goal, Student Advantage is continuing to acquire or form strategic alliances with companies in the higher education space.
- Continue to build brand. Student Advantage's market leadership position has been driven by its membership program and by partnering with leading national and local sponsors and universities. To sustain this leadership position, Student Advantage will continue its aggressive brand-building activities.
- Aggressively grow membership. Student Advantage has implemented a variety of initiatives to increase its membership. It is currently promoting memberships through its Web site and has increased its e-commerce partners to increase traffic to the site. It has expanded its on-campus marketing services, added corporate sponsors, and begun to offer programs to high school students and college graduates.
- Enhance relationships with students, businesses, and universities. Concurrent with its aggressive marketing to students, Student Advantage is also offering new services to its corporate sponsors, such as visitor and membership data that will allow Student Advantage and its business partners to better target advertising, make recommendations to students, and provide for a more personalized and engaging experience for students. Student Advantage will also continue to offer universities an outsourcing solution for specific online services, such as providing transcripts and grade reporting online, and Web development and maintenance for university athletic departments and campus newspapers.
- Continue to pursue strategic alliances and acquisitions. Student Advantage has acquired and fully integrated ten businesses that have helped it expand and

strengthen its online and off-line offerings to students. Such acquisitions and alliances will continue.

A business strategy challenge that Student Advantage faced was what Todd Eichler, Senior Vice President, calls "the chicken and egg" problem. What comes first, develop the corporate partners or the student members? The corporate partners are needed to create the "deals" that attract students, while the students are needed to attract the corporate partners. The solution was to do both at the same time.

COMPETITORS

Currently, Student Advantage has no competitors that compete across the board with a comparable set of products and services. However, over the years, Student Advantage has faced many competitors who have focused on one of two areas. The first area is competitors who provide either online or off-line student-focused products. This has included scores of young entrepreneurs offering discount coupon books and cards. Some of these competitors were hired by Student Advantage and their products were rebranded with the Student Advantage name. The second area is competitors who try to partner with universities and businesses to provide services to students. One of these was Collegiate Advantage who did events and promotions on campuses for companies. The competitive solution was to acquire Collegiate Advantage.

There have been numerous companies that have gone after specific niches in the college market. Some of them have been heavily funded by venture capitalists and were able to put much more money into their niches than Student Advantage. The founders (e.g., Ray Sozzi and Todd Eichler) internally funded Student Advantage until 1998. Competing against well-funded startups was one of Student Advantages major challenges. The disadvantage that these competitors faced was that they did not have the broad, synergistic set of products, services, and relationships that Student Advantage had developed. Many of these companies went out of business, while some of them (e.g., CollegeClub.com) were acquired by Student Advantage when it was felt that they could be made profitable within the Student Advantage business model.

Interestingly, the downturn of the dot.com world in 2001 reduced Student Advantage's competition. Venture capitalists became less willing to invest money in online businesses, including those that might compete with Student Advantage. This was a turning point for Student Advantage.

PRODUCTS AND SERVICES

Students can become a Student Advantage Member in several ways: (1) by paying an annual membership fee of $20; (2) by buying products or services from corporate sponsors, such as Barnes & Noble Bookstores and Wells Fargo, who "pay" for the students' memberships; and (3) through college or college-related programs where the sponsoring organizations purchase memberships in bulk for distribution free of charge to students. A Student Advantage Member has access to many products and services; see Figure 1 for examples of how students use their memberships.

Figure 1. How students use Student Advantage

10:02a.m.	Tim (Student Advantage Member #3756831954), a UCLA junior, checks out the basketball scores at Student Advantage's FANSonly Network, FANSonly.com
12:20a.m.	Deb (Student Advantage Member #3556493274), an American University senior, gets a 15% discount on her spring break Amtrak tickets
2:05p.m.	Phil (Student Advantage Member #3017359284), a recent Seton Hall graduate, plans his dream "post graduation trip" to Europe at railconnection.com
4:55p.m.	Tom (Student Advantage Member #3788075344), a Carnegie Mellon senior, orders a bouquet from 1-800-FLOWERS.com for his girlfriend and saves 15%
6:37p.m.	Yolanda (Student Advantage Member #3869625124), a freshman at Penn State, checks her grades at Student Advantage's getgrades.com
7:33p.m.	Kerry (Student Advantage Member #3941304554), an Azusa Pacific junior, on a deadline for the upcoming newspaper, downloads an article from Student Advantage's U-WIRE, at u-wire.com
9:12p.m.	Peter (Student Advantage Member 3068676514), a Boston College sophomore, gets $3 off a regularly priced CD at Tower Records

Student Advantage's products, services, and structure are organized around three groups: Student Services, University Services, and Business Services. Each group's offerings are described as follows.

Student Services

The Student Services group provides the leading online and off-line resources for information, services and commerce for the student community, including exclusive discounts. The division's offerings are available throughout the United States, locally on college campuses, and on the Student Advantage Network, giving students the "advantage" in every aspect of their daily lives, in partnership with the universities they attend.

The Student Advantage Network of sites provides content, community, and e-commerce to address the needs of college students. The sites offer services and information targeted to college students, including discount purchasing, travel alternatives, college sporting news, career and job searches, lifestyle and extracurricular decisions, and financial aid information. The Web sites:

- Enable access to approximately 500 college and university newspapers;
- Offer an e-commerce marketplace; and
- Include a searchable directory of sponsors that offer discounts for Student Advantage Members.

Business Services

The Business Services group serves the business-to-business market, offering experienced marketing information services, expertise in events and promotions, and database mining capabilities for national businesses that target students. Through this division, Student Advantage's business partners obtain critical information about this attractive demographic group.

Student Advantage reaches members through numerous channels: The Student Advantage Membership Program, the FANSonly Network, University Wire (U-Wire), Student Advantage Research, ScholarAid, Rail Connection, and Campus Direct. Other services include Student Advantage Cash and the SA Marketing Group.

Student Advantage provides a platform for businesses to market their products and services to a large, demographically attractive market. Student Advantage combines:

- Access to the college student market;
- Database marketing capabilities;
- A trusted brand;
- Program usage tracking;
- Quality online and off-line content; and
- Community interaction.

Student Advantage maintains contact with students throughout their college years and has established strong relationships with universities. In doing so, it benefits its sponsors by providing on-going targeted and continued access for advertising and marketing efforts. Additionally, sponsors also benefit from Student Advantage's experience, knowledge, and expertise in designing and implementing effective marketing techniques to reach college students.

University Services

The University Services group provides university-specific information services that are relevant to students' lives. The division's full range of capabilities creates tailored opportunities for each university by providing complete Internet content and data management, telephone grade reporting, networked news offices, sports information, and complementary school ID systems.

The Student Advantage Membership Program has been endorsed by more than 60 colleges, universities, and university organizations. The typical agreement is for schools to co-market the Student Advantage Membership Program to their students. This includes sending a letter to students explaining the program along with an application for membership, and receiving a percentage of the associated membership fees. Some universities have purchased Student Advantage Memberships in bulk, at varying discount levels depending on the number of memberships, and have distributed memberships to students free of charge.

Student Advantage has also entered contractual relationships with many schools whereby Student Advantage acts as a service provider to the school. Services provided include Athletic Department Web site operation and maintenance through FANSonly, school newspaper online publishing through U-Wire, grade and financial aid status reporting through the Campus Direct brand, and stored value card program operation and management through the Student Advantage Cash program.

THE EVOLUTION OF THE ENABLING TECHNOLOGY

Considering that Student Advantage in 1992 tracked no information about its cardholders, its transformation into an information-intensive business is remarkable. Before information technology provided Student Advantage with database capabilities, it was impossible to determine card usage electronically. Student Advantage would visit a campus, sell discount cards for $20 and leave campus with the sales revenues, but with no information about its customers. If Student Advantage wanted to know how much the cards were being used, it asked the retailers, and often got answers such as, "Yeah, we saw a lot of cards this week."

Fortunately, Student Advantage recognized early in its history that keeping all the data it did collect in one place was critical, regardless of the data's source. Whether the data came from student memberships, sponsor reports, corporate partners, or its fulfillment vendor, the Student Advantage ID number was the control for everything. Pulling the data together was never the issue; using it effectively was something Student Advantage had to learn. However, by never creating islands of data, Student Advantage successfully avoided a major stumbling block to data integration.

Still, in 1994, its internal IT capabilities were extremely limited. Erik Geisler, the Director of Product Operations, was the only IT-skilled employee, and he was not trained for the emerging Internet world. The first real database project happened almost by accident. When American Express made the Student Advantage Card available to its college card holding members, it sent Student Advantage a tape containing member information, and Student Advantage sensed the opportunity to create a database of its student member information.

By 1994, when AT&T came on board, Student Advantage, with a very limited internal IT support staff, was able to access its customer data, and even provide valuable data back to AT&T. AERO (the fulfillment vendor) created an interface to a FoxPro database with some baseline query capabilities, and Student Advantage could, for the first time, respond to customer inquiries and verify current address information for those students who failed to receive a requested discount card.

When Amtrak and Student Advantage formed their business alliance, customer information became more critical, and Student Advantage was ready for the challenge. Amtrak asked Student Advantage to provide student customer information it could not generate itself. When college students bought train tickets using their Student Advantage Card, they did not supply their names and addresses, but Student Advantage had that data and could provide it to Amtrak. Because Student Advantage was not a threat to either Amtrak or AT&T's business, but rather a resource, both companies were willing to help Student Advantage learn what it needed to know about their databases.

Student Advantage's first online initiative was begun in 1996. Initially, the development and maintenance of the Web site was outsourced. The site only provided information about the Student Advantage discount program. The material presented was nothing more than "brochureware."

Student Advantage took an unusual next step to expand its Web site. The company went to Boston University and created the Student Studio—a program whereby BU sent students to Student Advantage to develop, manage, and run a portion of its Web site. It paid the students—who signed on for a single semester—through work-study programs, and in return, Student Advantage had a Web site for use by college students that was designed by college students. The program, which ran until summer 1999, was an outstanding success for both partners. Boston University could offer its students a real-world work experience, and Student Advantage received excellent support and a fertile proving ground for new hires. During the time of the Student Studio agreement, Student Advantage's Web site was voted one of the top five college Web sites in the world.

As the Web site was evolving, Student Advantage added the magnetic strip to its cards. Now, for the first time, it was able to collect reliable and accurate information about the card's usage at retail outlets. Although not all stores had the technology to read the cards, data began to flow in. As Student Advantage evolved, acquired more businesses, and formed more strategic alliances, its information processing needs grew.

In late 1998, Student Advantage started bringing in IT personnel. It hired a vice president of technology and seasoned Web developers. Once it filed to go public in 1999, it became a "dot-com" and needed to develop a sustainable IT infrastructure. Its Student Studio program was no longer adequate—especially during exam time when many of its student employees were unavailable. Working with firms such as US Web and Handshake Dynamics, it began to strengthen its online position and bring the database in-house and under tighter control.

Decisions that Student Advantage made during this transition from off-line to online were critical to its successful migration. From the start, its online and off-line customer database was integrated, and when it sent a mailer asking a college student to visit its Web site, it made sure that the student, once there, would not have to input any data that Student Advantage already had. Student Advantage already knew its students, and it was critical that the Web-savvy students realized this.

Although consultants are still used, Student Advantage has built a highly competent technology team. It currently is doing most of its projects in-house, sometimes using the technical expertise obtained through an acquisition.

Figure 2 shows how data flows in Student Advantage's current technical environment. Everything begins with a Student Advantage member taking an action. The student may go to an off-line merchant, like a coffee shop, to make a purchase. If the merchant has a POS device, the student's magnetic card is swiped and the data related to the transaction is sent to Student Advantage's data warehouse. Some local merchants (as opposed to national chains) do not have the technology in place to read the student membership cards; consequently, data resulting from these transactions is lost.

A student may also go to studentadvantage.com and the details of this visit are recorded and sent to the data warehouse. While at Student Advantage's Web site, a student may link to a business partner's Web site, with the possible intention of making a purchase or obtaining information. The student may also go directly to a business partner's Web site, without first going to Student Advantage's. After authenticating that the student is a Student Advantage Member through a member ID number, the student is able to purchase at a discount. Data from students' visits to the business partners' Web sites is also sent to the data warehouse.

The data in the warehouse can then be analyzed using e-marketing tools. For example, the tools may be used to plan and execute a marketing campaign. If this is the case, the list of students to be included in the campaign, the campaign message, and the collateral materials are student to Student Advantage's SMTP server, where they are then sent to the targeted students.

Figure 2. The data flows in Student Advantage's technical environment

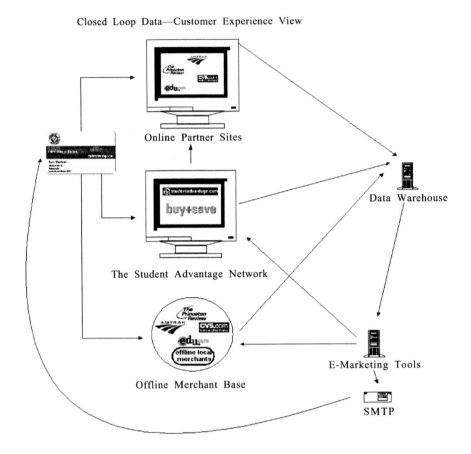

Third-party software provides Student Advantage with its e-marketing capabilities. The software resides on Student Advantage's hardware. Figure 3 shows how this software supports closed-loop marketing. The starting point is the entering of data to the data warehouse from Student Advantage's internal systems. These sources include the student membership database, internal fulfillment databases, customer service applications, and general leads. Another source is from external systems. These tend to be ad hoc and might include a business partner that wants Student Advantage to market to its customers and make its data available. Student Advantage's internal systems usually have the same student keys (i.e., Student Advantage Member Number), but this is not the case with external systems. The software utilizes a cross-reference table in assigning a unique, universal key to each student and for use within the e-marketing software. The cross-reference table also makes it possible to go back to the source data using the universal key.

Figure 3. Using Student Advantage's e-marketing system to provide closed loop marketing

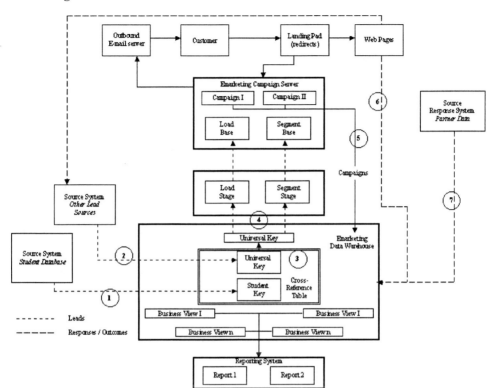

The e-marketing software then loads the data into its database. This is the basic extraction, transformation, and loading process associated with data warehousing. Once done, a process is used to import the data into the e-marketing campaign application. It is here that the market segment(s) are identified for the marketing campaigns. An outbound e-mail server then sends the marketing message to the leads (i.e., students) that have been selected. The landing pad is used to buffer the responses to the campaign. When a student responds to the message, the landing pad gets the instructions for what to do. For example, the instructions might be to present a particular Web page, ask a set of questions, follow a particular workflow, and track everything that transpires. It has a "lights out" functionality that allows it to process responses around the clock.

The responses to the campaign are automatically entered into the e-marketing software. Also returned to the e-marketing system is data collected when students go to Student Advantage's or a partner's Web site in response to the campaign. When the campaign is for a business partner, information about the campaign outcomes is passed on to the partner. For example, the outcomes might be that these (listed) customers purchased these (particular) items on the partner's Web site.

Student Advantage uses Brio software to analyze the e-marketing data. A user can either view predefined reports, drilldown into existing reports, or generate new reports by writing queries to the database. The ability to create and track campaigns from beginning to end provides a closed-loop marketing capability.

APPLICATIONS

Student Advantage has used its college student data in a variety of ways over the years.

Early Applications

One of the earliest target marketing campaigns was done for Amtrak. To help Amtrak build ridership on its weakest routes, Student Advantage identified all its members who attended a university within 30 miles of an Amtrak station. They then drilled down within this group of students to locate those students whose home addresses were also within 30 miles of an Amtrak station. To this select group, Amtrak offered deep discounts (up to 50%) and companion tickets in a major "Home for the Holidays" campaign. The campaign was highly successful for Amtrak and Student Advantage, not only because it had the desired effect of increasing Amtrak's ridership, but also because it validated how useful Student Advantage's student database could be. It began to take information technology very seriously, and started analyzing the data from all its partners.

Another successful campaign was one of the first e-mail campaigns. E-mails advertising a Web site to purchase textbooks were sent to 60,000 students. Many responded by going to the site and buying a book. The site had so much traffic it had to shut down and a new server had to be installed. Those students buying books were also asked to participate in a survey and responses indicated a high level of trust in Student Advantage.

Recent Applications

The e-marketing system software is used for many recent applications. It is employed for ad hoc and predefined analyses of Student Advantage's data. Of primary importance are historical relationships: How did each student come to be a member of Student Advantage? Was the membership card purchased, or was it given to the student by a university? Is the card a renewal or a first-time membership? Is there a mailing address on file, or just an e-mail address? In addition to the demographic profile, there is also a behavioral profile for each student. Has the student registered online, and shopped at one of the retailers? What has the student done lately? While the demographic profile is much more developed than the behavioral one, plans are underway to enhance this area.

Other applications analyze Web traffic and Web site performance. Most of this information is used for internal purposes, but a high level report is prepared quarterly and given to the financial community. The information is also used to report back the results of campaigns sponsored by Student Advantage's business partners.

Campaign planning and management are other applications that utilize the e-marketing system. A campaign might be designed to attract new members, generate business, and/or create traffic to a Web site. For example, an e-mail campaign designed for Textbooks.com should result in increased Web traffic and textbook sales. Once a campaign is designed, the budget and market segmentations are determined, and the campaign collateral (e.g., the messages, surveys) is developed. The campaign is then tracked, with the results fed back, to provide closed-loop marketing.

The first test campaigns using the e-marketing system were developed in February 2000. One campaign had Student Advantage's on-campus student representatives offering incentives to other students to visit studentadvantage.com. Here's how they did it. Using an on-campus "Wheel of Fortune" game, students either entered their e-mail address, swiped their Student Advantage card, or signed up for a card, and then spun a "virtual" wheel to determine a prize. Within 36 hours of spinning the wheel, the students received an e-mail message telling them what prize they had won and instructing them to visit the Student Advantage Web site to claim their prize. There was a 60% response rate to the e-mail messages, and of that group, 14% went beyond the prize-claiming page to become registered members. While one goal of the promotion was to have current Student Advantage Members visit the Web site, 2,600 new students became Student Advantage Members, at an acquisition cost far less than previous campaigns.

ASSESSING STUDENT ADVANTAGE'S BUSINESS MODEL

Over the last decade, Student Advantage has evolved its business model from being an off-line provider of a student discount card to being the leading online provider of content, products, and services for the higher education community and the businesses trying to reach the college market. This transformation has been achieved by a management team that has been willing to change organizational direction quickly, establish synergistic business relationships with business partners and universities, acquire other companies that complement the business strategy, and use information technology as the key enabler.

Like most dot-coms, creating market share is critical to long-term success. It is by this measure that Student Advantage has been especially successful. It has over 1.8 million college students as members—more than any other company that targets the college market. It also has established exclusive relationships with more than 15,000 business partners looking to attract college students. Student Advantage has also established an information technology infrastructure that allows it to develop and execute targeted marketing campaigns for itself and its business partners. Because of the data that Student Advantage has on college students and the ability to analyze that data, the company is well positioned to be the primary source of information on the most attractive demographic group in the country—college students.

An interesting problem that Student Advantage faces each year is the graduation of 20% of its members. There are ongoing discussions within Student Advantage about whether to try to retain these members by offering products and services designed specifically for them. An important complicating factor is that many of Student Advantage's business partners offer great deals to Student Advantage's members only because they are college students. Once they enter the workforce, it is hoped that they become lifetime "full value" customers. So, in addition to the question of whether Student

Advantage should expand its focus to include college graduates, there is the issue of whether and how its business partners would be part of such an initiative.

FUTURE DIRECTIONS

Student Advantage plans to capture and use more student data in the future. These plans include:

- Analyzing clickstream data more thoroughly and storing the findings with the member profiles. This will increase the ability to personalize interactions and messages with members;
- Incorporating behavioral data from all of Student Advantage's business units. This will provide a more comprehensive view of members;
- Installing tracking devices at a number of local and national business partners in order to better understand student behavior; and
- Developing an application that will eliminate the need for business partners to send back information about member activity at their Web site. Instead, Student Advantage will track its members' activities on the Web site.

Student Advantage is also striving to become more involved in the transactions between students and merchants, and as a result, is increasing its revenue stream. This initiative is associated with Student Advantage placing devices for swiping student cards in merchants' stores (both national and "mom and pop") and the growth of stored value debit cards like the Student Advantage Cash card. These cards typically allow students to make purchases both on (e.g., school cafeteria) and off (e.g., coffee shop) campus. When cards are run through the devices at Student Advantage's participating merchants, Student Advantage is able to understand student spending patterns and can sell the insights gleaned to business partners. Student Advantage is also in a position to receive a share of each transaction, much like credit card companies do.

LESSONS LEARNED

Important lessons have been learned at Student Advantage, including:

- Integrate data from different systems whenever possible. Student Advantage began to implement a formal data strategy at the same time that it developed its Internet strategy. This enabled Student Advantage to create a data strategy that took all data sources into account from the beginning, including off-line partner data, online data, e-marketing data, and customer service data. This approach eliminated inconsistencies in data across channels, thus better supporting data mining and creating the basis for providing a better customer experience.
- Partner data is valuable and sensitive. Much of Student Advantage's business model relies on obtaining student customer data from Student Advantage's network of business partners. Student Advantage had to present a strong business case for why its business partners should share its data. Student Advantage also

has had to earn and maintain the trust of its student customers. Student Advantage spends a considerable amount of time researching and modifying its privacy policies. In addition, they are extremely careful in how it shares and uses student data.

- Give marketers access to the data. Initially, only employees with strong technical skills had access to Student Advantage's data. It was soon recognized, however, that most of the people who knew "what to do" with the data were non-technical. Student Advantage implemented simple data access tools that "put the power" back in the hands of the marketers.

- Do not over-collect data. Student Advantage has learned the hard way that just because data is available, it does not mean that it should be tracked. At first, Student Advantage was tracking every aspect of what its customers did. After running into performance and storage problems, Student Advantage focused on capturing only the "necessary" parts of these transactions. Prior to capturing any data, Student Advantage asks the question, "What will this data be used for?" in an effort to reduce extraneous data capture.

- Maintain a unique identifier across all channels. Student Advantage was able to eliminate any discrepancies or match problems by maintaining the Student Advantage Member Number across all membership-related channels. As the business grows, e-mail addresses will be used as another identifier.

CONCLUSION

Ray Sozzi's original business model was to provide discount cards to college students who showed their Student Advantage Membership Card to participating merchants. This model changed as the Internet emerged and new business opportunities became apparent. The current business model focuses on college students and works closely with colleges and business partners, capitalizing on the information that Student Advantage has about the college market. A key part of Student Advantage's competitive position is the long-term relationships it had built with universities and business partners.

Like all dot-com companies, information technology is a vital, integral component of Student Advantage's business. Without it, there is no business. It is interesting to observe, however, that until recently, Student Advantage had little internal IT expertise and contracted out the required work. It even relied on Boston University students to maintain its Web site. What Student Advantage did have, however, was a strong management vision of how technology could be used. In the marketplace, it was able to acquire the technology and skills needed to implement the vision. For the long haul, Student Advantage recognized the need for in-house IT expertise to integrate, run, and manage an increasingly technologically complex environment and to provide leadership for future initiatives.

Student Advantage still has obstacles to overcome. It must continue to grow, evolve, and become profitable (targeted for Q4, 2001). It must continue to develop an internal IT staff and infrastructure that will allow the company to capitalize on its college student data.

Still, Student Advantage has done several things exceptionally well. It has successfully transformed from an off-line to a predominately online business. Through internal development and acquisitions, it has expanded the scope and content of its Web site in order to become the major electronic community for college students. It is poised to take advantage of its large membership base, the relationships it has carefully developed with colleges and business partners, and the unique information that it can generate from its database.

ACKNOWLEDGMENTS

The authors would especially like to thank Erik Geisler and Todd Eichler for the insights and information they provided.

Margaret T. O'Hara is an assistant professor of MIS at East Carolina University. After considerable work experience as a CIO, she completed her PhD in MIS at The University of Georgia. She specializes in understanding the impacts of technology-driven change, including the changes brought about by data warehousing. Maggie has also done considerable research in information systems education, including online learning and curriculum. She has published articles in both academic and practitioner journals, including Management Decision, The Journal of Computer Information Systems, Information Management, *and* Computerworld, *and has presented her work at numerous national and international conferences.*

Hugh J. Watson is a professor of MIS and a holder of a C. Herman and Mary Virginia Terry Chair of Business Administration in the Terry College of Business at the University of Georgia. He is the author of 22 books and over 100 scholarly journal articles. He is recognized for his work on decision support systems, executive information systems, and most recently, data warehousing. Hugh has consulted with numerous organizations, including the World Bank, Intel, IBM, Arthur Andersen, Conoco, and Glaxo. He is the senior editor of the Journal of Data Warehousing *and a fellow of The Data Warehousing Institute. He is the consulting series editor for John Wiley & Sons'* Computing and Information Processing *series.*

This case was previously published in M. Raisinghani (Ed.), *Cases on Worldwide E-Commerce: Theory in Action*, pp. 151-170, © 2002.

Chapter XV

Challenges in the Redesign of Content Management:
A Case of FCP

Anne Honkaranta, University of Jyväskylä, Finland

Airi Salminen, University of Jyväskylä, Finland

Tuomo Peltola, SysOpen Plc., Finland

EXECUTIVE SUMMARY

The Finnish Centre for Pensions (FCP) is a government organization acting as the central body for private pension institutions in Finland. One of its central tasks is to produce and publish guideline documents for ensuring that the pension institutions carry out pension provisioning in a unified way. Due to problems in the maintenance of the documents and requests for faster information delivery by the Internet, FCP carried out a content management development initiative during 2002-2004. The case follows the changes in components of the content management environment: in the activities of work processes, actor roles, systems, and content items. The case shows that in content management redesign, the work processes, roles of people in the processes, content items, and systems are deeply intertwined. Changes in one component often cause changes in others, and thereby iterative development efforts are needed. The case highlights the challenges encountered and describes the tools utilized for redesign activities.

ORGANIZATIONAL BACKGROUND

The Finnish Centre for Pensions (FCP) acts as the central body of the private sector pension institutions in Finland. It is overseen by the Ministry of Social Affairs and Health and supervised by the Insurance Supervision Authority. In 2002, there were 380 employees working at FCP, primarily lawyers, pension schema experts, and pension register systems experts. Its costs of operation for 2002 were 40 million euros (Eläketurvakeskus - Finnish Centre for Pensions, 2003). FCP is an expert organization carrying out multiple types of tasks (FCP, 2003). For legislative bodies, FCP provides expertise needed during the design of new pension-related laws and norms, and produces estimates on the pension use and coverage. For private persons and especially for pension institutions carrying out numerous pension-related tasks in a decentralized way, it provides information and guidance via telephone, e-mail, paper-print documents, and on the Internet.

Finland joined the European Union (EU) in 1995, and therefore statutes and regulations in Finland are currently dependent on the EU legislation. The material developed by government organizations like FCP to guideline private sector companies and citizens has to reflect the changes both in the national legislation and in the EU legislation. In each EU country, free movement of labor inside the EU also requires knowledge about other states' regulations and norms, and about mutual agreements. In 2004, the EU expanded with 10 new member states. Thus people working in government organizations developing regulations for pensions both in the old and new EU countries face major challenges in maintaining the national and local regulations. At the same time, there is an increasing demand to speed up acquisition and deployment of new technologies.

The case of FCP represents an interesting opportunity for investigating content management problems and solutions in the area of public administration. Possibilities to utilize current and future information technologies effectively in public administration are actively being investigated under the term e-government. The case description provides an example and accounts of experiences both for practitioners and researchers of e-government. Outside public administration, FCP represents a case where documents are essential sources of knowledge and act as boundary objects (Brown & Gray, 1995; Murphy, 2001) between organizations. It is likely that in several government organizations, both in the EU and outside it, similar needs for content redesign to those of FCP will evolve. A case study (Halverson & Ackerman, 2003) on document redesign in air traffic control shows that content redesign of documents critical for carrying out work in organizations is a challenging task in the private sector, too.

Data for the case description was gathered between June 2002 and March 2004 from various sources, and consisted of the following:

- Brochures, newsletters, and the Internet site of FCP (e.g., Eläketurvakeskus - Finnish Centre for Pensions, 2003; FCP, 2003);
- The reports of the content management initiative (e.g., Ahovaara, 2002, 2003; Peltola, 2003);
- Several discussions and five semi-structured or structured interviews with active development project group participants from various departments at FCP;

- Observing a workshop session at FCP; and
- A content management consultant who carried out the content items redesign at FCP was one of the authors of this article.

SETTING THE STAGE

This section introduces the content management model to be utilized throughout the rest of the article. From the case organization, content management concerning two major document types prior to the development initiative will be described. The last subsection discusses the reasons for initiating the content management initiative.

Content Management Model

The content management model creating the basis for the case description is a variant of the document management model described by Salminen, Lyytikäinen, and Tiitinen (2000) and Salminen (2003a). The original model has been applied to analyze document management and changes in document management caused by information technology acquisition in multiple cases (e.g., Päivärinta & Salminen, 2001; Salminen, Lyytikäinen, Tiitinen, & Mustajärvi, 2001). The variant of the model has been defined (Salminen, 2003b) to describe content management environments more widely, and not only management of documents. The model is illustrated in Figure 1. There are two basic types of entities in a content management environment: activities and resources. In the figure the oval represents the activities and the rectangles, the resources. The broken lines show the information flow between activities and resources.

An *activity* is a set of actions performed by one or more actors. On one hand, the analysis may concern content management around one single intra- or interorganizational business process as the main activity. In public administration such a process could be, for example, Creation of the State Budget. In the analysis the process is divided into smaller activities. On the other hand, the analysis may concern content management related to a set of related processes. Three kinds of *resources* are essential in any content management environment: actors, content items, and systems. *Actors* are the performers of activities. An actor is an organization or a person. In the Internet environments an actor may also be a software agent representing a person. *Systems* include the hardware, software, and standards used to support the performance of activities. *Content items* consist of stored data produced and used in the activities by actors. Many content items consist of documents and metadata related to them. Actors play different *roles* in relationship to activities. In relationship to content items and systems, actors are called *users*.

Figure 1. Content management model

Management of Directives and Circulars at FCP Prior to the Development Initiative

Within the *content items* worked with at FCP, there were two essential types of documents. These were directives and circulars. The main purpose assigned for them was to ensure that tens of independent pension institutions would carry out pension provisioning tasks, that is, pension admissions, calculations, and information gathering processes, in a coherent way. This was one of the major responsibilities of FCP. A *directive* issued the ordinances and rules for pension provisioning expressed in the laws and norms. It also gave guidelines on how to adjust new or enhanced norms into activities of pension provisioning in pension institutions. A simple categorization of directives into groups (A, B, C) had been developed, according to the division of pension-related matters into different departments at FCP (Ahovaara, 2002). The number of directives produced annually by various departments varied considerably. Ahovaara's report shows, for example, that the Law Department produced from 16 to 73 type A directives yearly. The length of the directives varied between 20 and 70 pages of print, and the preparation took from a few weeks to close to one year. In the distribution phase a type A directive was printed, copied, packed, and posted to 1,700 respondents. Requirements for long-term accessibility and maintainability of directives were high. Some producers transformed their directives to Adobe Acrobat® pdf format and made them available at the FCP's Internet site upon individual requests from pension institutions. At FCP, the directive documents were "no longer merely an aspect of organizational work; rather, they were the organizational work" (Orlikowski & Yates, 1994, p. 572).

A *circular* announced forthcoming changes in laws and norms, or in international affairs or labor regulations that affect provisioning. Circulars were also used for informing the pension institutions about revisions in published directives. A circular was less formal and less binding by its nature, and usually shorter than a directive.

The major organizational *actors* involved were the FCP and the private pension institutions in Finland. The most central human actors were the experts working at FCP and in the pension institutions. At FCP, the experts worked mainly as producers and publishers of directives and circulars. There were no explicit groups of directive or circular producers. When a need for a new directive was identified, a directive preparation project was launched. A person assigned as responsible for directive preparation project collected a group of experts from FCP, pension institutions, and elsewhere for the project. Printing, copying, and paper-print deliveries were managed by the personnel in the copy and distribution office where the paper documents were also archived. Experts in pension institutions acted as end users of the documents playing different roles in respect to pension provisioning. The actor roles were not explicitly defined, and were shaped and enhanced in the course of action.

The *activities* related to directives and circulars were conducted in a more or less ad hoc style at FCP. Work processes were not consistent across different departments. Since directives were more official by their nature, and a great deal broader by their content than circulars, the preparation processes for directives were far more complex and time-consuming than for circulars. The process of preparing a directive consisted of multiple activities, such as:

- Studying related laws, norms, directives, and other materials from internal and external sources, in multiple formats, and via different kinds of services;
- Planning the production process; scheduling, gathering an appropriate expert group with representatives from pension institutions;
- Preparing numerous versions according to the comments from the expert group; changing the state of a directive-in-process (e.g., "preliminary," "approved," "published," "valid," "replaced");
- Deciding the approval procedure and approval level required;
- Publishing the directive; and
- Instructing the printing, copying, and delivery process.

Some directive producers started using e-mail for commenting, and some directives were published on the FCP's Internet site. The Internet publication evolved gradually without detailed planning. The files were put up on the Internet mostly in an ad hoc style upon requests from end users rather than on a regular basis.

Systems support included several commonly used word processing systems which had been taken into use and replaced during the course of action. Directives and circulars were stored to separate locations, such as file servers and local hard disks, using various formats. A combined diary and archiving system was in use, but it did not provide support for efficient search of content items. There was no information technology support for managing flow of activities related to content preparation, nor on versioning or updating the states of content items during their life cycles. Directives were commented on by the experts of pension institutions mainly via e-mail.

Triggers for Initializing the Content Management Development Initiative

There were multiple problems and development needs identified, both concerning the content of the directives and circulars, and their preparation processes. Sometimes the experts at FCP had difficulties in reasoning whether a new directive was needed, or if a circular should be produced instead. Various information repositories had to be studied, including law databases and histories of previous directives and circulars about the subject matter. Locating directives and circulars from archives was often laborious. Not all of the old directives and circulars were available in an electronic form; also, on occasion, the content in an electronic form was incomplete. The content organization in directives and circulars was not always consistent (Ahovaara, 2002).

Changes in rules and provisioning processes needed to be negotiated with various expert groups, consisting of in-house experts as well as experts from external pension institutions. Scheduling the work to get all the needed statements and comments on a directive version was laborious. The overall processes could not be controlled by the experts in charge of production at FCP, since sometimes authorization from external administrative bodies with independent schedules and processes were involved. The use of paper-print deliveries led to many kinds of problems. Sometimes an expert responsible for preparation waited until a new directive was published so that the old paper-print versions used in pension institutions could be replaced as a whole. Sometimes a change was announced by a circular, but it could not be ensured that the changes announced by circulars were archived into the folders of pension institutions in a way that a change would be re-marked while a directive was employed. Since making changes to the content was difficult, the experts at FCP usually tried to prepare as polished and detailed a version of a directive as possible for publication—instead of risking having to tackle those changes soon after publication. This increased both the length of documents and the time needed for their preparation (Ahovaara, 2002).

As a consequence of the problems encountered, the producers as well as experts from pension institutions suggested improvements to the ways information was structured, processed, maintained, and distributed. Especially the length of the directive documents was considered as an obstacle for usable content both in electronic and in paper format.

In 2002, FCP established an initiative for developing the management of directive and circular content, and for initializing multichannel publishing. Multiple objectives were stated for the initiative (Ahovaara, 2002; Peltola, 2003):

- Improving the production, maintenance, and publishing processes, as well as the quality of the content of directives and circulars.
- Choosing and implementing a new content management system needed for content production and multichannel publishing.
- Creating a user-friendly and effective service for publishing the directives and circulars concerning earnings-related pension provision and related issues on the Internet.

CASE DESCRIPTION

The case description below is in two parts. In the first part, a chronological overview of the content management development initiative is given. The latter part highlights the major activities and challenges concerning the redesign of activities, actor roles, content items, and systems.

Overview of the Development Initiative

At the beginning, a steering group consisting of executives at FCP was founded. The steering group assigned a manager for the initiative from the information technology department of FCP. The manager had more than 15 years of experience in carrying out technology and software deployment projects. The development initiative planning was based on three principles:

- Participation of the users of the new system should be allowed on an early phase of system adaptation and tailoring (e.g., Weitzman et al., 2002).
- Broad participation of domain expert users should be emphasized by using suitable combinations of workshop, group, and individual work (e.g., Coughlan, Lycett, & Macredie, 2003; Doll & Deng, 2001; Honkaranta, 2003).

- Users should focus on non-technical aspects; requirements, best practices, and best solutions should be sought regardless of the contemporary technology (e.g., Doll & Deng, 2001; Honkaranta, 2003).

A clear distinction between non-technical and technical redesign activities was made in planning the initiative. The initiative was divided into three projects. The first one was to focus on the non-technical redesign and elicitation of requirements, the second on system piloting and enhancements, and the third on finalizing the technical redesign and implementation of the enhanced system. A project group for carrying out the non-technical design was founded. It consisted of the manager of the development initiative, a project assistant, and five to eight experts of substance areas from multiple departments at FCP. Numerous other experts were assigned to help the project group. The project group assigned for the first project continued their work in the following projects, too. The technical redesign group consisted of the manager of the development initiative, and a project manager and other staff from the supplier company of the content management software.

The content management development initiative was carried out as three projects in accordance with the plan. In the following, the initiative is described as it was carried out. The three projects of the initiative are depicted in Figure 2.

Project I was carried out during the first half of 2002. It started with development initiative planning as a whole. It focused on the non-technical redesign, that is, eliciting requirements for the new content management system and for redesigning the activities, actor roles, and content items. Needs for improvements in content management were elicited at FCP by interviews and group work. Actor roles were considered only at pension institutions, and the rest of the actor role design was assigned to Project II. The redesign of content items was initiated for the contemporary directives and circulars, but found more complex than expected. An individual subproject was founded for content item redesign to be carried out during Project II. A content management consultant was assigned to supervise and carry out the subproject.

Project II was carried out between June 2002 and June 2003. This project was focused on the selection and piloting the new content management system, defining enhancements needed for the system, and analyzing and redesigning the content items. The redesign of actor roles was continued from Project I. A new content management system called Hummingbird DM (2003) was selected, the prepared definitions of actor roles, activities, and content items were incorporated into a preliminary implementation

Figure 2. An overview of the content management redesign initiative

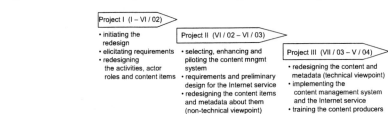

of the system, and tested by content producers. As a consequence, the definitions on the non-technical and technical side were both iterated. A preliminary version of the Internet service, its layout, and content organization were also prepared.

The redesign of content items was carried out by the FCP project group, led and managed by the content management consultant. The redesign considered the design of the metadata about the content items, too. Due to the complexity of content items design, only a portion of the most central kinds of content items were redesigned. As a consequence, the implementation had to be carried out in parallel with the contemporary solutions.

Project III started in June 2003. It was expected to last until February 2004, but was delayed for three months. This project focused on three aspects: completing the final (technical) redesign, training the content producers and users at FCP, and carrying out the system implementation. The layout and content organization, as well as the navigation mechanism provided by the new Internet service, were added and redefined. The maintenance and development routines for content management after the system implementation were planned, too. As new requirements surfaced during the development initiative, a part of content items redesign had to be postponed.

Redesign Activities and Challenges

Redesign of Actor Roles and Activities

The project group started by defining lists of known major *actor roles*, such as content producers, users, and maintainers. The user requirements at pension institutions were elicited. A number of experts from pension institutions took part in a workshop for explicating the requirements for the content of directives and circulars, as well as for the Internet service. The roles of internal actors at FCP were also explicated. The tasks of the roles basically consisted of familiar work. Some totally new actor roles were defined during Project III as a consequence of the changes in content production and management practices. The new actor roles included process controller, change manager, and content management developer. Avoiding drastic changes in the tasks of people was important since the old production practices remained partly in parallel with the new ones. For example, the roles of people taking care of printing, copying, and archiving the paper-print directives were still valid, since a portion of work with paper-printing remained in the new solution, too.

As the redesign of *activities* was started, a need for system support for the task was identified. The process design tool (QPRSoftware, 2003) was considered well-suited for supporting the work of FCP's project group (Ahovaara, 2002). The notation used in the tool was intuitively familiar by its looks, and the tool proved easy to learn and use. The tool provided support for production, maintenance, and versioning of the process models. The members of the project group were trained to use the process design tool, which took some extra resources but paid them back later on. Each project member explicated one or several contemporary processes with their colleagues. The redesign was carried out by enhancing and iterating these models. Figure 3 provides an example of notation used by the process design tool. It also describes a portion of the directive preparation process.

Figure 3. A portion of a process model in the process design tool

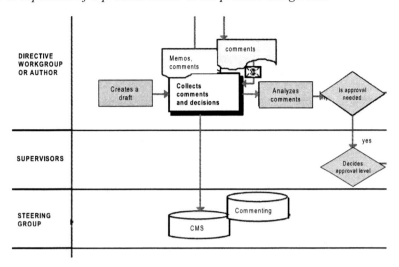

The work processes did not change in a drastic way. They were straightened up and enhanced by the new possibilities provided by the new content management solutions and the Internet service. There was still room for future process improvements. One member of the project group remarked:

I'm quite new in this organization...I had ideas for more radical changes, but I was afraid that the others would resist too drastic changes...especially now that everything related to our work is going to change so much.

Improvements in the turnaround times were identified soon after the adoption of the new processes. For example, the time needed for commenting the draft versions reduced from a couple of months to a few weeks, and the translators of directives reported that they received the texts for translation earlier in the process than before. These changes led to faster delivery cycles as a whole.

Redesign of Systems

The manager of the development initiative carried out the selection of the content management system. One of the reasons for choosing Hummingbird DM (2003) was its maturity as a product. In trial use it was found easy to use and fitting to the existing technological infrastructure at FCP. Its price/functionality level was considered reasonable and it provided support for electronic publishing. The system is based on relational database technology.

The deployment of the content management system took place gradually and multiple problems were encountered. A major reason for the problems was the FCP's heterogeneous technical environment and the integration of the new system to other software systems, maintained by different service providers. Incompatibility problems caused considerable inconvenience for the pilot users of the new system:

...the fault has not always been in the new system, but somewhere else...many times it remained unsolved whether the problem was caused by the user, the new system, or the technical environment.

The project manager was faced with multiple problems and found herself balancing on a rope between the existing and new technological solutions, internal and external users, and new and old system providers. She reported that:

It is essential that the coordination between multiple (software) service providers works seamlessly, and that the time schedules are kept tight..for coordination, one has to develop mutual terminology and language, and define rules for action.

The definitions of actor roles, activities, and content items were iterated multiple times, according to the findings from numerous system piloting and testing sessions. Also the metadata definition that was embedded to the system was enhanced multiple times. Managing the iterations, enhancements, and new requirements identified on the redesign posed a challenge for project coordination and management.

As a result of the redesign, two new add-in tools were embedded into the content management system. A tool that enabled collaborative commenting over content items on the Internet service was developed and implemented. The tool also allowed the comments to be tracked back easily. Albeit the content management system provided support for controlling and guiding the preparation and publishing activities of content items, broader support for tracking, guiding, and process automation was required. The second add-in tool was developed for this purpose. Due to the redesign activity itself, two additional tools were adopted. The process design tool (QPRSoftware, 2003) and the mind map tool (Mindjet, 2003) used on the content items redesign were found useful also for the purposes of the maintenance and development work after system implementation. In addition, word processing software was changed to a new, XML-enhanced version to facilitate further redesign.

In the new solution the content will be published via three digital channels: via an intranet service meant for the internal use at FCP, via a public Internet service provided and maintained by FCP, and via its replica on a public governmental Internet service. Multiple internal actors at FCP and external actors in pension institutions commented and took part in the design of the Internet service, which posed challenges particularly in reaching agreement on organizing and naming content items. A summary of the changes in systems is shown in Table 1.

Redesign of Content Items

Preliminary inspection carried out in Project I revealed that there were multiple kinds of content to be redesigned. In addition to the three types of directives (A, B, C), the paper delivery had enforced two kinds of directive content: ordinary directives and collections of them. With respect to subject matter, there were great variances on directives' content. There were also two types of circulars. Due to the complexity of the content types, the redesign had to be limited to directives concerning selected subject matters.

The redesign of content items was carried out by the FCP project group, led and managed by the content management consultant. The problem caused by the length of

Table 1. Summary of the changes in systems

System	Prior State	Resulting State
Content production tools	Commonly used word processing systems, such as Microsoft Word® and WordPerfect®; content stored as native formats of word processing systems	MS Word 2003® with XML support; content stored and archived in MS Word XML format + Adobe Acrobat pdf format
Content storage and maintenance tools	Diary system, file servers, local hard disks, paper	SQL-based content management system (Hummingbird DM, 2003)
Commenting tool	E-mail	Tailored Internet-based commenting tool built in to the content management system
Content publishing tools	Printers, ad-hoc transformations to Adobe Acrobat® pdf with Adobe Writer	Internet publishing system integrated to the content management system
Process tracking and controlling tools	No IT support	Tailored process control tool built in to the content management system
Process design tools	No IT support	QPR Process software (QPRSoftware, 2003)
Content item design tools	No IT support	Mind Manager software (Mindjet, 2003)

the directives was tackled first. It was studied whether the directives could be chopped into smaller units by their main sections, an approach commonly used to make content of long documents more usable on the Internet (e.g., Crowston & Williams, 1999). It was realized that the way content was organized within the directives was not consistent enough to allow such a simple partition. To find a way to organize and categorize the content within directives while making them smaller by their grain size, the consultant ended up on adopting a method (Honkaranta, 2003; Honkaranta & Lyytikäinen, 2003) in which communicational units of content are redesigned in a collaborative manner. A mind map software (Mindjet, 2003) was purchased and the project group was trained to deploy it for content redesign.

The redesign was carried out in two phases. In the *first phase*, the directives were redesigned by defining topics within exemplar directives by utilizing the mind map tool. The definition enabled reconsidering the content of the directives and defining the topics in the content as new documents. The approach required a new kind of thinking from the members of the project group, but after they grasped the idea, the redesign became easier. The new smaller document types were referred to as *statements* and the term directive was left out of use. Figure 4 gives an example of topic definition of a pension directive, visualized as a mind map diagram. The root of the topic tree is on the left, the subtopics are represented as branches extending to the right. In the figure, the topics that could constitute a future document are marked with a cross in front of the topic name. A sign with a notebook and pencil indicates that there are notes attached to the topic.

In the *second phase*, the new statement types were further defined by their substantial content for improving their consistency and quality. Due to the definition of topics, a new request for system support came into light. For some statement types there was a need for system support to access and manipulate topics appearing as parts of

Figure 4. Topic definition for the pension directive as a mind map

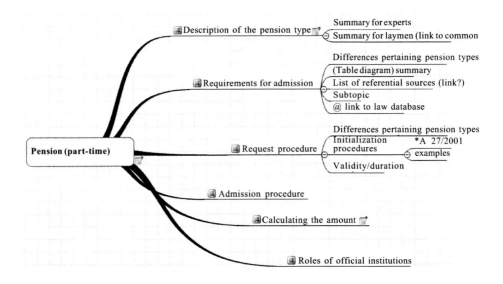

statements. The requirement led to trialing the deployment of XML (Bray, Paoli, Sperberg-McQueen, & Maler, 2000). The word processing software was switched to a new version with XML support (Cover, 2003), and the content producers had to learn to understand XML markup and the XML support in the new version of the word processing software.

Due to the redesign of directives, the circulars were quite easy to redesign. The kind of circular that was used to announce version changes to directives was no longer needed. The circulars were inspected and a classification according to their subject matter was prepared. To intensify the new uses of old circulars, they were renamed as *announcements*. Table 2 summarizes the content item types before and after the redesign.

Table 2. Content items at FCP before and after the redesign

Content Items Before Redesign	Content Items After Redesign
Directive - ordinance (10-30 pages in print) - collection (a folder, 50-100 pages in print) Categories: Ordinance-type directives grouped (A, B, C) with regard to the department in which the directive was produced.	**Statement** (two to 20 pages in print) Categories: Explicit categorization of statements with regard to the content type categorization (20 types).
	Aggregation (collections consisting of five to 20 statements and versions of them) Categories: according to the pension types.
Circular -announcement (one to three pages in print) -replacement/patch up for a circular (two to 20 pages in print)	**Announcement** (two to eight pages in print) Categories: a dozen categories according to the subject matter.

A new type of content item called *aggregation* was defined to replace the collection of directives. Aggregation is a set of statements and their appropriate versions pertaining to a subject matter. It is prepared manually by a content producer, since the versions needed for a case cannot be chosen by automated means. In the content management system, an aggregation was implemented as a virtual folder.

After the redesign of the primary content, metadata to be associated with statement, announcement, and aggregation instances for enhanced searching and grouping capabilities was designed. Prior to the design, the project group learned about metadata and its deployment in content management. Nevertheless, they found the idea and impact of metadata quite difficult to grasp. The design was constrained by the chosen document management system where the Dublin Core (1999) metadata scheme had been adopted. The Dublin Core scheme was originally defined for resource discovery on the Internet and it specifies 15 elements, for example, title, creator, and subjects, to be attached to resources. The design of metadata concerned renaming the Dublin Core elements, defining which elements should be mandatory, and developing lists of possible values for some of the elements.

Figure 5 illustrates the new content items and the new FCP Internet service with a sample screen dump. The service window is divided into three main components: the FCP service navigation bar on top, the pension type search and navigation bar on the left pane, and the content pane on the right.

In the figure the pension type is an aggregation consisting of related statements. The content of the statement selected from the left pane is shown in the right pane window. A user may request for navigation aid showing the topics within the selected statement by selecting a hyperlink that causes a navigation pop-up window to appear on the right pane content view.

Figure 5. A Screen dump from the new Internet service

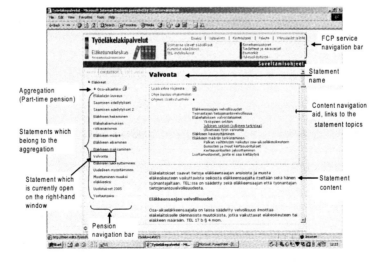

CURRENT CHALLENGES FACING THE ORGANIZATION

The content management redesign initiative was broad and long. Regardless of numerous efforts and hard work, the initiative can be seen as a starting point, not as an end to the development and redesign of content management at FCP. There are both similar and new kinds of redesign challenges ahead. The rest of the directives have to be redesigned, the metadata definition shall most probably be refined, and enhancements shall probably be needed to the Internet service, too. The redesign for utilization of XML (Bray et al., 2000) and related tools shall continue. Even though some new tools and methods were found useful to support the redesign work during the case, enhancements to these or even newer kinds of tools and methods may be needed for the future development.

The environment at FCP was heterogeneous at the time the development initiative was started, and the introduction of the new content management system further added to the heterogeneity. The number of system and service providers involved in content management increased. During the redesign work the participants from different organizations developed common terminology for communication and work practices to jointly solve the current problems. The knowledge about the terminology and work practices, however, remained tacit. That knowledge may be lost at the time personnel changes.

The new content management solution consists of multiple system components. A change in one component of the overall solution, such as deployment of a new word processing software or changes in the tailored tools with the content management system, may cause unexpected effects to the other parts of this system. The content management solution can be seen as a system ecology where continuous activities are needed to balance the equilibrium.

The need for parallel management of old and new document types and work practices poses a clear challenge for FCP. The new content production practices will be extended to cover all kinds of directive and circular content along with future content redesign. Yet the existing directives and circulars will need maintenance as legacy content for a number of years.

The pension system in Finland will undergo a massive reconstruction during 2005 -2007. The changes, without doubt, shall have an effect to the new content management solution *per se*. For ensuring the ability to carry out any necessary redesign to reflect the unforeseen changes in the national and EU regulations environment, a special task force for continuous development has been founded at FCP. One of the difficult tasks of the task force will be the management of the expertise needed to adhere to the evolving EU legislation, to national regulations, and to norms affecting pension provisioning, and information technology.

ACKNOWLEDGMENTS

The authors wish to thank the project group at FCP, and especially Riitta Ahovaara for enjoyable collaboration. The participants of the development initiative at the content management system vendor have also provided their assistance for the research.

REFERENCES

Ahovaara, R. (2002). *Yleiskirjehankkeen 1. Osaprojekti 10.01.-07.06.2002*. Helsinki: Eläketurvakeskus.

Ahovaara, R. (2003). *Väliraportti: Yleiskirjehanke, 2.Vaiheen osaprojekti: Palvelun sisällön määrittely ja suunnittelu*. Helsinki: Eläketurvakeskus.

Bray, T., Paoli, J., Sperberg-McQueen, C. M., & Maler, E. (2000). *Extensible Markup Language (XML) 1.0*. (2nd ed.) (W3C Recommendation). Retrieved April 1, 2003, from http://www.w3.org/TR/2000/REC-xml-20001006

Brown, J. S., & Gray, E. S. (1995). *The people are the company*. Retrieved February 4, 2002, from http://www.fastcompany.com/online/01/people.html

Coughlan, J., Lycett, M., & Macredie, R. D. (2003). Communication issues in requirements elicitation: A content analysis of stakeholder experiences [Electronic version]. *Information and Software Technology, 45*(1), 525-537.

Cover, R. (2003, 23 May). *Technology reports: Microsoft Office 11 and InfoPath (XDocs)*. Retrieved August 15, 2003: http://xml.coverpages.org/microsoftXDocs.html

Crowston, K., & Williams, M. (1999). The effects of linking on genres of Web documents. In R. H. Sprague (Ed.), *Proceedings of the 32nd Annual Hawaii International Conference on System Sciences. Genre in Digital Documents Minitrack*. Los Alamitos, CA: IEEE Computer Society Press.

Doll, W. J., & Deng, X. (2001). The collaborative use of information technology: End-user participation and system success. *Information Resources Management Journal, 14*(2), 6-16.

DublinCore. (1999). *Dublin core metadata element set, version 1.1*. Retrieved February, 17, 2000, from http://purl.org/DC/documents/rec-dces-19990702.htm

Eläketurvakeskus - Finnish Centre for Pensions. (2003). *Vuosikertomus 2002* (Annual Report, in Finnish) [Electronic version]. Helsinki: Eläketurvakeskus - Finnish Center for Pensions.

FCP. (2003). The Central Pension Security Institute: The Finnish Centre for Pensions. Retrieved August 25, 2003, from http://www.etk.fi/english/etusivu.asp

Halverson, C. A., & Ackerman, M. S. (2003). "Yeah, the rush ain't here yet—Take a break": Creation and use of an artifact as organizational memory [Electronic version]. In R. H. Sprague (Ed.), *Proceedings of the 36th Hawaii International Conference on System Sciences (HICSS)*. Los Alamitos, CA: IEEE Computer Society.

Honkaranta, A. (2003). *From genres to content analysis. Experiences from four case organizations*. PhD Thesis, University of Jyväskylä, Jyväskylä, Finland.

Honkaranta, A., & Lyytikäinen, V. (2003, June 4-6). Operationalizing a genre-based method for content analysis: A case of a church. In W. Abramowicz, & G. Klein (Eds.), *Proceedings of the Sixth International Conference on Business Information Systems,* Colorado Springs, Colorado (pp. 108-116). Poznan, Poland: Department of Management Information Systems at Poznan University of Economics.

Hummingbird. (2003). Hummingbird, Ltd. Homepage. Retrieved August 15, 2003, from http://www.hummingbird.com

Mindjet. (2003). MindManager software. Retrieved August 15, 2003, from http://www.mindjet.com/eu/

Murphy, L. D. (2001). Digital documents in organizational communities of practice: A first look. In R. H. Sprague (Ed.), *Proceedings of the 34ᵗʰ Hawaii International Conference on System Sciences* [Electronic version]. Los Alamitos, CA: IEEE Computer Society.

Orlikowski, W. J., & Yates, J. (1994). Genre repertoire: The structuring of communicative practices in organizations. *Administrative Science Quarterly, 39*(4), 541-574.

Päivärinta, T., & Salminen, A. (2001). Deliberate and emergent changes on a way toward electronic document management. In *Annals of Cases on Information Technology, Volume 3* (pp. 320-333).

Peltola, T. (2003). *Yleiskirjehankkeen sisällön määrittelyosio-väliraportti* (Report on FCP Content Items Redesign). Jyväskylä, Helsinki: Done Information Oy.

QPRSoftware. (2003). *QPR process guide*. Retrieved August, 15, 2003, from http://www.qpr.com/Products/QPRProcessGuide/index.html

Salminen, A. (2003a). Document analysis methods. In C. L. Bernie (Ed.), *Encyclopedia of library and information science* (2ⁿᵈ rev. ed., pp. 916-927). New York: Marcel Dekker.

Salminen, A. (2003b, October 29-30). Towards digital government by XML standardization: Methods and experiences. In XML Users Group Finland (Ed.), *Proceedings of the XML Finland 2003: Open Standards, XML and the Public Sector. Kuopio.* Espoo: XML Users Group Finland.

Salminen, A., Lyytikäinen, V., & Tiitinen, P. (2000). Putting documents into their work context in document analysis. *Information Processing & Management, 36*(4), 623-641.

Salminen, A., Lyytikäinen, V., Tiitinen, P., & Mustajärvi, O. (2001). Experiences of SGML standardization: The case of the Finnish legislative documents. In J. R. H. Sprague (Ed.), *Proceedings of the 34ᵗʰ Hawaii International Conference on System Sciences.* Los Alamitos,CA: IEEE Computer Society.

Weitzman, L., Dean, S. E., Meliksetian, D., Gupta, K., Zhou, N., & Wu, J. (2002). Transforming the content management process at IBM.Com. In *Conference on Human Factors in Computing Systems. Case studies of the CHI2002/AIGA experience design forum.* Minneapolis, Minnesota (pp. 1-15). New York: ACM Press. Retrieved Februrary 20, 2004. ACM Digital Library.

Anne Honkaranta is an assistant professor at the University of Jyväskylä, in the Department of Computer Science and Information Systems, Finland. She received her PhD in information systems from the University of Jyväskylä (2003). She has worked as a manager for Digital Documents Research in the Information Technology Research Institute, University of Jyväskylä, and as a project manager and researcher on several research and development projects with Finnish companies and public sector organizations. Her current research interests include content management in organizations, structured documents, e-government, e-learning, technical documentations, the genre theory, and participatory analysis and design of information systems.

Airi Salminen is a professor at the University of Jyväskylä, in the Department of Computer Science and Information Systems, Finland. She received her PhD in computer science from the University of Tampere (1989). She has worked as a visiting professor at the University of Waterloo, Canada, and headed several projects where research has been tied to document management development efforts in major Finnish companies and public sector organizations. Her current research interests include enterprise content management, structured documents, e-government, user interfaces, software maintenance environments, and Semantic Web.

Tuomo Peltola is a senior consultant at SysOpen Plc, which is one of the leading IT companies in Finland. He has worked as a consultant and as a project manager in several IT projects for private and public sector organizations. His professional interests include content and document management in large industrial and governmental organizations. He has co-authored several articles related to content and document management.

This case was previously published in the *International Journal of Cases on Electronic Commerce*, 1(1), pp. 52-69, © 2005.

Chapter XVI

Implementing and Managing a Large-Scale E-Service:
A Case on the Mandatory Provident Fund Scheme in Hong Kong

Theodore H. K. Clark, Hong Kong University of Science & Technology, Hong Kong

Karl Reiner Lang, Hong Kong University of Science & Technology, Hong Kong

Will W-K. Ma, Hong Kong University of Science & Technology, Hong Kong

EXECUTIVE SUMMARY

This case concerns a recently launched retirement protection scheme, the Mandatory Provident Fund (MPF), in Hong Kong. Service providers, employers, employees and the government are the four main parties involved in the MPF. The service has been implemented in two versions, that is, a bricks model and a clicks model. The former is based on conventional paper-based transactions and face-to-face meetings. The focus of this case, however, is on the latter, which introduces MPF as a service in an e-environment that connects all parties electronically and conducts all transactions via the Internet or other computer networks. The case discusses the MPF e-business model, and its implementation. We analyze the differences between the old and the new model and highlight the chief characteristics and benefits of the e-business model as they arise from the emerging digital economy. We also discuss some major problems, from both managerial and technical perspectives, that have occurred during the phases of implementing and launching the new service.

BACKGROUND

The case discusses the traditional and the new e-business model in providing retirement management services in Hong Kong, and examines how a Mandatory Provident Fund (MPF) service provider can benefit and gain competitive advantage through the application of current e-commerce technologies. The case provides comprehensive background information on the MPF scheme and the MPF market, and presents the newly developed MPF e-business model and its implementation as an electronic service (e-MPF).

The main purpose of this case is to develop and analyze the main components of this new e-service model, and to understand both its benefits and limitations in today's nascent e-environments (Westland & Clark, 1999). We present the issues and challenges that emerge from introducing and managing a new, large-scale service that involves several parties, each with different objectives and agendas. The government acts as the regulating body formulating the rules and overseeing the transactions between MPF service providers, employers and employees. The government's primary goal in introducing the MPF scheme is to provide basic retirement protection for Hong Kong's workforce in an effort to catch up with other developed countries that provide basic social welfare for its citizens. The service providers, on the other hand, see the emerging MPF market as a huge business opportunity. Employers and employees are forced by law to participate in the new scheme.

MPF and the New Economy

The Mandatory Provident Fund is an interesting business example in the emerging digital economy, and one of the first large-scale e-service projects in the public sector in Asia. The e-MPF model incorporates some fundamental e-business concepts as follows:

Electronic Money

There is no real physical activity or presence required in any of the transactions. Fund transfers, monetary transactions, contractual and regulatory settlements, and information exchanges are all done online.

Digital Distribution

In the traditional MPF model, distribution of paper documents and physical, contact-based customer service accounted for more than 30% of total cost. Moving to digital distribution and document management is expected to significantly reduce distribution cost.

Knowledge Management

In order to retain the best customers, MPF providers should supply their customers the most appropriate product and service information. Informed customers often prefer to make their own decisions in designing their MPF investment plan. The e-MPF business model suggests increasingly active and dynamic investment behavior.

Customer Relations

Being able to understand and anticipate the needs of the customer will be imperative in the new competitive MPF market. All leading MPF service providers will emphasize closer customer relationships as one of their priorities, and will employ modern IT systems to support customer relationship management.

MPF in an Electronic Marketplace

A truly electronic market is emerging for MPF services (Bakos, 1998). The entire value chain, including the post-sales investment asset management, can be conducted in digital space. All market participants, service providers, clients and the government share the same Internet-based business platform. However, the MPF service providers also offer a traditional, paper-based version of their service product. At least in the initial years, it is expected that most MPF clients will prefer face-to-face transactions and paper documents over electronic transactions. Especially low-wage workers and clients with low education are reluctant in using the electronic MPF (or e-MPF) services. But given that Hong Kong has one of the highest Internet penetration and growth rates in Asia and one of the best Internet infrastructures in place, it can be expected that more and more MPF clients will migrate to the e-MPF service platform over the years. Hence, all MPF service providers place strategic importance on e-MPF. Our discussion in this case emphasizes the electronic version of the MPF services.

Hong Kong is widely considered as a highly developed, ultra modern city-state. Its welfare system, however, is lacking. It is the family, not the government, that traditionally provides retirement support in Chinese societies. People with employer-provided retirement coverage accounted only for a minority until the launch of MPF. Retirement schemes were mostly arranged through either insurance or asset management companies. However, in an effort to bring Hong Kong up to par with other developed countries, the government has recently introduced the MPF Scheme, which would provide a safety net to much of its population. The particular scheme developed in Hong Kong is based on a similar scheme in Singapore. However, while the Singaporean model is strongly government-based, Hong Kong has opted for a more market-based solution. Specific details on the HK system can be found on the Mandatory Provident Fund Authority's official Web site (MPFA, 2001).

Hong Kong has a rapidly aging population. People aged 65 and above presently account for about 10% of the population. This proportion is estimated to increase to 13% by 2016, and to 20% by 2036. Only about one-third of the workforce has had some form of retirement protection. After decades of debates on the provision of retirement protection, Hong Kong took a major step forward in August 1995 when the Mandatory Provident Fund Schemes Ordinance was enacted to provide a formal system of retirement protection. The Mandatory Provident Fund Schemes Regulation was passed on April 1, 1998. The Mandatory Provident Fund Schemes Authority set December 1, 2000, as the enrollment deadline and for starting the collection of the contributions. From the period February to October 2000, HK's 251,000 employers had to complete the selection of an MPF service provider and arrange for employees to join the MPF scheme. The government set December 1, 2000, as the deadline for employers and employees to enroll in one of the approved MPF schemes.

The MPF System

The MPF System is an employment-related contributory system, under which members of the workforce aged between 18 and 65 are required to participate. There are three main types of MPF schemes:

1. Master trust scheme,
2. Employer-sponsored scheme, and
3. Industry scheme.

A *master trust scheme* is a scheme open to membership to the relevant employees of more than one employer, self-employed persons and persons with accrued benefits transferred from other schemes. This type of scheme is especially suitable for small- and medium-sized companies.

An *employer-sponsored scheme* is a scheme that is only open to the eligible employees of a single employer and its associated companies. This scheme is designed for big corporations and companies with a large number of employees.

An *industry scheme* is a scheme specially established for industries with high labor mobility, for example, the catering and construction industries. An employee does not need to change the scheme if he or she changes employment within the same industry. When changing employment, the employee has the choice of switching the benefits to the scheme of the new employer or remaining in the current scheme.

Trust Arrangement

All MPF schemes must be established under a trust arrangement that are governed by Hong Kong law. Scheme assets will be held separately from the assets of the trustees or the investment managers. This safeguards the interests of the scheme members from unnecessary financial risks.

Mandatory contributions are basically calculated on the basis of 10% of an employee's relevant income, with the employer and employee each paying 5%. Self-employed persons also have to contribute 5% of their relevant income. Mandatory contributions must be paid to registered MPF schemes managed by trustees. They must be paid for each period for which an employer pays relevant income to his or her employee. Investment managers will be appointed by the trustees of MPF schemes to make long-

Figure 1. Population statistics (percentage of population aged 65 and above)

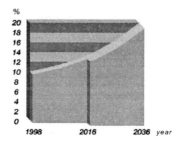

term investment of scheme assets and accrue benefits for the scheme members for their retirement protection. The diagram in Figure 2 shows the structure of the MPF arrangement and the interrelation of the various bodies.

The accrued benefits of an employee can be transferred to another scheme when the employee changes jobs. The MPF legislation has prescribed 65 as the retirement age. Scheme members who have attained age 65 may withdraw the benefits accrued from mandatory contributions in their MPF schemes in the form of a lump sum.

Scope of MPF Business

MPF-related services represent a potentially huge market. Before the MPF launch, less than one-third of the workforce of 3.4 million people already had some form of retirement protection. Those are exempted from participation in the MPF scheme. A further 400,000 do not qualify for inclusion for various reasons. The MPF scheme is targeting the remaining workforce. The Government has estimated that annual MPF contributions would amount to more than HK$10 billion (approximately US$1.3 billion) in the initial years, increasing to about HK$40 billion (~US$5 billion) when the system matures. However, this assumes that MPF service providers will have to be able to retain existing customers who join initially lest subsequent erosion in sales may occur. Increasing sales from the MPF business provides an ample opportunity for cross-selling, mainly other financial products, allowing the client base to broaden and business to expand. There is no doubt that a market transformation process has begun that will significantly change the way retirement protection services are used in Hong Kong.

The Playing Field

The MPF market is presently heavily regulated by the Mandatory Provident Fund Authority and the Security and Future Commission with detailed and specific responsibilities imposed on the trustee as well as the investment manager. The nature and business of providing MPF service and the high compliance requirements of the regulatory bodies has limited the entry of players. However, the banks, fund management houses and insurance companies are now all preparing to expand their business into the MPF market. Based on their own estimations, major players totally claimed 285% of the market share (Table 1).

Figure 2. MPFA scheme

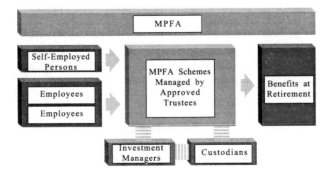

Table 1. Market share

Financial Institution Sectors	Claimed Market Share
Major Banks	120%
Major Insurance Companies	145%
Other Fund Management Houses	20%
TOTAL	285%

Obviously, this means that most players are overestimating their market share or market potential. However, the figures do reflect the relative market shares among the different sectors, with banks and insurance companies dominating the MPF market.

The Mandatory Provident Fund Schemes Ordinance was enacted in 1995 to set up and regulate the MPF system. MPF is a mandatory, fully funded contribution scheme that is privately managed. The Hong Kong Government's roles are mainly as policy maker, regulator and supervision body of the MPF market. The decision to put fund management in private hands and to create a competitive market environment was based on the belief that a market-based model would be more cost-effective and would ultimately benefit the retirees. At the end of 2000, there were 20 approved trustees and 31,927 registered MPF intermediaries competing to provide fund management services. Table 2 shows that despite the expiration of the legal deadline, about 20% of the workforce and 30% of the employers had not enrolled in MPF.

SETTING THE STAGE

Business strategies may be profit-oriented or may emphasize market share. The latter appear currently as the predominant strategy for most providers. In the beginning, there has been some uncertainty as to when employers will actually sign up for the MPF scheme. Many clients maintained a wait-and-see attitude while they tried to learn more about the offered plans and the providers before actually committing to invest in their preferred plan. Service providers have used this time window to improve their competitive position in the market (Clemons, 1986). For example, some have improved their e-commerce systems and user interfaces in order to make their e-MPF services more

Table 2. Some Crucial MPF statistics (as of February 15, 2001)

	Number
Approved Trustees	20
Registered MPF Intermediaries	31,927
Corporate Intermediaries	463
Individual Intermediaries	31,464
Enrollment	
Employers	70%
Employees	80%
Approved MPF products	243

attractive to clients, others have launched extensive promotion campaigns to educate the market about their services.

Intense competition exists among the MPF providers for supplying a convenient one-stop-shopping or outsourcing service. Most service providers view the MPF service as a complementary product within their entire product portfolio. For example, banks are increasingly competing on their e-banking capabilities and see e-MPF as an attractive new product to service their customers. Banks and insurance companies alike are developing customized, comprehensive packages that allow customers one-stop shopping for all financial service needs.

However, there are various costs such as those associated with the initial set up of a scheme, annual trustee and fund management services fee, switching fee, buy-and-sell spread, cash rebate, discount, associated benefit packages, payroll/MPF contribution conversion software as well as many others. In addition to after-sales service, it is a combination of some or all of the above that provides the appeal to the employer when making an MPF selection decisions.

The MPF market is dominated by big players with large promotion budgets that aggressively compete for new customers. Advertising campaigns typically elaborate on the theme that MPF is an investment for life, but they also emphasize the importance of the financial stability and security of the provider. Market leaders like HSBC and the Bank of China (BOC) currently have the edge. Distribution through retail bank customers is still a reliable tool. Appendix A shows the number of branches/agents in addition to the claimed market share.

The banking sector and the insurance sector hold about one-half of the MPF market share each, according to Table 1. The MPF provider has to incorporate expertise in trustee services, fund administration, custodial service and investment management. The banks have a distinct advantage over the other types of investors. Some banks, like HSBC and BOC, have developed their own integrated e-MPF platform. Others, like the Standard Chartered Bank, have decided to outsource some or most of the services. The wide range of financial products offered by the banks make this sector a unique battlefield. Traditional banking services, credit card business, mortgage, payroll, commercial loan and documentary credit facilities are products that can be enriched and value added if complemented with MPF services. However, they need to employ all their resources, as the business potential of cross-selling other types of banking products is substantial. Failure will ultimately mean losing a valuable customer and not just his or her MPF business.

Manulife is currently the only insurance company that has associated business units that can provide one-stop-shopping service. Some other MPF providers from the insurance or fund management background have a strong client base but lack expertise in some areas of the MPF service. Hence, forming alliances with other financial institutions is the preferred strategy of companies like, for example, CEF Life, CMG Asia or Principal Trust. Business is generated through their agents or other sales persons. Their traditional products are the various commercial and personal insurance products.

The competitors in the MPF market try to differentiate their services based on their fee schedules and, increasingly, on other product differentiators such as customer service and personalization (Hanson, 2000, pp. 151-219). At the early stage of introducing MPF services to the market, most providers view customer acquisition as the main business goal. Marketing strategies emphasize low fees to attract new customers (see

Appendix B for the comparison of schedule fees). HSBC was the first to offer fee waivers and bonus fund units. Manulife and AIA offered cash bonus while BOC and CEF offered fees as low as 1.5%. It is expected that the price war will continue and intensify for some time, with companies offering heavy rebates, discounts and fee waivers to attract and retain the customers and employers. But there are provisions in the participation contracts that allow service providers to increase fees in the future. Customers, however, demand more than just low fees when choosing a particular scheme. As a response, providers have begun to differentiate their service products through other criteria such as customer service, e-service friendliness and plan flexibility.

In the longer run, the fees charged will increase as all providers have similar provision in the participation agreement to allow fee adjustment. Hence, the ability for MPF service providers to provide a better customer service becomes an important means for both customer acquisition and retention. Leading banks are arranging MPF workshops for each employee in addition to call centers where representatives are on duty answering questions up to 16 hours a day. Interactive voice response systems help provide information to customers, and Web-based services now offer electronic document transfer as well as fund switching. All providers now routinely offer these basic services.

Providers also offer an assortment of bundled benefits such as waiving the annual fee for credit cards, offering preferential commercial or mortgage loan interest rates, free online banking membership, lower insurance premiums, better deposit rates, convenient payroll arrangements, gift coupons, cash rebates, souvenirs and other bonuses. Appendix C shows the non-fee competition offered by the key players.

CASE DESCRIPTION

We now introduce the e-business model underlying the MPF service in Hong Kong's public e-environment. Based on an analysis of the e-business model of one of the leading MPF service providers, we discuss how e-commerce technologies can be applied to achieve success in the competitive MPF market and provide benefit to the various players. Our case subject is a leading bank that engages in a wide range of businesses such as traditional banking, unit trusts, asset management, institutional, corporate and private client portfolio, trustee services, custodian services, as well as retirement fund services. The bank has over 200 branches and has been providing a full spectrum of banking services for a long time in Hong Kong. It has been managing hundreds of retirement fund schemes and billions of dollars in assets. The bank has especially targeted small and medium-size employers, that is, companies with 5 to 1,000 employees. It aims at gaining 15% of the market share, managing $4.8 billion annual fund inflow from 48,000 employer schemes and 480,000 employee accounts. It has launched three different investment schemes.

In the first phase of the marketing activities, MPF products have been sold through the existing clients of the bank. Later, this channel will expand to other potential targets including the valued customers of the other banking or insurance sectors. It will be up against both fee and non-fee competition and is more than aware of the importance of using technology to bring about a competitive advantage. Using this particular MPF service provider as the base case for this analysis, we examine the design of the main

Figure 3. The change of e-business world

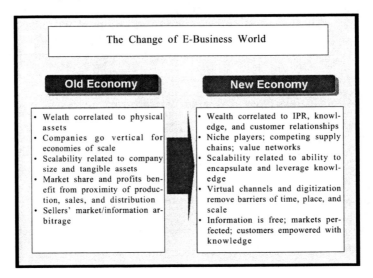

components of the e-service model, and discuss how e-commerce technologies facilitate B2E/B2C, B2B and B2G transactions (Timmers, 1998).

In the traditional business model of the old, physical economy, wealth is correlated to physical assets and companies go vertical for economies of scale. There is noticeable scalability that is related to company size and tangible assets. Market share and profits benefit from proximity of production, sales and distribution. It is a sellers' market with information arbitrage. In the new, digital economy, on the other hand, wealth is correlated more strongly with IP assets, knowledge and customer relationships. The new model emphasizes the creation of value networks (Tapscott, Ticoll, & Lowy, 2001). Scalability is related to the ability to encapsulate and leverage knowledge. Virtual channels and digitization remove barriers of time, place and scale.

The diagram in Figure 3 highlights the changes from the old to the new economy.

As Figure 4 indicates, the economy continues to transform. The suppliers are no longer at the center of business activities as the buyers instead take the leading role, enabling a more mature e-market and consumer-centered economy.

E-Service Benefits of MPF

Electronically supported Mandatory Provident Fund management (e-MPF) is a good example of the new business possibilities in the information age. We can identify several properties of the e-MPF business model, depicted in Figure 5, that provide benefit over conventional approaches:

- **Electronic money:** All monetary transactions are based on electronic money transfers.

Figure 4. Transformation of the eonomy

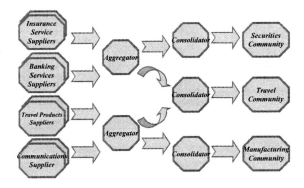

Source: FMM

Figure 5. e-MPF business model

- **Digital distribution:** In the old model, distribution of paper-based documents accounted for more than 30% of the total service cost. In the e-MPF model, all transactions and instructions are made in electronic form, which substantially reduces distribution cost.
- **Knowledge and information:** In order to retain their most profitable customers, MPF customers should be provided with the most accurate information. Customers are given access to a wealth of information that allows them to make their own decisions. More flexible and customized investment plans can be offered.
- **Other complementary products:** The banks, insurance companies and investment institutions are the three main providers in the MPF service. Their current products can be totally transformed into electronic formats and integrated with MPF products. The service providers can offer their entire product portfolio through the same transaction platform.
- **Re-intermediation:** Service providers no longer specialize in just one part of the value chain. They become aggregators who provide any financial service to their

customers in connection with MPF. We observe a move from value chain management to value network management.

- **Personalization:** New e-commerce technologies like WebBots and data mining enable the provision of cost-effective personalized information and transaction services at large scale. Several types of customer interactions can be automated, for example, contribution statement inquiries, plan switching, change of contribution percentage, change of employer or change of trustee.
- **Cross-selling:** Customer databases can be employed to automatically track transaction record and generate personalized recommendations for other service products that might be relevant and interesting to the customer.

The challenge of a successful e-MPF implementation is to develop a transparent, seamless alliance-based value network (Bakos & Brynjolfsson, 1998) that allows the customer to choose the best product combination for his or her personal needs without having to research the complex supplier market. Convenience and flexibility must be provided without compromising on security and privacy issues. Since e-MPF services have just been launched, it is too early to tell whether or not these challenges can be met. It will probably take some years before a reasonable assessment can be made.

Business-to-Consumer (B2C) and Business-to-Employee (B2E) Transactions

Account management and changes in chosen investment plans are very labor intensive in the conventional MPF model. Switching to the e-MPF model promises to significantly lower administrative cost while, at the same time, increases flexibility. As a contributor to an MPF scheme, each individual employee has an interest in checking how his or her contributions are invested and how much has accumulated in their MPF account. Providers have set up Web sites that provide personalized MPF account management and disseminate updated MPF information and investment decision aids.

Customers are able to access or download information selectively. Employing data mining tools and Web usage tracking technologies based on page hits and service

Figure 6. Workflow of change in contribution %

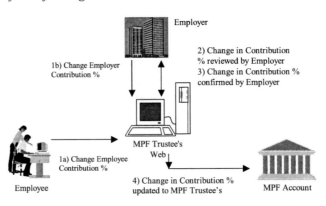

requests (Choi & Whinston, 2000), providers learn about their customers' interests. This allows them to respond more quickly to problems and newly arising demands. Expensive human resources can be shifted from sales and clerical activities to customer service.

Low operability and controlability in the traditional model gives the employees a sense of MPF basically being a salary deduction rather than investment for retirement protection. With a Web site capable of integrating the MPF system, employees are able to query the performance of their contributions online. This is especially critical when the financial markets show changes in volatility. For example, during a slump in the stock market, employees may want to change their schemes from high growth to stable growth in order to prevent or reduce losses.

The e-MPF model enables the transformation of the service process that adds value to providers and clients alike. For example, plan or scheme switching can be streamlined. Although it is an agreement between MPF providers and employees, in many cases, the employers act as middlemen to collect the data and input them into their payroll system and then notify the providers. This process incurs a high administrative overhead in the conventional model. In the e-MPF model, on the other hand, an automated MPF plan switching workflow can be setup on the Web to reduce administrative costs incurred by both MPF providers and employers. During month end, employers can print the change in employee plans, or download it from the Web and upload it into their payroll systems. New plan switching can be effective immediately upon employees' data input, or be effective after employers' confirmation.

Unlike the existing retirement schemes, the governing MPF authority body (MPFA) poses a legal requirement on MPF of a 5% minimum employer contribution and a 5% minimum employee contribution. However, MPF allows the employer or employee to contribute more than 5% voluntarily. However, changing the contribution percentage involves a tedious workflow among three parties namely the employee, employer and MPF providers. In the traditional MPF model, the employee or employer states his or her intention to change the employee or employer contribution percentage respectively. Then the employer, as a middleman, collects the changes, inputs data into the payroll system, notifies the bank to transfer correct funds to both employee and MPF, and finally notifies the MPF provider of the changes. The MPF providers will then credit the corresponding contributor's account upon the fund transfer.

In the e-MPF model, however, contribution percentage changes can be supported through a Web-based workflow system. Both employee and employers can change the employee or employer contribution percentage over the Web. Every month, employers can download the revised contribution percentage, confirm it and upload it into their payroll systems.

Web-based MPF service models can provide passive cross-selling through referral links to other bank products such as investment options, insurance products or online banking. A more proactive way is to adopt rule-based cross-selling. For example, if the contributor has a salary increase of more than 10%, it would indicate that he or she is likely to be more interested in a cross-sell of other investment products. If a contributor indicates that they wish to change the plan from high growth to stable, they are adopting a more conservative approach. The Web site can also be used to actively cross-sell other products.

Rule-based software agents can perform cross-selling functions in two ways. First, it can track and trace Web site access of customers, and activate cross-selling and/or up-selling offers if certain rules are matched. For example, if an employee is going to change to a high-risk plan, we can proceed to cross-sell some investment product. In alignment with appropriate marketing strategy, it is possible to use it to devise data-signaling programs, or data-screening programs for product customization. Second, employees could be allowed to set rule-based e-mail notification. For example, he or she could set a rule to receive e-mail, if the return of their plan is lower than 10%, or if the high-risk plan is gaining a return of over 30%. Also, the employee can choose to receive customized e-mail notifications on new investment products, insurance products or financial news. Web-based personalization methods can provide convenience and help strengthen the customer relationships.

The Web can also be used to provide other value-added services to the contributors, for example, investment analysis tools. This function can be used to primarily trace and track the contributor's expected risk and return and monitor the markets or stocks they prefer. Software agents can act as personal investment advisors and assist contributors in their investment decisions.

To achieve a reasonable level of data and transaction security, e-MPF models employ standard security management technology. Secure socket layers (SSLs) are adopted to provide authentication and data integrity. The users can simply login with an encrypted user ID and password. This ensures that the integrity of data transmitted from MPF providers, for example the MPF balance query, will be maintained. In addition, the secure electronic transfer protocol (SET) and digital signatures can be used to give enhanced security on eavesdropping and non-repudiation. However, this is currently not used much in MPF transactions at this stage because using SET and digital signatures require that the participants have obtained a personal digital certificate, which is currently rare in Hong Kong.

The introduction of the B2C and B2E e-commerce features discussed above are expected to bring the following benefits to both employers and employees:

- **Updated MPF information:** The first benefit is online, updated MPF information including MPFA regulation, MPF products, FAQ of MPF as well as links to other bank products. This is a unique feature that cannot be offered by other channels of communication such as television or newspaper. In addition, it provides another medium to perform pre-sales advertisement and collect feedback from employers and employees.
- **MPF service Web sites:** Secondly, MPF service Web sites can help to provide customers with a comprehensive and convenient one-stop-shopping place for a wide range of financial services. The higher switching cost of moving the entire service package to other providers may increase customer loyalty. Increased flexibility of MPF account management should increase customer satisfaction.
- **Customer relationship management:** As more employment and financial details can be collected from the Web, it helps to build better customer relationship management. Consumer databases help providers to better respond to customer needs. Providers can cost-effectively provide higher degrees of customization and personalization, and thus offer better products to their customers.
- **MPF service platform:** The MPF service platform can be integrated with e-banking and other e-services, and can be used for cross-selling and promotions.

Business-to-Business (B2B) Transactions

First, we discuss the business-to-business processes between the trustee and the company that employs individual MPF participants. After signing an agreement to join the MPF service provided by the trustee, the employer needs to send information about every employee to the trustee for creation of a new MPF account. Information about the percentage of the monthly contributions—a minimum of 5% of the salary, the particular scheme that the individual has selected, personal data and other transaction-oriented information—has to be sent to the trustee. When these initial stages are completed, the company is required to send payroll information to the trustee regularly so that contributions to the MPF funding can be arranged. After the monthly contributions from the employees are received, the trustee needs to send a receipt to the company. Meanwhile, if a new employee is hired or an employee leaves the company, updated employee information needs to be transferred to the trustee. At the end of each year, the trustee is required to generate an annual report about the company's contributions to the MPF schemes of its employees.

To sum up, high volume document exchanges are required between the trustee and the employer on a regular basis. All these exchanges are concerned with the transfer of information which suggest to automate this process using modern e-commerce technologies.

- **Employee information transfer:** Information about the employee can be transferred from the company to the trustee via the Internet. After setting up the employee's individual MPF account, the company can use the Internet to transfer and update information, including information about new employment or termination of employment contracts.
- **Payroll information transfer:** The company can send monthly payroll information about the each employee to the trustee in an electronic format. This information can automatically trigger the transaction of MPF contribution from the employer account to each employee's MPF account. To ensure security about the transaction, all details about to be transferred have to be predefined clearly before the transaction.
- **Confirmation information about contribution transaction:** After each successful transferral of the contribution from the employer's account to the employee's MPF account, a confirmation message is sent to the employer via the Internet to complete the process. These messages serve as formal receipts from the trustee. Annual reports about the employer's contributions are also transferred from the trustee to the employer over the Internet. As non-repudiation is required for the process, SSL is typically used as an encryption method.
- **Balance and analysis:** With all the above processes automated by electronic means, it is now possible for the employer to have online access to the balance of each employee account. In addition, report and real-time analysis about the investment of the MPF funding can also be offered over the Internet.

In the case that an employee leaves his company and joins a new employer with a different MPF trustee, the original employer should send updated employee information to its own trustee to terminate the contribution to the employee's MPF account. When

Figure 7. XML-tagged MPF document

```
<?xml version = "1.0" standalone ="yes"><
<transactionconfirm>
<trustee>MPFBank</trustee>
<company>ABC manufacturer</company>
<date>2000/04/30</date>
<periodstart>2000/04/01</periodstart>
<periodend>2000/04/30</periodend>
<contribution>HK$400,000</contribution>
<status>successful</status>
..........
</trsansactionconfirm>
```

the employee wishes to join the MPF scheme of a new trustee of the new company, he can send his request to the original trustee to ask for transmission of past MPF information to the new trustee, if the new trustee has also adopted an e-MPF model. In this case, switching employer and trustee is completely automated.

To provide a standard way for information exchange over the Internet, XML has been suggested as the most effective way to exchange standard MPF documents (Choi & Whinston, 2000, pp. 45-50). With XML, we can define information in a document by tags, that are predefined by the trustee, so that information can be automatically processed and trigger content-based actions. Figure 7 shows a simplified example of an XML-tagged MPF document.

Most of the MPF-related information exchanged between employers and trustees is confidential as it involves personal particulars as well as payroll information. Therefore, security concerns have to be resolved. Measures have to be taken to ensure confidentially, authenticity and non-repudiation of information being transferred. All data transmitted over the Internet are encrypted using SSL. In Hong Kong, the public key infrastructure that is required for SSL encryption has been established by the Hong Kong Post Office.

The transfer of the contribution between accounts needs a higher level of security as it involves transfer of money. Whenever a contribution is made, money has to be transferred from the employer's account to the employee's MPF account. All money transactions need to be predefined before the actual transaction occurs (e.g., from what account to what account, the upper limit of each transfer, the frequency of the transaction, etc.). The real transaction from the employee's account to the MPF account is done through the bank's secure transaction system instead of over the public Internet. The Internet only serves as the medium for the company to send payroll information to trigger the predefined transaction. In this way, money transfers are all done through the banking system's own computer network. The Internet only serves as the media to trigger predefined transactions securely. If the employer account and the MPF account are from the same bank, the process is much simpler.

After each transaction, the database is updated immediately so that the employer can verify the status of all transactions over the Internet.

The whole process can be summarized in the diagram that is shown in Figure 8.

Several benefits are expected from the automation of the B2B process in the MPF service schemes:

Figure 8. Summary of MPF process

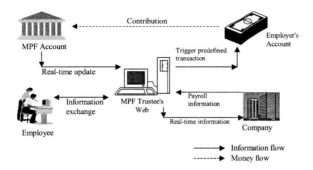

- **Reduction of administration cost:** Without the electronic process, the cost of exchanging information between the company and the trustee involves lots of manual work, use of paper documents, delivery charges and time delay due to delivery time. Using electronic information exchange, all these processes can be done speedier and at much lower cost.
- **Error reduction:** Without automation, data needs to be entered and reentered at several stages in the process. This inevitably introduces clerical error. With electronic data exchange, the data is only entered once and reused in all subsequent steps. Thus, human error in data entry can be significantly reduced.
- **Fast response:** Online transactions are executed almost instantaneously, which dramatically reduces cycle times and helps streamline the entire process.

Business-to-Government (B2G) Transactions

Employers have an obligation to report to the MPFA, the government body that supervises the MPF industry, about its progress when joining the MPF scheme, and inform about changes and provide updates on their regular MPF activities. They also have an obligation to send documents to the MPFA to prove that they have really contributed to their employee's MPF account. Trustees also need to send documents and reports about their investment policy, financial balance and investment details to the MPFA for inspection. This is required for supervision of trustees on their investment with the funding. The documents required for the MPFA are mostly legal documents and financial reports that include the following: employer application form, principle brochure, employer sales booklet, participation agreement, trust deed, proof of employer's contribution, MPF balance and MPF investment report.

As the processes between the employers, the trustees and the Government involve a large volume of information transfer, it is also very suitable to use the Internet as the platform to perform all these tasks (Nelson, 1998). The opportunity of B2G electronic process currently exists but it requires action on the part of the Government to initiate the process. Since the Hong Kong Government has recently, at the dawn of the 21st century, publicized its "Digital 21" initiative, which is aimed at promoting digital technologies to help transforming Hong Kong to a knowledge-based society, it can be expected that the e-MPF model will soon be extended to include the implementation of the B2G processes. The Hong Kong Government has already launched a series of electronic government services in other areas, and it is expected that a full e-MPF implementation, including the B2G part, will follow soon.

Current Challenges/Problems Facing the Organization

Government and industry have pushed the introduction of the MPF system. Only a few years after the initial decision, the MPF is up and running. This is certainly a success. As discussed in the previous sections, the MPF model is conceptually sound and the e-MPF model, in particular, promises great benefits to everyone. However, several serious problems emerged during the implementation, which we will summarize and discuss below. While some problem areas are concerned with technical issues, the most serious difficulties are related to managerial problems. Questions arise whether some of these problems could have been anticipated and better managed.

Challenges arise from the multiple levels of interactions between the parties involved. What are the fundamental features and components that would lead to a successful e-service model (Timmers, 1998)? The e-MPF model needs to include four sets of carefully designed relationships between the main parties: relationships between employers and service providers (business-to-business, or B2B relationships); service providers and clients (business-to-consumer, or B2C relationships); employers and employees (business-to-employee, or B2E relationships); and employers and service providers with government (business-to-government, or B2G relationships). We have introduced the e-MPF design and discussed how it implements the main stakeholder relationships. Complex information services involving multiple parties require a high degree of coordination to avoid friction and conflicts. Complexity arises from multiplicity of stakeholders, coordination requirements, new types of large-scale services and the different roles played by all parties involved. This results in a set of service implementation challenges. What are the main technical difficulties when implementing such a complex information service? And last, but not least, what are the main managerial issues in developing and launching a new service like MPF? What problems have occurred and what has their impact been? Who is responsible? Could some of the problems have been anticipated and perhaps avoided? Five areas have been identified as the main problem sources.

1.   **Market potential:** Many companies, especially small, family owned enterprises and self-employed professionals, did not fully cooperate in implementing the MPF model. As of May 2001, about 30% of the businesses and 10% of the employees have still not enrolled, although the enrollment deadline has long passed. The government is facing a big problem of how to deal with thousands of companies and employers violating MPF regulations. Prosecution has been threatened but mass prosecutions on that scale appears unenforceable. Critics have claimed that many small businesses could simply not afford the mandatory MPF contributions. Enforcing enrollment could then lead to layoffs. Some legislators have already blamed the MPF scheme for the recent rise in unemployment, which has gone up to 4.5% in February 2001, the first increase in 18 months. Many low salary workers who already suffer financial hardship cannot afford a 5% reduction of their net pay. The image of the MPF has suffered at large from negative press. The slowdown of the U.S. economy and volatile stock markets have negatively impacted the initial

performance of many MPF funds. More than half of the 290 MPF investment funds had posted negative returns by April 2001. Overall, the MPF has become quite unpopular, and most people only participate because law requires it.

2. **E-business limitations:** The e-MPF market is currently only a small fraction of the total MPF market. Many employers simply follow standard plans chosen by their company as default options, and do not use the flexible e-MPF mode. Despite the high Internet penetration rate in HK, there remains a large portion of the workforce that doesn't use computers at all or doesn't use sophisticated online services like the e-MPF. And even among the Internet-savvy professionals, e-MPF adoption has been relatively slow (Bhatnagar, Mistra, & Rao, 2000).

3. **System integration:** Multiple parties are involved in the implementation of the MPF system—the MPFA (Mandatory Provident Fund Scheme Authority) who enforces the law, the trustees who manage the funds, the intermediaries who provide daily administrative work and user interface, and the client companies who provide payroll data. All those organizations developed their own systems. A seamless integration of all business-to-business processes is an absolute requirement for e-MPF to work successfully. During the implementation phase, however, there were numerous coordination problems among the involved parties that delayed projects and led occasionally to ad-hoc style patchwork to fix system flaws. Back-end integration with payroll legacy systems at the employer's side with the MPF system is another important issue. There are very different legacy systems in place, running on different computing platforms. Many companies have had difficulties with the integration of their legacy systems. Similarly, service providers have encountered problems related to the integration of the e-MPF service with their other e-services. Each service provider has developed its own e-MPF system, which has also led to a proliferation of different user interfaces. Better coordination between the providers could have reduced or eliminated this problem.

4. **Project management:** During the software implementation phase of the MPF system, most service providers were running behind schedule and over budget. A large number of the MPF software implementations were outsourced to international software vendors and consultants. When the management realized that their projects were off target, it was often difficult to regain control, especially when the projects were outsourced. Only few clients from the employer's side enrolled in the early development stages so that the service providers could not really familiarize themselves with the client's systems. This led to some of the integration problems cited above. As deadlines approached, managing the relationships between banks and the contractors became increasingly challenging; extra resources had to be committed to meet the deadlines. There was little time for system testing. Testing with real data and cases was impossible because most companies had not enrolled until the very last moment before the legal deadline. System integration tests were impossible because the other parties were not ready yet. When the MPF systems were rolled out, most systems were not fully tested and there was a high risk of major problems. Fortunately, no disastrous failures have been reported, which many commentators attribute more to luck than to proper problem management.

5. **Flexibility:** At the moment, most e-MPF systems allow users only to adjust their investment plans one to several times a year, with only three kinds of investment choices, ranging from low risk to high risk. The industry is currently not fully

utilizing the e-MPF business model, which may deter employees from joining the e-service version of the MPF. At the same time, service providers postpone system upgrades and improvement, citing the currently low usage level of their e-services.

A final assessment of the success or failure of Hong Kong's MPF initiative, especially in terms of MPF as an electronic service, will have to wait a few more years until MPF has matured. An interesting future research project could be a longitudinal study that investigates how the MPF market matures and how the players respond to the various challenges.

ACKNOWLEDGMENTS

We would like to thank Sarah Cook for helping to prepare the manuscript of this case. We also express our thanks to Simon Leung and Philip Lee for contributions with the MPF market research. Our deepest gratitude, however, has to be extended to Norman Law who provided us with invaluable insights from the banking industry regarding the implementation of the MPF system.

REFERENCES

Bakos, Y. (1998). The emerging role of electronic marketplaces on the Internet. *Communications of the ACM, 41*(8), 35-42.

Bakos, Y., & Brynjolfsson, E. (1998). Organizational partnerships and the virtual corporation. In C. F. Kemerer (Ed.), *Information technology and industrial competitiveness: How IT shapes competition* (pp. 49-66). Kluwer Academic Publishers.

Bhatnagar, A., Misra, S., & Rao, R. H. (2000). On risk convenience and Internet shopping behavior. *Communications of the ACM, 43*(11), 98-105.

Clemons, E. K. (1986). Information systems for sustainable competitve advantage. *Information and Mangement, 11,* 131-136.

MPFA: Mandatory Provident Fund Schemes Authority. (2001). Official MPF Web site. Retrieved from http://www.mpfahk.org

Nelson, M. R. (1998). Government and governance in the networked world. In D. Tapscott, A. Lowy, & D. Ticoll (Eds.), *Blueprint to the digital economy* (pp. 339-354). New York: McGraw Hill.

Soon-Jong Choi, S. J., & Whinston, A. B. (2000). *The Internet economy: Technology and practice.* Austin, TX: Smart Econ Press.

Tapscott, D., Ticoll, D., & Lowy, A. (2001). *Digital capital: Harnessing the benefit of business Webs.* Harvard Business School Press.

Timmers, P. (1998). Business models for electronic markets. *EM-Electronic Markets, 8*(2), 3-8.

Ward Hanson, W. (2000). *Principles of Internet marketing,* Cincinatti, OH: Thomson Learning.

Westland, C. J., & Clark, T. H. K. (1999). *Global electronic commerce: Theory and case studies.* Cambridge, MA: MIT Press.

FURTHER READING

Castells, M. (1996). *The rise of the network society, 1.* Oxford, UK: Blackwell Publishers.

Galliers, R. D., Leidner, D. E., & Baker, B. (Eds.). (1999). *Strategic information management* (2nd ed.). Oxford, UK: Butterworth Heinemann.

Gulati, R., & Garino, J. (2000, May-June). Get the right mix of bricks & clicks. *Harvard Business Review*, 107-113.

Kalakota, R., & Whinston, A. B. (Eds.). (1997). *Readings in electronic commerce.* Reading, MA: Addison-Wesley.

Malone, T. W., Yates, J., & Benjamin, R. (1989). The logic of electronic markets. *Harvard Business Review,* May-June, 166-170.

Munro, A. J., Höök, K., & Benyon, D. (Eds.). (1999). *Social navigation of information spaces.* London; Heidelberg; New York: Springer.

Negroponte, N. (1995). *Being digital.* London, UK: Hodder and Stoughton.

Porter, M. (2001, March). Strategy and the Internet. *Harvard Business Review*, 63-78.

Strauss, J., & Frost, R. (2001). *E-marketing* (2nd ed.). Upper Saddle River, NJ: Prentice Hall.

APPENDIX A

Major Competitors

Table A. Banking

	MPF Organization Mode	Integral Parts of MPF Services	Number of Branches	Market Share (Claimed)
HSBC/ Hang Seng Bank	A separate business division	One-stop-shop	360+	40%
BOC	Joint venture with Prudential Assurance	One-stop-shop	270+	15%
Bank of East Asia	A separate business unit	One-stop-shop	100+	5-15%
Bank Consortium	Alliance with banking entity	Outsourcing Fund Management	280+	10-15%
Standard Chartered Bank	A separate business division	Outsourcing Fund Management, Trustee and Administration	80+	15-20%
TOTAL				*100-105%*

Table B. Insurance and fund management

	MPF Organization Mode	Integral Parts of MPF Services	Number of Agents	Market Share (Claimed)
AXA	A separate business unit	Outsourcing Custodian Service and Fund Management	3,000	20%
CMG	Partner up with Butterfield Trust	Outsourcing Custodian Service	2.500	20%
AIA/Jardine Fleming	Joint venture	One-stop-shop	8,000	25-30%
Manulife	A separate business unit	One-stop-shop	2,300	20%
INVESCO	Handles Fund Management only. Partner up with Bermuda Trust.	Outsourcing Trustee, Custodial & Fund Management	100+	10%
SUB-TOTAL				*90-100%*
OTHERS				*25-45%*

APPENDIX B

Table 1. The fee schedule (the initial offer)

	Initial Charges	Annual Management Fee-capital preservation fund	Annual Management fee - other funds	Special Feature
HSBC/ Hang Seng Bank	1.0%	2.200%	1.9500%	Clearest definition of the various types of fees
BOC	1.5%	0.800%	1.4875%	Cheapest preservation fund
Bank of East Asia	1.0-1.2%	1.200%	1.5000%	———
Bank Consortium	2.0%	1.400%	1.6250%	Least choice of available fund
Standard Chartered Bank	2.5%	1.675%	1.8000%	Most choice of available fund
AXA	1.0%	1.0000%	22.000%	Converting deposit into subscription is possible.
CMG	3.0%	2.500%	2.5000%	Lump sum fees available.
AIA/Jardine	0.5%	2.000%	2.0000%	Unlimited number of switch of fund over the net and phone

APPENDIX C

Table 1. Non-fee competition-technology and bundled benefit

	MPF specific Website	HRIS	IVRS	Associated Banking/Insurance Bundled Benefit
HSBC/ Hang Seng Bank	Yes www.mpfdirect.com	Payroll / MPF Packages	IVRS	Yes
BOC	No www.bocgroup.com	Payroll & MPF Adaptor	IVRS & MPF Workshop, Call center	Yes
Bank of East Asia	www.hkbea.com	Payroll & MPF Adaptor	IVRS	Yes
Bank Consortium	Yes www.bcthk.com	Payroll software	IVRS, investor education	Yes
Standard Chartered Bank	No www.standardchartered.com.hk	Payroll interface system	IVRS	Yes
AXA	No www.axa-chinaregion.com	TBA	IVRS, Call center	Yes
CMG	(TBA)	Payroll interface	IVRS	Yes
AIA/Jardine	Yes www.mpf-aiajf.com	Payroll system	--	Yes
Manulife	Yes www.mpf.com.hk	Contribution Software	Employee Seminar	Yes
INVESCO	No www.invesco.com.hk	Payroll Solution	IVRS, Employee Education, seminar, retirement investment center, MPF news update	Yes

Theodore H. K. Clark has taught information technology courses at the Hong Kong University of Science & Technology's (HKUST) Business School, Harvard University and Wharton Business School (University of Pennsylvania). He is an associate professor in information systems and serves currently as the deputy head of the ISMT Department at HKUST. His current research interests included electronic commerce, information technology (IT) strategy, business process reengineering, supply chain management and information infrastructure development. Dr. Clark has published a number of articles in leading research journals within the IT research community and has also written many case studies published by HKUST and HBS on electronic commerce, IT strategy and business process reengineering. In addition, he is the co-author of a book titled Global Electronic Commerce: Theory and Cases, *published by MIT Press.*

Karl Reiner Lang is an assistant professor in information systems at the Hong Kong University of Science & Technology (HKUST). Before joining HKUST in 1995, he had been on the faculty of the Business School at the Free University of Berlin. Dr. Lang has been teaching courses on information technology and electronic commerce at the undergraduate, postgraduate and executive levels. His research interests include management of digital businesses, decision technologies, knowledge-based products and services, and issues related to the newly arising informational society. Dr. Lang's recent publications have appeared in leading research journals such as Annals of Operations Research, Computational Economics, Journal of Organizational Computing and Electronic Commerce, *and* Decision Support Systems. *He has professional experience in Germany, the USA, and Hong Kong.*

Will Wai-Kit Ma is a research associate in the ISMT Department at the Hong Kong University of Science & Technology. Will had worked as marketing manager in a multimedia company coordinating multimedia projects and application training courses for five years. He then became an instructor training practicing teachers computer applications. He is also the author of a number of popular computer books, including Own Your Business on the Internet, A Guide to Hong Kong Web Sites, A Guide to Internet, *and* CD-ROM Practice Q&A. *His research interests are in information technology adoption, computer attitudes, electronic business and IT in education.*

This case was previously published in F. Tan (Ed.), *Cases on Global IT Applications and Management: Success and Pitfalls*, pp. 158-184, © 2002.

Chapter XVII

World Trade Point Federation:
Bringing E-Commerce Capabilities to Developing Nations

Nikhilesh Dholakia, University of Rhode Island, USA

Nir Kshetri, The University of North Carolina, Greensboro, USA

EXECUTIVE SUMMARY

This case provides an overview of the roles of the Global Trade Point Network (GTPNet) in facilitating small- and medium-sized enterprises' (SMEs') adoption of the Internet and e-commerce technologies. The GTPNet puts potential and actual traders in the position of suppliers and users of strategic information. Using the services provided by a Trade Point, traders can identify markets for their products, complete export formalities and procedures, and meet other international trade related requirements on the spot. The functioning of the Trade Points program is also discussed in terms of three core aspects of the program: Market Point, Knowledge Point, *and* Info Point.

ORGANIZATIONAL BACKGROUND

The United Nations Conference on Trade and Development (UNCTAD) was the initiator of the Trade Point program. UNCTAD was established in 1964 as the "focal point" within the United Nations (UN) system for assisting developing countries in diverse areas such as trade, finance, technology, investment, and sustainable development (UNCTAD, 1998b). With headquarters in Geneva, Switzerland, UNCTAD has 192 countries as its members.

UNCTAD aims to integrate developing countries into the world economy in a development-friendly manner. It undertakes research, policy analysis, and data collection to provide inputs to development experts and government representatives. UNCTAD works with member governments and interacts with organizations of the UN system and regional commissions, government institutions, non-governmental organizations, private firms, trade and industry associations, research institutes, and universities. Its technical cooperation emphasizes "capacity building" in four main areas: globalization and development; international trade in goods and services and commodities; investment, technology, and enterprise development; and services infrastructure for development and trade efficiency.

UNCTAD promotes simpler, less complex hardware and software platforms for developing countries (UNCTAD, 1993). As an element of its IT program and a core component of its Trade Efficiency Initiative, UNCTAD launched the Trade Point program in 1992 (UNCTAD, 1998a).

A timeline indicating major milestones in the evolution of the Trade Point program is presented in Table 1. These Trade Points are at various phases of operation (feasibility phase, development phase, and operational phase). Trade Points at operational phase also differ in terms of the types of services offered. The services provided by the Trade Points can be broadly classified into three categories: information, facilitation, and transaction.

Three main stages characterized the evolution of the Trade Point Program (UNCTAD, 1998a):

1. **The testbed period:** This began in 1992 and entailed setting up 16 pilot Trade Points.
2. **The launching of the concept of the Global Trade Point Network (GTPNet):** Starting from the 1994 United Nations International Symposium on Trade Efficiency (UNISTE), the Trade Points around the world were interconnected.
3. **The initiation of the movement "from contacts to contracts":** By the 1996 Executive Symposium on Trade Efficiency, UNCTAD put technical solutions in place that allowed enterprises to conduct e-commerce on an open but secure network.

Table 1. Development of the Trade Point program—Timeline

Year (Month)	Event
1964	Establishment of UNCTAD as the "focal point" within UN system for assisting developing countries.
1992	UNCTAD launches the Trade Point Program.
1994	Trade Points around the world interconnected.
1996	UNCTAD allows enterprises to conduct e-commerce on an open network.
2000 (September)	UNCTAD member states presented the concept of setting up the WTPF.
2000 (November)	Representatives of 58 Trade Points take the decision to establish WTPF.
2001 (May)	Registration process of WTPF completed.
2002 (November)	The Trade Point program completely taken over by WTPF.
2003 (February)	WTPF launches its Web site.
2003 (May)	GTPNet boasts a human network of 121 Trade Points in over 80 countries.

Source: Authors' research

The growing competition in the electronic marketplace led UNCTAD member states to realize the importance of cooperation and collaborations with external partners, especially from the private sector. The nature of the UN framework, however, does not allow unrestricted cooperation with private firms. At the September 2000 meeting of the UNCTAD member states, the concept of setting up the *World Trade Point Federation* was presented. During the sixth World Trade Point Meeting in November 2000, representatives of 58 Trade Points decided to establish the World Trade Point Federation (WTPF) as an international non-governmental organization under Swiss law. By December 2000, most of the Trade Points voted in favor of creating WTPF. The registration process of WTPF with the Register of Commerce in Geneva was completed in May 2001. The Trade Point program was completely taken over by the WTPF in November 2002. On February 19, 2003, the WTPF launched its Web site: http://www.wtpfed.org/newsite/index1.php.

SETTING THE STAGE

Through its technical cooperation, UNCTAD actively encourages the use of appropriate technology in developing countries usually by providing technical cooperation to in partnership with other agencies. The organization believes that such partnership and cooperation "helps to minimize the incidence of duplication, results in the creation of synergies, and insures sequencing of activities."[2]

The main objective of the Trade Point Program is to assist small- and medium-sized enterprises (SMEs) to take full advantage of global trading opportunities using modern ITs and to improve the capacity of developing countries to compete in global markets and by integrating in the value chains. The program has made it easier for smaller companies in developing nations to "meet" customers worldwide via the Internet and to export their products. (See Box 1 for an illustration of services provided by a Trade Point).

WTPF has outlined its vision to "be a global business facilitator for SMEs."[3] Its mission is to "become a global trade facilitator and trade information provider for SMEs, particularly those located in developing and least developed countries, through its human network with local know-how and its global e-business marketplace."[4] The main strategic objectives of the WTPF are to:

1.   Increase the participation of SMEs in international trade,
2.   Help SMEs trade more efficiently, and
3.   Assist Trade Points to become "one-stop-shops" where SMEs can obtain a full set of services pertaining to trade information, facilitation and transaction, as well as electronic commerce.[5]

SMEs and Internet Adoption

Touted as a technology that allows SMEs, even those from developing countries, to reach customers worldwide in a cost-effective manner, the Internet has increased international opportunities for SMEs (Hamill & Gregory, 1997; Lituchy & Rail, 2000). Internet technologies enhance SMEs' ability to compete with other companies, create the possibility and opportunity for a diverse range of entrepreneurs to start a business, offer a convenient and easy way of doing business transactions (not restricted to certain hours of operation), and offer an inexpensive way (compared to postage, fax, telephone, and travel) for small business to compete with larger companies (Williams, 1999, p. 20).

Surveys by various consulting and industry groups suggest that small firms recognize the advantages of e-commerce. For instance, a survey of small and mid-sized businesses by Arthur Andersen's Enterprise Group and National Small Business United (2000) cites various reasons for using the Internet. They include sending and receiving business e-mail (78%), researching goods and services (60%), sending and receiving personal e-mail (48%), conducting research (41%), and purchasing goods and services (40%).

Firm size is an important predictor of technology adoption by organizations (Mansfield, 1961). Smaller firms are thus less likely to adopt modern technologies such as the Internet compared to larger ones. In Japan, for example, firms with more than 300 employees were found to be four times more likely to adopt the Internet than firms with less than six employees (Coppel, 2000).

Functioning of the Trade Point Program

There are three core components of the Trade Point program: *Market Point*, *Knowledge Point*, and *Info Point* (Table 2).

Table 2. Core aspects of the Trade Point program and their functions

Aspect	Function	Remarks
Market Point		
Electronic Trading Opportunity (ETO) System	Trade related organizations can exchange Information in standardized form.	
Company Directory	Directory of firms related to international trade.	Unavailable as of August 2003.
Sector Information	Information on various sectors related to international trade.	Unavailable as of August 2003
Country Information	Basic as well as advanced profiles of countries across the world.	
World Trade Events	A database of trade events taking place all over the world.	
Trade-Related Sites	Can be searched by sectors such as economy, trade contacts, market information, market access, investment and tourism; by country; and by keyword.	
Useful Information	Available information includes customs authorities, statistical offices, standardization bodies, packaging institutes, export credit finance directories, and purchasing and supply management associations.	
Knowledge Point		
Trade Policy	Provides detailed information on various trade-related policies and agreements.	
Trade Terms	Provides dictionary of trade-related terms and detailed documents regarding some of them.	
Standards and Codes	Provides information on UN/LOCODE, country and currency codes, and codes for units of measurements.	
Trade Library	Information can be searched on subjects such as business cooperation, e-commerce, trade facilitations, trade information services, import-export related documents, and information technologies.	
Info Point		
World Trade Point Federation	Provides information about WTPF; its mission and vision; organization structure; membership benefits and the process of establishing a Trade Point.	
Global Trade Point Network	Provides information about Trade Points, services offered by them, and Trade Point directory.	

Market Point

Key elements of *Market Point* include *Electronic Trading Opportunity* (ETO) system, company directory, sector information, country information, world trade events, trade-related sites, and useful information.

The ETO system provides subscribers with a single point of contact for trade, investment and business opportunities using an international standard structured and using EDI-UN-EDIFACT[6] system. This is achieved via connection to the GTPNet. Through the ETO system, trade-related bodies can exchange trade information in standardized format. The ETOs are offers and demands for products, services, and investments. The system also allows automatic matching of inquiries made by buyers or sellers against offers. As of 2000, the ETO system connected over 20,000 trade organizations worldwide. To enable ETO users to conduct transactions without letters of credit[7] or other bank documents, the ETO system is also planning to provide a smart card capability (see Box 2).

As of late 2003, the *company directory* and *sector information* services were not available. GTPF has been working with Siemens, the German technology company, to make such services available in the near future.

Country information provides basic as well as advanced profiles of almost all countries of the world. Basic profile includes area, population, GDP, trade balance, and foreign direct investment. Advanced profile includes trade statistics, generalized system of preferences, trade policy reviews, investment fact sheets, corporate tax guide, and country credit rating.

The *world trade events* section of the *Market Point* provides a database of trade events taking place all over the world. Users can also search the database by sectors such as automation, animals and livestock, furniture and home supplies, and textiles; by continent; and by time period.

The *Market Point* has another database named *trade-related sites*. Users can also search this database by sectors such as economy, trade contacts, market information, market access, investment and tourism; by country; and by keyword.

The *Market Point* also has information about other *useful contacts* related to international trade. They include customs authorities, statistical offices, standardization bodies, packaging institutes, export credit finance directories, and purchasing and supply management associations.

Knowledge Point

The *Knowledge Point* deals with trade policy, trade terms, standards and codes, and trade library. *Trade policy* provides detailed information on various trade-related policies and agreements. They include General Agreement on Trade and Tariffs (GATT), agriculture agreement of the World Trade Organization (WTO), articles of customs valuations, agreements on import licensing, information technology products, rules of origin, safeguards, sanitary and phytosanitary measures, subsidies and countervailing measures, technical barriers to trade, textiles, goods schedules, general agreement of trade on services (GATS), and intellectual property. Dictionaries of trade terms are provided under *trade terms*.

The Standards & Codes section of the Knowledge Point provides information on UN/LOCODE, country and currency codes, and codes for units of measurements. The information provided promotes clarity in using the units of measurements for the fulfillment of commercial contracts as well as for the application of laws and regulations governing international trade procedures. UN/LOCODE provides agreed, unique coded designations for 36,000 locations in 234 countries.[8] Country and currency names and codes and codes for units of measurement used in International trade are also provided in this section.

In the trade library, users can search for information on subjects such as business cooperation, electronic commerce, trade facilitations, trade information services, import-export-related documents, and information technologies.

Info Point

Info Point provides information about WTPF and the Global Trade Points Network. Information about WTPF includes its mission and vision, organization structure, activities, benefits of membership, and procedures of establishing a Trade Point. This section will also have WTPF library and provides information on Trade Points, services provided by Trade Points, and Trade Point directory.

CASE DESCRIPTION

Actual adoption of the Internet by SMEs for e-commerce applications is limited even in developed countries (Dholakia and Kshetri, 2004). Some SMEs from developing nations, however, have been able to use the Internet to sell their products worldwide. For instance, SMEs from Bangladesh, China, Mexico, Pakistan, Russia, Thailand, and Zimbabwe have sold products such as bicycles, steel, salt, pharmaceuticals, stone materials, water and energy meters, flowers, and cosmetics using the GTPNet system. Box 1 documents the success of a small firm from Zimbabwe using the services of a trade point.

Box 1. How Trade Point program helped Misti-Flora's flower export business

Misti-Flora is a small firm in Zimbabwe that exports fresh-cut flowers. In the last three years, the firm grew from a family owned three-person enterprise to a small company employing 30 people.

In the early days of his export business, Paul Misti, president of Misti-Flora, used to book freight space only after cutting the flowers. Most of the time, the freight companies were unable to organize the transportation facilities in time. As a result, flowers used to sit in their boxes for a long time before they were delivered. This affected the freshness and quality of the flowers.

The nature of Misti-Flora's business makes it almost entirely dependent on exports. Hence, access to foreign markets is critical for the success of the company's business. After several bad experiences with unreliable freight companies, Paul Misti was hooked up with the Trade Point located at Harare, the capital city of Zimbabwe. The Harare Trade Point helped Paul at various phases of the business, including securing bank loans needed for exporting and identifying new markets that have demand for flowers. The Harare Trade Point also put Paul in contact with a freight-forwarder at the Harare airport. This freight-forwarder was much more reliable and guaranteed to get the products to their intended destinations on time. This solved his transport problem.

Misti-Flora has also developed its own homepage, including an online product catalog. The Harare Trade Point designed the homepage for Misti-Flora and updates it on a regular basis for a small fee. Since Misti-Flora is a member of the GTPNet, Trade Point Harare stores Misti-Flora's information free of charge on the main network server at the Trade Point Development Center.

Source: Adapted from UNCTAD (1998d) and "Blossoming Businesses"; available at http://www.gtpnet-e.com/UNCTAD/tptext.nsf/listcontents/COMPANY-STORIES and accessed on August 26, 2003

Box 2. The ETO system of the GTPNet

> The ETO System is probably one of the most important aspects of the GTPNet. It was started by the UN
> Trade Point Development Center (TPDC) in June 1993 and is the world's largest Internet-based business
> opportunities system. ETOs are offers and demands for products, services, and investment and are
> distributed point-to-point and company-to-company. They are forwarded to the GTPNet system by Trade
> Points and third-party information providers. The ETO system has been growing exponentially. A random
> survey of ETO users conducted in 1998 revealed that only 8% of them participated in the exchange of
> business opportunities before 1996 which increased to 22% in 1997 and 64% in 1998 (UNCTAD, 1998c).
> The same survey indicated that 48% of ETO users receive 1-10 responses per posted ETO, an additional
> 14% receive 10-30 responses, about 7% receive over 100 reactions. About a third of respondents made
> business deals on the basis of ETOs. About 34% of the transactions were of less than US$10,000 and in
> 53% of the cases the values ranged from US$10,000-1 million.
>
>   The number of ETO e-mails increased from 300 in June 1993 to over 60,000 in January 1996. In
> January 1996, the UNCTAD-TPDC also started distributing ETOs via newsgroups. The number of hits for
> the ETO newsgroups increased from 870,000 in January 1996 to 100,000 hits per day in March 1996.
>
>   In addition to e-mails and newsgroups, Trade Points employ a variety of media such as BBS,
> specialized databases, homepages, newspapers and other publications, and CD\ROMs to distribute ETOs.
> An estimate suggests that over 7 million companies received ETOs in July 1996 via a combination of e-
> mail, fax, bulletin board systems, newsgroup, newspaper, and publications. For instance, in 1996, the Trade
> Point Seoul in South Korea distributed the ETOs daily to its 67,000 customers through various media.
>
>   In India, the National Centre for Trade Information (NCTI) received a database of ETOs containing
> 27,345 demands/offers by September 2001. To provide value-added information to its customers, NCTI
> published 52 issues of its weekly publication *Trade Point India*. Four issues of NCTI's quarterly magazine
> *Trade Connect* were released and also posted on NCTI's Web site. NCTI regularly updated information on
> its Web site and also made available specialized CD- ROMs and electronic product catalogues. Similarly,
> the *Trade Point New Delhi* published ETOs on weekly publications to reach its subscribers, which
> exceeded 10,000 in 1998.

Sources: http://www.tptanzania.co.tz/about_body.html; Moreira (1996); NIC.in (2001); UNCTAD (1998c)

In 1996, while e-commerce[9] was still a technology of curiosity for many U.S.-based firms, about 100,000 SMEs in the Chinese city of Shanghai were involved in some types of international e-commerce activities, thanks to the services provided by the Shanghai Trade Point (Lu, 1997). Established in 1994, the Shanghai Trade Point works as a "one-stop shop" for firms involved in international trade. It does so by bringing together parties related to foreign trade such as government departments and customs; and providers of related services such as commodity inspections, foreign exchange control, banking and insurance, and transportation.

The Shanghai Trade Point performs these functions mainly by acting as a gateway to the Global Trade Point Network (GTPNet) launched by the United Nations Conference on Trade and Development (UNCTAD). Member units of the Shanghai Trade Point include Shanghai Customs, Shanghai Import and Export Commodity Inspection Bureau, Bank of China Shanghai Branch, Sinotrans (a leading provider of logistics services in China) Shanghai Branch, People's Insurance Company of China Shanghai Branch, Shanghai Foreign Trade Computer Centre, and State Administration Foreign Exchange Control Shanghai Branch.[10]

Of the queries processed by the Shanghai Trade Point in 1996, about 50% reached the intended parties and the sender companies received feedback; and 10% of the information resulted in business transaction (Lu, 1997). Many local companies were able to establish relationships with customers located in all continents through the GTPNet. Based on a computer networking system, the Shanghai Trade Point also provides companies with information about trade policies, regulations, tariff, license, statistics, products and markets, company profiles, and electronic trade opportunities (ETOs). It also assists companies to follow Customs and commodity inspection procedures, certificate issuance, transportation, and insurance business.

The Shanghai Trade Point was one of the first Trade Points in the GTPNet system along with the Trade Points in Bangkok and Lisbon. The GTPNet system gradually expanded its coverage worldwide. In mid-2003, GTPNet had a human network of 121 Trade Points in over 80 countries on the five continents.[11]

The last week of August of 2003 was as typical as any other week for hundreds SMEs that advertise their wares on one of dozens of Trade Point Web sites worldwide. For example, during August 2003, on the network of Trade Point Web sites, you could have stumbled upon[12]:

1. Solusindo, an Indonesian Trading Company, offering handcrafted furniture made from rattan, teakwood, bamboo, mahogany, and seagrass by small factories in the famed Java, Bali, and Lombok regions of Indonesia.
2. Nantong Haiwang, a Chinese fire hose manufacturer with ISO9001 and CCCF certification, offering dozens of varieties of fire hoses of excellent quality at reasonable prices, and quick delivery.
3. Agricole Machines, an exporter from India, purveying submersible water pumps, turbines, diesel engines, rice hullers, tractors, threshers, sprayers, sprinklers, and chaff cutters.
4. A small Chinese firm Yinfan, promising a range of beauty-care implements: manicure sets, tweezers, eyelash curlers, nail files, pedicure files, eyebrow brushes, mirrors, combs, and eyebrow pencil sharpeners.
5. Forever Time, a skilled maker of grandfather clocks from Thailand, extolling the virtues of its finely crafted clocks with engravings, embroideries, and mother-of-pearl inlays.

Trade Point

A Trade Point is a source of trade-related information that provides actual and potential traders with data about business and market opportunities, potential clients and suppliers, and trade regulations and requirements. The Trade Point system thus puts potential and actual traders in the position of suppliers as well as users of strategic information. Traders identify markets for their products, complete export procedures, and meet import-export regulatory requirements on the spot, in less time and at lower cost than before. Facilitators of foreign trade transactions—such as customs, foreign trade institutes, banks, chambers of commerce, freight forwarders, transport operators, and insurance companies—are grouped together under a single virtual roof to provide all required services at a reasonable cost. A survey conducted by UNCTAD (1997) indicated that a large majority of Trade Point customers (85.7%) were SMEs and micro-enterprises.

There are other alternative networks available to SMEs, but they provide only subsets of functions provided by the GTPNet systems and are intended for firms located in a particular country or region. For instance, governments, international organizations, and private companies provide information on business opportunities including various types of "match making" services. International Trade Center's (ITC) Web site, for instance, provides information on many other Web sites that contain business opportunities (da Luz, 2000). Similarly, Stat-USA (http://www.stat-usa.govtradtest.nsf) is a network provided by the U.S. Department of Commerce and is intended for U.S. SMEs. Likewise, the site of the Federation of International Trade Associations (FITA) comprises over 300 international trade associations in the United States, Canada, and Mexico, and maintains a searchable database of more than 2,500 world trade Web resources (da Luz, 2000).

Trade Points thus allow SMEs and firms from developing countries to reach customers and suppliers world wide in a timely and cost-effective manner. It is the world's biggest system of this type. As early as in 1997, the combined GTPNet sites accounted for approximately 5 million hits every day (UNCTAD, 1998d). The system has also been able to achieve a reasonably high response rate. For example, as discussed in the previous section, 50% of the inquiries processed by the Shanghai Trade Point in 1996 reached the intended trade partners, and they received feedback and 10% of the inquiries resulted in business deals (Lu, 1997). Similarly, in 1998, 27% of the ETOs resulted in some types of business transactions.[13]

The majority of Trade Points are located in developing countries. For instance, out of 149 trade points at different phases of operations in 1998, 115 were located in developing countries and 16 of them in least developed countries (Bangladesh, Benin, Burkina Faso, Cape Verde, Eritrea, Ethiopia, the Gambia, Guinea-Bissau, Maldives, Mali, Mauritania, Mozambique, Sao Tome and Principe, Uganda, the United Republic of Tanzania, and Zambia) (UNCTAD, 1998c).[14] Developing countries also have a much higher share in the ETOs than in the overall global e-commerce. A United Nations Trade Point Development Center's (UNTPDC) analysis of ETOs posted on the GTPNet during March 1-July 15, 1998, indicated that 20% of them were posted by U.S.-based companies, followed by companies in China (19%), South Korea (11%), and India (7%) (UNCTAD, 1998c). It is interesting to note that the U.S. accounted for 74% of the global Internet commerce market in 1998 (Wang, 1999).

All Trade Points are interconnected in a worldwide electronic network—the Global Trade Point Network (GTPNet)—and equipped with efficient telecommunications tools to link up with other global networks to facilitate participation by traders, especially SMEs, in the emerging electronic commerce economy.

International institutions such as UNCTAD possess unique capabilities that allow them to take a wide range of measures to attack the sources of problems plaguing the underutilization of modern information and communications technologies by SMEs mainly in developing countries. Because "almost all nations observe almost all principles of international law and almost all of their obligations almost all of the time" (Henkin, 1979), these institutions carry enormous power. They can influence developing countries' policies so as to foster and strengthen the ICT sectors. These include increasing ICT budgets; opening ICT sectors for competition; and removing tariff and non-tariff barriers to ICT products. International institutions can also work to match multinational corporations' (MNCs) philanthropic as well as a profit motives with the ICT needs of developing countries. They can also use the resources at their own disposal to facilitate ICT use among firms and individuals in developing countries.

CURRENT CHALLENGES/PROBLEMS FACING THE TRADE POINT PROGRAM

Over nearly a decade of existence, including over five years of e-commerce facilitation, Trade Points have become important nodes for the flow of global import- and export-related inquiries and information. For instance, in late 2003, thousands of inquiries and offers similar to these could be found on Trade Point Web sites[15]:

1. An exporter in India looking for international buyers of fancy bags, baskets, purses, decorative items, tabletop mats, doormats, disposable plates and cups, and trays made out of banana, palm, and similar plant leaves and fibers.
2. Jiangnan Enterprise of China offering pharmaceutical machines such as high-efficiency film coating machines, three-dimensional fixers, capsule filling machines, and aluminum-plastic blister packing machines.
3. Gulf Food Products of Jordan prepared to export a variety of jams, sauces, canned vegetables and fruits, and seasonings.
4. Cellenas Creations of Australia wanting to buy a variety of beads, jewelry findings, party supplies, novelties, packing items, and display stands.
5. OAS of Singapore offering to sell identification accessories such as lanyards, badge clips, pull reels, and badge holders.

While Trade Points provide a vast e-business network geared to the needs of SMEs, a lot needs to be done to make the program more usable by SMEs. In particular, GTPNet sites are vast and not well organized (Lehrer, 2003). At a recent international forum on ways to improve the Trade Point programs for SMEs, the following suggestions came up[16]:

1. Encourage and assist non-exporting companies in entering the international marketplace, perhaps even creating some special e-commerce programs open to "new exporters" only.
2. Develop ways for SMEs to enter new markets, alerting SMEs to the pitfalls involved, and provide guidance for the management of the export process to the new markets.
3. Address issues of lack of quality and low production volumes of many SMEs.
4. Provide speedy, low-cost translation services so that import-export business can be conducted in multiple languages.
5. Provide convenient online payment mechanisms.
6. Provide skilled, efficient, and rapid Web search services to SMEs—using trained human Web surfers—to locate trade-related information and trading opportunities.
7. Simple and robust Web development tools whereby SMEs can input their company and product information to automatically generate Web pages and electronic catalogs.

The rationale for establishment of the WTPF was to increase the involvement of the private sector and other external partners in the Trade Point program. The future success of the program would hinge on WTPF's success in identifying such partners and using them strategically. Towards the end of 2003, WTPF was in the process of identifying strategic partners, particularly in the technical component of the program.

Most of the Trade Points are mainly located in big cities. Moreover, many least developed countries are still deprived of the services of Trade Points. SMEs using the services of Trade Points are also required to follow its format, and hence GTPNet system lacks flexibility. Third, GTPNet will be an effective system for a firm only if its existing and potential trading partners also use the services provided by the system.

Questions for Discussion

1. What are the advantages and disadvantages of the Trade Point program for SMEs compared to the SMEs having their own Web sites for e-commerce transactions?
2. What are the major challenges that are facing WTPF? What do you recommend to overcome them?
3. What incremental contribution would the World Trade Point Federation provide compared to UNCTAD for SMEs' adoption of e-commerce technologies?
4. Visit the Web site of the Trade Point Directory at http://www.wtpfed.org/newsite/tp/. Comment on the distribution pattern of Trade Points over the world.
5. How do the three categories of services provided by the Trade Point program differ in terms of their role in SMEs' adoption of the Internet in international business?

REFERENCES

Coppel, J. (2000). *E-commerce: Impacts and policy challenges* (Economics Department Working Paper No. 252). Organization of Economic Cooperation and Development (OECD). Retrieved December 24, 2000 from http://www.olis.oecd.org/olis/2000doc.nsf/c5ce8ffa41835d64c125685d005300b0/c12568d1006e03f7c12569070052efe3/$FILE/00079760.PDF

Dholakia, R. R., & Kshetri, N. (2004). Factors impacting the adoption of the Internet among SMEs. *Small Business Economics, 23*(4), 311-22.

Hamill, J., & Gregory, K. (1997). Internet marketing in the internationalization of UK SMEs. *Journal of Marketing Management, 13*(1-3), 9-28.

Henkin, L. (1979). *How nations behave* (2nd ed.).

Kotok, A. (1999). EDI, warts and all. *XML.com*. Retrieved August 4, 1999, from http://www.xml.com/pub/a/1999/08/edi/index2.html

Lehrer, B. (2003). *Finding business opportunities on the Internet*. Retrieved from http://www.fita.org/aotm/tbird.html

Lituchy, T. R., & Rail, A. (2000). Bed and breakfasts, small inns and the Internet: The impact of technology on the globalization of small businesses. *Journal of International Marketing, 8*(2), 86-97.

Lu, J. (1997). *Project manager for China*. UNCTAD-TPDC. Retrieved from http://www.arraydev.com/commerce/JIBC/9704-28.htm

Mansfield, E. (1961). Technical change and the rate of imitation. *Econometrica, 29*(4), 741-66.

Moreira, C. (1996). *Why the GTPNet is now the largest trading network on earth*. Retrieved from http://www.arraydev.com/commerce/JIBC/9603-5.htm

National Small Business United. (2000). *Survey of small and mid-sized businesses: Trends for 2000.* Retrieved from http://www.nsbu.org/survey/index.html

NIC.in. (2001). India Trade Promotion Organization. Retrieved from http://commin.nic.in/doc/annual/ch_7.htm

UNCTAD. (1993, October 7). The Trade Point: Concept and implementation. *United Nations Conference on Trade and Development, Ge.93-53859* (pp. 3-4).

UNCTAD. (1997, July). Trade point survey results. *United Nations Conference on Trade and Development*, Geneva. Retrieved June 16, 2001, from http://www.untpdc.org/untpdc/library/te/survey/

UNCTAD. (1998a, December 14). In-depth evaluation of UNCTAD's Trade Point Program. *United Nations Conference on Trade and Development*, Geneva. Retrieved June 2, 2003, from http://www.unctad.org/en/docs/wpd110a.pdf

UNCTAD. (1998b). *Synoptic record of the Proceedings of the Trade and Development Board at its 18th Executive Session.* Geneva: United Nations Conference on Trade and Development. Retrieved July 10, 1998 from http://www.unctad.org/en/docs/tb18d3.pdf

UNCTAD. (1998c). Trade Point review. *United Nations Conference on Trade and Development*, Geneva. Retrieved from http://www.sdnp.undp.org/mirrors/lc/pan/untpdc/gtpnet/tpreview/#2.%201%20The%20current%20status%20of%20Trade%20Points

UNCTAD. (1998d, October 22). UNCTAD press release (PFD/4). Retrieved from http://www-partners.unctad.ch/english/R2/pfd4.htm

UNCTAD. (1998e, September 17). Policy issues relating to access to participation in electronic commerce. *United Nations Conference on Trade and Development.* Retrieved from http://r0.unctad.org/stdev/compendium/documents/TD.B.COM.3.16.pdf

Wang, A. (1999). Verio expands global reach of e-commerce. *E-Commerce Times.* Retrieved April 26, 1999, from http://www.ecommercetimes.com/perl/story/143.html

Williams, V. (1999, July). *Small businesses venture into e-commerce.* Office of Advocacy, U.S. Small Business Administration.

WTO. (1998, May 18, 20). Declaration on global electronic commerce. *Ministerial Conference, Second Session, WT/MIN(98)/DEC/2*, World Trade Organization, Geneva.

ENDNOTES

[1] See UNCTAD's technical cooperation at the service of trade and development—http://www.unctad.org/Templates/Page.asp?intItemID=1479&lang=1.

[2] See http://www.tradepointathens.gr/TPENGL/homeengl/wtpffinal.htm.

[3] See http://www.tradepointathens.gr/TPENGL/homeengl/wtpffinal.htm.

[4] See http://www.eurobc.com.mk/tp_p_wtpf.htm.

[5] UN/EDIFACT standard is mainly used outside North America for electronic data interchange (EDI). UN/EDIFACT in many ways resembles X12, which is used in North America, but still has many differences. Although X12 has implemented some of the features of UN/EDIFACT, they are different standards (Kotok, 1999).

6   A letter of credit (LOC) is a written document issued by a bank at the request of a buyer (importer) to pay a seller (exporter) upon presentation of import documents specified in the document. LOCs are employed widely in import-export transactions to enable trading partners who may not know or trust each other to conduct business through the mediation of trusted banks.

7   For example, Yerevan, the capital of Armenia, has the LOCODE of AM EVN, and Cartagena, a coastal city in Colombia, has the LOCODE of CO CTG.

8   Following WTO (1998) we define e-commerce as any transaction in which *at least one* of the following activities—production, distribution, marketing, sale, *or* delivery—takes place by electronic means.

9   See the *Shanghai Trade Point* Web site: http://sunsite.icm.edu.pl/untpdc/incubator/chn/tpsha/stp.html (accessed December 19, 2003).

10   See Introductory word by the WTPF President (May 23, 2003) at: http://www.wtpfed.com/newsite/index1.php#.

11   The examples are from the Web sites of Trade Points of Iran, China, Thailand, and Macedonia.

12   See http://www.spyrus.com.au/content/pressroom/releases/1998/pr_seal.asp.

13   It should, however, be noted that all of the Trade Points are not fully operational.

14   These are from the Trade Point Web sites in India, China, Jordan, and Australia.

15   These suggestions are condensed from UNCTAD/WTO e-mail discussions on SMEs, reported at http://www.intracen.org/e_discuss/sme/welcome.htm (accessed August 27, 2003).

Nikhilesh Dholakia is a professor of marketing, e-commerce and management information systems at the University of Rhode Island (URI). He has published extensively in the fields of marketing, e-commerce, and consumer culture. Among his books are: Essentials of New Product Management *(Prentice-Hall, 1987);* Consumption and Marketing: Macro Dimensions *(South-Western, 1996);* New Infotainment Technologies in the Home: Demand-Side Perspectives *(Lawrence Erlbaum Associates, 1996);* Consuming People: From Political Economy to Theaters of Consumption *(Routledge, 1998); and* Worldwide E-Commerce and Online Marketing: Watching the Evolution *(Quorum, 2002). Dr. Dholakia has won the Charles Slater award of the* Journal of Macromarketing.

Nir Kshetri is an assistant professor at the Bryan School of Business and Economics, University of North Carolina, Greensboro. He has published and presented more than 30 academic articles, mainly in international business and global IT areas. His works have been published in journals such as IEEE Software, Electronic Markets, Small Business Economics, *and* Pacific Telecommunications Review. *He has also contributed chapters to several books, including:* Handbook of Information Security *(John Wiley & Sons, 2004);* The Internet Encyclopedia *(John Wiley & Sons, 2003);* Wireless

Communications and Mobile Commerce *(Idea Group Publishing, 2003);* The Digital Challenges: Information Technology in the Development Context *(Ashgate Publishing, forthcoming);* Architectural Issues of Web-enabled Electronic Business *(Idea Group Publishing, 2003); and* Internet Marketing *(2nd edition, Stuttgart, Germany: Schaeffer-Poeschel, 2001).*

This case was previously published in the *International Journal of Cases on Electronic Commerce,* 1(1) (pp. 39-52), © 2005.

Chapter XVIII

Assessing the Introduction of Electronic Banking in Egypt Using the Technology Acceptance Model

Sherif Kamel, The American University in Cairo, Egypt

Ahmed Hassan, Maastricht School of Management, The Netherlands

EXECUTIVE SUMMARY

The developments taking place in information and communication technology are increasing competition in financial institutions worldwide. Thus, the deployment of advanced technologies is essential to achieve a competitive edge. Recently, the banking industry was highly affected by the technology evolution that transformed the way banks deliver their services, using technologies such as automated teller machines, phones, the Internet, credit cards, and electronic cash. In line with global trends, retail banking in Egypt has been undergoing many changes. In the past, banks faced significant uncertainty regarding investments in advanced technologies, but recently, banks have been investing heavily in technology to maintain a competitive edge. However, to better forecast the future, banks need to understand the different factors influencing customers' choice between traditional and unconventional banking instruments. This case covers the introduction and diffusion of retail banking in Egypt and the development in electronic delivery channels and payment systems in its marketplace. The case represents a model for the application of advanced information and communication technology in the context of a developing nation.

BACKGROUND

Global changes are penetrating all societies and communities around the world, bringing more innovations, competition, products, and services and introducing new trends, directions, and ways to do things differently. The Internet and the World Wide Web have introduced new ways for doing business (Kamel, 2001). This has created many challenges and opportunities in the global market-place to the main players of the business cycle; among which are financial institutions. Respectively, in order to face its increasing competitive pressures, they were required to recognize the need to perform a balancing act between achieving strategic goals and meeting the continuous changing customer needs and requirements. While strategic goals are usually corporate-specific and can be achieved in different ways, understanding and meeting customer needs may be studied and analyzed at the industry level. Today, the use of cutting-edge information and communication technology is becoming a cornerstone in dealing with the competitive pressure faced by different businesses around the world.

Over the last few decades, the banking industry has been highly affected by such technology evolution, with an emphasis on the way services are delivered to retail banking customers. For more than 200 years, banking was a simple branch-based operation. However, things started to change since the early 1980s, with the use of multiple technologies and applications that surfaced with the penetration of computing in various sectors and industries, including banking. Among such technologies were the growing number of technology-based remote access delivery channels and payment systems, such as automated teller machines that displaced cashier tellers; the telephone, represented by call centers that replaced the bank branch; the Internet that replaced snail mail; credit cards and electronic cash that replaced traditional cash transactions; and shortly, interactive television that will replace face-to-face transactions (Kamel & Assem, 2002).

In Egypt, in line with global trends, the retail banking business has been undergoing tremendous changes over the last two decades. As a result, the banking industry was always facing a significant uncertainty regarding the potential investments in advanced banking technologies required to implement the different electronic delivery channels and payment systems. Regardless of the return, currently, banks in Egypt are investing large amounts of money in technology, not only to maintain a competitive edge but also to remain in the business. In order to make better forecasts for business planning and decision-making, banks need to better understand the different factors influencing the Egyptian customer choice among traditional and electronic banking instruments (Kamel & Assem, 2002).

The success in the application of different information and communication technology in retail banking delivery channels and payment systems relies to a large extent on the ability of customers to accept and adopt such systems. In Egypt, most of the technology-related decisions are based on reactions to other decisions taken by the competition, without a real study of actual customer needs or perceptions, which leads to the creation of a high level of risk associated with such strategy. An overestimation of the level of customer acceptance of the technology can misguide decision-makers to get involved in investments, which are not ready to give return, while underestimation of the acceptance level can lead to the loss of substantial market share.

Figure 1. Technology acceptance model (TAM)

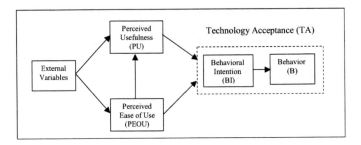

This case analyzes the banking sector in Egypt and the deployment of information and communication technology in the sector in terms of adoption, diffusion, and innovation, while providing an understanding of the acceptance level of consumers of different technology-based delivery channels and electronic payment systems and the extent to which various factors influence consumers' willingness to use different technologies. The case depends on the use of the technology acceptance model (TAM) (shown in Figure 1)—introduced by Davis in 1985 to study the level of customer acceptance to new banking technologies in Egypt. TAM, by definition, considers user perceptions of ease of use and usefulness as the main factors affecting the acceptance level of any technology. The case will also consider the role of trust as an external variable affecting consumer adoption of electronic banking delivery channels and payment systems, which is a factor that is much associated with the cultural aspect of the society in Egypt, which for a long time was not accustomed to the use of banking services and facilities (Kamel & Assem, 2002).

The research variables tested that were directly extracted from TAM include perceived ease of use (PEOU), perceived usefulness (PU), and technology acceptance (TA). PEOU and PU were simultaneously acting as dependent and independent variables, while TA was merely a dependent variable that depended on PEOU and PU. Moreover, trust (T) was used as an independent variable, which was indirectly affected by TA through its direct effect on variables PU and PEOU, as shown in Table 1.

In addition to TAM, the case used a PEST analysis to study the different environmental factors affecting the banking sector in Egypt and its deployment of different technology-based systems. The case study focused on a number of research issues, including the identification of the main environmental factors affecting the Egyptian

Table 1. Research variables

Variable	Description	Type	Associated Data Type	Scale
TA	Technology Acceptance	Dependent	Ordinal	Discrete (0-7) 0: Accept, 7: Reject
PEOU	Perceived Ease of Use	Independent /Dependent	Ordinal	Discrete (0-7) 0: Easy, 7: Not Easy
PU	Perceived Usefulness	Independent /Dependent	Ordinal	Discrete (0-7) 0: Useful, 7: Not Useful
T	Trust	Independent	Ordinal	Discrete (0-7) 0: Trustful, 7: Trustless

Table 2. Research hypotheses

Null Hypotheses	Alternative Hypotheses
PU has no significant effect on TA	PU has a significant effect on TA
PEOU has no significant effect on TA	PEOU has a significant effect on TA
PU has no significant effect on PEOU	PU has a significant effect on PEOU
T has no significant effect on PU	T has a significant effect on PU
T has no significant effect on PEOU	T has a significant effect on PEOU

banking sector in general, and the electronic retail banking delivery channels and payment systems in particular; the extent to which banks were encouraging their customers to use technology-based systems, and the degree of support provided to them; and the determination of the main patterns of customer usage of different electronic delivery channels and payment systems. A number of hypotheses were formulated and tested during the study that mainly describe the relationships between different research variables as proposed by TAM; such hypotheses are shown in Table 2.

Based on the analytical nature of the study, the methodology used in the research was based on a combination of quantitative and qualitative approaches, where a research questionnaire was distributed among a sample of different bank customers. The survey instrument is shown in Appendix 1. The objective of the questionnaire was to demonstrate and investigate the relationship between the research variables by measuring the salient beliefs and intentions of bank customers in Egypt toward technology-based delivery channels and electronic payment systems. Moreover, the questionnaire measured the level of awareness among customers, and how this awareness was built. The subjects chosen to respond to the questionnaire consisted of a random sample of bank customers with varying demographics and different professions. All questionnaires were sent by electronic mail, facsimile, and, in some cases, it was handed to the respondent in person in an interview session, to provide the opportunity to explain the purpose of the research and to guide the respondent through the questionnaire. Moreover, a number of interviews were conducted with top executives and managers working in the banking sector or in the field of information and communication technology to include policy makers, major players, and decision makers as part of the survey. Most of the results of the questions in the questionnaires and the interviews were of a quantitative nature, with the intent to measure each of the research variables extracted from TAM and to understand the relationships between them.

Technology Acceptance Model (TAM)

The complexity of adopting new technologies was first popularized by the theory of diffusion of innovations (Rogers, 1983), where Rogers summarized the key influences of user acceptance behavior as relative advantage, complexity, compatibility, trialability, and observability. Rogers stated that an individual's perceptions are the basis of a widely studied model from social psychology entitled the theory of reasoned action (TRA), which was first proposed by Ajzen and Fishbein (1980). TRA is a model that has demonstrated success in predicting and explaining behavior across a wide variety of domains (Davis, 1989). Additionally, an extension of TRA is the theory of planned behavior (TPB) (Ajzen, 1991), which accounts for conditions with which individuals do not have complete control over their behavior (Taylor & Todd, 1995). Based on the three above-mentioned user acceptance research areas, diffusion of innovation, TRA, and

TPB, TRA has emerged as a prominent model that has served as a basis for expanding user acceptance research. Specifically, a modified TRA model defined in the F. D. Davis study (1985) resulted in a concise, complete, reliable, and valid model for predicting user acceptance, entitled the technology acceptance model (TAM), that has repeatedly shown viability in predicting user acceptance of new and different technologies (Adams, Nelson, & Todd, 1992; Taylor & Todd, 1995; Davis & Venkatesh, 1995; Doll et al., 1989).

The basic goal of TAM is to provide an explanation of the determinants of technology acceptance that are capable of explaining user behavior across a broad range of end-user technologies and user populations, while at the same time, being both parsimonious and theoretically justified (Davis et al., 1989). According to TAM, perceived usefulness and perceived ease of use are the fundamental determinants of attitude toward usage intentions and actual technology usage. In TAM, behavior in terms of technology usage has been explained by investigating the perceived usefulness and ease of use the individual experiences or expects when using a specific technology. According to TAM, the easier the technology is to use, and the more useful it is perceived to be, the more positive one's attitude and intention toward using the technology; therefore, technology use increases. During the last few years, TAM has offered researchers and practitioners a relatively simple and cost-effective way to predict the ultimate measure of system success, whether or not that system is actually used (Morris & Dillon, 1997). It has been used to explain the use of a number of technologies including databases, communication technologies, and electronic mail, among others. The empirical evidence indicates that increasing the PEOU of the system will increase PU and will translate into an increased behavioral intention (BI), resulting in a larger margin of TA. However, research also indicates that the influences of PEOU on PU diminish over time, as users become proficient with the target system (Chau, 1996; Davis et al., 1989). Therefore, the literature suggests that PEOU determinants will have the greatest contribution to user acceptance in the early stages of system deployment, when users have limited experience with a target system. This concept is significant to consumer acceptance of banking technologies, and as customers are offered use of an unfamiliar banking technology, they can quickly become discouraged if that specific technology is not easy to use, regardless of the technology usefulness. However, it is important to note that the cultural differences that exist between different countries may affect the adoption and diffusion of new technologies.

Trust in Banking Technologies

The level of uncertainty avoidance plays an important role in building trust. Therefore, the research considered the effect of trust on the adoption and usage of advanced banking technologies as an extension to the basic TAM. Within the literature, organization theory provides a cross-disciplinary definition of trust that applies to a large range of relationships among individuals and organizations. In that context, trust implies benevolence, integrity, and ability in an exchange relationship (Mayer et al., 1995).

In a study conducted in Egypt in 2001 on the delivery channels for retail banking products, focusing on measuring the satisfaction levels of customers of banks with the in-person bank branches and their possible shift to alternative delivery channels, results indicated high dissatisfaction levels due to lack of bank awareness of customer needs. The research showed low loyalty levels, where 62% of customers surveyed stated their

Figure 2. Effect of trust as an external variable

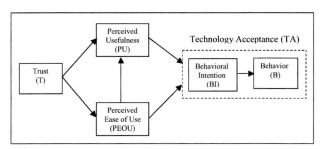

Table 3. Customer preferences for different delivery channels

Delivery Channel	Extremely Important	Important	Not Important
Bank Branches	36.96%	35.87%	27.17
ATMs	70.65%	26.09%	3.26%
Mobile Banking	19.02%	33.70%	47.28%
Call Centers	32.07%	51.63%	16.30%
Internet banking	17.39%	35.87%	46.74%

willingness to change their banks if offered more convenient banking alternatives. Responsive service was found to be the major satisfaction driver, followed by a 24-hour accessibility feature. Moreover, 71% of surveyed customers showed interest in using e-banking, if their banks guaranteed its security. When customers were asked to rank the importance of the five delivery channels, automated teller machines (ATMs) came first. See Table 3 for the rest of the results.

SETTING THE STAGE

The Banking Sector in Egypt

The banking sector in Egypt is among the oldest and largest in the region. The National Bank of Egypt (NBE) was the first bank to begin operation in the country in 1898; also in the year 1898, the stock exchange was established. In that time, central bank functions were partially performed by the National Bank of Egypt, which was the sole body licensed to issue Egyptian banknotes. The size of the banking sector has grown rapidly during the first half of the 20th century. In 1956, a total of 32 banks were operating in Egypt. Those banks included 26 commercial banks, four mortgage banks, one agricultural bank, and one industrial bank. All were foreign banks except the National Bank of Egypt and Bank Misr (Huband, 1999).

During the period 1957-1974, nationalization had a dramatic impact on Egypt's financial system. The closure of the Egyptian stock market and the confiscation of all foreign banks turned the financial system into a stagnant, non-competitive sector. Only fully owned Egyptian banks were permitted to operate. In February 1960, the National

Bank of Egypt was nationalized, and in 1961, the Central Bank of Egypt was established to perform its responsibilities as the unique entity responsible for setting banking system regulations (World Investment News, 1998). Starting in the mid-1970s, the Egyptian banking sector expanded markedly, along with the country's open door policy that aimed at an outward-looking growth, with an active role for the private sector to promote economic performance, which was coupled with a new banking law enacted in 1975 defining the nature and mode of operations for all banks. Today, Egypt has a total of 62 banks, with more than 2400 branches, as well as 28 representative offices of foreign banks and three unregistered banks, which do not report to the Central Bank of Egypt (CBE, 2001).

Evolution of Retail Banking in Egypt

Capitalizing on its comparative advantages in the service sector, financial-sector growth potentials, and noticeable economic growth, Egypt is currently moving steadily toward becoming the biggest financial center in the region. Owing to the flourishing privatization program and the prospering domestic bond market, banks have encountered new investment fields, which helped them, diversify their portfolios and lower their financial risks. Retail banking was the most important among those new fields (Egypt SIS, 1999). Retail banking is that part of commercial banking concerned with the activities of individual customers, generally in large numbers. Retail banking is considered less risky compared to corporate banking, as it involves a more diversified loan portfolio across a mass market. Retail customers provide reliable low-cost sources of funds for asset management and good opportunities for retail securities placement and fund management. However, the retail business requires heavy investments to increase the number of branches, enlarge staff size, expand the ATM network, and establish various delivery channels (Grant, 1984).

Since the mid-1990s, the banking sector in Egypt has been changing fast, and after decades of focusing on generating corporate assets, most public and private banks are starting to recognize the potentials for retail business represented in the relatively under-branched banking sector, compared to the high population and the rising per capita income. Accordingly, most banks started to penetrate the retail market. Recently, the number of individual bank customers reached 9 million (*Business Monthly*, 2000), and a variety of retail products are currently offered by a large number of banks, including payroll accounts, car financing, mutual funds, credit cards, and personal loans. Moreover, banks are competing in expanding their branch networks and diversifying their delivery channels to include ATMs, call centers, mobile banking, and Internet banking. As part of the research, an environmental PEST analysis was conducted to study the political, economic, social, and technological factors affecting the banking sector, with a focus on retail business activities and the deterrents facing the development and growth of the banking sector.

Political Factors

The political system in Egypt played a significant role in the growth and expansion of local and international banks and played a major role in attracting banks and financial institutions worldwide to establish joint ventures or representative offices in Egypt. The banking sector has been entirely public since the late 1950s, when it was nationalized. However, in the mid-1970s, an open-door policy allowed the establishment of private banks. In 2002, there are a number of international players in the market, including Barclays, American Express, Citibank, HSBC, and recently, Standard Chartered Bank (CBE, 2000). Moreover, a number of laws and regulations were established to help the banking sector grow, especially focusing on the retail banking business, including an electronic law, which is expected to have a positive effect on the growth of the credit card market of different banks. Additionally, the expected approval of the new mortgage law represents another opportunity for banks to expand their retail activities in the area of housing loans (*Business Today*, 2001).

Economic Factors

Since the mid 1980s, Egypt started to follow an economic reform program, which was designed to establish a stable and credible economy. Macroeconomic indicators look positive, with a growth rate at 6.5%, inflation rate at 2.8%, and budget deficit at 3.6% of gross domestic product (BSAC, 2001). Egypt's success on its macroeconomic agenda secured the stability necessary to establish investor confidence and stimulate the capital market (BSAC, 1999). The growth rates of banks' assets, deposits, and loans are direct reflections of the economic growth of the banking sector, yielding a CAGR of 12.6% during the period between 1995 and 1997 (CBE, 2000).

Social Factors

The Egyptian population of more than 68 million in December 2001, represents many attractions for local and foreign banks to expand their business. The current individual bank customers represent around 13% of the population. Among those customers, the number of credit and debit cardholders is less than 7%, which directly reflects the great potential for plastic money in Egypt (*Business Monthly*, 2000). According to age, bank customers can be divided into three segments:

1. Youth (20-30 years old) represent the most important target group, with their accounts and student loans. They easily adopt technology, but their loyalty to the bank they deal with is not guaranteed, requiring continuous innovative financial services to attract them and cost switching to keep them.
2. The second age group, 30-50 years old, represents good potential due to the large number of housewives within that segment who are willing to use different electronic delivery channels, like ATMs and phone banking.
3. The last segment, above 50 years of age, shows some reluctance to deal with banks in general, and to using technology-based services in particular, requiring special care and incentives, such as retirement packages and special senior accounts.

Market Assessment of Banking Services

For a long time, the market in Egypt was dominated by cash society values, with people reluctant to go to the bank and open an account for purely cultural reasons, opting to keep their cash at home. However, recently, the private sector started to include their employees in various payroll plans offered by different banks. As a result, the number of individual bank customers increased, and a relatively high level of awareness was established among certain segments of the society, which started to recognize the benefits of retail banking. However, it is important to note that the society highly values human interaction, which affects the penetration of retail banking through electronic delivery channels, especially among the less-educated, who are not comfortable dealing with technology-related equipment. Moreover, among the other current problems is the fact that credit cards are scary for some people due to the high interest rates; very few people are using ATMs for deposits or are willing to use their credit cards over the Internet. It is important to note that the average illiteracy among the population is more than 39% (EFG-Hermes, 2001), and a large portion of the remaining 61% is considered under-educated. Consequently, ease of use, simplicity, and Arabic interfaces are key factors for the adoption of new services provided by banks. In general, consumers in Egypt are considered flexible and fast to adopt new habits, which is obvious in the penetration rates of mobile telephony, which was first introduced in 1997. There are now more than 3.5 million subscribers, even though telephony was introduced early in the last century and to date, there are only 7.1 million land lines (www.mcit.gov.eg). However, in order to capitalize on such an advantage, banks need to familiarize consumers with the services and products they offer through solid marketing communications strategies. Such services have to provide an attractive value proposition to the local market.

Technological Factors

The rate of information and communication technology adoption in the banking sector was increasing steadily over the last decade as a result of the growth in retail banking activities, opening of competition within the sector, and noticeable government support of-automation efforts. Offering retail banking services involves providing customers with electronic payment systems, such as plastic money debit and credit cards, as well as technology-based delivery channels for performing their daily transactions. Such channels, which are known as remote access systems or self-service banking, include ATMs, call centers, phone banking, Internet banking, and mobile banking. The use of plastic money has a number of benefits, including reducing the cost of printing money and the proliferation of money not fit for circulation. Moreover, the introduction of remote access electronic delivery channels relatively increases access to customers and significantly cuts the cost of transactions, as shown in Figure 3 (Beck et al., 1999).

Since the mid 1980s, Egypt has focused on building its information and communication technology infrastructure, which was reflected in the introduction of the liberalization program of Telecom Egypt in 1998, and the establishment of the Ministry of

Figure 3. Lower transaction costs through technology

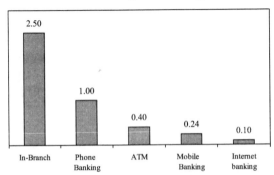

Communications and Information Technology (MCIT) in 1999. The tremendous improvements in telecommunications infrastructure cost, reliability, bandwidth, and reach achieved are providing a strong impetus to substantial technology investments in the banking sector in Egypt (Magued, 2001). However, despite the increasing technology investments made by banks, the sector is still considered in the early development stages in terms of banking technology infrastructure necessary for future large-scale card issuing, widely distributed ATM networks, efficient call centers, and automated clearing operations.

In the mid-1980s, banks started to install point-of-sale machines and encouraged members to accept payment by credit cards, correspondent to the growth in international and business travel. By the early 1990s, the first locally issued credit card found its way to the local market. Currently, 26 banks in Egypt issue debit and credit cards, but the number of cardholders is small, estimated at 600,000 locally issued cards, among which, more than 400,000 are credit cards, representing less than 7% of bank customers, which is estimated to be around 9 million. However, the market for debit and credit cards has great potential and is expected to reach one million cardholders in 2002, according to the forecasts of Visa International (*Business Today*, 2001). One of the indicators for such potential is the success that Citibank Egypt realized in the issuance of 50,000 credit cards in less than two years. In addition to the traditional debit and credit cards, banks are competing to introduce a number of innovative card products. For example, in 2001, Citibank and Vodafone, Egypt's leading mobile operator, launched a co-branded credit card to add a new product to the variety of credit cards issued in the Egyptian market (*Business Today*, 2001). Moreover, the use of ATMs, as a remote access channel to banks, has been in place since 1994; however, the rate of growth and adoption is fairly low, and according to the Commercial International Bank, Egypt's leading retail bank, the average number of ATM transactions performed monthly by a bank customer is currently four times the number recorded in 1998. The installed ATM population is currently low, but the rate of installation growth is relatively high. In August, 2001, the total committed ATM population in Egypt was 721, expected to double in 2002, which is still a relatively small number in comparison to the United States, with its 197,500 machines. Moreover, several banks have installed interactive voice response (IVR) systems and are considering the installation of call centers to follow the Citibank Egypt initiative introducing the concept of call centers in Egypt in 1999, known as Citiphone (Kamel & Assem, 2002).

With respect to Internet banking, Internet access in Egypt dates to 1993, mainly through governmental and educational organizations. Commercial Internet access was available since 1994. However, it was in January, 1996, that the government made an official address authorizing the private sector to step into the provision of Internet services. By April, 2002, Egypt's 51 private-sector Internet service providers delivered service to an estimated one million subscribers (www.mcit.gov.eg). The government is currently in the process of increasing Egypt's transmission capacity on the Internet in order to meet the increasing number of Internet users, who are expected to reach two million by the end of 2002. Moreover, the government, starting January 14, 2002, underwent a major step to diffuse the use of the Internet across its 26 different provinces by providing Internet connectivity for free (www.mcit.gov.eg). Internet banking, also known as online banking, is still not fully introduced in Egypt, mainly due to the relatively low number of Internet users. However, since late 2001, Citibank offers the first of such services as a prototype, allowing customers to check their account balances, perform internal transfers, and pay their monthly credit card bills through the Internet. Most of the other commercial banks have short-term plans to launch Internet banking as well.

With respect to mobile telephony, the GSM service started in 1996 by the government was soon after privatized, and competition was introduced. However, despite the rapidly increasing number of mobile subscribers, mobile banking is currently only offered by the National Societe Genarale Bank and is still not very popular among bank customers. Therefore, more efforts need to be made in that area in terms of increasing the simplicity of the user interface and conducting customer education and awareness programs.

To conclude, retail banking is strongly affected by political, economic, social, and technological factors. The current environment of the retail-banking sector includes many opportunities, as well as a number of risks. Although the potentials are high, the challenges are much higher. Therefore, in order to succeed in the market and build a respectable customer loyalty, banks operating in Egypt need to work on increasing customer awareness, and to carefully study and understand customers' social and economic needs. Such understanding can be achieved through different marketing communications tools, which can provide banks with customer feedback about the products they offer.

CASE DESCRIPTION

The study covered five different leading banks operating in Egypt, including Commercial International Bank (CIB), Misr International Bank (MIB), National Societe Generale Bank (NSGB), Egyptian American Bank (EAB), and Citibank Egypt. The cases highlighted their strengths and weaknesses with respect to retail banking activities and strategies, in order to provide a general understanding of the present environment as well as some insight into the future of retail banking. Table 4 demonstrates the profile of the different banks surveyed.

CIB and MIB were chosen as being the largest private sector banks in terms of assets, deposits, and market share. The EAB was chosen because of its perceived service leadership in the banking sector through a widely diversified range of products and

Table 4. Bank profiles

	CIB	MIB	NSGB	EAB
Growth in assets	10.77%	11.85%	20.71%	9.05%
Growth in loans	6.18%	8.37%	10.17%	-2.84%
Growth in deposits	11.66%	11.65%	21.19%	8.95%
Loans per branch	156,676	339,394	313,448	117,850
Deposits per branch	162,502	482,839	391,617	172,689
Market share loans	6.40%	3.50%	2.00%	1.98%
Market share deposits	5.20%	4.00%	1.97%	2.09%
Number of ATMs	90	14	19	25

Table 5. Overall subject demographics

	21-30	31-40	41-50	Total
Male	42	14	8	64
Female	27	7	5	39
Total	69	21	13	103

services, including retail banking. The NSGB was chosen as a result of its high retail business growth rates over the last two years, beginning in 1999, as well as for being the first bank to introduce mobile banking services in Egypt. Finally, Citibank Egypt was selected, because it is setting the pace in the market through its innovative products and trends in retail banking; and over the last few years, it has been taking the lead in continuously diversifying and introducing new technology-based services for bank customers.

The sample population was randomly selected with varying demographics and professions. It was small due to the fact that the population capable of responding to the survey instrument, as perceived by the researchers, and that represent active online users of the technology with willingness to receive bank information online, was small. It was easy to identify those groups, because only a few hundred customers met those criteria after searching online bank databases and selected customers' databases with e-mail accounts used corresponding with at least one of the banks. The questionnaire was distributed among 200 bank customers; the valid response rate was 103, including 64 (62.14%) male and 39 (37.86%) female of three age categories: 21-30, 31-40, and 41-50 years old. Table 5 shows the distribution of the respondents. It is obvious that a larger sample would have provided more accurate results and would have led to the development of more concrete findings. However, it is important to note that this research represents the initial phase of more comprehensive coverage of the sector, which should lead to more macro-level findings (Czaja & Blair, 1996).

In addition to basic demographic data, subjects were asked to name the banks they dealt with. Responses included the names of 19 public- and private-sector banks: 56.29% of the respondents indicated that they were using private-sector banks, and 43.71% reported using public-sector banks. Some of the major issues addressed in the survey included the role played by banks in technology adoption, and general customer perception of the banking sector services. In that respect, the private-sector banks took the lead in technology introduction and diffusion at the retail banking level.

With respect to the role of banks in technology adoption, 72% of respondents felt that banks provided the necessary support and assistance when using different electronic delivery channels. Moreover, 70% of respondents felt that banks encouraged them to use remote-access technology-based delivery channels instead of visiting bank branches. The relatively high positive values may have been due to recent efforts exerted by many banks in order to direct customers toward using different electronic delivery channels after recognizing the large benefits they could realize, including reducing the load on bank branches, improving the quality and efficiency of the services offered, and introducing additional added-values to various customers.

With respect to general customer perceptions, 47% of respondents ranked trust as the most important feature they look for in technology-based delivery channels and

Figure 4. Technology acceptance model and research hypotheses

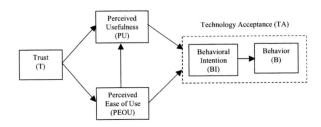

payment systems, followed by 31% for ease of use and 23% for usefulness, as the primary factors that can encourage them to use such systems. These results seemed logical and in compliance with the high level of conservatism and uncertainty avoidance, which are common characteristics of the society in Egypt. In general, those results implied that for most bank customers, it is of highest priority to be convinced that the technology is secure and trustful, and only then may they try to use that technology. If it is easy and simple, they will be able to use it and, accordingly, find out whether it is useful or not.

A statistical analysis has been performed based on the hypotheses testing on the data collected, in order to test the association between different research variables, as shown in Figure 4. The objective was basically to find out whether the results would succeed or fail to reject the null hypotheses, and accordingly, determine the significance of the alternative hypotheses. Following is the assessment and perceptions of survey respondents of the different electronic delivery channels and payment systems.

Automated Teller Machines

The results obtained for ATMs, shown in Table 6, indicate that most of the alternative hypotheses were confirmed with different significance levels, except H_4 (trust will have a significant effect on perceived usefulness). Accordingly, the relationship between trust and perceived usefulness was not clear in the responses received. The lack of such relationship implies that perceiving ATMs to be secured and trustful delivery channels does not affect the customer perception of its usefulness. Such a conclusion may be valid for ATMs, although at this point, there is no proof whether this will also apply for other systems. However, such indications could set the pace for preliminary expectations with regard to customer acceptance of various electronic retail banking delivery channels. According to the resulting *p*-values, which are measures of the

Table 6. Association foefficients for the model on ATM ($\alpha = 0.05$)

Dependent Variable	Independent Variable	R^2	Association Coefficient	Significance of (p-Value)
TA	PU	0.07367	0.138	< 0.01
	PEOU	0.07905	0.123	< 0.005
PU	T	0.01235	0.097	> 0.1
	PEOU	0.4585	0.642	< 0.005
PEOU	T	0.3479	0.322	< 0.005

significance of the alternative hypotheses and the strength of the relationship between any two variables, perceived ease of use has a relatively significant effect on technology acceptance, as well as on perceived usefulness.

Similarly significant is the effect of trust on perceived ease of use, while the effect of perceived usefulness on technology acceptance was shown to be the least significant. Those results adhere, to a large extent, to the general results highlighted earlier, and they comply with the conclusion previously stated, that trust is the major factor affecting perceived ease of use, which in turn, drives perceived usefulness and eventually technology acceptance. It is also important to note the element of cultural adaptation and local market conditions in Egypt. In that respect, it is useful to mention that until the mid-1980s, retail banking was hardly diffused among the population. Therefore, the gradual increase in the retail banking population from three million to more than 10 million in less than 20 years is a major development. However, it has to be implemented gradually to avoid cultural deterrents and resistance to change.

Credit Cards

The responses addressing the acceptance of credit cards as a payment system have confirmed the alternative hypotheses H_{2a}, H_{3a}, and H_{5a}, while they disconfirmed H_{1a} and H_{4a}, as shown in Table 7.

The table shows the significant effect of perceived ease of use on technology acceptance as well as the significant role of trust in building such perceived ease of use. However, unlike the case of ATMs, credit cards' results confirmed the relationship between perceived usefulness and trust, but did not confirm the relation between perceived usefulness and technology acceptance of credit cards as a technology-based payment system. The results obtained for credit cards imply that trust is a major factor in the usage of electronic payment systems, and its indirect effect through perceived usefulness and perceived ease of use is the most significant determinant of the acceptance level. Such results were expected for credit cards, which, for many bank customers, may involve a relatively non-affordable level of risk compared to a technology like ATMs.

Phone Banking

The results obtained for phone banking were consistent with all five hypothesized relationships between the research variables. The significance of each of those relationships is shown in Table 8.

The results indicate that the majority of the responses confirmed that technology acceptance is directly related to perceived usefulness and perceived ease of use, and is

Table 7. Association coefficients for the model on credit cards ($\alpha = 0.05$)

Dependent Variable	Independent Variable	R^2	Association Coefficient	Significance of (p-Value)
TA	PU	0.02723	0.190	> 0.05
	PEOU	0.18349	0.249	< 0.01
PU	T	0.39682	0.311	< 0.005
	PEOU	0.06466	0.007	> 0.1
PEOU	T	0.26798	0.226	< 0.01

Table 8. Association coefficients for the model on phone banking (α = 0.05)

Dependent Variable	Independent Variable	R²	Association Coefficient	Significance of (p-Value)
TA	PU	0.21489	0.561	< 0.005
	PEOU	0.14849	0.558	< 0.005
PU	T	0.23272	0.371	< 0.005
	PEOU	0.66378	0.870	< 0.005
PEOU	T	0.17264	0.138	< 0.01

indirectly affected by the element of trust in technology. The significant relationships indicated from the above diagram imply that phone banking is considered of high potential, as it allows customers to access their accounts in a fast and easy way through the phone and does not involve the effort of moving from one place to another, as is the case with ATMs. However, if we go further in comparing phone banking with ATMs, it is important to mention that phone banking lacks an important feature—cash access.

Internet Banking

Similar to phone banking, the results obtained for the acceptance of Internet banking were consistent with the hypothesized relationships. However, the significance levels (*p*-values) of all relationships were relatively low compared to those obtained for phone banking. The similarity between the results of Internet and phone banking is attributed to the fact that both technologies provide bank customers with the same range of banking services, namely, balance inquiry, transfers between accounts, and bill payment, without direct access to cash. The low significance of different relationships shown in Table 9 is most likely due to other factors affecting the usage of Internet banking, such as the availability of a PC and an Internet connection and knowing how to use them. This is also affected by the fact that computer literacy in Egypt is only 8% (www.mcit.gov.eg). In addition, the perception of the relatively high risk associated with performing financial transactions over the Internet, as well as the low level of awareness of that technology, have played significant roles in forming these results.

Summary of Results

The analyses of Tables 6 to 9 indicate that the questionnaire responses failed to confirm the alternative research hypotheses in three out of 20 cases, with varying significance levels. This implies that TAM can be considered as a useful tool when used

Table 9. Association coefficients for the model on Internet banking (α = 0.05)

Dependent Variable	Independent Variable	R²	Association Coefficient	Significance of (p-Value)
TA	PU	0.16974	0.028	< 0.01
	PEOU	0.14154	0.083	< 0.01
PU	T	0.13388	0.067	< 0.01
	PEOU	0.09032	0.068	< 0.01
PEOU	T	0.29107	0.095	< 0.01

to determine the customer acceptance of electronic banking delivery channels. It is also useful in identifying the related aspects that affect the behavior of different customers with respect to various technologies.

Accordingly, banks can rely to a fairly large extent on the perceptions of their customers regarding any new or existing technology-based service to predict and measure the acceptance levels and the potentials of that service, bearing in mind the effects of other external factors that differ from one technology to the other. With respect to usage patterns of banking technologies, the respondents, as shown in Figure 5, revealed that most of them are using ATMs for cash withdrawals and balance inquiry, while few of them are using it to perform cash or check deposits, and fewer are using it for bill payment. Respectively, such patterns can be attributed to the low level of awareness and lack of trust, which implies that the focus of the banks' efforts should be directed at building such trust and awareness among their customers.

The patterns of credit card usage show that most customers are using the cards for cash advance, as if they were bank loans. The usage of credit cards over the Internet is still in a premature stage, with 7.77%, while their usage for other purchase transactions involving human interaction, such as shopping, restaurants, and hotels, is approaching 50%, as shown in Figure 6.

Figure 5. ATM usage patterns

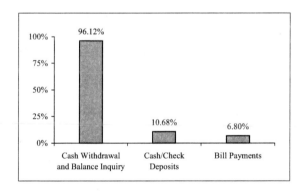

Figure 6. Credit card usage patterns

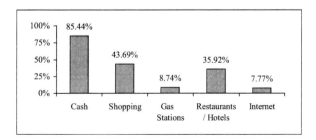

Figure 7. Phone banking usage patterns

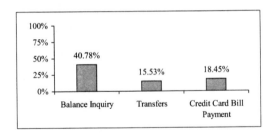

Figure 7 includes the patterns of phone banking as a technology-based delivery channel, which shows less than 50% of customers using or willing to use such a channel to inquire about their account balances. Despite the high potential for phone banking, less than 20% of the customers have shown interest in using the phone to perform transfers between their accounts or pay their credit card bills. The fact behind such results is that phone banking is still a recent development and is offered only by two banks in Egypt. However, with some marketing efforts, it is possible to build the necessary awareness and trust among different customers and increase their willingness to use such a channel.

The usage of the Internet as a banking delivery channel was shown to be of minimal interest among the respondents (Figure 8). As mentioned earlier, the challenge faced by that channel is lack of awareness as well as the cost associated with the hardware and the Internet connection, which may not be affordable except to a few specific socioeconomic segments. To conclude, it is worth noting that the research succeeded in confirming most of the alternative hypotheses for all banking technologies, and the results clearly highlighted the potentials for each technology as well as the overall perceptions of Egyptian banking customers and their willingness to use electronic delivery channels and payment systems, provided that they are trustful, secure, and easy to use. However, there are extensive efforts that still need to be exerted from banks operating in the retail business in Egypt, especially in the area of building awareness and trust among their customers.

Figure 8. Internet banking usage patterns

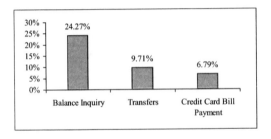

CURRENT CHALLENGES AND PROBLEMS FACING THE ORGANIZATION

Electronic retail banking delivery channels are becoming important not only for competitive purposes among banks but also for their survival, development, and growth. Thus, banks in Egypt have realized the challenge to cater to the growing needs of the market to channel their interest in improving the infrastructure, while focusing on customers' needs rather than solely serving their competitive strategies. It is important to note that the more the banks will be able to provide a convincing value-proposition to their customers, the more they will realize their targeted objectives and increase their market share, which represents a vital challenge relating to the banks' visibility in the market as a technology service provider. However, at the same time, banks must cater to local values and cultures of the society and smoothly adopt, diffuse, and adapt such technologies to serve their customers' needs without facing major resistance.

The challenges also include the diffusion of innovation among the community and the development of the infrastructure required. Also challenging, is diffusing it among Egypt's 27 provinces, while avoiding the creation of communities of haves and have nots and attempting to leverage the statistics of technology penetration, which currently stand at 15% of the population engaged in retail banking and benefiting from its services. There are a lot of questions that need to be answered that represent a set of challenges. If turned into opportunities, these challenges could help boost the banking sector. Can banks cater to changing customers' needs? Can they provide a convincing value-proposition? Can they provide customers with easy-to-use trustful technology tools and delivery channels? Can they make that shift and still focus on their organization-based competitive strategy vision? With continuous development in electronic banking, banks in Egypt have realized that there are no easy solutions. At the same time, they realized that a change of strategy has to take place in order for them to remain in the competition, not only globally but also locally, and that represents the main challenge for the main players in the industry.

The research study results showed that despite the challenges faced while adopting various technology-based retail banking systems in Egypt, there are still strong indications that, over time, technology will permit banks to provide useful services to customers while improving their marketing and communication, increasing their efficiency, and reducing cost of delivery. Moreover, the analysis showed that, consistent with TAM, perceived ease of use and perceived usefulness are playing relatively important roles in defining the acceptance level of different banking technologies. Additionally, the role of trust as an external variable affecting the acceptance level proved to be significant for all systems, including ATMs, credit cards, phone banking, and Internet banking. To summarize, it is believed that major efforts in infrastructure build-up, including technology and human resources development, need to take place not only by banks but also by all players in the new digital economy, including governments and the private sector.

REFERENCES

Adams, D. A., Nelson, R. R., & Todd, P. A. (1992). Perceived usefulness, ease of use and usage of information technology: A replication. *MIS Quarterly, 16* (2), 227-247.

Ajzen, I. (1991). The theory of planned behavior. *Organizational Behavior and Human Decision Processes, 50,* 179-211.

Ajzen, I., & Fishbein, M. (1980). *Understanding attitudes and predicting social behavior.* Englewood Cliffs, NJ: Prentice Hall.

Beck, D. A., Fraser, J. N., Reuter-Domenech, A. C., & Sidebottom, P. (1999). Personal financial services goes global. *The McKinsey Quarterly, 2.*

Business Monthly. (2000, August). *Journal of the American Chamber of Commerce in Egypt.*

Business Studies and Analysis Center (BSAC). (1999, September). *The Egyptian banking sector.* American Chamber of Commerce in Egypt.

Business Studies and Analysis Center (BSAC). (2001, June). *The Egyptian capital market.* American Chamber of Commerce in Egypt.

Business Today. (2001, August). *Sector survey: Business and finance.*

Central Bank of Egypt (CBE). (2000). CBE 1999/2000 Annual Report. *CBE Publications.*

Central Bank of Egypt (CBE). (2001). CBE 2000/2001 Annual Report. *CBE Publications.*

Chau, P. Y. K. (1996). An empirical assessment of a modified technology acceptance model. *Journal of Management Information Systems, 13*(2), 185-204.

Czaja, R., & Blair, J. (1996). *Designing surveys: A guide to decisions and procedures.* California: Pine Forge.

Davis, F. D. (1985). *A technology acceptance model for empirically testing new end-user information systems: Theory and results.* Doctoral Dissertation, MIT Sloan School of Management, Cambridge, MA.

Davis, F. D. (1989). Perceived usefulness, perceived ease of use and user acceptance of information technology. *MIS Quarterly, 13*(3), 319-339.

Davis, F. D., Bagozzi, R. P., & Warshaw, P. R. (1989). User acceptance of computer technology: A comparison of two theoretical models. *Management Science, 35*(8), 982-1002.

Davis, F. D., & Venkatesh, V. (1995). Measuring user acceptance of emerging information technologies: An assessment of possible method biases. *Proceedings of the 28th Annual Hawaii International Conference on System Sciences* (pp. 729-736).

Doll, W., Hendrickson, J. A., & Xiaodong, D. (1998). Using Davis's perceived usefulness and ease-of-use instruments for decision making: A confirmatory and multi-group invariance analysis. *Decision Science, 29*(4), 839-869.

EFG-Hermes. (2001, August). *Macroeconomic ipdate document.*

Egypt State Information Service (SIS) Publications. (1999). *The Banking Sector in Egypt.* Retrieved September 29, 2001, from www.sis.gov.eg/inv99/html/bank1.htm

Grant, A. (1984). *The insider guide to the financial services revolution.* New York: McGraw Hill.

Huband, M. (1999). Egypt leading the way: Institution building and stability in the financial system. *Euromoney Publication Plc.*

Kamel, S. (2001, October 20-31). The Implications of emerging electronic delivery channels on the banking sector. *The 11ᵗʰ BIT Conference Proceedings on Constructing IS Futures*, Manchester, UK.

Kamel, S., & Assem, A. (2002, April 3-5). Using TAM to assess the potentials of electronic banking in Egypt. *ISOneWorld Conference Proceedings*, Las Vegas, Nevada, USA.

Magued, M. H. (2001). *IT in financial services* (Working Paper).

Mayer, R. C., Davis, J. H., & Schoorman, F. D. (1995). An integrative model of organizational trust. *Academy of Management Review, 20*(3), 709-734.

Ministry of Communication and Information Technology (MCIT). Retrieved March 31, 2002, from http://www.mcit.gov.eg

Morris, M. G., & Dillon, A. (1997, July/August). How user perceptions influence software use. *IEEE Software*, 58-64.

Rogers, E. M. (1983). *Diffusion of innovation.* New York: Free Press.

Taylor, S., & Peter, A. T. (1995). Understanding information technology usage: A test of competing models. *Information Systems Research, 6*(2), 144-176.

World Investment News (WIN). (1998, November). Interview with Mr. Ismail Hassan, Governor of the Central Bank of Egypt (CBE). Retrieved September 20, 2001, from http://www.winne.com/Egypt

APPENDIX 1

Research Questionnaire

The following questionnaire is intended to measure the customer acceptance of advanced retail banking technologies and electronic payment systems, as well as the main factors affecting the customer decision to use such system. The data collected by this questionnaire is exclusively for research purposes and will not be used or distributed elsewhere.

Age
- ☐ Less than 20
- ☐ 20 to 30
- ☐ 30 to 40

- ☐ 40 to 50
- ☐ More than 50

Gender   ☐ Male

☐ Female

Current Profession

Average ANNUAL Income:

- ☐ Less than 10,000 EGP
- ☐ 10,000 - 20,000 EGP
- ☐ 20,000 - 50,000 EGP

- ☐ 50,000 - 100,000 EGP
- ☐ 100,000 - 200,000 EGP
- ☐ More than 200,000 EGP

Bank customer since: How many banks are you dealing with?

Please list the banks that you are dealing with:

Which of the following services are provided by your bank(s):

- ☐ ATMs
- ☐ Credit Cards
- ☐ Phone Banking

- ☐ Internet Banking
- ☐ Others (Please specify)

To what extent is your bank supporting you in using such technologies? (Please give a percentage)

To what extent is your bank encouraging you to use such technologies? (Please give a percentage)

In general, what is the main feature that would make you use a certain banking technology?

☐ Safety and Security   ☐ Usefulness   ☐ Ease of Use

In terms of their importance for the users of advanced banking technologies, how do you rank the above factors?

☐ a.b.c   ☐ b.c.a   ☐ a.c.t
☐ c.a.b   ☐ b.a.c   ☐ c.a.t

Other than the above, what other features do you think should be available in any new technology provided by a bank to its customers? Please rank them from the most to the least important from your point of view. *(Hint: You can think about availability, reliability, cultural acceptance, cost of service, etc.).*

ATMs (Automated Teller Machines):
ATMs are used by bank customers to perform a wide range of financial transactions, ranging from balance inquiry to cash withdrawal, deposit, transfer, and, recently, bill payment. Each customer should have a unique PIN to access his bank account through the ATM using his/her card.

Are you aware of that technology?

☐ Yes   ☐ No

IF YES: How was it introduced to you?

☐ Through Bank Staff   ☐   Just by Chance
☐ Through Media Advertisements ☐   Others

What are the main functions that you are using it for?

☐ Cash Withdrawal   ☐ Transfer between Accounts
☐ Deposits   ☐ Bill Payments
☐ Balance Inquiry   ☐ None of the above

For the following questions, please give your rating from 1 to 7 as to how you agree/ disagree with the argument.
1:Strongly Agree   2:Agree   3:Somewhat Agree   4:Neutral   5:Somewhat Disagree 6:Disagree 7:Strongly Disagree

a) I would prefer using the ATM over visiting the bank branch.
☐ 1   ☐ 2   ☐ 3   ☐ 4   ☐ 5   ☐ 6   ☐ 7
b) Using the ATM in different financial transactions is safe and secure.
☐ 1   ☐ 2   ☐ 3   ☐ 4   ☐ 5   ☐ 6   ☐ 7
c) I would find the ATM useful and convenient.
☐ 1   ☐ 2   ☐ 3   ☐ 4   ☐ 5   ☐ 6   ☐ 7
d) My interaction with the ATM would be easy and understandable.
☐ 1   ☐ 2   ☐ 3   ☐ 4   ☐ 5   ☐ 6   ☐ 7

Credit Cards:

Credit cards are used by bank customers to perform their different payments in different retail stores, restaurants, etc. In addition, they are commonly used for Internet shopping. Credit cards can also be used for cash advance, but usually in that case, the customer would have to pay cash advance fees. The most common credit card brands are MasterCard and Visa.

Are you aware of that technology?

☐ Yes   ☐ No

IF YES: How was it introduced to you?

☐ Through Bank Staff   ☐ Just by Chance
☐ Through Media Advertisements   ☐ Others

What are the main functions that you are using it for?

☐ Shopping   ☐ Gas Stations
☐ Restaurants/Hotels   ☐ None of the above
☐ Internet   ☐ Others

For the following questions, please give your rating from 1 to 7 as to how you agree/ disagree with the argument.
1:Strongly Agree 2:Agree 3:Somewhat Agree 4:Neutral 5:Somewhat Disagree
6:Disagree 7:Strongly Disagree

a) I'm very likely to use my credit card rather than than pay in cash.
☐ 1   ☐ 2   ☐ 3   ☐ 4   ☐ 5   ☐ 6   ☐ 7
b) I don't feel comfortable giving my credit card to a salesperson in a shop or in a restaurant.
☐ 1   ☐ 2   ☐ 3   ☐ 4   ☐ 5   ☐ 6   ☐ 7
c) Using the credit card would enable me to accomplish my payment transactions more quickly.
☐ 1   ☐ 2   ☐ 3   ☐ 4   ☐ 5   ☐ 6   ☐ 7
d) The process of paying my bills using the credit card is easy and clear.
☐ 1   ☐ 2   ☐ 3   ☐ 4   ☐ 5   ☐ 6   ☐ 7

Call Centers / Phone Banking:

Bank call centers are used for different transactions, like checking the account balance and performing internal transfer between the accounts. It is also used by some banks to pay the credit card bill, if the customer has an account in that bank.

Are you aware of that technology?

☐ Yes   ☐ No

IF YES: How was it introduced to you?

☐ Through Bank Staff ☐ Just by Chance
☐ Through Media Advertisements ☐ Others

What are the main functions that you are using it for?

☐ Balance Inquiry ☐ Credit Card Payment
☐ Transfers ☐ None of the above

For the following questions, please give your rating from 1 to 7 as to how you agree/ disagree with the argument.
1: Strongly Agree 2: Agree 3: Somewhat Agree 4: Neutral 5: Somewhat Disagree 6: Disagree
7: Strongly Disagree

a) If my bank had a call center, I would have used it to do my transactions.
☐ 1   ☐ 2   ☐ 3   ☐ 4   ☐ 5   ☐ 6   ☐ 7
b) I don't trust giving my account number over the phone.
☐ 1   ☐ 2   ☐ 3   ☐ 4   ☐ 5   ☐ 6   ☐ 7
c) Learning to use the call center would be easy for me.
☐ 1   ☐ 2   ☐ 3   ☐ 4   ☐ 5   ☐ 6   ☐ 7

Internet Banking:
Internet Banking refers to using the Internet to perform different non-cash transactions, like viewing the account balance and conducting internal transfers.

Are you aware of that technology?

☐ Yes ☐ No

IF YES: How was it introduced to you?

☐ Through Bank Staff ☐ Just by Chance
☐ Through Media ☐ Others
   Advertisements

What are the main functions that you are using it for?

☐ Balance Inquiry ☐ Credit Card Payment
☐ Transfers ☐ None of the above

For the following questions, please give your rating from 1 to 7 as to how you agree/ disagree with the argument.
1: Strongly Agree 2: Agree 3: Somewhat Agree 4: Neutral 5: Somewhat Disagree
6: Disagree 7: Strongly Disagree

a) I would have used Internet Banking if it was provided by my bank.
   ☐ 1   ☐ 2   ☐ 3   ☐ 4   ☐ 5   ☐ 6   ☐ 7
b) Accessing my financial information over the Internet is safe and secure.
   ☐ 1   ☐ 2   ☐ 3   ☐ 4   ☐ 5   ☐ 6   ☐ 7
c) Using Internet Banking would save my time.
   ☐ 1   ☐ 2   ☐ 3   ☐ 4   ☐ 5   ☐ 6   ☐ 7
d) It would be easy for me to become skilled at using Internet banking.
   ☐ 1   ☐ 2   ☐ 3   ☐ 4   ☐ 5   ☐ 6   ☐ 7

In the following space, please feel free to add any comments that you may have:

_____

_____

_____

Sherif Kamel is an assistant professor of MIS and associate director of the Management Center at the American University in Cairo, Egypt. Previously, he was the director of the Regional IT Institute (1992-2001) and the training manager of the Cabinet of Egypt Information and Decision Support Center (1987-1991). In 1996, he was a co-founding member of the Internet Society of Egypt. Dr. Kamel has many publications in IT transfer to developing countries, e-commerce, human resources development, decision support applications, and knowledge management. He serves on the editorial and review boards of a number of IS journals and is the associate editor of the Annals of Cases on Information Technology Applications and Management in Organizations. *Dr. Kamel is currently the VP for communications for the Information Resources Management Association (IRMA). He is a graduate of the London School of Economics and Political Science (UK) and The American University in Cairo (Egypt).*

Ahmed Hassan graduated in 1995 from the Faculty of Engineering, Cairo University. He began his career as a systems analyst in the area of electronic payment systems in the Egyptian Banks Company for Technological Advancement. In 2000, he moved to Citibank Egypt as a project manager responsible for electronic retail banking systems. In 2001, he got his MBA from Maastricht School of Management (MSM).

This case was previously published in *Annals of Cases on Information Technology*, Volume5/ 2003, pp. 1-25, © 2003.

Chapter XIX

Bringing E-Business to the World's Largest Flower Auction:
The Case of Aalsmeer

Tim van Dantzig, Aalsmeer Flower Auction, The Netherlands

Albert Boonstra, University of Groningen, The Netherlands

EXECUTIVE SUMMARY

This case history takes place at the biggest flower auction of the world, the Aalsmeer Flower Auction. Directors of the Aalsmeer Flower Auction felt that the Internet might play an important role in the future of their business. They believed that an active and leading position in applying electronic networks could secure and even strengthen their dominant position and that a policy of restraint could be a threat if other parties should enter this market with electronic auctions. At the end of the 1990s, they started various e-business initiatives. The case study describes the different e-business initiatives and the responses from suppliers, customers, managers and other stakeholders on each of these initiatives. Readers will be challenged to analyze this material and offer advice to the management of the auction about future directions with respect to e-business.

ORGANIZATIONAL BACKGROUND

History

At the beginning of the 20th century, Aalsmeer growers as a cooperative joined forces to counterbalance the power of the middlemen. This resulted in the foundation of two local auctions, both located in this little village in the west of the Netherlands, near Amsterdam Airport.

Growers in eastern Aalsmeer founded an auction named "Flowerlove"; they auctioned their export flowers in a café, where the first auction took place on the 4th of December 1911. In January 1912, the other auction, "Central Aalsmeer Auction" (CAV) in Aalsmeer Village, was started. Also in Aalsmeer Village, the first flowers were auctioned in a café.

Both auctions were thriving from the beginning, their turnovers not varying very much. In 1918, CAV was the first auction to reach a yearly turnover of 1 million guilders ($560,000). In 1971, the last year of both auctions, Flowerlove realized a turnover of 107 million guilders ($60 million). CAV achieved a turnover of 113 million guilders (almost $65 million).

After four years of preparations, Aalsmeer Flower Auction (AFA) was born when the two auctions merged on March 6, 1968. However, they continued to operate quite independently. The vast majority of the growers backed this merger, realizing that further development would only be possible in a new physical complex and on new premises with sufficient room for expansion for many years to come. The merger was accelerated by the repeal of cultivation constraints and the explosive growth of the export of flowers and plants in the 1960s. During the first three years, only cut flowers were auctioned. These included cut flowers from foreign production areas such as Spain, France and Italy. One of the first measures of the board of Aalsmeer Flower Auction was permission to import under certain conditions.

An important fact in the year 1972 was the completion of a brand new huge auctioning complex near the former building of Flowerlove. In this complex, all facilities for auctioning, storage, processing and logistics were concentrated together. A year later, a mediation agency for the trading of large uniform batches of plants was established. The cash-and-carry center "Cultra," where wholesalers serve smaller buyers, dates from 1980.

The growth of the Aalsmeer Flower Auction was a result of the fact that, until 1985, there had only been one main flower exporting country in the world: the Netherlands (Yearbook 1985, Statistics Netherlands). This explains that almost every aspect of the world trade in flowers was controlled from auctions in this country: pricing, packaging distribution, and quality control. But around that time, the first signals for change could be picked up. New countries, including Israel, Spain, Kenia, Tanzania, Ecuador and Colombia started to produce flowers with the intention to trade these products via the Netherlands in order to gain hard currencies and to be connected with a fine-meshed distribution network. This development made the Aalsmeer Flower Auction become an international center for supply and demand of floricultural products.

Auctions

Auctions involve determination of the basis for product or service exchange between a buyer and a seller according to particular trading rules that help select the best match between the buyer and seller (Chaffey, 2004). Klein (1997) identifies different roles for the auction:

- **Price discovery:** By means of buyer gatherings in which there is a bidding for products that do not have standardized prices, auctions can help establish a realistic market price.
- **Efficient allocation mechanism:** The sale of items that are difficult to distribute through traditional channels falls into this category. Examples include "damaged inventory" that has a limited shelf life or is only available at a particular time, such as aircraft flights or theatre tickets.
- **Distribution mechanism:** As a means of attracting particular audiences.
- **Coordination mechanism:** Here, the auction is used to coordinate the sale of a product to a number of interested parties.

To understand auctions, it is important to distinguish between offers and bids. An offer is a commitment of a trader to sell under certain conditions, such as a minimum price. A bid is made by a trader to buy under the conditions of the bid, such as a commitment to purchase at a particular price (Reck, 1997).

Current Situation

Today, Aalsmeer Flower Auction offers globally-producing growers and globally active wholesalers and exporters a total concept: a central marketplace for the buying and selling of floricultural products with a range of marketing channels, facilities for growers and buyers and logistics. This makes the Aalsmeer Flower Auction a prominent link in the international chain of flower and plant sales. In 55,000 transactions, an average of 19 million flowers and 2 million plants change hands every day within a surface area of 1 million m². The flowers and plants are supplied by around 7,000 growers worldwide, and bought by 1,375 wholesalers and exporters. Within a couple of hours they are exported to almost every country in the world.

Aalsmeer Flower Auction's market share is 44%. With approximately 2,000 employees, an annual turnover of over 1.5 billion Euro ($1.9 billion) was achieved in 2002. Cut flowers yielded around 1 billion Euro, while plants yielded 5 million Euro. The greater part of this turnover came from Dutch products, supplemented by foreign products.

Of all the products traded via the flower auctions in the Netherlands (over 3.4 bn Euro in 2002), over 44% have been auctioned directly through Aalsmeer Flower Auction. Products originating from other auctions are also processed at Aalsmeer Flower Auction. In total, Aalsmeer Flower Auction has a 55% market share in Dutch floricultural exports. By now, the exporting countries with the highest growth shares are those in Eastern Europe, like Poland and Russia. See the appendix for more financial and organizational data.

Value Chain and Industry

Traditionally, Holland is a flower-exporting country; the two largest flower auctions of the world are established in the Netherlands. One of them is Aalsmeer Flower Auction. Therefore, Dutch flower auctions play a leading role in the international chain of flower and plant sales.

Within this floricultural value chain, growers are the initial suppliers. Demand comes from exporters, importers, wholesalers, cash & carries and retailers (see Figure 1). Within this chain, auctions play a mediating role between growers and exporters. This role primarily consists of bringing supply and demand of floricultural products together and by doing so, determining market prices. In some cases, these prices have the status of world market prices, since many parties throughout the world use them as important indicators for price setting.

Another role of the auction in the chain is to increase the efficiency of transactions by breaking up large numbers of uniform products from growers into smaller amounts for buyers. This "break-bulk" function generates for both parties a large number of complementary financial, IT, housing and logistic services.

This chain originated in the time that it was supply-driven. Since the 1910s, growers have united to gain more market power to push their products through the chain. However, different developments, which will be described in more detail, explain that this value chain is under pressure. Electronic networks, changing customer needs, mergers and acquisitions of buyers and professionalization of growers pressure parties to move to a value chain that is as cost-effective and responsive as it can possibly be.

Structure of Aalsmeer Flower Auction

As noted, Aalsmeer Flower Auction is a growers' cooperative. Around 3,500 growers in 15 sections are members of the cooperative society and thus joint owners of the auction building. The members appoint a board of nine from among their ranks to determine policy. A chairman, a vice-chairman and a secretary are selected from this board. The management and implementation of policy are in the hands of three general management members: a managing director, a commercial director and an operational director. A supervisory board provides policy recommendations and verification.

The organization chart shows this structure (Figure 2).

As illustrated in the organization chart, the Aalsmeer Flower auction uses two main channels to play its role as a mediator among growers and buyers:

- **Auction:** By using the auction clock, most of the supply from growers is divided into smaller units to be sold by exporters and wholesalers.

Figure 1. Value chain of flowers and plants

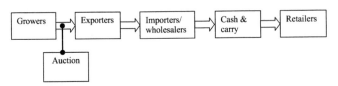

- **Direct mediation:** Teams of mediators combine specific supply and demand to generate transactions for day trade and futures. In this process, they often follow the auction prices.

Between the auctioning and mediation departments, there is a cultural difference. Employees of both departments see each other as competitors. In the past, the emphasis was clearly on auctioning, while mediation was mainly a by-product. Now, business is gradually moving to mediation, but the mediation process is following the price setting at the auction.

As a result, both channels are strongly interrelated. Just the cooperation of the two channels gains advantage for growers and buyers. They can choose which percentage of selling or buying they want to do via each channel and therefore they are almost always assured of selling or buying what they want.

Operational departments, such as logistics, information technology (IT) finance and human resource management (HRM), are providing all kinds of services to the commercial auctioning and mediation departments. The e-selling unit displayed in the organization chart plays an important role in the e-business initiatives of the Aalsmeer Flower Auction, as will be discussed next.

Auctioning and Mediating Processes at the Aalsmeer Flower Auction

Each night, the auction prepares the products for auctioning the next day. This means: loading the products on special carts for internal transport and presentation, checking the quality of the products, and entering information about the products into the auction system.

At about 5 a.m., all the interested buyers can check which products will be auctioned that day by addressing the "clock supply online" system of the auction. They can also see the products "live" at the lineup area. At 6 a.m., buyers group together in one of the auction halls. Each hall has its own products; for example, roses and tulips are auctioned in a separate hall. The buyers are wholesalers and exporters from all over the world. Therefore, the auction also offers "remote buying," which is an Internet application in which each of the auction halls can be simulated. By using this system, online and off-line buyers can buy products.

Figure 2. Organization chart Aalsmeer Flower Auction

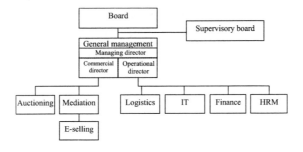

For each (bunch of) cart(s) with products, the auctioneer sets a starting price. Next, that cart is automatically transported into the auction hall, where it passes the auction clock (about three meters in diameter). The auctioneer starts the clock, in which red lights are moving fast from the start price towards a price of zero. The buyer who is the first to press the button from his or her seat in the hall (or from his or her computer) will become the owner of the cart. In this way, the optimal price based on supply and demand is achieved. Immediately after a cart has been sold, auction employees transport it to the location of the buyer. This is possible because about 65% of the buyers are physically present in the auctioning complex. In the meantime, the money involved in the transaction is transferred from the bank account of the buyer to the bank account of the grower.

Apart from the auction clock process as described, the Aalsmeer Flower Auction also plays an important role as a mediator for day trading and future trading. Many exporters and wholesalers (see Figure 1) wish to make contracts with their customers (e.g., supermarkets, outlet stores, chains of florists) for months in advance. Therefore, they want to be sure that they can deliver the contracted products at a certain price. At the auction clock, they are not sure of that. So these buyers can use the services of the mediation department of the auction. The mediating employees help these buyers to find growers to supply the products. After that, they help them draw up the contract with these growers and check up on the quality of the products on a continuing basis to guarantee the contracted amount and quality.

SETTING THE STAGE

In the mid 1990s there were several simultaneous changes in the environment of the Aalsmeer Flower Auction. The most relevant of these contextual issues were:

1. The increasing internationalization of the industry, for example, the opening of new markets in Eastern Europe and the advent of new entrants (foreign growers for South America and North Africa);
2. Increasing trade outside the auction;
3. New technological opportunities, including the adoption of the Internet;
4. Increasing power of retailers leading to demand for fresher products, more varieties, smaller quantities and higher delivery frequencies.

Each of these contextual issues will be discussed next.

1. *Increasing Internationalization of the Industry*
    As, for example, Russia and Poland became more oriented to Western Europe, they were seen as a whole new buying market for the flower industry with its own characteristics. Also, mergers and acquisitions among buyers as well as professionalization among growers led to a more formal way of doing business. With their increasing size and power, the buyers gained more industry dominance. As a result, most growers familiarized themselves with a more professional style of selling.

2. *Increasing Trade Outside the Auction*

The trade of flowers from countries in Africa and South America became stronger in 1990s. Not all these products were sent to the flower auction for selling; a lot of growers in these countries have direct agreements with buyers. By passing the auction, the auction misses income and interesting sorts of flowers and plants that do not grow in Europe. Also, this direct selling was seen as a threat to existing Dutch growers, who are obligated to sell via the auction with higher costs for the buyers.

3. *New Technological Opportunities*

In the mid 1990s a new flower auction (Tele Flower Auction), which operated fully electronically, entered the market. This caused a shock with the established parties; this shock was intensified by the relative success of this newcomer. It also led to further discussions about technological opportunities to change the auctioning process as well as ideas to use multiple channels rather than the one physical flow auctioned by the auction clock. Separate channels, linked or unlinked from the auction clock, were seen as a serious possibility.

This idea was also boosted because towards the end of the 1990s the Internet became a more common phenomenon.

4. *Increasing Power of Retailers*

Critics argued that the auction was too far away from the customer; they stated that the auction was mainly directed to market the products of the growers and not to address the needs of customers. But since the 1980s, critical consumers with changing needs have increasingly affected demand. To respond to that change, retailers asked for fresher products, more varieties, smaller quantities and multiple deliveries each week. This led to the idea of "chain reversal" and "chain reduction": not that supply should determine demand, but that demand should determine supply in a much more direct way.

The board of the Aalsmeer Flower Auction felt that they had to react to the previously mentioned developments in the market. Otherwise, the other parties in the value chain could become a threat for the position of the auction in that chain. Until then, the auction had always been in the comfortable position of serving a supply market that kept on growing. The auction could determine which instruments to use to serve the market. This resulted in a quite passive role.

However, due to the changing market developments, it was necessary to start a strategic reorientation of the Aalsmeer Flower Auction, which included a discussion about using electronic networks and reinventing the value chain to enable strategic change.

CASE DESCRIPTION

Part of the outcome of the strategic reorientation was the attempt of Aalsmeer Flower Auction to use electronic channels to support its business processes and to connect its processes with those of suppliers and buyers (Andal Ancion et al., 2003). Initial objectives of these e-business activities were to enable innovation, to redefine the value chain, to reduce transaction costs, to strengthen the link with wholesalers and retailers and to increase market share.

The director of commercial affairs, John Stevens, was, in particular, responsible for the deployment and extension of e-business applications. In 1997, he formed a group of 10 employees to help achieve these objectives and to develop, implement and maintain effective e-business applications. This group consisted of people with different backgrounds: IT, marketing and logistics. Manager of the group became Marrianne Groothuis, a marketing manager. In order to keep this group open-minded, creative and ambitious, it was located in a separate building, outside the huge auction complex. Within its own atmosphere and in relative autonomy, this group—named e-selling—started to develop its first e-business application.

E-Business Phase 1: FlowerAccess

This first e-business application was named FlowerAccess (www. floweraccess.com). This application consisted of an ordering system directed to retailers. It enabled retailers to place orders online to exporters and wholesalers, who would then pass it on to growers. The growers, in their turn, were to transport the products to the wholesalers, who put the orders together and take them to the retailer, for example, the florist. This process is illustrated in Figure 3.

To use FlowerAccess, wholesalers received the accumulated supply of all FlowerAccess growers and offered this to retailers. Based on information that the system generated, growers were able to adjust their supply to the demand from retailers. The following screen shots show how the ordering process can take place. Figure 4 illustrates the ordering via FlowerAccess and Figure 5 the order confirmation.

Up until then, Aalsmeer Flower Auction had had no business relations with retailers; therefore FlowerAccess can be interpreted as an attempt to redefine the value chain. By using FlowerAccess, Aalsmeer Flower Auction tried to increase its grip on the value chain as a whole, also by including retailers and other clients (cash & carries). By being the first with such a system, Aalsmeer Flower Auction also aimed at creating market dominance and making attempts of others to introduce similar systems less successful.

In 1999, the implementation of FlowerAccess started. Marrianne Groothuis and her team visited a large number of growers, wholesalers and retailers to demonstrate the system and its potential benefits. This initially led to 60 participating growers, seven wholesalers and 1,200 retailers (spread out over various European countries). Unfortunately, only 20% of the 1,200 connected retailers made regular use of FlowerAccess. A main problem was that the amount of ordered flowers was too small to be attractive

Figure 3. Flow of activities with FlowerAccess

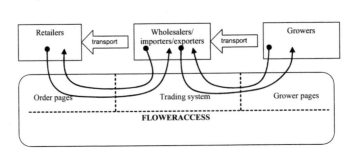

Figure 4. Ordering via FlowerAccess

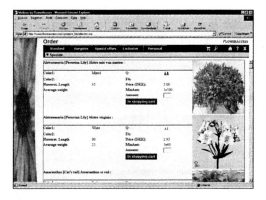

Figure 5. Order Confirmation via FlowerAccess

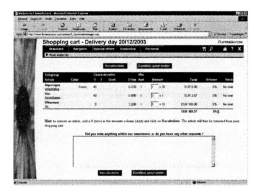

enough for growers to keep on participating in FlowerAccess. Moreover, many growers did not really believe that they would gain much efficiency by using the system. They were not accustomed to using computers in their business processes, so it took them more time to make electronic offerings via the computer than via the traditional faxes. The share of FlowerAccess in the returns was no more than 1% of the total auction turnover. This meant that FlowerAccess could not live up to the realization of the initial objectives.

At the start of FlowerAccess, retailers were not so experienced with Internet based applications. An exception was retailers from a number of Northern European countries, especially Denmark, who were relatively used to the Internet. For them, but also for retailers in the UK, France, Switzerland and Germany, the FlowerAccess system could be interesting because it offered them a wide range of new and fresh products that was becoming easily accessible. In these countries there are not many cash-and-carry stores to obtain the products by self-service, so ordering via Internet saved them a lot of time. However, this did not count for Dutch and Belgian retailers who always have a cash-and-carry in the neighborhood. Reasons for not using the system were the lack of personal contacts with competitors, as was the case with the cash-and-carries, and the impossibility to touch or smell the products before buying.

In a management meeting, Marrianne Groothuis had to report these disappointing figures to the general management (Clegg et al., 2001; Coltman et al., 2001). John Stevens did not understand why the FlowerAccess initiative had failed so far.

"There are several reasons for it," Marrianne Groothuis began. "Many wholesalers and retailers seem not to be prepared or willing to move to the new system. Wholesalers seem to be reluctant to become too dependent on the systems of our auction, because they provide insight into profit margins and other sensitive business information. Besides, many retailers prefer to look and smell flowers prior to purchase. They can do this in cash & carry outlets. This also enables them to maintain personal contacts with colleagues, who can also provide them with important market information. Only in Denmark and Switzerland, which have few purchasing channels for these products, FlowerAccess is relatively successful. My final argument," Marrianne Groothuis said, "is that the technology and speed of Internet is not as fast as we expected. Sometimes, it takes more than a minute before all flower pictures are build up on the screen of the retailers' PCs."

"Well Marrianne, my conclusion is that FlowerAccess has led to a cost increase of our auction due to the development and maintenance of the system," John Stevens said. "So far you are right," Marrianne answered, "but I still see possibilities to enhance the volumes for growers. Internet speed problems are also expected to disappear in a short period. Please give me another chance to demonstrate that our e-business strategy is the right way to achieve our commercial objectives." The management decided to give Marrianne Groothuis the benefit of the doubt: some managers had serious doubts about the appropriateness of using the Internet in their business, but they also felt that it was not appropriate to stop the initiatives altogether.

E-Business Phase 2: Flower XL

And so, while the FlowerAccess formula was kept alive, the knowledge created by developing this system proved to be useful for the development of the next e-business initiative of Marrianne Groothuis and her e-selling team. They named this new e-business application FlowerXL, because it was exclusively aimed at wholesalers instead of retailers.

Figure 6 shows a screen print of an ordering page of Flower XL.

Aalsmeer Flower Auction had already established relations with wholesalers, which meant that this system would complement and strengthen the existing value chain and was not a threat to existing parties. Because Aalsmeer knows most wholesalers very well, it was better able to adjust this system to the specific needs and expectations of these parties. Another rationale behind this system, according to Marrianne Groothuis, was that the transaction volumes of wholesalers were much higher than those of retailers, which made it much more profitable for all parties.

Consequently, FlowerXL appeared to have more potential than FlowerAccess. However, after one year, Marrianne Groothuis had to report again that the sales figures of FlowerXL were quite limited. Just like the retailers, the wholesalers also tended to largely base their business on personal and informal contacts, which were maintained at

Figure 6. Ordering page where wholesalers choose products and place them in shopping cart

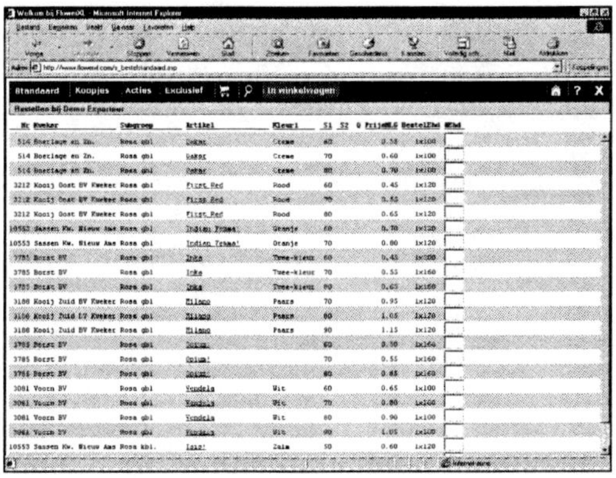

the auction hall. From the perspective of many wholesalers, an exclusive Internet-based ordering system undermined this informal information exchange.

Therefore, John Stevens and the other directors of Aalsmeer Flower Auction believed that a successful e-business system should be integrated into the existing business and be complementary and supportive rather than that it replacing the traditional business (Huang et al., 2003). This view dominated the next stage of e-business at Aalsmeer Flower Auction.

Phase 3: Electronic Trading Place

Although many directors had become skeptical about the effectiveness of e-business initiatives, they decided to set up a new application in 2002, named Electronic Trading Place, also directed at exporters and wholesalers. This new application had the aim to add service, to support wholesalers and exporters in the cost-effectiveness of their transactions, and to complement rather than replace the traditional auction. The objective to reduce costs and to transform the value chain was put to the background. The management, with John Stevens as front man, also decided to use pilot studies to adapt initial designs and to work very closely with prospective users.

During these pilot studies, Marianne and her team became increasingly aware that for wholesalers, using auction systems is very much an issue of security and trust. Amongst many wholesalers, there is a high degree of competition, and by using auction systems, they can be sure that auction employees monitor their transactions. This involves sensitive and secret information, which has to be kept from their competitors. Following the concept of the Electronic Trading Place, auction management decided to deal with this issue by separating mediation employees into different teams, which are not allowed to communicate about transactions of customers.

Within the Electronic Trading Place, a wholesaler (or exporter) purchased plants or flowers from a grower. Account managers from Aalsmeer Flower Auction helped

Figure 7. Product detail page where growers specify product characteristics

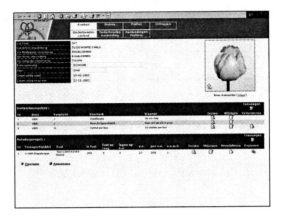

Figure 8. Ordering page where exporters choose products and place in shopping cart

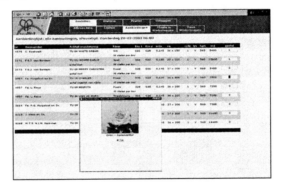

wholesalers analyze for which products they had a permanent need, and which growers may be used to fulfill this need. The system helped connect the wholesalers with the growers in order to make the transactions as cost-effective as possible. Figure 7 shows a screen print of a page where growers can specify the characteristics of their products. Figure 8 shows a page where exporters can choose products and place them in their shopping cart.

After six months of experiments, the pilot received a positive assessment from all parties involved. According to Marrianne Groothuis, who was still leading the e-selling unit, an important reason for this was that the system was based on trust among wholesalers and growers. Buyers and sellers became known to each other and the electronic transaction helped them to make the routine processes more cost-effective. The pilot system, which was based on the old FlowerAccess system, was totally modernized by means of new Internet techniques. Also, comments from users in the pilot were used to improve the application.

The acceptance of this application by users grew slowly after the market introduction at the end of 2002. Important improvements to the system were applied, including the monitoring of orders via the internal ordering system of the mediation department, the enclosure of digital photos to written descriptions and also more standardized qualifications of products.

Since the system was integrated in other sale channels, including the auction, traders became more used to it. This promoted acceptance and explained the gradual increase of use. Another factor was that the auction hall (but also canteens and corridors) still remained as a place to exchange business information.

Technical Aspects of Different E-Business Systems

At the end of the 1990s, FlowerAccess was one of the first Internet ordering applications. This meant that there were not many standards at that time. Because different software companies were involved, the system consisted of separate components that were connected by different exchange formats, such as comma separated files (CSV) and file transaction protocol (FTP). Because FlowerAccess was a stand-alone system developed outside the auction, there was no connection with the (financial) systems of the auction. So transactions made between wholesalers and growers had to be re-entered in the auctioning system. By now, the auction is still suffering from the negative consequences of this fact. FlowerAccess does not really fit in with the current auction IT standards and technical support, which regularly causes technical problems. By 2004, there will be a plan ready to transfer all the components of the system to a modern environment, similarly to the Electronic Trading Place.

FlowerXL was technically similar to FlowerAccess. Except for the grower pages, all the components of FlowerAccess could be used; only the ordering pages had to be adjusted to the specific needs of wholesalers, the target group of FlowerXL. In order to publish order lists, the wholesaler system rather than the grower pages was used to enter the offerings into FlowerXL To run FlowerXL next to FlowerAccess, a new Web server was installed, but the database server as well as the database design were the same as those of FlowerAccess.

By the time the Electronic Trading Place was build, the technology of FlowerAccess and FlowerXL systems became outdated. By that time, also the auction had set standards, based on experiences of other Internet systems. The coupling of different components became easier because of the shared technical platform.

Another difference of the Electronic Trading Place compared to FlowerAccess and FlowerXL is the exchange of data by means of a connection to the different systems of the auction. In this way, the mediators can monitor orders made via the Electronic Trading Place in their own system. Further, all the basic "information needs" (e.g., name and addresses of growers and buyers, codes for flowers and trolleys) do not have to be re-entered into the Electronic Trading Place. The necessary back office of the Electronic Trading Place is also minimal compared to the previous systems. Table 1 describes the most important technical differences between FlowerAccess/ FlowerXL and the Electronic Trading Place, and shows some further details about the development of the different systems mentioned in the case.

Organizational and Cultural Implications

During the third phase (Electronic Trading Place), John Stevens and his management team decided to integrate the e-selling unit (see Figure 2) with the mediation unit.

Table 1. Technical aspects with respect to e-business systems at Aalsmeer

	FlowerAccess/ FlowerXL	Electronic Trading Place
Developers	External parties	Internal IT staff
Development time	About eight man-years	About one man-year
Development tools	RDS, Access	UML, use cases
Automatic connections with other auction systems	No, only by hand	Yes, automatically
Designed according to auction IT standards	No, no standards available	Yes
Designed according to auction graphic standards	No, no standards available	Yes, corporate image lay-out of websites
Use of backoffice	Needed for almost every function	Only need for by mutating users
Platform database	SQL server 6.5 (now migration to Windows 2000)	Windows 2000 clustered
Coupling between websites and database	Embedded SQL directly on tables and on stored procedures	Visual basic com+ components which trigger stored procedures

E-business systems were no longer perceived as separate systems and separate lines of business (Gulati et al., 2000). According to the directors, only a strong integration complementing other channels would prove to be promising in the short run. They believed that in the long run channels might gradually transform to more electronic forms (Barley, 1990; Boddy, 2000; Jackson et al., 2003; Porter, 2001).

Problems during the integration of the e-selling group were the diverse cultures of both units. The employees of e-selling were relatively autonomous and received plenty of resources to develop the initial systems. These systems cost millions of Euros, while the proven revenues remained unclear. Many employees from mediation did not understand that the management funded this unprofitable unit for such a long time. After the integration, both units had to cooperate and to integrate their processes, which appeared to be a complicated process of organizational change and integration.

Summary of the Case Description

The following tables (Table 2 and Table 3) summarize this case history by comparing the different phases of using e-business applications (Table 2) and by putting the different relevant events between 1997 and 2004 in a time frame (Table 3).

CURRENT CHALLENGES AND PROBLEMS FACING THE ORGANIZATION

As said before, the FlowerAccess system is still operational alongside the Electronic Trading Place. FlowerXL was turned off after the start of the pilot with the Electronic Trading Place.

Today, FlowerAccess is increasingly becoming a commercial success, at least for the wholesalers who are working with the system. After years of intense contact between the wholesalers and their retailers, mostly via local wholesalers and retailer organizations, more and more retailers are ordering via FlowerAccess. Recently, retailers in Spain and Sweden were offered to join FlowerAccess. Right now, about 800 retailers are

Table 2. Summary of e-business applications of Aalsmeer Flower Auction

e-Business application / Dimension	Phase 1 FlowerAccess	Phase 2 Flower XL	Phase 3 Electronic Trading Place
Role in the value chain	Connecting retailers with exporters and wholesalers	Connecting wholesalers and exporters with growers	Connecting wholesalers and exporters with growers
Objectives	Domination in value chain Disintermediation Lowering transaction costs Increasing market share	Strengthening position towards importers and wholesalers Lowering transaction costs Increasing market share	Improving service Strengthening existing activities Strengthening trust and loyalty Integration with other business processes
Degree of realization of objectives	Limited	Moderate	Satisfactory
Degree of contrast with existing processes	Radical	Moderate	Small
User acceptance	Initially low, now slightly growing in some countries	Low	Increasing
Trading volumes	Relatively low	Relatively low	Increasing
Position of e-Business in the organization	Separate	Separate	Integrated

Table 3. Main events and time frame

Date	Event	Information on objectives, costs and realization of goals
1997	Development of FlowerAccess	– Foundation of an e-selling unit – Development in time and costs: about 8 man-years – Goal is to develop e-system to realize innovation, redefine the value chain, reduce transaction costs, strengthen links with customers and increase market share
1997-1998	Introduction of FlowerAccess on test market	– Defining e-business process – New market opportunities by increased Internet speed – One wholesaler operating in France and Germany – E-selling employees visit growers and retailers
1999-2000	Wider implementation of FlowerAccess	– Partnering with new growers and wholesalers – 60 growers, seven wholesalers and 1,200 retailers (20% ordering)
2001-2002	Use of FlowerAccess	– Promotion of the 'e' concept – 150 growers, 15 wholesalers and 1200 retailers (80% ordering) – Integration of e-selling with Mediation department: from 15 to three e-selling employees
2001	Development of FlowerXL	– Primary goals are to enhance the volume of growers, and to strengthen the position compared to that of importers – Development at very low cost by the use of the FlowerAccess system as a basis
2001	Introduction of FlowerXL on test market	– One agent using the system to connect his own growers to his own customers – Two e-selling employees guiding the import agent – Goals are not reached, but experiences show opportunities for e-selling with flower exporters – Finally, FlowerXL system is turned off
Begin 2002	Development of Electronic Trading Place	– Developing modern e-selling system for exporters – Development costs: about one man-year – Goals are to provide efficient ordering service to growers and exporters and to strengthen links with these existing partners
Mid 2002	Introduction of Electronic Trading Place on test market	– Connecting five growers of roses to one exporter – Intensive role of Mediation employees to adjust supply and demand and to get users adapted to the electronic way of purchasing – User acceptance partly gained, giving the 'go' for the next step
End 2002 and begin 2003	Implementation of Electronic Trading Place	– Connecting 30 growers of tulips to 15 exporters (30% ordering) – Intensive support by Mediation employees – Goals are not reached: transparency of supply not appreciated by growers, exporters prefer telephone over e-system, fixed prices not appreciated by growers and exporters
End 2003 and 2004	Use of Electronic Trading Place	– No external users of e-system – Internal use by Mediation employee to gain user experience and to explore future opportunities of the system and the concept
2003-2004	Current phase of FlowerAccess	– Five wholesalers, 1,000 retailers (80% ordering) – No growers involved due to lack of volume – Only two dedicated e-selling employees – Goals only partially reached (innovation and stronger link with participating wholesalers) but FlowerAccess is being kept alive as a motor for future innovation

ordering and that is far more than the about 200 in the beginning. But this volume is still relatively small to gain enough turnover for the Aalsmeer Flower Auction to cover the costs of the system.

Also, the returns of the Electronic Trading Place are still quite small. Many growers and exporters as well as some employees of the auction are hesitant to use the system because of all the reasons mentioned before.

Recently, the mediation department began to use the system internally to confirm orders on contract. Instead of the grower or exporter as an actor, a mediator makes the offerings and orders for them. Through this operating procedure, Aalsmeer Flower Auction tries to gain more knowledge regarding the opportunities and limitations of the system and its formula.

The management of Aalsmeer Flower Auction believes that the auction still has a long way to go to use electronic networks in the most optimal way. Actual questions and challenges are:

- How can acceptance and use of electronic channels effectively be promoted among internal and external parties?
- How can Aalsmeer gain market dominance without threatening wholesalers and growers?
- How should e-business be positioned: as a separate activity or as an integrated part of the organization (Gulati et al., 2000)?
- Is e-business the future and should Aalsmeer go through a transformation process or is e-business only one of the many channels that should be integrated?
- How do the e-business initiatives of Aalsmeer Flower Auction fit in with the other electronic means that have entered the floricultural sector in recent years (e.g., the introduction of standard EDI messages between grower, auction, exporters/wholesalers)?
- How can e-business enhance the strategy of the auction to disconnect product information from the logistic processes?
- How can the different e-business initiatives function as a catalyst for new electronic systems of Aalsmeer Flower Auction in the future?

REFERENCES

Andal Ancion, A., Cartwright, P. A., & Yip, G. S. (2003). The digital transformation of traditional businesses. *Sloan Management Review, 44*(4), 34-41.

Barley, S. (1990). The alignment of technology and structure through roles and networks. *Administrative Science Quarterly, 35*(1), 61-103.

Boddy, D. (2000). Implementing interorganizational IT systems: Lessons from a call centre project. *Journal of Information Systems, 15*(12), 29-37.

Chaffey, D. (2004). *E-business and e-commerce management.* London: Prentice Hall/Financial Times.

Clegg, C. W., Icasati-Johanson, B., & Bennett, S. (2001). E-business: Boom or gloom? *Behaviour & Information Technology, 20*(4), 293-298.

Coltman, T., Devinney, T., Latukefu, A., & Midgley, D. (2001). E-business: Revolution, evolution or hype? *California Management Review, 44*(1), 57-86.

Gulati, R., & Garino, J. (2000). Get the right mix for bricks & clicks. *Harvard Business Review, 78*(3), 107-114.

Huang, J., Makoju, E., Newell, S., & Galliers, R. D. (2003). Opportunities to learn from 'failure' with electronic commerce: A case study of electronic banking. *Journal of Information Technology, 18*(1), 17-26.

Jackson, P., & Harris, L. (2003). E-business and organisational change. Reconciling traditional values with business transformation. *Journal of Organizational Change Management, 16*(5), 497-511.

Klein, S. (1997). Introduction to electronic auctions. *International Journal of Electronic Markets, 4*(7), 3-6.

Porter, M. E. (2001). Strategy and the Internet. *Harvard Business Review, 79*(2), 63-78.

Reck, M. (1997). Trading characteristics of electronic auctions. *Journal of Electronic Markets, 4*(7), 17-23.

Statistics Netherlands. (n.d.). *Yearbook 1985.* The Hague, SDU.

APPENDIX

Total annual turnover (in million Euros)

	2002	**2001**	**2000**	**1999**	**1998**
Cut flowers	1.021	977	981	885	895
House plants	455	418	401	375	369
Garden plants	108	93	86	80	79
Total	*1.584*	*1.488*	*1.468*	*1.340*	*1.343*

Annual turnover via auctioning and mediation for cut flowers (in million Euros)

Year	Auctioning	Mediation	Total	% auctioning	% mediation
2002	929	92	1.021	91%	9%
1998	843	52	895	94%	6%

Annual turnover via auctioning and mediating for house plants (in million Euros)

Year	Auctioning	Mediation	Total	% auctioning	% Mediation
2002	202	253	455	44%	56%
1998	198	171	369	54%	46%

Annual turnover via auctioning and mediating for garden plants (in million Euros)

Year	Auctioning	Mediation	total	% auctioning	% Mediation
2002	57	51	108	52%	48%
1998	42	37	79	54%	46%

Export countries for cut flowers (in million Euros)

Country	Volume 2002
Germany	922
United Kingdom	555
France	421
Italy	154
United States	135
Switzerland	96
Belgium	89
Austria	81
Denmark	69
Russia	66
Others	402
Total	*2.990*

Export countries for pot plants (in million Euros)

Country	Volume 2002
Germany	550
France	167
United Kingdom	153
Italy	111
Belgium	65
Austria	44
Switzerland	43
Spain	33
Denmark	32
Sweden	29
Others	167
Total	*1.394*

All data from annual report Aalsmeer Flower Auction 2002.

Relevant facts

- Aalsmeer Flower Auction sells more than 20 million flowers and plants every day.
- 7,000 specialized growers from all over the world offer their flowers and plants via Aalsmeer Flower Auction every day.
- The auction has an essential "break-bulk' function: large lots are sold within a couple of hours and divided into smaller lots.
- The customers who are situated at the auction (wholesalers and exporters) can be on their way to the consumer, anywhere in the world, within a few hours.
- With its 1 mln m² of floor space, the auction building is the largest commercial building in the world.
- Today 130,000 auction stacking carts are in use.
- Aalsmeer Flower Auction turns over 6 million Euro every day.

Tim van Dantzig, MscBA, has worked in the E-Business Department of the Aalsmeer Flower Auction for almost three years. He is primarily responsible for the functionality of the e-business applications. In that role, he coordinates the Mediating Department and IT Department activities (both mentioned in the case). He holds a Master of Science in business administration from the University of Groningen, The Netherlands.

Albert Boonstra, Bec, MBA, PhD, is an associate professor at the University of Groningen, The Netherlands. He specializes in human and organizational issues when implementing and using information and communication technologies. Examples of this include e-business strategies and organizational change issues around information systems. He teaches IT-management-related courses for students as well as for experienced managers. He also consults for many profit and not-for-profit organizations on the management of information systems. Books include ICT, People and Organizations: A Management Approach *(with D. Boddy and G. Kennedy) and* Managing Information Systems: An Organisational Perspective, *all with Financial Times/Prentice Hall. He has recently published in the* Journal of General Management, European Management Journal, Journal of Management and Organization, New Technology, Work & Employment, *and the* Journal of Information Technology.

This case was previously published in the *International Journal of Cases on Electronic Commerce*, 1(1) (pp. 1-25), © 2005.

Chapter XX

The Impact of E-Commerce Technology on the Air Travel Industry

Susan Gasson, Drexel University, USA

EXECUTIVE SUMMARY

This case study examines the impact of online reservation systems and e-commerce on the travel industry. Two questions are examined:

1. *How can competitive advantage be obtained from the exploitation of new information technologies—in particular, e-commerce technologies?*
2. *How has the role of travel agents changed because of the new information technologies being used to achieve competitive advantage in the air travel industry?*

Initial discussion concerns the impact of the American Airlines SABRE system, as this has often been touted as giving American Airlines first-mover advantage in the industry. The wider impact of remote-access, computerized reservation systems, or Global Distribution Systems, and e-commerce access to online reservations in the travel industry is analyzed, using Porter's five-force model of industry competitive forces, to understand how the travel industry has shaped and has been shaped by information systems. The case study concludes with a comparison of the impact of information technologies between the U.S. and European travel industries. It concludes that technology alone does not affect the roles of industry players, but the development of winning technologies exploits structural factors in the environment. Constant evolution of strategic information systems is critical to producing competitive advantage, but opportunism also plays a strong role.

BACKGROUND: THE USE OF INFORMATION TECHNOLOGY IN THE AIR TRAVEL INDUSTRY

In the 1960s, when air travel first became affordable for the individual, travel agents provided an essential service. A travel agent would find a suitable flight in the printed schedules published by individual airlines and telephone the airline-booking agent to make a reservation. At a later time, the airline booking agent would return the call to confirm the reservation, or to suggest an alternative flight if no seats were available. The airline paid the agent a flat commission fee for the booking. The structure of the air travel industry prior to computerization is shown in Figure 1. The airline industry was regulated, so most routes were served by a single airline. Travel agents mainly served the individual travel market, while corporate travel was booked directly with an airline, to achieve corporate discounts (Clemons & Hann, 1999). The role of the travel agent was to advise clients on travel destinations and to act as an intermediary in the complicated process of arranging travel bookings.

The discussion below presents a case study of how the use of new technologies have affected the air travel industry, analyzing two waves of information technology that have had a major impact on the industry. The first of these is the development of direct reservation systems, such as the American Airlines SABRE system. The second is the development of online sales channels via the Internet.

SETTING THE STAGE: THE DEVELOPMENT OF THE AMERICAN AIRLINES SABRE SYSTEM

American Airlines is a division of AMR Corporation, employing over 128,000 people worldwide and reported net revenue in 2000 of $19.7 billion. One of the largest airlines in the world, AMR Corp. operates American Airlines, TWA and American Eagle. In August 2001, American Airlines announced a competitive alliance with British Airways, allowing them to codeshare (run a flight-schedule jointly, for a certain route) across the entire breadth of their respective global networks and opening up a completely new range of destinations to their customers.

Figure 1. The pre-computerization air travel industry structure

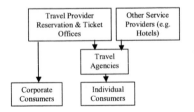

SABRE (Semi-Automated Business Research Environment) was developed by American Airlines in conjunction with IBM. Launched in the early 1960s, SABRE was the first computerized airline reservation system, serving American Airlines reservation counters from coast to coast in the USA and from Canada to Mexico by 1964. SABRE was expensive to develop and, when it came online, competitors filed lawsuits claiming that it gave American Airlines (AA) an unfair advantage (mainly because AA flights were listed first by the system). Other airlines rushed to develop their own reservation systems: United Airlines' system created the Apollo system, TWA developed PARS (TWA is now owned by American Airlines), and Delta developed DATAS.

Over 90% of the 40,000+ travel agents in the U.S. now connect into various direct reservation systems, but as the learning curve is high for a new system and space is limited, each agent tends to be connected to only one system. Appendix 1 gives the ownership of the major direct reservation systems (now called Global Distribution Systems, or GDS) and the major online travel agencies. Different airlines' reservation systems communicate with one another in real time. An agent can access and book flights on other carriers via its primary system, allowing a travel agent, for example, to book an American Airline flight through Amadeus (the direct reservations system owned by Air France, Iberia and Lufthansa) or to book a Lufthansa flight through SABRE (the American Airlines system). The airline consortium that owns the reservation system receives a fee for each reservation made for a competing airline and the airline providing the agent's reservation system is more likely to receive bookings on its flights. Because of this, each airline tries to maximize the number of travel agents connected directly to its own system and minimizes bookings for its flights via other systems.

The initial competitive advantage provided by the SABRE system has continued to operate to the present day: approximately three out of five airline flight tickets are booked through SABRE (Hopper, 1990; SABRE, 2002). Thus, SABRE gave American Airlines a first-mover competitive advantage that persisted, even after other airlines had developed their own computerized reservation systems. American Airlines made more money from SABRE than they did from flying passengers: revenue from the SABRE reservation system consistently accounted for more than 50% of the company's total revenues (Hopper, 1990; SABRE, 2002). In 1992, talking about legislation that would force American to divest itself of SABRE, American Airlines Chairman Robert Crandall said: "If you told me I had to sell either the airline or the system, I'd probably sell the airline." However, in 2000, American Airlines completed the process that turned the Sabre Technology Group into its own company. Sabre is now an S&P 500 company and has a 70% stake in Travelocity, the online travel agent (SABRE, 2002).

It could be argued that the competitive advantage conferred by the SABRE system has persisted, but only because of *continual* technical and product innovation:

- Initially (in the 1960s), SABRE served only American Airlines ticket and reservations staff.
- In 1976, travel agents were first offered a direct, remote-access service; by year end the system was installed in 130 locations, serving 86% of the top 100 agency accounts (AMR, 2002; SABRE, 2002).
- In 1985, SABRE was the first system that allowed consumers to access airline, hotel and car rental reservations directly, using an IBM PC (the world's first business-oriented personal computer) (AMR, 2002; SABRE, 2002).

- By 1986, the SABRE system was extended to the United Kingdom, paving the way for widespread international expansion. SABRE also installed the airline industry's first automated yield management system in this year: this prices airline seats to yield the maximum revenue for each flight (SABRE, 2002).
- By 1987, SABRE had become the world's largest private real-time data-processing system, serving more than 10,000 travel agents worldwide (AMR, 2002).
- In 1990, SABRE had 40% of the air travel booking market. To quote Hopper (1990), "If SABRE doesn't do the job, another system will. SABRE's industry-leading market share of 40% means that rival systems account for three out of five airline bookings."
- In 1996, the SABRE Technology Group exploited the increasing popularity of the Internet by launching Travelocity.com, a leading online business-to-consumer (B2C) travel site.
- In 2001, SABRE connects more than 59,000 travel agents around the world, providing content from 450 airlines, 53,000 hotels, 54 car rental companies, eight cruise lines, 33 railroads and 228 tour operators (SABRE, 2002), making it the largest Global Distribution System (GDS) for travel services.
- New innovations include wireless connectivity via mobile consumer devices and the use of a hand-held device by American Airlines gate staff, to make seat assignments and print boarding passes, making it simple for airlines to accommodate passengers who have missed connecting flights.

Therefore, SABRE can be seen as an *evolving set* of systems, developed in response to business needs and technical opportunities. Continual evolution itself is not the success factor, it is continual evolution in combination with the opportunistic exploitation of opportunities offered by the industry environment. However, while airlines were developing information systems to exploit new technologies and structural changes in the competitive environment, travel agents were not in a position to do so.

CASE DESCRIPTION: THE IMPACT OF NEW TECHNOLOGIES ON THE AIR TRAVEL INDUSTRY

The Advent of Global Distribution Systems

In the mid-1970s, airlines began to offer travel agents access to direct, computerized reservation systems (see the discussion of the SABRE system, below) and in 1978, the airline industry was deregulated, leading to more price and service competition between airlines on the same route. Providers of computerized reservation systems provided access for travel agents via dialup telephone connections (and eventually permanent or broadband connections). This changed the way in which travel agents completed a transaction and gave them faster and better information about price and availability, compared with the previous, asynchronous process of booking direct with the airline. Travel agents were still essential to the process of booking a flight, as access to the

Figure 2. The air travel industry structure as affected by GDS (e.g., SABRE)

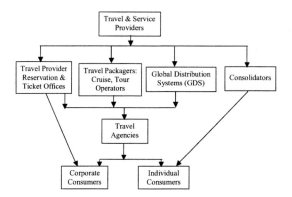

specialized technology required to obtain this knowledge was unavailable to the consumer. Although unavailable for direct consumer use, computerized reservation systems allowed travel agents to provide a more effective service. The travel agent could confirm the booking in real time and seek alternatives if a flight was full, while the customer waited. A real time booking with an airline-booking agent was better than relying on an asynchronous transaction, conducted over several hours or days. The travel market became segmented, as travel agents increasingly targeted corporate customers, providing value-added services like negotiation of bulk fares and arranging complex itineraries (Clemons & Hann, 1999).

Direct reservation system terminals and connections were often offered free to travel agents, as airlines competed for market share with travel agents. A travel agent would normally not use more than one direct reservation system, since they took a great deal of time and training to use. Not all systems initially carried all airlines, but this changed as direct reservation systems became ubiquitous. However, a particular airline's direct reservation system would usually display that airline's flights first, giving them an advantage. Airlines also had to pay a fee to have their flights included in a competitor's reservation system, which would add to the cost of booking with that airline through a travel agent who used a competitor's reservation system. Over a period, direct reservation systems became more prevalent and encompassed a wider range of products and services, to become global distribution systems (GDS).

GDS enabled travel and service providers (such as hotels and car-hire) the ability to market to customers in remote locations. The role of the travel agent changed as time went on, from knowledgeable travel and destination expert, to an intermediary, who saved the customer time and effort in booking a whole package of travel-related products and services. Another development in the 1980s was the emergence of consolidators: companies who purchased blocks of unsold seats from airlines and so were able to sell direct to the customer at a lower price than the travel agent could offer using GDS pricing. This trend fragmented the market, to some extent. Customers became aware of the differential pricing strategies used by airlines and became more price-sensitive as a result.

By the mid-1990s, the market had changed and travel agents became less buoyant. The airlines engaged in price wars and margins were reduced—the airlines sought to cap or to cut commission in an attempt to remain profitable. Although some of the larger agents had replaced dialup connections with broadband or permanently connected links, they were still relying on third-party providers for their information and level of service (the various airline reservation systems). The technology employed (direct access terminals) was becoming outdated, often having cumbersome, text-based interfaces, with difficult-to-negotiate menus and user-interfaces. Most travel agents relied on the same type of local knowledge that they had always used, to differentiate their value to the consumer.

Travel agents that focused on corporate customers could use information systems to provide better fare-search and point-of-sales tools such as ticket printing and this gave them some short-term competitive advantage during the 1990s. However, travel agents still faced two significant threats to their competitiveness during this period (Clemons & Hann, 1999): rebating (commission-sharing with corporate customers), by competitor travel agents, and commission caps and cuts by the airlines.

Internet Technologies

More recently, travel agents have faced additional threats to their profitability, enabled by the widespread use of the Internet. The first is disintermediation (cutting out the middleman) by the airlines and the computer-reservation system operators. The economics of individual transaction processing have been turned on their head by the ubiquity of Internet access: it is now justifiable even for the airlines to serve individual customers, as the cost of processing an electronic transaction is so low, compared to the cost of processing a purchase transaction performed by a human salesperson. Airlines are attracted even more by the profitability of corporate electronic transactions. With sophisticated information systems, it is now possible for airlines to offer complex discounts on bulk purchases across many different routes and classes of travel, for corporate customers. It is also possible for them to use data-mining techniques to target dynamic discounts and value-added service offerings at high-value corporate customers, increasing the business that they attract through using direct sales channels.

The second threat is competition from online travel agents whose overhead costs are much lower and who can achieve much wider economies of scale in processing large numbers of relatively low-margin purchase-transactions. Online travel agents use new technologies to access the direct reservation systems of multiple services in real time, allowing individual and corporate customers to directly coordinate flight, car hire, hotel and other services, as shown in Figure 3. However, there is a cost to using online travel booking services. The search cost can be high: air ticket prices may change from day-to-day or hour-to-hour. The time and effort involved in putting together a complex package of air and land travel services and hotel bookings is often too high for individual customers to contemplate. The online market may well be focused on the most price-sensitive segment of the air travel market: those willing to spend a disproportionate amount of time and effort in obtaining a low-cost ticket. Many customers may also visit an online travel agent's site to obtain information and then book elsewhere.

Following e-commerce developments, the travel industry is segmented between:

Figure 3. Structure of the air travel industry following e-commerce expansion (modified from Heartland, 2001)

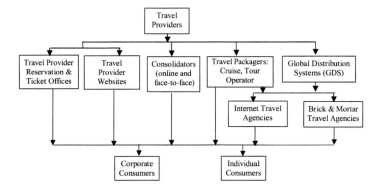

1. Traditional (brick and mortar) travel agents serving an increasingly smaller pool of individual customers who do not wish to spend the time and effort in searching for lower-priced travel.
2. Traditional travel agents serving the corporate market, whose margins are increasingly eroded by competition on customer rebates and by commission-limiting strategies on the part of airlines and other travel providers.
3. Consolidators whose business is increasingly threatened by the dynamic pricing strategies of online and direct sales channels.
4. Online travel agents who serve the corporate market and price-sensitive individuals.
5. Travel providers selling directly to companies and individuals, all of whom are price-sensitive and have excellent information about alternatives.

A Competitive Analysis of Changes in the Air Travel Industry

This section uses Porter's five-force model to analyze the impact of new technologies on competition in the air travel industry (Porter & Millar, 1985). This model analyzes the relative competitive pressures exerted on a firm (or type of firm, in this case) by five different industry "forces": direct competitors, new market entrants, substitute products/services, suppliers and customers of the firm. The most significant threats to the firm are then analyzed to determine how information technology can be used to reduce or sidestep the pressure.

Initially, the search time and cost that an individual would have to incur, in telephoning to discover information about alternative flights and airfares far outweighed the inconvenience of visiting a travel agent. The commission fees paid to travel agents were also applied to direct bookings made by individuals, so there was no cost or convenience advantage in not using a travel agent. Travel agents only competed with each other on service rather than cost. The service element mainly consisted of local knowledge about which airlines offered the best schedule from local airports to a

Figure 4. An industry analysis of the non-computerized airline industry

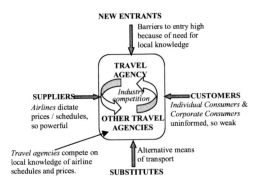

particular destination and which airline's price structure was most attractive. The role of specialized system knowledge and local knowledge about airline schedules and pricing structures gave individual agents an advantage over other agents.

The use of direct reservation systems by travel agents raised the barriers to entry for those agents who were not early adopters of these systems. As airlines were competing with each other, to achieve market penetration, direct reservation system terminals and connections were often installed free of charge by the airlines. However, the investment required in training was high and late adopters of the new technology struggled to keep up. Once a critical mass of directly connected travel agents was achieved and flights could be entered in multiple systems, airlines were able to offer dynamic pricing, raising fares during periods of high demand and lowering fares during periods of low demand. Local knowledge on the part of travel agents became less important, as it rapidly became out of date and travel agents could only compete on the level of personal service that they offered. Exploiting their power, in the 1980s, the airlines began to adopt differential pricing, favoring travel agents purchasing more than a certain value of flights from in a month. Many small agents lost business as a result and had to introduce an additional fee to consumers, making them even more uncompetitive. Consumers lost out, as there was an incentive for larger agents to place as much business as possible with a preferred airline, whether or not this airline offered the best deal for the consumer. However, direct reservations were still not available to consumers, so consumers remained uninformed about choices and locked in to travel agents.

Two recent trends have affected the air travel product-market. An IS application that has radically changed the market for travel agents is the emergence of global distribution systems (GDS), which serve as the main channel for airline ticket distribution in the USA. The evolution of SABRE from a direct reservation system for airline tickets into a GDS serving airlines, hotels, car rental, rail travel and cruise lines is one example. Many other GDSs are in operation today, lowering the costs of entry into the travel agent market immensely, although the subscription and booking fees are now more significant for small companies (Elias, 1999). The advent of GDS has changed the balance of power and the main players in the air travel industry and diversified travel agents into selling multiple products, all of which can be reserved in real time. As shown in Appendix 1, most of the major Global Distribution Systems are owned by consortia of airlines, allowing them to specialize in dynamic pricing over a subset of travel providers.

The second development is an increasing familiarity with Internet technology, on the part of consumers. The second is the replacement of traditional travel agents with online travel agents. As an initial response to use of the Internet by consumers, airlines attempted dis-intermediation (cutting out the middleman). By selling direct to the consumer, airlines were able to offer prices and value-added services unavailable to travel agents. Nevertheless, while dis-intermediation offers cost and value-added benefits to the consumer, it does not add a great deal of convenience. Online travel agents, such as Travelocity (a vertical integration venture by the SABRE Technology Group), Expedia and Orbitz emerged to fill the void. The specialized technology required to make direct bookings is now available to the consumer, often at lower cost (in terms of time and effort) than booking through a traditional travel agent. However, an examination of the major online travel agents and Global Distribution Systems shows that airlines are once again consolidating their ownership of the major distribution channels, to the probably disadvantage of bricks and mortar travel agents.

A Tale of Two Markets: How Local Environments Affect the Strategic Impact of IS

It is interesting to examine the differences in e-commerce impact between the USA and Europe. The single derivation of most USA Telcos (local telephony providers, which mainly originated from the demerger of the Bell Corp group of companies) meant that they adopted a homogenization of charging structures. USA telephony charging structures earn revenue mainly through the provision of long distance and value-added services. The provision of local telephony services has, until recently, been seen as a base cost of providing access to the network and has been charged accordingly, leading to essential free (or very low cost) local telephone calls. In Europe, on the other hand, a multiplicity of small nations, each with different cultures and funding structures led to a telephony environment which was, until fairly recently, hostile to cross-company traffic. Revenue was therefore earned mainly through local (and local long-distance) calls, rather than long-distance traffic in the USA sense of the word. Peak-hour local calls in the USA average at about seven cents per call (of up to 24 hours). Peak-hour local calls in Europe can cost 50 cents a minute.

Figure 5. The air travel industry as affected by global distribution systems

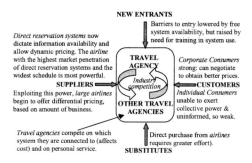

It is not surprising then that the uptake of Internet access has been much higher in the USA than in Europe. While most companies in the USA have a Web site and the majority of these conduct some sort of business via that Web site (even if not fully automated), most of the smaller companies in Europe are still trying to figure out how to install a Web site and what to do with it, once they have it. Consumers are relatively unsophisticated, compared to American consumers, with a commensurately lower level of trust in Internet transactions (IBM, 2000). The travel industry in Europe has not been affected by new information technologies to anywhere near the same extent as the USA travel industry. Internet-based travel sales constituted only $2.2 billion or 1.2% of the European market in the year 2000 (Marcussen, 1999, 2001). However, this figure was an increase from 0.45% in 1999 and even the European bricks-and-mortar travel market is beginning to be described as "beleaguered." In contrast, USA Internet-based travel bookings are booming. In 1998, 2.08% of the travel market (by value) was transacted over the Internet. This figure is predicted to rise to 7.5% by 2003 (Elias, 1999). The winnings European travel agents will; be those who respond to changes in the market environment by employing newer technologies early in the game. As with the development of SABRE and the success of the online travel agent Orbitz (see the next section), exploiting market structures opportunistically through IT innovation leads to high rewards.

CURRENT CHALLENGES/PROBLEMS FACING THE ORGANIZATION

Trends in the Travel Industry

Influences on the air travel industry include increased competition through globalization, changing customer lifestyles, and the perception of risk that consumers attach to air travel. Some market trends include increased consumer knowledge about product offerings (driven by more direct marketing and also the ease of comparison that the Internet affords), higher customer expectations of convenience, added value through the customization of offerings, increased consumer affluence and the more intense exploitation of leisure time to "get away." All of these factors tend to increase consumer power, allowing consumers to exert more leverage on the industry in terms of pricing and choice. However, they also increase the total market size: sales in the first quarter of 2002 exceeded those in the first quarter of 2001 significantly (Jupiter, 2001). In 2000, leisure travelers (55%) outnumbered business travelers (37%)—the other 8% of travelers were those who combined business and pleasure (Heartland, 2001).

The bundling of a variety of products and services into an attractive package is made possible by the exploitation of preferential pricing to a value-added provider (normally a travel agent). The ability to access "value-added" services has recently been offered to travel agents through a variety of real-time, online reservation systems. Travel agents who exploit online reservation systems do not have to sell their packages to consumers online, although they may have to strive to compete with the convenience of those who do. Bundling gives travel agents more power, as they can present the consumer with more attractively priced product bundles than if the consumer buys these services separately and may add value with items that the consumer would not have thought to add, such as a bottle of iced champagne waiting in the room!

Air travel bookings provide U.S. travel agents with the majority of their revenue (Heartland, 2001). On average, 54% of travel agents' revenues accrue from air travel bookings. Cruises account for 19% of revenue (margins are higher on sale of cruises, but this also may be threatened as cruise operators increasingly employ direct sales channels). Hotel bookings provide 11% of revenue, car rentals 8% and sale of rail tickets and other services provide 8%. Hence, direct and online sales of air tickets represent a huge threat to the survival of most travel agents. Coupled with the year-on-year cuts in airline commission payments to travel agents, as a percentage of sales value, and a similar trend in other commissions, such as hotel bookings (Heartland, 2001), travel agents may well struggle to survive. Unless they can find a way to differentiate their products and services, the smaller travel agents will not survive for long.

Technology trends include the ever-increasing sophistication of data mining and customer relationship management software (providing detail on both patterns of purchases and hypotheses for the motivation behind purchases), increasingly seamless connectivity between systems and the ubiquitous availability of trustworthy, secure online purchasing. Such technological advances mostly benefit the airlines. Because of the amount of information that they can collect about their customers and the impact of various pricing and marketing strategies—all in real time and collated by geographical region and some demographics—airlines can leverage direct sales channels to a high degree. They can then exploit the brand recognition of their direct channel online sites and can offer differential pricing to preferred customers. Airline direct channel sales could well offer a challenge to online travel agents, in the future, particularly when catering to frequent flier consumers. This may cause tension between the preference and price structures allocated to indirect sales channels (travel agents) and direct sales channels (their own online reservation systems), as there is obviously more profit in disintermediation. There has been a recent trend of airline mergers, which effectively combine multiple travel routes and result in less competition on any particular route. Airlines have significantly increased their direct sales, and in some cases doubling these sales between 2000 and 2001 (Heartland, 2001). Effective customer relationship management systems may now permit airlines to lock customers into using their airlines, through frequent flier programs, an element that has been missing in the industry until now, since most frequent fliers belong to several airline schemes.

The Challenge for E-Commerce Transactions

Individual e-commerce customers are demanding and often unforgiving. They expect page downloads in less than eight seconds and expect to complete the shopping process in less than ten minutes from when they open the retailer's homepage. They demand convenience, speed and a seamless buying experience. Nearly a quarter of online shoppers stop using the site after a failed transaction. In fact, failure has a serious impact—10% never shop online again (BCG, 2000).

The challenge for airlines, in common with other businesses, will be to offer a consistent customer experience across channels. Customers shopping on an airline Web site expect the same level of service that they would get through a travel agent. Customers buying airline tickets via a third-party Web site, such as Travelocity, expect the same sort of treatment, including recognition of frequent flier privileges. In an increasingly connected world, online customers expect a consistent experience via Palm devices and mobile phones. There may well be a role in the future for e-commerce wireless portals, connecting consumers to online travel agents, direct channel sales and perhaps even allowing the consumer to customize their own, value-added bundle of travel products. If travel agents are proactive in their use of online technologies, they may survive and even remain competitive. However, the corporate market is more susceptible to disintermediation by the airlines, which see the development of business-to-business markets as the most significant of their long-term strategies (IBM, 2000). It is ironic that the industry that originally limited direct sales to corporate customers because the cost-overhead of dealing with individual customers could more profitably be mediated by travel agents is now returning to that position once again.

A consequence of e-commerce purchasing is the commoditization of products and services sold via e-commerce direct distribution channels (Kalakota & Whinston, 1996). With increasing information about product and service features and pricing, consumers tend to treat direct channel products and services as interchangeable. This is particularly true for online services, such as travel bookings, where the service provider is acting as an intermediary for third-party products and services. Consumers will increasingly see both online and traditional service-providers as interchangeable, as their experience of comparing online prices increases. The theory is that consumers select their service-provider based on price. However, Gallaugher (199) argues that both product and service brands are significant in reducing the impact of commoditization. Users have difficulty locating product and service information on the Internet and so rely on known brands to reduce the effort in locating a trustworthy purchase. This presents a way for travel agents to reduce the threat from direct sales by airlines. However, the challenge for travel agents is to differentiate their offering. Some ways of achieving this are by building a strong agency brand, by identifying a less price-sensitive niche target market segment (e.g., affluent senior citizens) whose needs they anticipate better than competitors, or by reducing search time and effort. Analysts at Jupiter (2001) found that poor customer service in the travel industry disproportionately affected consumer perceptions of a travel agency or airline brand. Seventy-nine percent of consumers said they would be less likely to buy airline tickets online a second time from a company with which they had a poor experience and 54% said that the experience would adversely affect their future off-line relationship with that company. Most consumers appear to prioritize communication about delays and cancellations—this is a differentiated service opportunity for the right travel agent.

Increasingly, we see online travel agents attempting to differentiate their service from that of their competitors. Expedia promotes their service on the basis of a powerful information system search capability that allows users to find more combinations on pricing and schedules than their competitors; users can sort flights by price, flight duration and departure times. Travelocity has responded by revamping its information systems to provide innovative search facilities—for example, a user can select a flight based on destination and fare, and then view a three-month calendar of the flight's availability. This echoes the lesson learned from SABRE: branding is not enough to provide competitive advantage in a high-rivalry, turbulent product-market characterized by rapid technological change. However, most of the online travel agents are owned by, or have very close ties to, a major Global Distribution System company (GDS are global, computer reservation systems). The exception to the dominance of a few major GDS companies is provided by Orbitz (see Appendix 1 for ownership), who have created their own GDS software. GDS fees accounted for 4.72% of an air ticket's cost, in 2000 (Kasper, 2000). Orbitz created their own software in response to their perception that there are flaws in the major GDS software packages that eliminate "the overwhelming majority of itineraries from consideration before they are checked for prices" (Kasper, 2000). Coupled with the high concentration of the market between the major players (see Appendix 1 for the year 2000 online travel market share figures), the major GDS companies dominate the market and bias the competitive offerings (Kasper, 2000). Orbitz strategy is to offer access to all airfares—including the very small percentage of fares offered only by airlines directly through their own Web sites (as airlines pay no GDS fees on these fares, direct-booking fares may be significantly lower). In return for providing Orbitz with all fares that they offer, the airline receives a significant discount on the booking fees that a carrier pays for bookings through an online travel agent such as Travelocity or Expedia. Complaints from competitors, accusing them of giving preference to major airlines, resulted in a DOT audit of Orbitz that concluded that they had spurred competition in the market. However, this innovative technology may not change the face of competition and lower prices for consumers in the long term. Orbitz introduced a booking fee for customers in December 2001. It is debatable whether this is because of low online sales margins (a consequence of highly price-sensitive customers) or an experiment on the part of the major airlines that own Orbitz (see Appendix 1), to test the market's willingness to pay for online bookings.

It can be seen, then, that an effective information system platform is the basis for success in this market, whether the service provider is a brick and mortar travel agent, an online agent or a direct-channel airline provider. Successful companies need to *evolve* a set of systems, developed in response to business needs and technical opportunities. Continual evolution alone is not the success factor, but continual evolution in combination with the opportunistic exploitation of opportunities offered by the industry environment. As we saw in the comparison of the European market with that of the USA, differences in the structure of the local market environment require different technical responses.

The Future of the Air Travel Industry

All is not doom and gloom: brick and mortar travel agents are beginning to exploit the new technologies, to add value and information services to their basic service package. To this factor is attributed the rise of travel agent revenues in the USA, which rose 25% in 1998 (Kellendar, 1999). A report by Heartland (2001) argues that smaller travel agents are becoming increasingly uncompetitive, given squeezed margins, reducing commissions and cherry picking of higher-value custom by online travel agents and by airlines. The question is, to whom is the increased business going?

In the individual consumer market, are sales going to the traditional travel agent, hampered by older technology in booking flights and tinkering at the margins? Alternatively, are they going to the new, online travel agents, establishing radical brand images and innovative ways of obtaining a low-cost, high-quality package?

In the corporate travel market, are sales going to the traditional travel agent, who reduce the search time and effort of corporate travel buyers, but whose profit margins are squeezed at both ends: by corporate rebate negotiations and by airline commission reductions? Are they going to the online travel agents, whose economies of scale can support radical discount strategies? On the other hand, are they going to the airlines, whose direct sales channels can offer dynamic bulk pricing and who have the ability to squeeze out indirect channel service providers by limiting availability and by employing differential pricing? The major airlines see corporate direct sales as their most strategic market opportunity, long-term. Given the airlines' ownership of the major online travel agencies and their ability to set commission levels for their competitors, this strategy may well be highly successful.

REFERENCES

AMR. (2002). History section from corporate Web site. Retrieved from http://www.amrcorp.com

BCG. (2000, March). *Winning the online consumer* (Consultancy Report). Boston Consulting Group.

Clemons, E. K., & Hann, I-H. (1999). Rosenbluth international: Strategic transformation of a successful enterprise. *Journal of Management Information Systems, 16* (2) 9-28.

Elias, E. (1999). *Internet commerce: Transforming the travel industry* (Business Report). SRI Consulting.

Gallaugher, J. M. (1999). Internet commerce strategies: Challenging the new conventional wisdom. *Communications of the ACM, 42*(7) 27-29.

Heartland. (2001). *E-commerce's impact on the air travel industry* (Report SBAHQ-00-M-0797). Heartland Information Research Inc. Prepared for U.S. Govt. Small Business Administration, Washington, DC.

Hopper, M. D. (1990). Rattling SABRE—New ways to compete on information. *Harvard Business Review, 90*(3), 118-125.

IBM. (2000). *eBusiness: Is Europe ready?* (Consultancy Report). Commissioned jointly with *The Economist.*

Jupiter. (2001, December). *Relationship management in the travel industry: Improving customer retention cost-effectively through proactive alerts* (Consultancy Report). Jupiter Media Metrix.

Kalakota, R., & Whinston, A. (1996). *Frontiers of electronic commerce.* Reading, MA: Addison Wesley.

Kasper, D. (2000). *The competitive significance of Orbitz* (White Paper). LECG Consulting. Retrieved from Orbitz corporate Web site.

Kellendar, P. (1999). E-travel: The future takes flight. *Computing Japan, 6*(1).

Marcussen, C. H. (1999, March). *Internet distribution of European travel and tourism services.* Report for Research Centre of Bornholm, Denmark.

Marcussen, C. H. (2001, March). *Quantifying trends in European Internet distribution.* Report for Research Centre of Bornholm, Denmark (original from March/May 2000; updated March 2001).

Porter, M. E. & Millar, V. E. (1985, July-August). How information gives you competitive advantage. *Harvard Business Review*.

SABRE. (2002). History section from corporate Web site. Retrieved from http://www.sabre.com

ENDNOTES

[1]   Year 2000 *online travel sales market* share figures, obtained from Kasper (2000).

[2]   Year 2000 *GDS bookings market* share figures, derived from Sabre investor relations section on corporate Web site.

[3]   American turned Sabre into an independent company in March 2000.

[4]   The market share figure given is that of CheapTickets.com, another brand used by the same company.

[5]   Terra Lycos is the world's third largest Internet portal (according to the Amadeus corporate Web site).

[6]   Worldspan is a key strategic business partner of Expedia.com, but not owner.

[7]   USA Networks Inc., a Microsoft business partner, acquired Expedia from Microsoft in July 2001.

[8]   Source: Priceline.com corporate Web site

[9]   Rosenbluth is a large bricks-and-mortar travel agent.

APPENDIX 1

Ownership of Online Travel Agents and Major GDS

Online Agency (Market Share[i])	Owning/Partner GDS (Market Share[ii])	Part-Owners	Notes
Travelocity.com (39%)	Sabre (50%)	American (divested)[iii]	Sabre manages US **Airways** reservations systems. **Yahoo.com** is also a strategic partner.
Trip.com (4%[iv])	Galileo (24%)	United, Cendant	Also operates **cheaptickets.com**
OneTravel.com	Amadeus (8%)	Air France, Iberia, Lufthansa	Acquired **Advantage Travel**, a large Texas travel agency and have a strategic partnership with **Terra Lycos**[v].
Orbitz.com (Kasper (2000) predicts 2% share by 2004)		American, Continental, Delta, United, Northwest	Orbitz "reengineer older technologies", using their own software, to avoid Computer Reservation System fees
Expedia.com (24%)	Worldspan[vi]	USA Networks Inc.[vii]	Microsoft market Expedia through their MSN network. Ticketmaster is a strategic partner.
	Worldspan (18%)	Northwest, Delta, TWA	TWA merged with American Airlines in 2001
Priceline.com (10%)	Strategic alliance with OneTravel.com announced in 2001		Almost 20% of business comes from online partner sites such as AOL and Travelocity.com[viii]
Biztravel.com		Rosenbluth[ix]	Discontinued operations, Sept. 2001

Source: Heartland (2001), airlines' and their business partners' corporate Web sites

Susan Gasson is an assistant professor in the College of Information Science and Technology at Drexel University, USA. Following a career in data communications systems design and consultancy, she earned an MBA and a PhD from Warwick Business School in the UK. Dr. Gasson's research interests include agile IS support for competitive organizations and collaboration in cross-functional IS requirements analysis and design.

This case was previously published in *Annals of Cases on Information Technology*, Volume 5/ 2003, pp. 234-249, © 2003.

Chapter XXI

Management & Delivery of Digital Print via the Web:
A Case Study of Gaia Fulfilment

Savvas Papagiannidis, University of Newcastle upon Tyne Business School, UK

Feng Li, University of Newcastle upon Tyne Business School, UK

EXECUTIVE SUMMARY

In this chapter, we use the experience of Gaia Fulfilment to demonstrate the challenges of developing and deploying collateral fulfillment, that is, short-run print on demand via the Web. By discussing the technological innovations that Gaia achieved we will outline their product development steps and the solutions the technology enabled. We also show the benefits of collateral fulfillment by presenting two examples of customers that use Gaia's technology. The chapter concludes with the challenges that Gaia faced and ways they attempted to resolve them.

ORGANIZATIONAL BACKGROUND

The Internet has revolutionized the way SMEs and SoHo (Small Office Home Office) companies do business. A small organization can have the same "footprint" on the Web as a much larger one. Indeed, some forward thinking organizations are virtual companies, with a huge online presence. However, an area where large enterprises still reign supreme is that of printed material.

There is a long established relationship between volume and price in printing; so the more copies required the greater the quality per unit cost spent. SMEs often present their products well on the Web, but cannot justify expensive traditional printing for short runs. Inevitably, products that have taken years of work are ultimately presented on print from inexpensive desktop printers. Even larger organizations face major challenges when it comes to short print runs.

In 2001 Gaia Fulfilment (http://www.gaia-fulfilment.com), with support from Xerox, started developing a print-on-demand solution. Not unlike Gutenberg, who took existing technologies like ink, paper, a wine press, metal letters and created a new technology, Gaia took the Internet, Lotus Domino (or simply Domino) and the Docucolor 2060 and invented a new technology—collateral fulfillment—true full color short run digital print over the Web.

Offering collateral fulfillment over the Web was the key to the success of the technology as the Internet can facilitate the effective ordering and monitoring process, which is extremely important especially when it comes to a large number of transactions, e.g., in B2B. Although printing over the Web rarely features at the top of the Internet based "killer applications," such as video-on-demand (Ayres & Williams, 2004), it is hard to see how this technology would have been viable without the Internet. As "the use of the Internet will lead to a generation of a wider range of new product ideas" (Ozer, 2003) more technologies like digital printing will find their way to market.

"Given its speed, convenience, interactivity the Internet can help firms collect, categorize and use information needed for product development, enable them to understand their market better and, hence, help them reduce the fuzziness in the new product development process. In addition, the Internet can facilitate the collaboration of different people who are involved in product development, increase the speed and the quality of new product testing and validation and improve the effectiveness and the efficiency of manufacturing development and new product launch. Thus, there seems to be a match between the offerings of the Internet and the different requirements of the new product development process" (Ozer, 2003), which can result to the minimization of risks, especially when developing new technologies.

Gaia was established as a Private Limited company for the sole purpose of delivering print-on-demand over the Web. Its founders were Andy Bex (technical director) and Ian Scanlan (sales director). Both of them still (2004) lead the company. Andy Bex has been the managing director of two other IT companies: an IBM partner software development house and an IT-training agency. He is a principal certified Lotus professional and a member of the Association of Project Managers. Ian Scanlan worked for 15 years with Xerox, in sales, before starting Gaia. Their combined skill set and experience naturally lead to a printing solution over the Web. These skills are of key significance as lack of managerial, technical and marketing skills are a common component of underperformance in start-up companies (Kakati, 2003). Added to their skills was the entrepreneurial attitude of the two directors which led them to attempt to exploit a market opportunity. In a Schumpeterian view they carried out a technological innovation through a new combination of tools: by introducing a new method of production, Gaia contributed in the establishment and expansion of a new market (Schumpeter, 1934).

Gaia chose a flat management structure, with nearly its entire business process being outsourced, apart from the Domino-related development, marketing and support. All administration and facilities are bought in from a print partner. Development and infrastructure is managed by Andy Bex with all development being outsourced to two companies. Sales and marketing activities, managed by Ian Scanlan, are through a two-tiered reseller channel with the first tier being the print partners who have licensed Gaia's technology and the second tier being independent resellers interacting via a dedicated Web technology. This effectively reduced to a minimum standing overhead and allows the company to be managed with by a handful of staff.

This allowed the two directors, to focus on what they are best at. Andy Bex said:

As managing director of my last development house, I found that most of my energy was spent managing people; so for Gaia I chose not to have any staff and to outsource everything. This has allowed the company to reduce its cost base and to quickly change direction, if needed.

Indeed, Gaia had to change their direction a few times while developing their products in the first two years, mainly addressing rising customer demand and expectations. In this way Gaia was able to generate not only the necessary funds to keep the business going, but also continue the development work.

Gaia's revenue model is based on retaining a small percentage of the value of each document printed. The benefits of this model are that there no direct costs and the solution is scalable without a significant increase in overheads; the disadvantage with this model is that it takes time to grow the revenue, which is why it is crucial to minimize ongoing overheads. For the fiscal year 2004-2005 Gaia forecast sales of around one million pounds, with sales generated by their five products:

1. gMail, a mailer tool for direct mail applications, with direct access to more than 47 million UK business and residential names and addresses.
2. gBuild, a document building tool, which utilizes variable data, such as text, images, font and color properties and PDF (Portable Document Format) pages to compile a document.
3. gBrand, a tool that prints PDFs directly and also delivers branded collateral (for example resellers can have their information on their brochures).
4. gCRM, a template driven tool that imports information through an XML (eXtensible Markup Language) file, for example to create property window cards for real estate agents.
5. gMailPDF, a tool to mail a PDF file to multiple recipients.

These applications are appropriate for most market places. However, certain vertical markets have been targeted specifically (for example IT and real estate) as these have ongoing fulfillment challenges. The IT sector faces challenges with obsolescence due to product specifications changing regularly, while the real estate sector have significant management, cost and quality issues with property details sheets, a continuing print requirement.

In addition, Gaia's marketing has targeted larger SMEs, because for corporate clients it was perceived that the sales cycle was too long and for smaller SMEs and B2C solutions the setup and management was too lengthy.

This case focuses on the benefits that digital printing can bring to an organization.

SETTING THE STAGE

Since Gutenberg first pressed ink onto paper in 1452 traditional printing has had an undeniable relationship between cost and volume. Traditional color print presses take a good deal of setting up to produce the first document and create a lot of waste. As a result the first document is extremely expensive, but as the volume increases this overhead is absorbed until the customer is only paying for the ink and paper. It is common to be offered print at a cost of x, but then to be offered double the amount of print for only $x+x/10$.

This creates an inevitable cycle:

Print more than is needed because reprint is expensive.

Remove specific or local information to maintain shelf-life.

Logistical infrastructure to store and distribute remnant.

This cycle has several issues:

- Resistance to change print output.
- High volume requirement, which results into low volume being excluded.
- Fear of error increases lead time from concept to print.
- Distribution on a push system with excessive documents distributed.

The print industry has tried to resolve this over the years, with organizations like Xerox, Indigo and Xeikon developing digital technologies. These were initially in black and white and then in full color. As with all new technologies, the first large scale color digital presses were expensive, unreliable, complex and with poor quality output. By the start of the new millennia Xerox (http://www.xerox.com) had finally produced an inexpensive, simple to use printer, capable of matching any press for quality—the Docucolour 2045/60.

It had then become possible to achieve short run color print with very little setup cost, effectively giving digital print a flat line for cost. Theoretically this meant that the per unit cost was the same for one, 10 or 1,000 copies, so digital presses could cost-effectively provide short run jobs.

Technically digital print had come of age, but theory did not match reality. Although it was quick and easy to set up print jobs on digital presses; there still remained many complex business and quality processes, which increased costs, such as manually invoicing and manually proofing a job.

Added to this was the print industry's resistance to change and its focus on customer service; historically the print industry is very conservative and sees technical innovation as a threat rather than an opportunity. Most print organizations perceive their differentiator as customer service requiring significant manual intervention in the print process and therefore are not open to automated customer self-help solutions. As a result, although the technology was capable of producing a single print at cost y, the printer still needed to proof the print, impose it on the printer RIP (Raster Image Processor: a device, usually hardware but can be software, that takes information about a page and converts it into a bitmap for printing), distribute and invoice the customer. The invoice alone could easily cost $10*y$.

The answer to this final element was to create a "no touch" solution streamlining the process from customer to printer, which requires little human interaction. The obvious means for this solution was the Internet.

CASE DESCRIPTION

While working together delivering a print solution for a large UK building society Andy Bex and Ian Scanlan recognized the potential collateral fulfillment and incorporated Gaia Fulfilment for the sole purpose of developing a collateral fulfillment software solution.

The solution that Gaia developed consists of two elements, the back-end which is based on Lotus Domino (http://www.lotus.com) and the front-end based on PHP (Figure 1).

The back-end manages the user accounts, storage of files (such as JPG, EPS and PDF files) and also allows printer partners to set up, to manage and to track the print jobs. The data kept in Domino is stored in three databases. User accounts are kept in gUser, resource files such as images and PDFs are kept in gStore, while orders are kept in gPrint. A fourth database, gSite, is used as a global database, containing documents that are shared among the clients, for example image libraries or generic templates.

A key feature of Domino that made it an attractive option is its advanced replication technology. Replication allows a no-touch synchronization of the printer's server with the Gaia servers. Lotus has been leading this technology for many years. Andy Bex had experienced this whilst developing several document management solutions in Domino. The replication technology is crucial to the solution, as it allows files to be moved intelligently across the relatively narrow pipes of the Internet, ensuring that all the significant file transfers occurred locally on the printers relatively wide-band local area network (LAN).

This is crucial in Gaia's concept of decomposition of print. Most online printing solutions aim to create a PDF document live on the Web and then move it to the printer, usually via file transfer protocol (FTP). If the document is then re-ordered, the whole

Figure 1. Back-end and front-end structures of Gaia's technology

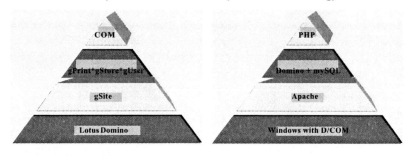

document must be moved again. With Gaia's decomposition technology the constituent parts of the print job are moved using replication. If the job is re-ordered or even modified and re-ordered, these elements do not have to be moved again, as they are already resident on the printer's LAN, thus massively reducing the usage of bandwidth. The technology used to compose the documents when they arrive at the printer's end is Xerox's proprietary VIPP (Variable Intelligent Postscript PrintWare).

The front-end is based on PHP (http://www.php.net) and mySQL (http://www.mysql.com) running on Apache (http://www.apache.org). All three of them are open source software. They have been extensively used in demanding projects and were found to be reliable. In fact, Apache is the leading software in the Web server market. A decision not to hold all data in Domino was taken early in the development process as Domino is well-suited to store rich text, but not relational data; so mySQL was employed to store relational application data.

In the early stages of development an order was generated in PHP, consisting of a DBF (a text file format, specific to VIPP and not dBase) file. This, with all the order elements and an XML file containing order information, were e-mailed to the Domino server. Although this was easy to implement, it had many disadvantages (for example it consumed a lot of bandwidth) and naturally the development process led to the integration of PHP with Domino.

Gaia faced many technical challenges while attempting this integration and found that this area was not well supported or documented. The lack of any similar projects made each development step a formidable task. As such, Gaia's development team first developed a toolkit to perform the required functions and then proceeded to develop the application.

PHP and other ancillary programs communicate with the back-end using the Component Object Model (COM). COM allowed a common interface between the two ends and direct access to Domino, that is, it made possible to read and write directly in the Domino databases from the Web. The team was also able to deploy the Distributed version of COM (DCOM) which made it possible to run the applications in more than one server. For example, a server running the data sources was used to perform queries and return the results to the main Web server without affecting the Web server's normal operation (Figure 2(a)).

An additional important feature of the solution's front-end part is the previewing of the documents, before printing. All Gaia's solutions can produce a low resolution PDF of the final document allowing the client to verify that everything is correct.

Ordering a Document

This section explains in detail how the technology works in order to produce a document. In this example we follow the order process of a mailer, often used in one-to-one marketing. As a result, mailers require the highest level of personalization. "In customer-relationship management it is VDP's (Variable-Data Printing) ability to generate higher response rates and sales through delivery of truly unique, custom documents—including both text and graphics—personalized to each message recipient that has fired the imaginations of marketing people" (Morris-Lee, 2001).

Gaia's gMail application can personalize a template by using data (text and images) that the user provides while ordering. (See Screenshot 1 & 2).

Figure 2(a). All front-end elements communicate with Domino through PHP & COM

Screenshot 1 & 2. Once authenticated, the user is presented with the documents available to Order

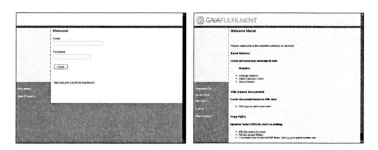

The client enters the Gaia Web site by using his unique username and password. Once the user is authenticated the system offers a list of type of documents available to order, for example mailers or PDFs. The list is generated by accessing the gPrint database and requesting all the templates that are associated with the user's account. (See Screenshot 3 & 4).

Corporate users may have a list of bespoke templates that they can use for their mailing campaigns. These carry all the corporate artwork and the appropriate print settings. If bespoke templates are not found, the system offers generic templates that can be customized using artwork that is uploaded by the user.

Each template has a number of options that the user has to respond to. For example, if the mailer is for a real estate company the template may ask the user to specify the type of property (e.g., semi-detached) or ask the user to select an image from an image library. The images come from gStore, if they have been uploaded by the user, or from gSite, if

Screenshot 3 & 4. User is asked to select type of mailer and enter corresponding content-related options

Screenshot 5 & 6. Using the electoral roll to perform a search for recipients who live in an area of a specific postcode and the user is asked whether an extra copy is required for verification purposes

they belong to a generic image library. The template options are stored in the mySQL database, as they are relational.

The user responds to these options by entering the answers in a form-based tool, as shown in Screenshot 4. The answers are then used to compile the content that will be used for the final document. In this case, entering "semi-detached house" results in: "We are currently instructed to sell a semi-detached house".

The user then performs a search using one of the available data-sources (e.g., the electoral role which contains 1.5 million organizations and more than 46.5 million people) and specifies whether an extra copy for verification is required or not. Alternatively, the user can upload a CSV (comma separated value) file with the recipients' information. This format was selected as it is widely used in Microsoft's Office applications (e.g., Excel or Access). When the user places an order the recipient's information is stored in a DBF file which is attached to the order document, stored in gPrint (see Figure 2(b)).

Before ordering, the user has the option to preview the document. The solution generates a low resolution PDF document, which is fully branded with the organizations artwork (e.g., logo), the sender's information (e.g., contact information and signature) and the recipient's details (e.g., "Dear John"). To generate the preview the solution saves

Figure 2(b).

an order (exactly the same as a real order with the exception of single value that specifies the order as of preview type) and all the required files in gPrint. It then outputs all required files (e.g., images, the DBF file, the template and so on) in a temporary directory and process them to create the PDF used for the preview. In this case the final PDF was only 55kb which would only require a few seconds to download.

Printing Process and Distribution

Once an order is received, it is distributed to the print partners (printers) based on the printing requirements. Print partners are printers who are licensed to use the Gaia technology who also have a responsibility to drive print volume up by engaging directly with customers and resellers.

The fulfillment process starts automatically two hours after the order is received providing the user with sufficient time to cancel. This allows Gaia's print partners to print, finish and distribute back to the customer, in most cases, within 24 hours (Figure 3).

This also allows international customers to deliver next day in the United Kingdom, significantly reducing time and postage costs. As international print partners join the Gaia network, Gaia's customers will be able to deliver next day to the countries in which these printers are based (Figure 4).

With Gaia acting as an electronic hub for many print partners across the United Kingdom, Gaia becomes one of the largest printing organizations in the country. The combined print capacity of the Gaia network is approximately 20 million digital color page-prints per month (2004). This number will continue to increase as new print partners join the network. Apart from increasing the print capacity, a new partner could also bring

Figure 3. Flowchart of order processing

Figure 4. Gaia acting as a print broker for many different organizations

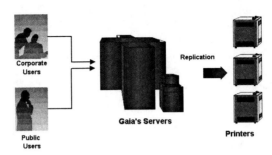

additional finishing capabilities, like binding, stapling, laminating and others, allowing for more varied print runs.

As discussed earlier, the print industry is extremely conservative and even amongst the most innovative digital printers, acceptance of new technology has been difficult to achieve. Gaia's current print partners tend to have entrenched processes and focus on specific vertical markets. Migration of current print partner customers and development of new customers has been slow for a variety of reasons, the most important of which are:

- The print partners lack specific skills for management of digital print over the Web, for example authoring VIPP documents.
- Customers on existing technologies that are working are left as they are even though significant benefits can be gained by migrating to Gaia's technology.
- Print partners are generally themselves SMEs and tend to lack the required resources to fully implement Gaia's technology.

Benefits of Collateral Fulfillment

Technology itself is not an innovation unless it delivers real benefits. Instead of listing the benefits that collateral fulfillment can deliver, these are discussed by presenting the benefits that two organizations operating in different markets, Perle and Chesterton, gained when using collateral fulfillment. The two examples aim to demonstrate that collateral fulfillment can deliver value to any organization that faces print-challenges.

Perle: Background

Perle Systems is a leading developer, manufacturer and vendor of high-reliability and richly featured networking products. These products are used to connect remote users reliably and securely to central servers for a wide variety of business applications. Product lines include serial/terminal servers, console servers, multi-port serial cards, multi-modem cards, routers, remote access servers, emulation adapters, print servers and network controllers. Perle has offices and representative offices in 12 countries in North America, Europe and Asia and sells its products through distribution channels worldwide.

The Challenge

Perle's challenges were like those of many other organizations operating through a global distribution channel: printed collaterals for many products, to many customers, often in several different languages. Historically, this problem had been resolved by printing 5,000 of each product brochure for each language, resulting in a good price per page. Each new product would then be shipped immediately in blocks of 50, with any remnant being stored. Once a product brochure ran out, another order of 5,000 would be placed. In total Perle supported 134 documents. This solution caused many problems:

1.   **Print cost:** Although the actual cost per page was attractive using runs of 5,000 on litho press, the true cost was not. The reality was that many of the documents were either not being delivered due to obsolescence or were being distributed to channel partners who did not want them. For example, a channel partner may have only been selling one or two main product lines, but would still receive brochures for all products.

2.   **Storage:** A hidden cost to the brochure supply was the time and effort of staff to manage the storage and distribution of the brochures. In addition the physical storage space came at a cost.

3.   **Obsolescence:** Perle's products changed quickly and the brochures needed to keep up with these changes. However, once a brochure had gone to print it was impossible to update. This meant either scrapping the print and reprinting an updated version or sending out obsolete brochures.

4.   **Content:** Perle extended the shelf life of their product brochures by not including time sensitive information, but this in itself reduced the value of the collateral.

5.   **Language:** As all print runs were for 5,000 this was excessive for some languages making these documents extremely expensive with huge wastage. Often, this meant that these brochures simply were not printed.

6.   **Time to market:** Time to market was poor, because the content and print took a long time to achieve. Furthermore, if a channel partner required additional prints these had to be handled manually and may have required the printing of a whole new batch.

7.   **Environment:** Perle were concerned about the effect this wastage had on the environment.

8.   **Accountability:** There was very little accountability in the system. Effectively, brochures were dispatched to all channel partners, whether they wanted them or not. It was then almost impossible to gauge interest, knowledge or to compare the brochure requirement directly to sales.

The Solution

In late 2001, Perle migrated onto collateral fulfillment technology. This allowed all of Perle's brochures to be put online and printed-on-demand, by direct request of the channel partner or Perle office. At the time Gaia proposed this technology to Perle there were no alternative digital solutions available at the market. Even after the solution was implemented, competitors who were using Web interfaces were still fulfilling via traditional lithographic printing and therefore lost the benefits of short run digital print.

The benefits that Perle gained were:

- A 60% reduction in print expenditure, mainly due to channel partners and Perle offices only ordering what they required.
- Collateral obsolescence has all but disappeared. As the solution was print-on-demand there was no stock, no stock logistics and therefore no obsolescence.
- Collaterals could be more detailed and could support more languages.
- Partner loyalty was increased as the new technology could brand the printed output with their logo and details.
- A MIS (management information system) and audit trail was available in real time. Perle could directly view who required what product, even to the degree of being able to predict production shortfalls, if a particular product sheet was ordered extensively.
- Time to market was improved both logistically and because management decisions to produce and print new collaterals were no longer cost driven.
- Environmental friendliness. Less print with less waste meant Perle was operating an environment-friendly process.

Perle's challenges were met, with the cost of development being recouped with in the first year, due to the massive print savings. However, at the top of Perle's agenda was always the effective support of their partner channel. Gaia's solution allowed partners to enjoy brochures that were more accurate and timely than before.

Chesterton: Background

As a second example of a real-life application of Gaia's technology we present the experience of Chesterton Residential, a real estate organization based in the United Kingdom. Real estate is a good example of what industries may undergo as they are transformed to information-intensive organizational forms that are supported by ICT according to Nohria and Berkley (as cited in Sawyer, Crowston, Allbritton, & Wigand, 2000).

Chesterton Residential has been at the forefront of the property market since 1805. They have 20 offices (2004) mainly across London, offering a broad selection of properties to buy or rent. They also have specialist departments dealing with new homes and investment properties. Chesterton has approximately 180 members of staff. Their management team consists of a managing director, three main directors and 10 associate directors. They also have 22 managers and 12 assistant managers. Their annual turnover is around £19 million.

Challenges

A key element of an estate agent's daily routine is direct mail to existing and potential customers.

The message of the letters is usually one of the following:

- We have potential buyers, who want to buy a property like yours.
- We have recently sold a property like yours in your street, but have disappointed buyers, who may wish to buy your property.

- We are selling a house near yours; do you know any friends or family that would be interested?

As these messages are location-sensitive they need to be delivered accurately to the correct streets. The simplest solution for most agents is to manually print the letters and walk the appropriate streets mailing these letters, a process that is very inefficient.

Chesterton's main issues were:

- **Cost:** Mail runs were produced on local desktop machines, which were extremely expensive. In addition, the mail runs were taking a long time to manage and distribute.
- **Quality:** The content of the letter was not consistent; each letter was composed by an agent with no company standard. The letters also tended to lack specific information to which the customer could relate to.
- **Accountability:** Chesterton found it impossible to measure the level of mailing activity and therefore could not measure its level of success.

Solution

Gaia Fulfilment deployed gMail for Chesterton, a Web-based solution that enabled local knowledge combined with leading edge print technology to fulfill mailings to the main contact within a household. The one-to-one marketing message was the key to the response success of this product.

The only viable alternative for Chesterton other than their legacy process and Gaia's new solution was to engage with a volume mail house. Many businesses use such facilities but there are significant drawbacks: volume has to be high (10000+) and significant amount of planning and preparation and delay are involved in each mailing. While this is suitable for a general marketing mailer it is not suitable for the activities of real estate agents.

The key benefits that Chesterton received were:

- The cost of each mailer was significantly reduced.
- Significantly less time was required to produce and distribute the letter, freeing up the staff and allowing them to be more productive.
- The company agreed each mailer's content centrally, with the individual agents only being allowed to enter location and property description.
- Each mailer was highly branded with very specific local information that was of interest to the user. For example, the letters sent to a specific property had the recipient's name and address actually in the letter content. Other document elements, such as local images, could also help attract the recipient's attention.
- Accurate online reports were available, allowing Chesterton to manage and monitor the mailing activity. Since the implementation of the new solution Chesterton's management have been able to set accurate budgets for this activity.
- gMail has access to names and addresses of 1.5 million organizations and more than 46.5 million people, allowing Chesterton's much greater scope for their mailing campaigns.

By employing Collateral Fulfilment (gMail) to target specific streets in high value areas of Central London, Chesterton enjoyed a 10-fold increase in listings.

Discussion

In the above two examples, Perle and Chesterton, enjoyed the benefits that Gaia's technology brought. Both organizations committed in using Gaia's technology and assigned one member of staff to monitor the entire process who was trained by Gaia. In many instances the administrator placed orders for the other members of staff, who were later gradually involved in the order process themselves. In such a way they achieved a smooth change of the print fulfillment process, without compromising daily operations. When training was required it was provided by the organization's administrator with Gaia's support.

In order for corporate accounts, like Perle and Chesterton, to be deployed the client has to gather the necessary content that will be used to generate the documents. To streamline this process Gaia produced a checklist of the things that the client was expected to provide.

Gaia's technology is generic and does not have to be "tweaked" in order to be offered to an organization. Hence, Perle and Chesterton users used the same system to place their orders, like all Gaia's customer. This also applies for B2B and B2C usage. With this approach Gaia monitored only one tool that simplified developing and supporting the technology.

Although Gaia's technology can be seen as an automation tool that replaces existing ways of obtaining quality print, in Chesterton's case it has also resulted in a significant reengineering of the company's employees daily routine. As the technology deals with printing and distribution of mailers, they have more time to spend on more productive tasks, like customer support and marketing. This can be of great importance in a market like real estate. "In the past realtor's traditional role was that of an information intermediary. That has been contested by ICT, for example real estate agents once had complete control over access to the MLS listings, this control has been weakened by the development of alternative sources of listing information" (Sawyer et al., 2000; Wigand, Crowston, Sawyer, & Allbritton, 2001). As a result real estate agent found themselves in a defending position against information technology, which they had so openly embraced (for example, the penetration of computer usage grew from 5% of licensed agents in 1995, to nearly 95% in 1999 according to the National Association of Realtors (Sawyer et al., 2000). Still, technology and applications like Gaia's can provide them with the tools to reinvent their marketing strategy and to keep up with the requirements that the market conditions impose.

If "successful reengineering requires that companies first concentrate on crucial business processes that effect competitive factors, customer service, cost reduction, product quality and time-to-market" (Attaran, 2004), then Gaia's solution has certainly achieved this for Chesterton. Of course the focus was not on reengineering the real estate agent's operations. Still the introduction of a new technology naturally led to a chain reaction.

This type of changes may not be met in other organizations using Gaia's technology. For example, Perle used Gaia's technology as a replacement of an existing print source and as such none of their existing processes (apart from ordering print) had to change. In Perle's case Gaia's technology is providing "a new mechanism for performing an old process" (Attaran, 2004), although of course this has brought significant benefits in its own right. Perle were mainly interested in the effective fulfillment of their resellers marketing campaigns, strengthening the resellers access to market and also their perception of the value of working with Perle (Simpson, Siguaw, & Baker, 2001). "A common supplier complaint is that the reseller does not have enough time to adequately represent its product, effective supplier-provided marketing tools, such as lead-generation programs, may encourage the reseller to engage in desired activities" (Gilliland, 2004). By providing high quality branded brochures, Perle provided an effective incentive to enforce their relationship with their resellers and encourage them to market their products.

In Perle's case, Gaia provided a branded frond end that matches Perle corporate site. This allows Perle to direct their resellers to a solution which appears as an integrated part of their site, enforcing their brand awareness. This was not required for Chesterton as the solution was used "internally." Being able to brand the front-end of their technology enables Gaia to offer the solution to resellers, who can then undertake independent marketing and sales initiatives. This allows Gaia to maintain low overheads, as a significant part of their marketing and support is delegated to resellers.

CURRENT CHALLENGES/PROBLEMS FACING THE ORGANIZATION

Since the beginning Gaia has faced a lot of challenges, many of which have yet to be resolved:

- **Too early:** "Right timing of opportunity exploitation is important for high-technology firms as this opportunity window usually lasts only a short time" (Katila & Mang, 2003), especially when it comes to Internet-related technologies. Gaia was keen to get to market first in an attempt to obtain higher market share, although the reality was that the technology was delivered too early. Most of the customer base could not perceive what the offering was. At the same time many in the print industry either wrongly believed that they had a solution or could not see the benefit of it. Since 2001 Gaia has experienced a growing momentum in the digital print revolution and should be well-placed when the market matures. "Variable data printing, or VDP, is evolving from its technological roots to its marketing destiny" (Fultz, 2000).

  In fact this seems to be a matter of time according to digital print professionals surveyed at the 2001 On Demand Digital Printing & Publishing Strategy Conference and Exposition. According to Direct Market (2001), 96% of them expected digital printing or a combination of digital and offset, to replace offset-only as the printing technology of the future.

  Also, the Xerox Corporation survey of commercial printers, quick printers, graphic arts services providers, and other professionals reveals that:
  - 89% of print professionals feel today's (2001) digital color presses provide appropriate quality for most short-run printing jobs;

- 88% of print professionals see digital color as a way to increase their profits; and
- More than 20% expect the amount of variable data printing to increase dramatically in the next year (2002) with 67% expect the amount to increase somewhat.
- **Inertia of printers:** For many years printers have built their reputation on quality, or more accurately on manually resolving all the customer-caused short falls of each job. Collateral fulfillment depends upon short run, but high quality prints, which require a "no-touch" solution. Gaia came across significant resistance to this approach from the print industry that continually wants to map user interaction into the process. With a combination of partner selection, education and positive results Gaia has tried to convince print partners to re-configure their processes. Early feedback indicates that Gaia's efforts have started making a difference.
- **Setup costs:** The deployment of each customer and customer solution takes time and resource, which does not always add up commercially. Gaia is therefore looking at solutions that require no setup and also at ways that could move more of the process to the users.
- **The marketing challenge:** Although in principle print partners could be resellers of Gaia solutions, they have not shown the necessary willingness to commit to marketing the solutions. Among the possible ways forward that Gaia was looking at the beginning of 2004 was the introduction of resellers. A reseller could help Gaia market the products in a wider range covering more markets. They could also help reduce customer management, as resellers would manage their own clients.

By allowing access to their technology but still maintaining ownership and control of it, Gaia can continue to influence their market, past the entry point, which is important as "a pioneering advantage is likely to last longer when firms can impede technology diffusion within the industry" (Coeurderoy & Durand, 2004). In addition as "technology-based innovations require a 'critical' number of adopters in order to be effectively used" (Montaguti, Kuester, & Robertson, 2002) Gaia can increase the pace by allowing partners and resellers to access their technology.

Finding the balance can help Gaia foster the expansion of the market while maintain a leading role in it.

These ongoing challenges have delayed the development of both product development and market penetration. Gaia's management team believes that what is required is a clearer proposition to the market place. More specifically they believe they need to clarify what the technology can achieve, in order to find more applications, and reduce the technical barriers for both print partners and users.

REFERENCES

Anonymous. (2001). Print professionals say digital printing will prevail over offset (Brief Article). *Direct Marketing, 64,* 19.

Attaran, M. (2004). Exploring the relationship between information technology and business process reengineering. *Information & Management, 41*(5), 585-596.

Ayres, R. U., & Williams, E. (2004). The digital economy: Where do we stand? *Technological Forecasting and Social Change, 71*(4), 315-339.

Coeurderoy, R., & Durand, R. (2004). Leveraging the advantage of early entry: proprietary technologies versus cost leadership. *Journal of Business Research, 57*(6), 583-590.

Fultz, P. (2000). Closing the one-to-one loop. *Direct Marketing, 62,* 28.

Gilliland, D. I. (2004). Designing channel incentives to overcome reseller rejection. *Industrial Marketing Management, 33*(2), 87-95.

Kakati, M. (2003). Success criteria in high-tech new ventures. *Technovation, 23*(5), 447-457.

Katila, R., & Mang, P. Y. (2003). Exploiting technological opportunities: The timing of collaborations. *Research Policy, 32*(2), 317-332.

Montaguti, E., Kuester, S., & Robertson, T. S. (2002). Entry strategy for radical product innovations: A conceptual model and propositional inventory. *International Journal of Research in Marketing, 19*(1), 21-42.

Morris-Lee, J. (2001). Getting ready for real-time marketing: Part three. *Direct Marketing, 64,* 26.

Ozer, M. (2003). Process implications of the use of the Internet in new product development: A conceptual analysis. *Industrial Marketing Management, 32*(6), 517-530.

Sawyer, S., Crowston, K., Allbritton, M., & Wigand, R. (2000). *How do information and communication technologies reshape work? Evidence from the residential real estate industry.* Paper presented at the International Conference on Information Systems, Brisbane, Queensland, Australia.

Schumpeter, J. A. (1934). *The theory of economic development.* Cambride: Harvard University Press.

Simpson, P. M., Siguaw, J. A., & Baker, T. L. (2001). A model of value creation: Supplier behaviors and their impact on reseller-perceived value. *Industrial Marketing Management, 30*(2), 119-134.

Wigand, R., Crowston, K., Sawyer, S., & Allbritton, M. (2001). *Information and communications technologies in the real estate industry: results of a pliot survey (Research in progress).* Paper presented at the The 9th European Conference on Information Systems, Bled, Slovenia.

Savvas Papagiannidis graduated from the Physics Department of the University of New Castle upon Tyne. Upon completion of his PhD, he joined the eBusiness Group at the Business School, in the same university. He has started a number of e-business ventures and also worked as a freelance Internet developer. His research interests include management of Internet and emerging technologies, high-technology related entrepreneurship and e-business models.

Feng Li is chair of e-business development at the University of New Castle upon Tyne Business School. His research has centrally focused on the interactions between information systems on the one hand, and strategic and organizational innovations on the other. A particular focus of his current research is on the Internet and e-business, and emerging strategies, business models, and organizational designs in the new economy. He has worked closely with companies in banking, telecommunications, car manufacturing and electronics industries through research, consultancy and executive management programs. His recent work on Internet banking and on telecom pricing models and value networks have been extensively reported by the media.

This case was previously published in the *International Journal of Cases on Electronic Commerce*, 1(1), pp. 1-18, © 2005.

Chapter XXII

Web-Enabling for Competitive Advantage:
A Case Study of Himalayan Adventures

Luvai Motiwalla, University of Massachusetts, Lowell, USA

Azim Hashimi, University of Massachusetts, Lowell, USA

EXECUTIVE SUMMARY

This case emphasis is on the reduction of the logistical aspects of adventure travel and increase in the customer base by using the Web-enabling *information technology resources. A global travel company, Himalayan Adventures (HA), based in Pakistan wants to build a one-stop electronic commerce store for its customers. Through this Web site, HA hopes to provide all of their travel services, visa details, health and safety insurance, weather information, flight reservations, police registration, currency exchange, travel itineraries, sale and purchase of equipment, souvenirs and communication requirements. To implement the online store for HA, the owner, Abdul Bari, is planning to utilize the Porter electronic business model in analyzing the market needs, and identifying the appropriate information technology to gain a strategic advantage. This project, once implemented, will compliment the already existing HA* brick *model with a* bricks-and-clicks *model. On the initial investment of $70,000 per year for three years, the incremental net present value created by the project is $174,079.*

BACKGROUND

Abdul Bari, president of Himalayan Adventures (HA), sat in his office in central Gilgit bazaar looking at the sun set in the majestic Himalayan Mountains. The tourist season for 1998 in Northern Areas of Pakistan (NAP) had just ended. For the next seven months, until April 1999, the foreign or domestic tourists would not be visiting the NAP for climbing, trekking or hiking.

The 1998 season was a turbulent year for the Pakistani tourist industry in general and NAP's tourist industry in particular, which provides the developing country with more than 50% of its $14 billion tourism revenue. Although this turbulence was attributed to the overall decline in customer base after Pakistan and India tested their nuclear devices in summer of 1998, Abdul Bari thought otherwise. After talking to many of his clients, AB knew the real reason was the better logistical arrangements, customer service and lower costs that other foreign competitors were providing to their clients in HA's market segment, namely adventure tourism in the Himalayan and Karakorum mountain ranges of Central Asia. These competitors included the tour operators from Australia, England, Germany, India, Nepal and Bhutan.

As estimated in the World Bank Country Development Report (1999), the travel and tourism market provides Pakistan a total of annual revenue of $14 billion. Four of the 10 highest peaks in the world lie in the NAP, which houses the mountain ranges of Karakorum, Himalaya, Pamir and Hindu-Kush. The rugged beauty of the region, along with its unique culture, offers a potential tourist an experience that is enjoyable, challenging and enriching. The Pakistani Tourism Development Corporation estimates that foreign visitors to the country have explored only 20% of the NAP territories.

HA started as a partnership between a mountain climber and a business student in January of 1995. The main niche or specialty market of the company is trekking, bicycling and the cultural safari tour market, though the company has facilitated mountaineering

Figure 1. Map of Pakistan and the NAP

Table 1. Customer nationality

Country	Market Share
Germany	30%
Australia	25%
New Zealand	20%
Great Britain	10%
Spain	10%
Japan	5%

expeditions in the past. During the tourist season, i.e., May to September, based on tours that have been reserved, the company hires porters and guides, who are then assigned to each visiting group and stay with the group for the duration of the tour. To achieve economies of scale, and for logistic and client safety reasons, the company has always focused on selling its packages to a group of five people. The average customer load per season for the company is between 130-160 customers, with an average profit margin per head at $500.

The Market

One-hundred percent of HA's customer base is of foreign origin. The breakdown in terms of nationalities is shown in Table 1.

Due to the nature of NAP (NAP as supposed to a province of the country, is a federal controlled territory under the supervision of Pakistani Army), all foreigners visiting the area have to appear for a personal interview at the Pakistani Embassy or Mission office in their respective countries before they can be given a permission to visit the NAP. This is often a cumbersome and expensive procedure for potential clients of the HA. In addition, there is often no updated information available to the potential clients on visa details, health immunizations and insurance, currency, weather conditions, baggage and fitness requirements. Furthermore, tourists have no quick way of finding information on the trip packages offered by HA or other travel operators. They often get this information via word of mouth from people who have visited the NAP. To further add to their woes, the marketing and information channels adopted by government departments are inadequate, outdated or incomprehensible. As it currently stands, customers have to refer to many different sources of information for planning their trip. This information is generally gathered in a piece-meal style from multiple Web resources, the Lonely Planet bookstore and other mass media resources.

Himalayan Adventure's Financials

The Profit & Loss statement, since its inception, is shown in Table 2.

SETTING THE STAGE

The Northern Areas of Pakistan (NAP) attract two distinct groups of travelers. First, there are the thrill seekers, who come for the sheer challenge of navigating the challenging landscape of the area, and include the mountain climbers and trekkers. Second, there are groups comprising the mild natured—at least in terms of their adventure spirit—travelers who find less challenging ways to explore NAP, be it through biking, hiking,

Table 2. Income statements of Himalayan adventures

	1995 ($'000)	1996 ($'000)	1997 ($'000)	1998 (Estimated) ($'000)
Revenues	80	100	117	110
Porters	20	20	22	22
Guides	10	10	12	12
Equip. Rental	10	15	15	15
Hotel Rental	25	25	30	30
Other	5	0	5	3
Cost of Sales	70	80	84	82
SG&A Expenses	22.5	10	15.5	13
Pre-Tax Income	(12.5)	10	17.5	15
Taxes (Savings)	(5)	4	7	4
Net Income (Loss)	(7.5)	6	10.5	9

cultural safaris or just visiting the Gilgit, Hunza or Chitral valleys. Unlike major tour operators, who competed aggressively for mountain climbing parties sponsored by local companies, HA due to the limited marketing, logistical and budgetary constraints, competed only in the trekking, mountain biking and the cultural safari tour markets.

Climbing expeditions are contingent on two factors—cooperation of the Pakistani government in granting climbing passes and most importantly the availability of good climbing weather. Out of 12 years that he had been involved in this business, the first five of them as a guide for mountaineering expeditions, Abdul Bari surmised that the actual scaling rate[1] for mountain climbers had been less than 5%. This statistic had a major role to play in turning people away from climbing towards the more rewarding trekking adventures, which are 14-day-plus *hike-a-thons* designed to take tourists to either one or more base camp sites around the mountain ranges and are less contingent on weather severities due to the low altitude exposure. Most of the trekking expeditions are carried out between the altitudes of 9,000 to 17,000 feet. Most importantly they are less expensive and, depending on the tourist demand for a particular Trek,[2] economies of scale are achievable by merging two or more groups, hence reducing the cost for the trek. Seventy percent of HA's clients comprised this group, with the rest being in either the biking (two popular routes are the Karakorum Highway or the silk route ride, and the Gilgit-to-Chitral ride; both rides are in excess of 600 km) or the cultural safari category.[3]

Abdul Bari—The Indigenous Adventurer With an Entrepreneurial Dream

Born in a village in Astore valley, the oldest of seven siblings and made to work at his family's livestock rearing operation when he was just 10, Abdul Bari had little in terms of formal education. Just like many other teenagers in the villages of Northern Areas, he always wanted to work as a guide due to the attractiveness of the wages offered to porters or guides. (A porter can expect to earn $10-15 per day, and in one month can earn more than the average per capita income of the whole Northern Areas; guides generally earn twice the wages offered to porters). As a result, when he was just 15 years old, Abdul Bari started working as a porter, then as a trekking guide and later as a climbing guide for visiting tourists. In just 10 years Abdul Bari had guided through almost every major trek in the Northern Areas and led climbing parties to K-2 (also known as Mount Godwin Austin— the second highest in the world), as well as Nanga Parbat (ninth highest mountain).

CASE DESCRIPTION

Realizing the immense potential that the seasonal adventure tourism offered, Bari took a loan of $20,000 from family members and in 1994 was looking for a business partner when he met Mohammed in January of 1994. Mohammed, who had come to work with an international infrastructure and agricultural development agency operating in the Northern Areas, had been born in Pakistan, but grew up in Europe and did his post-secondary education in Canada.

In 1994, advertising for travel operators was limited to informal referrals to potential customers in Japanese, European and Australian markets through satisfied clients, most of who had actually come to Pakistan and found their own way to Gilgit (570 kms away from a major international airport). Travel operators generally played a passive role in which the potential clients would come to them and negotiate the prices per trek. There was little or no formal line of communication in the pre-trip phases and as such no accurate measure of the demand that tour operators faced could be gauged. This resulted in a loss of potential clientele who would either select tour operators in other countries before they came to Pakistan (through better advertising tactics and security of pre-trip communications) or come to Pakistan's Northern Areas looking for favorable prices, and if the tour operators were over-booked with potential clients, a likely possibility, would end up forfeiting the trek. Abdul Bari wanted to capitalize on this opportunity by starting HA.

Mohammed was interested in Abdul Bari's idea and promised him that while he could not work a full-time position in the company due to his job commitments, he would invest $10,000 in HA for a 30% share and also help Bari start up his company. Thus, in January of 1995, Himalayan Adventures was formed with a start-up capital of $30,000. Their initial marketing strategy included contacting clientele who had visited the NAP, did a trek under Abdul Bari's guidance and had indicated that they knew friends or relatives who would be interested in similar treks, biking tours or safaris.

Operations of Himalayan Adventures

As the tourist season of 1995 began, HA operations comprised the following:

*   A staff of three employees, Bari and two other guides;
*   A leased Jeep for transporting guests in and out; and
*   An office space in central Gilgit Bazaar, and a rented guest lodge serving as a base of operations and as a transit place for trips from and to the airport.

In 1995, HA hosted a total of 13 groups—12 in trekking and a cultural safari—and the company registered a loss due to high start-up costs. The next years saw further increases in business activity and increase in profits, however well below the normal profit levels of other domestic competitors. In the summer of 1996, after working (assisting) at HA for two years, Mohammed left for the United States to pursue an MBA at a university in the Commonwealth of Massachusetts.

In 1998, Abdul Bari expected that, for the third straight year, HA would register a profit of around $10,000—an amount five times lower than its competitors in the domestic market. Abdul Bari would have to sit down and figure out a way to set a direction for his business and turn it into a more profitable venture. One option was an alliance with other tourist operators in NAP. Another option was collaborating with the Pakistan Tourism Development Corporation. A third option was expanding HA business via the Internet. Some of Bari's international clients had mentioned that Internet was becoming a useful business tool, and how they could use the Internet to speed up their pre-adventure planning and allow them to keep in touch with their contacts during their trip. Thus, Abdul Bari was considering which of these three options would be ideal for HA, as the official tourist season came to a close in the NAP.

In late 1998, after having returned from the U.S. only three weeks earlier, Mohammed's phone rang at his desk at the Marketing Division of Citibank in Islamabad, Pakistan. After the pleasantries were exchanged, Abdul Bari informed Mohammed about his concerns for Himalayan Adventures. The conversation is as follows:

Abdul Bari (AB) You know because of the security concerns and better logistics, a lot of tourists who could be our customers are choosing different destinations altogether. This is quite frustrating, and I have had talks with other Tourist Operators in NAP. Business is steadily declining, but HA is in real bad financial position.

Mohammed (M) I see. I am aware of the general decline in the tourist industry, but HA has always under priced its tours to gain competitive advantage.

AB That probably is not enough any longer. Tourists are getting frustrated and tired of the hassles they have to put up with just to get into Pakistan.

M I know your concern, but since I have been out for such a long time, can you perhaps explain to me what you mean. Give me an example of the hassles you have encountered.

AB Okay. You remember the first trek you went to; the Fairy Meadows Trek? You remember the group that went along with you?

M Yeah, there a couple from New Zealand, an Australian, a German and a Spaniard.

AB Right. Well this year that German, Ziegfried, referred us to his brother Hans and his girlfriend Petra, who wanted to do the trek to K-2 base camp (see Appendix B for more details).

M Interesting. I was thinking that perhaps we should no longer focus on lower prices. While I was in the U.S., I learned some new marketing and customer service techniques. Perhaps a better strategy might be to differentiate the tours of HA from others. One option I'm considering is using the Internet. This new technology could help us in marketing the tours worldwide, improve our service quality, and allow us to simplify the visa and permit process with the Pakistani government. What do you think, Abdul?

AB I think this is a good idea because I have heard about the Internet from our clients and the other travel firms in this area.

M Okay then, why don't you come over to Islamabad and I will try to explain a couple of ideas that I have for HA.

AB Okay, I will be there next week.

At the end of the conversation, Mohammed knew that the Internet held a place in adventure tourism and may be the key to salvaging HA. But, how? What e-business implementation strategy should he use? Mohammed had read a *Harvard Business Review* article in which he found there were two Internet strategies available for business: a *pure dot-com* strategy or the *bricks-and-clicks* strategy (see Appendix A for more details).

CURRENT CHALLENGES/PROBLEMS FACING THE ORGANIZATION

The Internet Approach

The Internet- (or Web-) based economic model is staggeringly more efficient at the transaction cost level (Wigand & Benjamin, 1995). For example, the cost of processing an airline ticket through traditional approach is $8, but is only $1 through the Web. Similarly, other efficiencies can be derived from marketing and advertisements, online information processing with forms that are electronically linked to databases and online customer support (Hoffman et al., 1995). Elimination of middleman in the distribution channel (or disintermediation) also can have a big impact on the market efficiency (Michalski, 1995). Other efficiencies are generated due to less or no inventory, storage or real-estate space, larger customer base and 24x7 access at no additional cost (Steinfield & Whitten, 1999). Marketing on the Web can result in additional unit sales at very low unit cost. In addition to the lower cost, the Web also enables a higher level of customization to the needs of individual clients (Choi & Winston, 2000). Auto manufacturers, such as Ford and GM, are experimenting with custom-designed cars that can be delivered in less than two weeks to a customer's home (White, 1999). Thus, Web-enabling business processes is particularly attractive in the new economy where product lifecycles are short and efficient, while the market for products and services is global.

The Web allows organizations to expand their business reach. One of the key benefits of the Web is access to and from global markets (Economist, 1997). The Web eliminates several geographical barriers for a corporation that wants to conduct global commerce. Political, trade and cultural barriers may still make it difficult to take true advantage of the global business environment.

While traditional commerce relied on value-added networks (VANs) or private networks, which were expensive and provided limited connectivity (Pyle, 1996), the Web makes electronic commerce (e-commerce) cheaper with extensive global connectivity. Businesses have been able to produce goods anywhere and deliver electronically or physically via couriers (Steinfield & Whitten, 1999). This enables an organization the flexibility to expand into different product lines and markets quickly, with low investments. Secondly, 24x7 availability, better communication with customers and sharing of the organizational knowledgebase allows an organization to provide better customer service. This can translate to better customer retention rates, as well as repeat orders.

Finally, the rich interactive media and database technology of the Web allows for unconstrained awareness, visibility and opportunity for an organization to promote its products and services (Senn, 2000). This enhances organizations' ability to attract new customers, thereby increasing their overall markets and profitability. Despite the recent dot-com failures (Francis, 2000), e-commerce has made tremendous in-roads in traditional corporations. Forrester Research in their survey found 90% of the firms plan to conduct some e-commerce, business-to-consumer (B2C) or business-to-business (B2B), and predicts e-commerce transactions will rise to about $6.9 trillion by 2004. As a result, the travel industry has started to believe in the Internet because of its ability to attract and retain more customers, reduce sales and distribution overheads, and increase global access to markets with an expectation of an increase in sales revenues, and higher profits.

Given the information needs of potential customers and to spawn new business growth, the Internet has been identified as a potential weapon and can be utilized to accomplish the following competitive advantages for HA (for an example of how a customer experience changes after HA invests in the Web, please refer to Appendix B):

In Existing Markets

- A Web site can help to expedite communication and also act as a marketing tool for HA, by creating a comprehensive customer database through which targeted promotional campaigns such as information newsletters, discounts, special deals, etc. are carried out.
- An information portal—with relevant links to all the relevant government authorities (such as through an extranet provision with these government agencies), as well as useful adventure tips and links to other adventure-related information.
- An online auction which brings sellers of used gear and buyers together as mountain/trekking gear is very expensive and usually outside the monetary reach of the "one-time adventure seeker." Alternatively HA can have a referral program with outdoor equipment manufacturers who would offer discounts to HA customers.
- A chat room and discussion boards similar to the ones offered by Excite, Yahoo! and Hotmail portals, to be used by adventure patrons and HA members to share their experience, selling second-hand gear, for group matching, etc. Discussion boards (such as the ones offered by Lonely Plant) can also be used to match like-minded groups with one another, and hence achieve the cost savings which are present in a group package (as compared to the high price individuals or couples pay, if they buy a package for less than three people).
- An FAQ section could be created on the Web site to answer basic questions that customers have on relevant topics.

In New Markets

- Target the 10,000+ foreign nationals (ex-pats and foreign workers) currently residing in Pakistan at virtually little or not cost.
- A new and emerging trend among the smaller business companies, especially those in the software market, is on building the group dynamic spirit. This idea, which is borrowed from military training ideology, is being capitalized upon by both Harvard and Columbia universities, which offer corporate team-spirit-building courses by taking the study group to a rugged outdoor surrounding and making them work together to build a team spirit. NAP offered a perfect surrounding for this kind of adventure, and HA could design a special targeted package for this kind of team-building adventure[4] suited to the needs of domestic and international corporate sectors.

Web Site Development and Implementation Plan

It is anticipated that it would take HA at least three years to come up with funds and invest in the Web initiatives. As HA cannot afford a major investment at the onset of the project, it is proposed that the Internet investment should be done in a piece-meal fashion. A brief Web site development and implementation plan is as follows:

- Registering for a domain name for the Web site in the USA for a dot-com (top-level) domain.
- Creating a static Web site with links to relevant government agencies, bookstores, travel stores, etc.
- Creating an e-commerce Web site (B2C) for customer reservations and trip planning activities.
- Investing in back-end applications and a database, which is compatible with major Internet service providers (ISPs).
- Purchasing server hardware and PCs (this should be bought from corporate auctions within the country due to cheaper prices as compared to the international market prices).
- Accessing a secure Web server to transmit sensitive information via the 128-bit SSL encryption standard from the Web site.
- Setting up a merchant account for processing customer payments via credit cards, and other electronic cash and checking options.
- Developing a closed instant messaging or chat and discussion bulletin board for HA's clients and business partners.
- Choosing an e-commerce platform, like Microsoft's Site server, to quickly build shopping carts, search engines and order fulfillment systems.
- Choosing an automated booking system that can check for availability for tours and dates, and confirm a place to a potential customer.
- Developing a data mining system to analyze the profitability of various tours that HA offers and their popularity.
- Developing B2B extranets with relevant government agencies and other mountain gear vendors.

Web Site Implementation Issues

While implementing the Web site, HA's development team must select from among the various Web technologies. Although HTML is a standard protocol which works on all operating systems and browser platforms, several problems can occur in the implementation of dynamic HTML technologies. For example, the HA design team must decide very early whether their Web site will support both Netscape™ and Internet Explorer™ browsers. Also, what browser versions will be supported? The older versions of these browsers do not support the dynamic scripting languages such as VBScript and JavaScript. Finally, some of these scripting technologies work on Microsoft's Windows™ but not on Unix, Linux or Apple's Macintosh™ operating systems. With more emerging Web platforms such as PDA devices and wireless phones, it would be advisable for the HA team to select a minimum operating standard for their development.

One option for developing the Web site with minimal budget is for HA to introduce a new hiring program for Web programmers. Under this program, HA would use its existing network of clients and offer one free trip, with all expenses paid, to a group of programmers who will assist HA in the areas of Web design and development. This is done due to cost considerations, and inviting our customer ensures that theWeb site final Web site design and outlook is reflective of HA and its customers' passion for the outdoors. Another implementation option would be to syndicate the Web site development with one of the major travel Web sites like Expedia.com or Travelocity.com, which provide syndicated content for small travel agencies that do not have the necessary resources.

Web Security Issues

The security in the Web environment is perhaps one of the most prominent concerns for businesses and customers alike. In this regard the proposed project in no way alters the payment policy that HA has adopted since its inception in the late 90s. As is the norm, the payment scheme will stay the same, with 50% of the tour price due at the beginning of the trip and 50% halfway through. HA, however, should still considering outsourcing it to TRUSTe.com or VeriSign.com security organizations to increase customer confidence. It should further explore the in-vogue merchant accounts for accepting payments via credit card, e-Cash (like PayPal.com) and e-Wallet.com. Mohammed thinks that due to the e-payment method's popularity, 100% of similar business would be conducted through online payment systems by 2005.

Long-Term Considerations

Financial resources permitting, HA would like to incorporate the following features onto its Web site in addition to its current operations in the near future:

- A strategic alliance with the Pakistan Tourist Development Corporation (PTDC) so as to have HA's Web link on the PTDC's Web page, which is generally the primary source of tourism information within Pakistan.
- A comprehensive GIS system (database), with route and cost information, which allows customers to build their own trips by selecting the destinations (cities, mountain peaks, trails, etc.) they would like to visit. This obviously would require a very large capital investment. However, this vision of future adventure travel should be kept in mind when HA considers more IT strategic alternatives in the future.
- Providing e-mail access at major check-in points to allow customers to stay in touch with their loved ones. Another option is the video SAT phones which can be bought second hand in domestic market at nominal prices. This equipment could be rented to customers to facilitate their needs. The provision for this equipment (three per year) has been allowed in the costs and benefits analysis section.

Costs and Benefits

Pre-Project Status (number of trips and customers are averages):

No. of Trips:	25	
Heads per trip:	6	
Profit Margin (PM)	$500	
Pre-Interest and tax Profit	**$75,000**	A

Post-Project Status (assumes that number of trips double in the first year and the number stays the same for the next three years; also there is an increase in the PM as HA takes advantage of technology):

No. of Trips:	50	
Heads per trip:	6	
Profit Margin	$650	
Total PM	**$195,000**	**B**
Profit from equipment sales	**$20,000**	**C**
Less Annual Cost (estimated)		
Equipment & Software	$40,000	
HR costs	$30,000	
Total Investment/year	**$70,000**	**D**

Incremental benefit/year for next three years ($\{B+C\} - \{A+D\}$) = **$ 70,000**
Net Present Value of project @ discount rate of 10% = **$ 174,079**
$(70,000/1.10) + (70,000/\{1.100^2\}) + (70,000/\{1.100^3\})$

After understanding the details provided by Mohammed, Abdul Bari has to make final decision on whether HA should opt for a pure *dot-com* approach, closing its office in Islamabad and investing all the money on the Web environment. Or should HA opt for a *bricks-and-clicks* model using the Web environment to supplement its existing offices? Abdul Bari would like to see business growth, more operational efficiencies and an increase in his profit margins. But, he has to work within the technology, business, regulatory and societal environment of a developing country. In addition, Bari and Mohammed have to consider the various Web site development, implementation and security issues in making their final decision.

FURTHER READING

Article I. Web Enabling Strategy Supplement

A review of the Web-enabling strategy literature reveals two business models used by the e-business enterprises. One model highlighted by Mahadevan (2000) shows the different economic streams targeted by the pure-plays to succeed in the new Internet economy. Another model highlighted by Gulati and Garino (2000) shows how clicks-and-mortar firms have successfully integrated their online channels with their off-line, traditional ones.

Mahadevan's article, "Business Models for Internet-Based E-Commerce" (2000), focuses on classifying the business models as portals, market makers and product/service providers who rely on three economic streams for surviving in the new economy. They are value stream, revenue stream and logistical stream. To succeed, the dot-com companies must rely on some unique combination of each of the three streams. Although Mahadevan has done a good job in identifying the various revenue streams for the dot-com companies depending on their market structure, these economic streams may never materialize for companies. For example, free offerings do not always result in paid purchases by the customer. Both Pets.com and Petco gave away free advice to pet owners on care, wellness, behavior, etc., through their e-commerce Web sites. This counsel was not exclusive to these two companies, as similar information could be obtained from other non-commercial sites. Therefore this advice did not have the anticipated impact on potential customers. Nor does the amount of dollars spent on advertising compensate for all the expenses incurred trying to capture sales for the site. For example, eToys and Pets.com spent significant advertising dollars trying to steer customers to their Web sites. Some of these advertising contracts were upwards of $27 million.

Mahadevan (2000) also directly contradicts some of the core strategies that must be followed in order to succeed with any form of business as stated by Porter. Mahadevan states that giving the customer more and more choices with more suppliers available is in the best interest of the e-commerce firm. As we now know (with all dot-com failures), giving away too much bargaining power to the consumer has an adverse affect on the firm and the industry as a whole. Mahadevan also states that the pure-play has larger margins than the brick-and-mortar firms do. This may have been true last summer, but now the pure-play margins are thinner or negative as opposed to margins for large brick-based establishments.

Gulati and Garino (2000) are proponents of integrating the e-commerce channel and Web presence with the core brick-and-mortar establishment. In their article titled, "Get the Right Mix of *Bricks & Clicks*," they discuss the values and advantages of being a fully integrated firm or at least tending to lean toward that end of the integration scale. They go on to evaluate four major strategies that firms can take when it comes to running an extension of their business channel on the Internet. This scale ranges from in-house division (high integration), to joint venture, to strategic partnership, to the other side, which is spin-off (high separation). They state that the benefits of being fully or partially integrated are greater than the advantages of independence as a pure-play Internet business.

The integrated business does seem to have a greater advantage over its pure-play counterpart. The only difference is that instead of solely concentrating on the clicks-and-mortar approach, we want to investigate both sides of the coin. We believe that HA can still survive in today's economic conditions. However, its management must follow certain basic business strategies as outlined by Porter.

Porter's Model

The framework for our analysis is built upon the theories of Michael Porter's recent article, "Strategy and the Internet" (2001), in which he defines several business fundamentals that must be followed in order to be successful regardless of the type of firm. Porter outlines two major fundamentals that are influenced by the Internet to more of a degree than was once thought previously. They are *industry structure* and *sustainable competitive advantage*. Without at least acknowledging these essentials to be crucial to the profitable operation of the firm, a fight for survival will always exist.

The Internet has an inherent adverse or beneficial effect on each of the Porter fundamentals. An important aspect to note is that the Internet is based upon an open technological architecture. This architecture has the largest effect on these competitive elements. Since the technology platform is common, and little or no capital investment is required, anybody with minimal know-how can set up a Web site and start conducting e-commerce. Enterprising individuals that want to set up a side occupation can now have additional disposable income, thereby helping to fuel the economy. This also results in the barrier to entry being nearly non-existent in certain industries, not to mention that the number of competitors coming on board every month, or every day, is astronomical. This increases the rivalry that already exists between competitors, and even compounds it logarithmically.

The Internet has opened up the availability of the vast amount of information that can be acquired by potential buyers. This is great for buyers because they can perform in-depth research before buying the product. It seems that this would cut down the number of returns because the consumer would be more knowledgeable about the different features of a product. They can even get cost information that was not readily available to them before the emergence of the Internet. An example of this is, the actual invoice paid by a car dealer is now available at a buyer's mouse click. This puts bargaining power into the hands of the consumer and puts the dealer at a disadvantage. The consumer will get the deal of her choice or go elsewhere. The bad part of all of this is that the retailers (brick-and-mortar firms *and* pure-plays) now compete solely on the basis of price, and switching costs are lowered, meaning that consumers can readily change vendors without penalty.

Because of the Internet, suppliers gain an increase in the number of potential customers causing the number of middlemen to be reduced. The ease in which these potential customers are reached means more direct sales are possible from large suppliers. This is good for suppliers, but has mixed results for consumers. The consumer has only one outlet for a certain product, such as a well-known brand of computer that he really wants, and he has to pay the exact price stated. There are no middleman-type companies to play off each other for a reduced price (haggling). On the other hand, the middlemen inflate the actual price in order to profit form the sale, so the supplier may realistically have a lower price.

The last competitive element is the threat of substitute products. The speed and organization of the Internet, with its database storage capabilities and set standards, has the ability to make industries more efficient and expand the industry. This expansion leads to more competitors and newer, better technologies that increase the threat of substitutions. As Internet technologies change rapidly and get cheaper, it gets easier and cost effective for customers to switch to a better product or service. If suppliers are not quick in their development, implementation and time to market, they will soon be filing for bankruptcy.

Operational effectiveness is described as offering the same product or service that your competitors do, except doing it better. This can refer to the speed at which something is done, the amount of customization that can be accomplished, the overall efficiency of operations or even the manner at which something is sold. Operational effectiveness is what many referred to as "Internet Speed"—how quickly can a company come up to speed to meet or exceed the operations of its competitors? As it turns out in the Internet world, duplicating a firm's operations is so easy to do that operational effectiveness becomes a non-issue. This is no strategic advantage because a firm's competitor can replicate its product and operation in a very short time. And with technology changing on a daily basis, the competitor could end up exceeding the baseline set by the original firm. The process becomes a vicious cycle.

The real advantage for sustainable competitive advantage comes from strategic positioning. The key to success is to provide something that a consumer or business needs and then be an exclusive provider for it. To accomplish this, the firm must offer something of high or inimitable value to the buyer, with no other competitor that can match this value. Sellers compete on providing unique services or offerings to buyers rather than competing on price, which can lead to failings in business. Please take a look at the challenges and problems faced by HA, and how the Porter model can be utilized by HA.

Article II. Customer Experience at HA: Pre- and Post-Web Site Phases

The following is a walkthrough of a trekking trip that a young outdoor and adventure-loving couple, Hans and Petra (H&P) from Hamburg, Germany, takes with Himalayan Adventures (HA).

Action	Pre-Website	Post-Website	HOW WAS THIS DONE?
Finding and selecting the tour, reserving the place in the tour and making travel arrangements	H&P ask friends and family, read travel magazines to find HA. Communication between H&P and HA is primarily done through regular mail or phone. After numerous exchanges of information (including convincing a couple of like-minded friends to go on the tour in order to achieve economies of scale on the cost of the package), H&P decide on the package. Additionally they also have to do research on best airfares. Once booked there is another exchange of mail to finalize the itinerary of the trip.	H&P go to search engines and find HA website. Tour packages promotions are available on the HA website. H&P register their name and travel plans; find another three members to join their trekking tour. Within hours, they have replies from like-minded travelers who will be going on the same tour. HA website allows them to make all their travel arrangements and confirms everything electronically. Secure access is provided for H&P to select and pay for a variety of travel options for Air, Hotel, and Trekking packages.	• E-Marketing • Secure Access • Electronic Payment Options
Tourist Visa acquisition	This process requires, first receiving the application in mail and then showing up in person at the nearest embassy or consulate (Berlin or Bonn) for an interview with the visa officer so as to establish legitimacy of the travel plans (estimated time: 2 weeks).	On HA website there is a link to all the relevant visa information and policy along with a online visa application form with relevant information on the tour provider i.e. HA. By filling out the information H&P would not have to travel in person for the visa approval. Instead everything can be done online. The whole process would take less than three working days.	Issues: • Online Forms • Database Integration • Back-End Application Integration
Actual trip: staying in contact with loved ones	Once in Pakistan, H&P buy calling cards (for a 7 minute call to Germany, it costs $3-4 a minute on a calling card) which allows them to periodically call their family and friends at home.	The day they land in Pakistan, H&P send e-mails to their families and friends and can talk to their loved ones using the HA website. Once H&P arrive in Gilgit mountains two days later, H&P send another e-mail or talk to their relatives. Once they are on the trek, H&P rent a laptop and a digital camera from HA. Every day of the trek, they call home, download and send their digital images and stay in constant contact with their family, in addition to having 24x7 accesses to Instant Messaging, chat and e-mail.	Issues: • Customer Service • Community Boards, Chats, IMS, Etc. • M-Commerce • Collaboration
Aftermath	H&P are very happy with their tour. In writing they send their photographs to HA and thank HA for hosting the trip. HA management is extremely happy to receive the letter of thanks and appraisal. It is stored in the personal archives of the manger, perhaps never to be looked at again in the near future.	H&P thoroughly enjoyed their trip. They go back to Hamburg with all of these memories of a wonderful and safe trek. They upload their trip experiences with images/photographs on the HA website applauding them for their memorable experience. H&P's story appears in the next issue of the monthly online outdoor adventure newsletter that HA offers to its members. Potential clients have a chance to read H&P's story and view the breathtaking photographs.	Issues: • Post Purchase Experiences • Repeat Business

REFERENCES

Adventure Tours Pakistan. Retrieved from http://www.atp.com.pk

Choi, S., et al. (1997). *The economics of electronic commerce.* Indianapolis, IN: Macmillan.

Economist. (1997, September). Going digital: How new technology is changing our lives. *Economist.* Retrieved from http://www.economist.com/editorial/freeforall/14-9-97/ec4.html

Francis, D. (2000, November 20). Despite dotcom failures, e-tail's future is bright. *Christian Science Monitor,* 17.

Government of Pakistan. (1998). Census Results. Government of Pakistan, Division of Statistics.

Gulati, R., & Garino, J. (2000, May-June). Get the right mix of bricks and clicks. *Harvard Business Review.*

Hoffman, D., Novak, T., & Chatterjee, P. (1995). Commercial scenarios for the Web: Opportunities and challenges. *Journal of Computer-Mediated Communications, 1*(3).

Lonely Planet. Retrieved http://www.lonelyplanet.com

Mahadevan, B. (2000). Business models for Internet-based e-commerce: An anatomy. *California Management Review, 42*(2), 55-69.

Michalski, et al. (1995). People are the killer APP. *Forbes, 155*(12), 120-122.

Pakistan Tourism Development Corporation. (1997). Report.

Porter, M. E. (2001). Strategy and the Internet. *Harvard Business Review, 79*(3), 63-80.

Pyle, R. (1996). Commerce and the Internet. *Communications of the ACM, 39*(6), 23.

Senn, J. (2000, Spring). Business-to-business e-commerce. *Information Systems Management,* 23-32.

Steinfield, C., & Whitten, P. (1999). Community-level socio-economic impacts of electronic commerce. *Journal of Computer-Mediated Communications, 5*(2).

Turban, McLean, & Wetherbe. (2001). *Information technology for management.* New York: Prentice Hall.

White, G. (1999, December 3). How GM, Ford think Web can make a splash on the factory floor. *Wall Street Journal,* 1.

Wigand, R., & Benjamin, R. (1995). Electronic commerce: Effects on electronic markets. *Journal of Computer Mediated Communication, 1*(3). Retrieved from http://www.ascusc.org/jcmc/vol1/issue3/vol1no3.html

World Bank Country Development. (1999). Report.

ENDNOTES

[1] Defined as number of times at least one person from the whole climbing expedition had reached a summit. Most expeditions make it up to the third or the fourth (generally the last camp before the summit) base camps and have to abandon their attempts due to poor weather.

[2] Treks can be customized to fit the needs of a particular group as well. However, most people opt for the standard 10 treks, which generally covered all the major mountain ranges. All of these were offered by Himalayan Adventures.

3   Cultural Safari's are generally 5+ day jeep rides to and from major tourist destinations in the Northern Areas and are customized for each group—generally no more than four people per group.

4   A company by the name of Adventure Tours Pakistan already offers this kind of adventure opportunity to the 1st Battalion 51st Highland Rangers of UK Army by taking a 25-member team every summer to a 23-day 105 km Baltoro Glacier Trek.

Luvai Motiwalla is currently an associate professor of MIS in the College of Management at the University of Massachusetts, Lowell, USA. He has a PhD and MS in management information systems from the University of Arizona and a BBA from Penn State University. He has published articles in several national and international journals, including Journal of Internet & Higher Education, Information & Management, Information Resource Management Journal, Journal of Organizational Computing & e-Commerce, *and* Journal of MIS. *He has also consulted or worked on research projects funded by Connecticut Department of Health Services, IBM, NCR, and U.S. Army.*

Azim Hashimi is currently an MBA student at the College of Management at the University of Massachusetts, Lowell, USA. He did his undergraduate studies at the Memorial University of Newfoundland, Canada. Prior to enrolling in the MBA program, he interned for the World Bank and worked in the fields of micro-credit and enterprise development at major NGOs in Pakistan and USA.

This case was previously published in *Annals of Cases on Information Technology*, Volume 5/ 2003, pp. 274-289, © 2003.

About the Editor

Mehdi Khosrow-Pour, D.B.A, is executive director of the Information Resources Management Association (IRMA) and senior academic technology editor for Idea Group Inc. Previously, he served on the faculty of the Pennsylvania State University as a professor of information systems for 20 years. He has written or edited more than 30 books in information technology management. Dr. Khosrow-Pour is also editor-in-chief of the *Information Resources Management Journal*, *Journal of Electronic Commerce in Organizations*, *Journal of Cases on Information Technology*, and *International Journal of Cases on Electronic Commerce*.

Index

business-to-business (B2B) transactions 273
business-to-business e-commerce 107, 130, 142, 190
business-to-business markets 352
business-to-consumer (B2C) 270, 381
business-to-employee (B2E) 270
business-to-government (B2G) transactions 275

C

C++ 53
cash rebate 266
cell phones 194
change management 158, 165
changeover 117
Chile 193
circular 246
clicks and mortar 38, 73
clicks model 260
clickstream 240
closed-loop marketing 236
collaborative planning, forecasting, and replenish 110
collateral fulfillment technology 367
college market 228
Colombia 191
commission rates 54
commodity business 161
common gateway interface (CGI) 53
common student identifier 226
competence-enhancing discontinuities 223
competition 48, 266
competitive advantage 35, 261, 341
competitors 35
component-based computing 53
computer ownership 191
configuration 157
consulting services 97
consumer comfort with electronic commerce 66
consumers 22, 212
content 367
content items 245
content management model 245
content management service 98

conventional advertising 27
copyright 83
copyrighted music 216
cost 52, 369
credit card 19, 266, 309
credit card fraud 191
credit card penetration 194
cross-border issues 188
cross-border negotiations 192
cross-selling 270
cultural differences 192
currency 188
customer interaction 174
customer loyalty 52
customer relations 262
customer relationships 262
customer service 54
customer-managed orders 161
customers 172, 237
customers' orders fulfillment 115
cyberspace 21
cyberspace marketing 21
cycle-time reduction 163

D

DataNaut 98
David Pottruck 38
day traders 54
declining sales 220
dematerialization 83
development initiative 248
digital distribution 261
digital economy 260
digital radio/TV station 79
digital signal processing (DSP) 159
direct access terminals 346
direct e-mail advertisement 23
direct mail advertisement 24
direct marketing 24
discount 266
discount brokerage firms 50
disintermediation 83, 213
distribution 266
distribution networks 191
distribution of IPOs 67
distributors 212

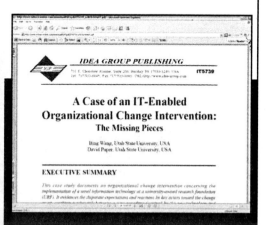